Social Work with Latinos

Social Work with Latinos

A Cultural Assets Paradigm

Melvin Delgado

OXFORD

UNIVERSITY PRESS

OXFORD
UNIVERSITY PRESS

Oxford University Press is a department of the University of Oxford.
It furthers the University's objective of excellence in research, scholarship,
and education by publishing worldwide.

Oxford   New York

Auckland   Cape Town   Dar es Salaam   Hong Kong   Karachi
Kuala Lumpur   Madrid   Melbourne   Mexico City   Nairobi
New Delhi   Shanghai   Taipei   Toronto

With offices in

Argentina   Austria   Brazil   Chile   Czech Republic   France   Greece
Guatemala   Hungary   Italy   Japan   Poland   Portugal   Singapore
South Korea   Switzerland   Thailand   Turkey   Ukraine   Vietnam

Oxford is a registered trade mark of Oxford University Press
in the UK and certain other countries.

Published in the United States of America by
Oxford University Press
198 Madison Avenue, New York, NY 10016

© Oxford University Press 2007

First issued as an Oxford University Press paperback, 2013.

Library of Congress Cataloging-in-Publication Data
Delgado, Melvin.
Social work with Latinos: a cultural assets paradigm / Melvin Delgado.
p.   cm.
Includes bibliographical references and index.
ISBN: 978-0-19-530118-2 (hardcover); 978-0-19-932893-2 (paperback)
1. Hispanic Americans—Services for.   2. Social work with minorities—United States.
3. Hispanic Americans—Social conditions.   I. Title.
HV3187.A2D444 2006
362.84'68073—dc22   2005037213

About the cover artist: Born in 1956 in Harlem, New York, Soraida Martinez is a formally
educated artist and designer of Puerto Rican heritage who since 1992 has been
promoting tolerance and diversity through the "Verdadism" art style of paintings
juxtaposed with written social commentaries. For more information on Soraida,
the art of Verdadism, and the ideas behind "The Battle of the Rice and Beans"
see www.soraida.com.

This book is dedicated to Denise, Laura, and Barbara

PREFACE

Invariably, the undertaking of a major writing project such as a book brings with it a tremendous amount of satisfaction, not to mention a great amount of learning and insights that transpires along the way. Although by most objective standards I can be considered somewhat of an "expert" on Latinos, the writing of this book has had the opposite effect upon me. To say that the experience of writing this book has been humbling would be a serious understatement! A little knowledge is dangerous; a lot of knowledge is simply very dangerous.

No person, regardless of his or her talent, commitment, time, and resources, can speak for any one group in this society, unless they have been duly elected to do so. I certainly do not fall into that category. The explosion of the Latino community in the United States has made the process of writing a comprehensive social work book on this population group impossible to achieve. Mind you, it does not mean that I did not try to do this with this book. It simply means that I could not achieve it. The Latino community is far too complex in composition and geographical context to be captured in its essence in this country at this point in time, let alone in the next 10 to 20 years. The politics of immigration is impossible to predict, particularly post–September 11, 2001, as this nation ventures to militarily influence the fates of nations across the world.

As readers work their way through this book from chapter to chapter, this realization will no doubt take hold in a very profound manner, and I wish to "normalize" this realization. I say this not wishing to overwhelm the reader. Instead, my sole purpose is to better prepare the reader for this journey, which will result in a more in-depth appreciation of how the Latino community is both transforming this society and being transformed in the process of doing so. Absolute answers, I am afraid, are not possible, but it is possible to anticipate themes and issues related to the Latino explosion. The presence of Latinos in this country can only be fully appreciated from a multidimensional perspective, such as the one social workers possess. Our embrace of an ecological-contextual and multimethod interventionist perspective prepares the profession to make significant contributions to helping the Latino community make a successful transition in this country, particularly those who are newcomers. Anything short of this goal would constitute a serious shortcoming on the part of social work and its mission!

The reader familiar with my writings will find that the Latino cultural assets paradigm presented in this book incorporates many of the constructs found in my previous scholarship, such as capacity enhancement, nontraditional settings, natural support systems, and urban community–centered practice, to list a few. The proposed paradigm represents a synthesis of all of these and other constructs in a manner that emphasizes a cultural and group-specific perspective. These constructs can also be applied to other groups, but may take different manifestations, depending on the group they are being applied to and the context within which they are situated.

ACKNOWLEDGMENTS

I want to take this opportunity to thank Boston University School of Social Work for its continued support of my research and scholarship on marginalized urban-based communities of color. I also want to extend a special thank you to Ms. Alison Conway, Research Assistant, for her work on all facets of this book from beginning to end. It would have been very difficult to complete this book without her support!

CONTENTS

Part I

Setting the Stage

Chapter 1

CONTEXT GROUNDING

Whatever the domain of social work practitioners, whether in child welfare, juvenile justice, mental and physical health, or community and policy practice, social work must be able to serve individuals, families and households, and communities living in an era of globalization. . . . The profession must be equally active as a local, global, and transnational agent.

Gregory Acevedo, "Neither Here nor There: Puerto Rican Circular Migration" (2004)

The profession of social work has faced numerous challenges over the course of its history in reaching out and serving undervalued population groups in the United States. Very often these undervalued groups have been newcomers to this country, with Latinos being one such community. With the exception of Puerto Ricans, who have been United States citizens since 1917, as will be noted in chapter 2 in greater detail, the legal status of Latinos is increasingly a serious factor to be considered in the designing and implementation of services (Cornelius, 2002; Coutin, 2003; Hagan & Rodriguez, 2002; Swarns, 2003a,b). De Genova and Ramos-Zayas (2003) argue that it is impossible to understand the economic position of Latinos, in this case Mexican and Puerto Rican, without understanding the meaning of and relationship to it of citizenship.

The importance of reaching the Latino community, however, has never been more striking than it is today, as a result of an interplay of various factors. The highly politically charged atmosphere in this country post–September 11, 2001, has compounded a difficult enough challenge for all helping professions, particularly those attempting to reach newcomers, and more specifically, those who are undocumented (Capps et al., 2004; Drachman & Paulino, 2004). In addition, the rapid demographic expansion of this community throughout the United States finds very few communities, particularly those in urban areas, not affected by this demographic trend.

High immigration rates involving newcomers of color, documented and undocumented, is having an important sociopolitical impact in this country, particularly in areas that have historically conceptualized race as either white or black (Abrahams, 2005; Bean et al., 2005). Tensions have arisen within communities of color, and between these communities and white, non-Latino residents (Egan, 2005b; Gibbs & Bankhead, 2001; Gonzalez, 2001; Hutchinson, 2005; Kasindorf & Puente, 1999; Landsberg, 2005; Martinez, 2005; New Latino nation, 2005; Perez, 2001; Quinones, 2005; Suggs, 2005; Wood, 2005).

The emergence of border patrols, enforcement of local ordinances against trespassing targeting the undocumented, and voter initiatives targeting undocumented immigrants, particularly Latinos, are examples of these tensions (Brooks, 2005; Cullen, 2005; C. Rodriguez, 2005). In Connecticut, a group called Connecticut Citizens for Immigration Control has demanded a legal investigation into McDonald's restaurants' hiring practices, claiming that the company disproportionately hires Latinos (Crowder, 2005). Socially, issues emanating from the crossing of ethnic and racial circles can result in Latinos and African Americans minimizing contact with outside groups (Jones, 2005).

The following description of an antiimmigration confrontation in San Diego, California, illustrates this tension (Gaona & Graham, 2005, p. B1):

> Police from several jurisdictions, most wearing riot gear, formed a barrier to keep the peace between those attending a forum on illegal immigration and protesters who ranged from Latino activist to Muslim students. While more than 100 protesters jeered, the public forum featuring Rep. Tom Tancredo, R-Colo., and other vocal opponents of illegal immigration expounded on how health care, homeland security, education, the economy and the environment are affected by undocumented immigrants.

Ironically, increased border security may also have an unintended consequence, keeping the undocumented in this country from returning home and encouraging them to settle in the United States (Porter & Malkin, 2005b).

The term "Juanito-come-lately" has emerged to capture sentiments by some African Americans about Latinos benefiting from civil rights advances without paying the requisite "dues." Sentiments on the part of some Latinos toward African Americans are captured in the following statement by a Latina (Kasindorf & Puerte, 1999, p. 12): "Whatever blacks want, they get. . . . They lead by intimidation. They threaten to riot or boycott. People don't feel threatened by us because we haven't threatened to burn the city down."

One community organizer in North Carolina (Martinez, 2005, p. 2) addressed this very point:

Most of the tension between African Americans and Latinos arises in the poultry industry. . . . In Silver City, where the David Duke rally took place, 80 percent of the poultry workers are Latinos. There is not a lot of tension in agriculture, where 60 to 70 percent of the Latinos work, because blacks don't "own" these jobs.

Although these tensions have involved the Latino community in general, they have taken on particular meaning when discussing undocumented Latinos, and the perceived beliefs that they have substantially changed the labor market by depressing wages. Save Our State (SOS), a California anti-immigration group, recently tried but was unsuccessful at creating a coalition with the Los Angeles African American community (Richardson, 2005).

The Nation of Islam's Louis Farrakhan, responding to the controversial comments of Mexico's president, Vicente Fox, on Mexican immigrants taking jobs away from African Americans/blacks, noted (Iowa's Hispanic population, 2005):

that blacks do not want to go to farms and pick fruit because they already "picked enough cotton. Why are you so foolishly sensitive when somebody is telling you the truth?" . . . [Farrakhan] said blacks and Latinos should form an alliance to correct differences and animosity between the two communities.

Pickel (2005, p. 1F) notes that differences of opinion on the undocumented have split two groups with conservative values (evangelical Christians and Republicans):

[they] find themselves on opposite sides of the thorny immigration issue. As Atlanta's Hispanic evangelical population continues to grow, conservative Republicans are grappling with how to relate to this group. Evangelical Hispanics tend to share conservatives' views on social issues such as gay marriage and abortion, but disagree strongly on illegal immigration.

Tensions have also arisen within specific Latino subgroups (Egan, 2005a; Feuer, 2003; Kugel, 2002; Spinelle, 2005), and between those who are in this country undocumented and those who have legal status. The following two scenarios in New York City and San Diego further highlight these tensions. Feuer describes an El Barrio (New York City) incident that typifies how these tensions can get manifested, and the challenges that social workers, particularly those within cohesive communities, face in bringing various sectors of the Latino community together (2003, p. A10):

This summer [2003], for example, tensions worsened when several Mexican restaurants complained to the police about a group of Mexican women selling tacos and empanadas on the sidewalks in front of their doors. The women, in turn, have said that selling street food is the only way that they can survive. . . . "I can understand these women need to make a living. . . . But I pay taxes, they don't pay taxes. I'm here legally and they are not."

The San Diego incident described by Deison (2005, p. 1) is a West Coast example of these tensions:

Lupe Moreno knows the immigrant struggle. She has lived all her life in Santa Ana, a gateway community for Mexican immigrants. Her father helped smuggle them into the country, her former husband sneaked in illegally. Now Moreno is part of the growing movement to stem the flow of illegal immigration. "I want people to know that there are Latinos who are law-abiding. . . . We need to protect our borders." Although polls suggest that the majority of Latinos are sympathetic to illegal immigrants once they have settled in the United States, opinions vary by generation, home country, economic class and personal values. Some Latinos are strongly opposed to crossing the border illegally.

A 2005 national survey by the Pew Hispanic Center found that 60 percent of Latinos native to the United States surveyed favored restricting undocumented immigrants from obtaining driver's licenses, with 66 percent of those born outside of the United States favoring granting licenses (Lester, 2005; Suro, 2005a). In addition, foreign-born Latinos overwhelmingly (90 percent) view immigrants as strengthening the country; those who are native born also do so, but to a lesser degree (66 percent).

The early part of the twenty-first century has continued to witness a dramatic increase in the number of Latinos in the United States (Schodilski, 2003). High birth rates, low death rates, and increased immigration rates (particularly among those who are undocumented) have largely fueled the Latino numerical explosion (Delgado, Jones, & Rohani, 2005). The interplay of these three factors has resulted in a significant net increase in the size of the Latino community, and with it the increased need for social workers and other helping professionals to engage Latinos in a wide variety of contexts and circumstances. The slowing down of white, non-Latino birth rates further emphasizes this numerical explosion. The United States is now listed as one of eight "low-fertility countries," along with France, Germany, Italy, Japan, the Republic of Korea, the Russian Federation, and the United Kingdom (Jolly, 2004).

Massey, Zambrana, and Bell (1995) identified five critical considerations that must be addressed in any form of culturally competent social intervention with Latinos: (1) the diversity of Latinos must be recognized; (2) race as a mediating factor in the lives of Latinos must be recognized; (3) residential segregation, along with its deleterious consequences, must not be blamed on Latinos; (4) immigration confounds other social processes affecting this community; and (5) the Spanish language plays a unique role in shaping the social, economic, and political reality of Latinos in the United States.

The social work profession has been faced with a number of challenges in how best to engage and meet the needs of an increasingly diverse population group that is no longer concentrated in certain geographical areas of the country, and to do so in a manner that affirms cultural values and assets (Delgado, Jones, & Rohani, 2005; Gutierrez, Yeakley, & Ortega, 2000; Kossak, 2005; Suarez-Orozco & Paez, 2002; Yan & Wong, 2005). It should be noted, however, that this challenge is not restricted to social work and other helping professions. Academic Spanish departments, for example, are debating how best to teach this content in light of the significant number of students taking Spanish to further their careers, rather than for the "love of the language" itself (Reyes, 2005; Stavan, 2005).

There is no geographical region of the country that has not experienced a dramatic, if not a rapid, increase in the number of Latinos, as I will address in greater detail in chapter 2. Urban areas that have historically attracted Latinos such as Chicago, Miami, Los Angeles, and New York, for example, continue to do so, in record numbers, and areas with limited histories of doing so have changed (Jones-Correa, 1998; Lao-Montes & Davila, 2001; Waldinger & Bozorgmehr, 1996; Waldinger & Lee, 2001; Wilson, 2003). Demographic trends starting in the 1980s have continued well into this century (Hayes-Bautista, Schink, & Chapa, 1988; Portes & Rumbaut, 2001).

California is one state that has experienced significant changes as a result of net Latino population increases (Baldassare, 2000; Mahler, 1995; McCarthy & Vernez, 1997). In 2001, the state experienced a significant shift in birth rates, with Latinos constituting a majority of all births for the first time in history (Jablon, 2003). The implications of this milestone will be felt as this cohort enters primary school in six years, and eight years later as they enter high school.

States such as Alabama, Georgia, Iowa, Missouri, Nevada, New Hampshire, North Carolina, and Utah, to list but a few, have historically not had significant numbers of Latinos within their borders (Baird & Guidos, 2004). However, that has started to change, and in some instances, the increases have been quite significant. Clark County, Nevada, which includes Las Vegas, is such an example. This is the fastest growing county in the fastest growing state in the United States, nearly doubling in size to 1.4 million from 1990 to 2000. This increase has been largely due to the increase of its Latino residents (Schmitt, 2001).

The engagement of and service to Latinos has proved to be challenging to the profession of social work and other helping professions. Factors such as acculturation, legal status in this country, sexual orientation, religiosity, and heterogeneity, among others, have effectively made the provision of culturally competent services more arduous to achieve, particularly when social workers do not share a similar background to the consumer and his or her community (Bertera, Bertera, & Shankar, 2003; Cabassa, 2003; Koss-Chioino & Vargas, 1999; Montero-Sieburth & Villarruel, 2000a; Zambrana, 1995).

However, even when there are no background differences between the social worker and the consumer, issues related to socioeconomic class, skin pigmentation, formal educational level, and cultural values on gender roles, such as machismo and Marianismo, could possibly serve to hamper a positive working relationship with Latinos and their community. Gender role–related cultural values of machismo and Marianismo, for example, raise serious questions about which cultural values should be fostered in this society, and which should be extinguished whenever possible because they violate basic human dignity (see chapter 6). This division often places social workers in an untenable position of trying to assess to what extent culturally competent practice is predicated upon gender-dictated values that are detrimental to this population group within the context of life in the United States? (Hondagneu-Sotelo, 1994; Hurtado, 1995).

Vega's (1995) observations based on social science research on Latino families made over a decade ago have not been substantially superseded since that period, and typify how helping professions, including social work, must seek to balance cultural values, in this case gender-related, and the structural changes of Latino families that are inherent in the resettlement process. Latino family research has historically fallen into two primary camps, so to speak (p. 4): (1) the role and internal dynamics of families and social networks; and (2) the changing family structure and gender-role patterns, or "how Latinas experience and perceive their family situations and how they are managing domestic role obligations and associated strains and conflicts in the context of outside employment."

The field of social work has embraced cultural competence principles and strategies and in the process of doing so has helped define congruent behaviors, attitudes, and policies necessary to work effectively in multicultural situations (Delgado, Jones, & Rohani, 2005; Fong & Furuto, 2001; Greene & Barnes, 1998; Lee & Greene, 2003; Lum, 2003). This contribution on the part of the profession can only be expected to continue into this century.

This book is an attempt to help shape how the profession can do this in the immediate future for one population group in particular. However, although this book is specific to Latinos, it is important to emphasize that the Latino community no longer consists of primarily three types of groups (Mexicans, Puerto Ricans, and Cubans). Numerous other Latino groups have entered the United States in sizeable numbers over the past decade and a half, and this demographic change is reflected in this book. This book, in addition, has implications for groups other than Latinos in this country, too, in that it raises parallel considerations and issues for groups occupying and competing for the same physical space and other resources. As already indicated, potential tensions and even conflicts between Latinos and other non-Latino groups and subgroups, and even within Latino groups, necessitates that social workers be cognizant of this potential.

Book Goals

This book will purposefully take a broad view of how best to reach Latinos in the United States across a lifespan and a variety of organizational settings. Every effort is also made to address topics usually not found in books focused on Latinos, in an effort to further social work's understanding of Latinos in the United States. An emphasis on examining how social work programs and services must be designed and structured to take into account cultural assets facilitates an overview perspective. There are a variety of principles, strategies, and techniques that must ultimately form the basis of any effective cultural assets–based interventions with Latinos.

This book, as a result, addresses eight interrelated goals: (1) to provide an updated social demographic profile of the Latino community and highlight significant trends with direct implications for social work; (2) to highlight the challenges typically faced by social workers in reaching and serving this community; (3) to identify some of the most pressing current and projected future needs of this community; (4) to raise emerging and rarely covered topics related to Latinos, and in the process to help the social work profession develop strategic initiatives that are both innovative and meet critical needs; (5) to provide a cultural assets paradigm incorporating a strengths and community assets perspective to conceptualize social work interventions; (6) through the use of case studies and illustrations, to show how a cultural assets perspective can be operationalized across population groups and organizational settings; (7) to draw upon various constructs and concepts from a variety of academic and professional disciplines in order to ground the Latino experience in the United States within a broad context, encompassing social, economic, and political considerations; and (8) to provide a series of organizational practice recommendations that systematically addresses how to tap and mobilize cultural assets in service to community.

The reader would be well advised that any effort to capture the diversity and rapidly changing nature of the Latino community in the United States necessitates reliance on multiple sources of information. Use of scholarly material is always advised. However, the very nature of scholarship requires expenditure of a considerable time period before a scholarly publication comes to press and makes its way into the hands of students and practitioners. Thus, it is strongly suggested that use of multiple sources for information is in order, including the use of ethnographic research, asset and needs assessments, and popular media. In essence, changes are quick and require constant vigilance on the part of practitioners if they are to stay informed! This book, I believe, has made extensive use of these sources when "scholarly" material is either dated, limited in scope, or absent.

Author Qualifications

The reader has every right to ask what are the qualifications, or what is the "legitimacy," of this author in writing a book on Latinos, particularly one advocating an assets paradigm. I have a long history of practice, research, and scholarship on Latinos in the United States. I have published four books specifically on Latinos over the past seven years: (1) *Social Services in Latino Communities: Research and Strategies* (1998b) (a collection of previously published articles); (2) *Alcohol Use/Abuse among Latinos: Issues and Examples of Culturally Competent Services* (edited volume, 1998c); (3) *Latino Elders and the Twenty-First Century: Issues and Challenges for Culturally Competent Research and Practice* (edited volume, 1998d); and (4) *Latinos and Alcohol Use/Abuse Revisited: Advances and Challenges for Prevention and Treatment Programs* (edited volume, 2005). In addition, I have authored over 100 articles and book chapters on Latinos and social work practice. Finally, I am a second-generation Puerto Rican, born and raised in New York City. Thus, my interest in Latinos is not only professional but also very personal.

This book's goals build upon the books just mentioned, other scholarship, and practice with Latinos over the past 30 years. This book not only represents a synthesis of this experience but also seeks to break new ground by taking into consideration the latest developments in the field, and new demographic information on Latinos in the United States.

The primary focus of my current research and scholarship is on urban practice with marginalized communities of color using a capacity enhancement paradigm. This paradigm embraces a central premise, namely, that all groups have assets that must be identified, sustained, and incorporated into any culturally meaningfully social intervention. However, this book also seeks to address the growing number of Latinos who do not reside in urban areas of the country. Migrant or seasonal workers, for example, are a group that has historically not been a part of the urban scene, and present a unique set of needs and challenges (Lopez, Nerenberg, & Valdes, 2000). Thus, every effort has been made to take an inclusive perspective, but never losing sight of the fact that over 90 percent of the Latino community in this country still resides in urban areas.

Outline of the Book

This book consists of three parts, each of which systematically builds upon the previous one. Although it is always tempting to jump around from part to part depending upon one's interests, this is not advised. This book consists of nine chapters divided into three interrelated sections:

Part I, "Setting the Stage" (chapters 1–4), grounds the reader, utilizing a variety of concepts and constructs in order to better understand and appreciate the Latino experience in the United States. Part II, "A Conceptual Foundation: Access, Culture, and Assets" (chapters 5–7), utilizes the material covered in Part I and introduces a conceptual foundation and social paradigm that systematically builds upon Latino cultural and community assets as a central feature of a social intervention that bridges both micro and macro social work practice perspectives. Part III, "A View from the Field" (chapters 8 and 9), presents a series of case illustrations to highlight how a Latino cultural assets paradigm can be implemented, and an opportunity to present recommendations, raise issues for the field, and reflection on the process of writing this book.

Key Concepts Defined

A series of definitions of key constructs follows as a means of facilitating the reading of this book. The following definitions of three key concepts are not intended to be exhaustive in nature. Clearly, each of these concepts deserves to have a book or series of books devoted to it, as is the case with cultural assets. I believe it is of sufficient importance to address the following three concepts in this chapter.

Definition of Latino

How a people are defined plays an instrumental role in how they view themselves and how the external world views them (Comas-Diaz, 2001; Garcia, 1999; Hernandez, 2004; Omi, 2001). Attempting a definition of any construct, particularly one that garners a consensus of opinions, is never easy in the social sciences (Swarns, 2004). In fact, this journey, by its very nature, must traverse numerous obstacles and may never achieve a true destination, namely, a consensus definition (Camarillo & Bonilla, 2001). Ultimately, this passage may result in a clearer understanding of the boundaries, elements, and tension areas that must be addressed in order to achieve a definition with wide appeal and meaning, or at the very least to clarify what the construct does mean (Borak, Fiellin, & Chemerynski, 2004).

The historical evolution of how Latinos have been labeled from a human service perspective has followed a path that can probably be traced back to the late 1960s and early 1970s, when the terms "Spanish-speaking" and "Hispano" emerged in the professional literature to capture the importance of group-specific service provision. The middle and late 1970s, in turn, witnessed the emergence of the term "Hispanic" to bring together people from disparate backgrounds but sharing a common language and cultural heritage (Del Olmo, 2001). This term effectively served as a sociopolitical construct that had relevance within and outside of the helping professions. The commonalties of conditions caused by social and economic injustice very often served as a basis to create a unified image of this community. The term "Hispanic," however, is not new and is traced back to the sixteenth century by the *Oxford English Dictionary*, which makes reference to residents of the Iberian Peninsula (Del Olmo, 2001). Thus, the evolution of this term can be traced back five centuries!

The popular media, for example, *Time* magazine in 1978, reinforced the use of this construct, and the phrase "The 1980s, the Decade of Hispanics," and the emergence of Hispanic Heritage Month in 1988 symbolized how most Americans in this era sought to view this population group (Davila, 2001; DeSipio & Henson, 1997; Olivarez, 1998; Rodriguez, 1997). A tremendous amount of national publicity resulted from the use of this term, representing both the novelty of the perspective but also the understanding of how this population group had grown demographically. The term served to effectively unify a group with many similarities and differences and at the same time served to reduce it to one simple term. To say that the emergence of the term "Hispanic" was bittersweet would be an understatement. The specific marketing of goods and services to this group is one of the most direct and profound implications of this categorization, however (Davila, 2001; Russell, 2004; Torres-Saillant, 2002).

The use of this term by the U.S. Census Bureau in the 1980 and 1990 censuses resulted in creation of data that further reinforced the use of the term "Hispanic," particularly in the development of policies and programs targeting this population through grants and other funding mechanisms. Availability of funding for research, demonstration programs, and projects highlighted the presence of Hispanics in the country during the era of the 1980s and 1990s (Becerra, Karno, & Escobar, 1982; Vega & Miranda, 1985).

Further, the coining of this term played an effective role within human services and among helping professions and their corresponding credentialing programs, by highlighting how this population group was slowly emerging from being invisible to warranting further attention, and how important it was to better prepare students to meet the challenges inherent in serving a group that does not speak English and are newly arrived in this country. Articles and books with titles like "Planning Mental Health Programs for Hispanic Communities" (Scott & Delgado, 1979), *Hispanic Families* (Montiel, 1978), and *Transcultural Psychiatry: An Hispanic Perspective* (Padilla & Padilla, 1978), for example, emerged to symbolize this approach toward human services, legitimizing this area of scholarship and research.

The emergence of the term "Latino," in turn, can arguably be traced to the early 1990s, and it has endured up to the present moment as this book goes to print, although it is not uncommon to see the terms *Hispanic* and *Latino* used interchangeably, with corresponding debates usually associated with the labeling of a people from within and outside of the group, or to see the combined term *Hispanic/Latino* used as a means of politically bridging different constituencies (Garcia, 1999). Oboler (1995), for example, examines the evolution of the term "Latino" and puts this evolution within a sociopolitical context, particularly with regard to the use of this term to represent this community within an urban context.

The term "Chicano," however, has a distinctive history and must not be confused with the terms *Hispanic* or *Latino*, and has been traced back to the Southwest and the early part of the twentieth century. The term generally has been used to refer to Mexicans who are either citizens of the United States or refugees from the Mexican Revolution residing in this country (Blea, 1988; Del Olmo, 2001; Keefe & Padilla, 1987). The term's political association with social and economic justice emerged in the 1940s and 1950s, and symbolized pride and self-assertion (Del Olmo, 2001, p. 2): "It was 'our' word, the argument went. It emerged from the barrio and was not a label imposed on us by outside society, like Mexican American (or, later on, Hispanic)."

Suarez-Orozco and Paez (2002, p. 9) note that the term "Latino" integrates various points and considerations:

> The most robust case for the analytic use of the panethnic Latino construct emerges from various shared sociohistorical processes that are at the heart of the Latino experience in the United States . . . the experience of immigration, the changing nature of U.S. relations with Latin America; and the processes of radicalization as Latinos enter, and complicate, the powerful "black-white" binary logic that has driven U.S. racial relations.

It is becoming more common to see the term "Afro-Latino" as an attempt to capture the role of race in the lives of Latinos, particularly those whose skin pigmentation would convey an outward appearance of African/black. The term *Latino*, as a result, serves to capture many disparate factors into a collective sense of identity that stresses commonalties over what many would argue are very different circumstances and backgrounds.

Needless to say, there are numerous definitions of what being a Hispanic or Latino means. The Historical Society of Pennsylvania (2005, p. 1), however, does a wonderful job of defining the term "Latino" by highlighting a multifaceted perspective of what this term seeks to capture and convey to the general public:

> "Latino" is a term used to describe people from Spanish-speaking countries of the Americas. Latino/a is an overarching term intended to include many aspects of cultural and linguistic identity. A Latino may be an immigrant or someone born in the United States; may have fair-skinned or dark-skinned; may be a professional or a day laborer; may speak Spanish, English, be bilingual or not speak Spanish at all; may be Catholic, Jewish, Pentecostal, Mormon, Quaker or agnostic. This term is a unifying term meant to include all people who share a common Latin American ancestry.

This definition of *Latino* by the Pennsylvania Historical Society brings to the foreground this highly dynamic and complex construct and is the one used in this book. The embrace of a term such as "Latino" primarily seeks to empower this group socially and politically and has less to do with the creation of an identity that permeates all aspects of someone's life.

The reader may have difficulty grasping this point, however. Terms related to race and ethnicity in this society have very politicized connotations; the context of the discussion plays a critical role in determining what term is used to capture a group's commonalities and differences. The term "Latino" has currency when addressing the common struggle Latino subgroups face in this country, and there is a concerted effort to attract national attention from the popular media or governmental entities. However, this term loses much of its meaning when the Latino being served by a social worker on a one-to-one scale has El Salvador as his country of origin, for example.

From a broader perspective involving the creation of a program or service, the more specific the term used, the better. If the program or service is targeting recently arrived Mexicans, then, this term should be used in the programs' title. However, if it involves multiple Latino subgroups, as it is often the case in urban-based programs, the broader term "Latino" has greater usage and meaning.

Lowe (1996) utilized concepts such as *heterogeneity, hybridity,* and *multiplicity* to emphasize the point, in this case referring to Asians in the United States but with applicability to Latinos, that this community is quite complex in composition, and therefore defies any efforts at making it a monolithic community. Arana (2001, p. 1) quite eloquently makes this very point regarding the Latino community in this country:

> We are not a seamlessly uniform people. We do not necessarily share culture of a common history. We are South Americans, Central Americans, Mexicans and Caribbean's, scrambled and sliced in different ways. We are jungle people, mountain people, coastal people, desert people, island people, urban people. We have—even as Latinos—a melting pot of our own.

Most commonly, Latinos prefer to use their countries of origin as their primary definition within and between Latino subgroups. Mexicans, El Salvadorans, Dominicans, Cubans, and Puerto Ricans, for example, will tend to embrace this classification. A 2002 Pew Hispanic Center national poll bears this interpretation out (Pew Hispanic Center, 2002b). This national poll found that 54 percent of Latinos surveyed said that their country of origin is the first or second choice for identifying themselves, compared to 25 percent of Latinos who say that "Latino" or "Hispanic" is their first choice, and 20 percent who give "American" as their preference. More specifically, 68 percent of foreign-born Latinos primarily choose their country of origin. The children of Latino immigrants also prefer to identify themselves by their parents' country of origin (38 percent) or as American (35 percent).

The general public, however, may find the term "Latino" specific enough to develop perceptions and, in the case of social work, develop social interventions. The emergence of combined identities such as Mexican American, Peruvian American, and Puerto Rican American, for example, has been referred to as *diasporic nationalism*. This term embraces the sentiment, particularly of newcomer youth, being caught between two worlds, the world of their ancestors and the New World (Tambiah, 2000).

However, this New World, so to speak, has these Latino youth still living in predominantly Latino communities. Combined identities, as a result, seek to "address the concerns and politics inherent in accommodation, acculturation, integration, and assimilation, and having newcomer groups achieving equal rights with natives" (Delgado, Jones, & Rohani, 2005, p. 136). The emergence and popularity of dual citizenship among Caribbean and Central and South Americans in the United States reinforces the importance of combined identities not just among youth but also among their parents (Larkin, 1999).

Flores (2000, pp. 191–192), in discussing community and identity, presents an excellent statement on the challenges of arriving at a definition of a group that has universal acceptance:

> "Where I come from, in New Mexico, nobody uses Latino, most people never even heard the term. We're Mexicanos, Chicanos, Mexican-Americans, Raza, Hispanic, but never Latino. Anyone who comes around talking about Latino this or Latino that is obviously an outsider." Or, from a contrary perspective, it is "Hispanic" that raises the red flag: "Hispanic? For me, a Hispanic is basically a sellout, un vendido. Anyone who calls himself Hispanic, or refers to our community as Hispanic, just wants to be an American and forget our roots."

Niemann, Romero, Arredondo, and Rodriguez (1999) posit, in this case regarding Mexicans, that ethnic identity has a social construction that shapes how ethnic and racial groups view and define themselves. Racism, as a result, can negatively influence ethnic identity, undermining confidence in self and others sharing the same ethnic identity. The subject of racism and discrimination will be addressed again in chapter 2, in examining how help-seeking behavior is influenced by these experiences.

Clemente (2004, p. 23) raises a cautionary point pertaining to the fostering of Latino pride and what it can mean within this society: "Latinos need a true exploration of cultural pride and not vulgar superciliousness manifested in stereotypical behavior that promotes antagonism, anger, violence, and resistance by members of other ethnic groups." Latino pride, as a result, becomes a two-edged sword, so to speak. I believe it parallels the experience that African Americans had during the 1960s when the slogan "Black is beautiful" became equated with *If black is beautiful, then white must be ugly.* When groups of color embrace a position of self-pride, it is bound to have a negative reaction from the dominant group. On a more positive note, Hayes-Bautista (2002) proposes that Latino identity be viewed in a similar fashion to how Texans identify themselves. Every Texan is an American. However, not every American is a Texan (Loera, 2005).

Finally, it is important to note that as a result of intergroup marriage, Latino identities related to countries of origin have blurred (Logan, 2003b). I participated in a conference in 2004 in Lawrence, Massachusetts, which is approximately 30 miles north of Boston. The theme of the conference was Dominican–Puerto Rican community relations. Lawrence has a Latino population that is almost evenly split between Puerto Ricans and Dominicans. Although the islands of Dominican Republic and Puerto Rico are often considered sister islands because of their geographic proximity to each other, tensions existed between these two groups in Lawrence. Out-group marriage, in turn, does occur in significant numbers, with 20 percent of Latinos marrying a non-Latino (Pew Hispanic Center, 2002c).

There was a panel of three discussants on one theme, namely, how these two communities are merging, particularly for future generations. One panelist was born in the Dominican Republic, but was raised in Puerto Rico since a very early age; another panelist had one parent who was Puerto Rican and other who was Dominican and was raised in New York City; one panelist was Puerto Rican but married to a Dominican and was raised in Lawrence; and one panelist was born to two Dominican parents but was born and raised in Puerto Rico. If this panel typifies the Latino community in other sectors of the country where different Latino groups reside, the Lawrence scenario raises important questions about how identity labels will undergo drastic adjustments as new generations of Latino youth emerge in the twenty-first century.

Social workers must never jump to conclusions that having a Latino identity is all-defining, as in the case of newly elected Los Angeles mayor Antonio Villaraigusa (Uranga, 2005a, p. N1):

> The rest of the nation is becoming more like Southern California as the much-talked-about "Latinization" of America slowly accelerates. . . . Indeed, when Villaraigosa was elected in May as the city's first Latino mayor in more than a century, he quickly became a media darling. . . . But Villaraigosa . . . has told . . . interviewers and others that his ethnic background does not define him, just as the Latino population itself does not easily fit into categories.

Definition of Culture

The subject of how *culture* is defined can easily take an entire book, and often has done so. This construct historically has been defined and operationalized by academic fields such as anthropology and sociology, and more recently, psychology. However, in the 1960s the construct found increased significance within human services, social work not being an exception, because of an understanding and appreciation of how culture influences help-seeking perceptions and behaviors. Culture forms, as a result, an integral part in the programming and structuring of the helping process (Greene, Watkins, McNutt, & Lopez, 1998; Waites et al., 2004).

Cauce (2002), in examining culture within a quantitative-empirical research framework, advances three constructs (acculturation, ethnic identity, and ethnic minority socialization) that lend themselves to measuring various key dimensions of culture in a research endeavor. Each of these dimensions will be addressed in various degrees in this and subsequent chapters.

Social workers cannot assume or be expected to know all cultures; thus they become "perpetual" learners in order to become and remain relevant practitioners. No social work educational program, regardless of how progressive it is, can provide all of the information social workers will need in addressing ethnic and racial communities in the United States. No postgraduate certificate can stamp a social worker as being "culturally competent," and therefore not needing further formal or informal education to remain "current." However, a good educational or training program provides its students with the necessary tools and attitudes that legitimize their learning process, and prepares them to learn from a variety of sources, particularly from the consumers and their community. They, after all, are the ultimate experts on their situations, backgrounds, aspirations, and concerns, and their voices must be tapped whenever possible.

For the purposes of this book, the definition of culture developed by Locke (1992, p. 10) will be used because of its emphasis on social navigational skills that, I believe, are essential for survival of any group: "Culture is a body of learned beliefs, traditions, principles, and guides for behavior that are commonly shared among members of a particular group. Culture serves as a road map for both perceiving and interacting with the world." This definition, though simple, touches upon the complexity of this construct and how it manages to manifest itself in daily interactions. Culture plays a multifaceted role in the lives of people. It not only provides meaning and purpose but also serves as a protective factor in helping people to navigate stressful and even tumultuous times. This all-encompassing role makes any definition of culture arduous to achieve, and that should be expected. An operational definition of culture would be extensive in nature, covering music, art, folklore, history, customs, and so on. The concept of culture I subscribe to is elastic in quality, expanding and contracting to emphasize or deemphasize certain elements depending upon the group being addressed, and the circumstances they find themselves in.

Further, any definition of culture must also take into account how this construct goes far beyond what is conventionally referred to as culture. In fact, a host of sociodemographic variables, such as age, gender, socioeconomic class, religion, profession, educational level, sexual orientation, marital status, political affiliation, physical and cognitive abilities, and urban versus rural based—to list but several of the most prominently mentioned ones—also serve to interact with and change cultural values and beliefs (Beck, Williams, Hope, & Park, 2001).

Lum (2003, p. 35) summed up quite well the types of contextual considerations or questions that must be answered in order to be effective in providing assistance:

> In order to fully understand a person, one must take into account the total context of how the texture of the person has been woven together to form a unique being. What pieces or ingredients have been put together to form a mosaic or detailed pattern? What is the total context that transcends the person and the environment and MUST be understood for helping to proceed?

Culture is an integral part of this context.

This context may also involve elements that we do not necessarily think about. The contextual reality of a Puerto Rican with dark skin pigmentation and green eyes, for example, will differ from that of a person who is white with blue eyes and blond hair. Both can share a common identity of being Puerto Rican. However, the latter one will have an easier time socially navigating in this society, with potentially different outcomes regarding success and wealth (Fears, 2003; Gonzalez, 2003; Montalvo, 1999, 2004; Navarro, 2003b; Poe, 2003). For example, in 2002, the unemployment rate for Latino blacks was 12.3 percent, compared to 8 percent for all Latinos; their poverty rate was 31.5 percent, compared to 26 percent for all Latinos; and their median household income was $35,000, compared to $38,500 for all Latinos (Gonzales, 2003).

In the 2000 U.S. census, only 2 percent of Latinos identified themselves as being black. However, almost 28 percent of those doing so resided in New York City (Navarro, 2003b). New York City, in turn, has the largest concentration of Caribbean Latinos in the nation. Poe (2003) comments that Latinos who self-identify themselves as black share a socioeconomic status more in common with African Americans/blacks than with other Latinos or white, non-Latino Americans.

Nevertheless, terms such as "white" and "black" do not have the same significance for many Latinos. Latinos have created terms such as "Moreno," "trigueno," and "indio," for example, to attempt to capture skin shades and ancestry, and in so doing, attempt to take into account different hues, rather than the traditional white-black classification used in this country (Navarro, 2003a). One Latina (New York City Puerto Rican) summed up this dilemma quite well (Navarro, 2003a, p. 12): "I feel that being Latina implies mixed racial heritage and I wish more people knew that. Why should I have to choose?"

Choosing, however, if it is at all possible, essentially amounts to having to deny a part of a Latino heritage or ancestral line that may have relatives that are near and dear. This will cause great pain and negative results for Latinos who do so, as they become ever vigilant that their histories stay buried. A tremendous amount of energy must be devoted to this goal, energy that, I believe, can be better spent on other socially challenging pursuits such as achievement of social and economic justice for all Latinos.

A 24-year-old Dominican New Yorker, who immigrated at the age of 11, and who is black in his physical features and identifies as such in this country, brings an added dimension to this dilemma (Navarro, 2003a, p. 12): "In the Dominican Republic . . . he was called 'Indio,' Indian. That is because even the darkest-skinned Dominican often regards 'black' as a synonym for Haitian; the two nations, which share the island of Hispaniola, have a long history of conflict." An understanding of history does not always equate to positive outcomes; history can also bring "baggage" in relating to newcomers to this country.

Montalvo (2004, p. 39) goes on note the implications of phenotype for social work practice:

> Practitioners . . . have paid scant attention to phenotype in the assessment of problems in identity development, family dynamics, and intergroup relations judging from the absence in the literature. This is curious since Latinas consistently reported that skin color prejudice was a key factor in their lives, and research evidence has consistently pointed to it as a major stressor.

Thus, the interplay of numerous social factors, phenotype being one, creates a social experience for each Latino that may share commonalties across subgroups, but still manages to retain unique features for that individual, depending upon his or her social demographic profile (Ortiz, 1995).

Practitioners as well as academic researchers have much to learn about how this emerging community views itself and others. It is highly recommended that Latino consumers and community be provided with an opportunity to answer how they define themselves rather than make assumptions or be expected to fall into a small range of categories on ethnic or racial groupings. There is clearly no consensus on how best to label this population group, and as time passes, it is becoming even more arduous to find labels that can characterize the experiences of this group!

Definition of Cultural Assets

The definition of cultural assets that will guide this book is premised on the fundamental belief that all human groups possess some forms of assets or strengths, as well as needs. The question of what these assets are takes precedence over the typical question of whether there are any assets or strengths. Wording takes on great importance in any dialogue. However, this importance weighs especially heavily in how providers, in this case social workers, view undervalued communities in this society. Emphasizing "What are they?" rather than "Are there any?" represents a sociopolitical viewpoint with immense implications for how helping professions view the people they seek to assist.

Cultural assets is a construct that represents the beliefs, traditions, principles, knowledge, and skills that effectively help people, particularly those who have been marginalized economically and socially by a society, to perceive and succeed in spite of immense odds against them. The collectivity of these elements forms a groups' or community's cultural assets. These assets, as will be addressed in subsequent chapters, are not fixed in time or substance, and are subject to changes as the context changes. Nevertheless, the presence of cultural assets remains throughout a group's lifetime in various forms and shapes, ready to be tapped in times of need.

Conclusion

As this introductory chapter has hopefully pointed out, the subject of social work and Latinos is not only timely but one that must be ever present in how the profession views its historical mission of addressing the needs of America's newcomers. The challenges posed by that mission, however, are not to be minimized or overlooked as the United States continues to witness an unparalleled expansion in the number of Latinos within its borders. The complexity and challenges are equally matched by the rewards and the realization of the potential contributions of this expanding community across all geographical sectors of the country, but particularly in its urban centers (Logan, 2002b; Wilson, 2003).

Numerous concepts and issues will be touched upon and, in some cases, delved into in great depth in this book. No one book can possibly do justice to all of the dimensions associated with social work practice with Latinos. This book, unfortunately, is no exception. Nevertheless, the quest for a paradigm to guide all forms of social work interventions is equivalent to a search for an all-encompassing theory of the universe. Although it is not currently available, hope springs eternal that it is within the grasp of science, and the challenge never dissuades scientists from articulating and embracing this goal. This book is about this goal, to bring all facets of social work together in common pursuit of social interventions that affirm, empower, and, ultimately, serve Latinos in the United States.

Chapter 2

DEMOGRAPHIC PROFILE, TRENDS, AND COMMENTARY

Latinos are changing the way the country looks, feels, and thinks, eats, dances, and votes. From teeming immigrant Meccas to small-town America, they are filling churches, building businesses, and celebrating this nation's heritage. . . . In America, a country that constantly redefines itself, the rise of Latinos also raises questions about race, identity, and culture—and whether the United States will ever truly be one nation.

Brock Larmer, "Latino America" (1999)

It is quite appropriate to start this chapter with Brock Larmer's statement because it captures the challenges this country is facing in the early part of the twenty-first century as the Latino community continues to expand numerically and influence all facets of this society. There is no geographical sector of the United States that does not have either a significant Latino presence or one that is starting to emerge to the point where there is recognition of this as an up-and-coming community (Logan, 2002a, 2003a). These population changes in some instances can be seen as dramatic or just a continuation of a pattern of growth that can be traced back decades, as the case may be. At any rate, there is no mistaking a sense in the air that the times are changing in many communities across this nation.

Viglucci and Henderson (2003, p. 1) address the multitude of ways these changes will transform the country:

Even as sociologists and political scientists debate the implications of this shift, one thing is certain: Much faster growth in the Hispanic population, fueled by immigration and higher birth rates, means the numerical gulf [with African Americans] will only continue to widen. . . . What this means is unclear. Many foresee increasing Hispanic economic and political clout, potentially at blacks' expense. Some see little prospect of a Hispanic national monolith, noting that the label groups people of widely differing—and sometimes rivaling—cultures, national origins and races. Others note the effects are already evident: Hispanic voters are a growing factor in state and national elections, in which they often serve as swing voting blocs.

Latinos, in essence, have joined the groups of "soccer moms" and "NASCAR" dads as a unit of analysis. However, the diversity of this community makes it difficult to consider this group a cohesive bloc (Betancourt, 2005).

The history of the United States has witnessed numerous periods during which this country has encountered significant changes in the composition of its residents, with no century not having experienced this. This coming century will probably enter into the history books as being comparable to that of the nineteenth century when the shores of the United States were teeming with newcomers. However, there is probably no period in U.S. history where the overall composition has changed as dramatically as it has in the past 20 years. The changes have received considerable national public attention and have only slowly been recognized in the scholarly literature.

In the mid-1990s, this country's shifting demographics first received increased national attention (Seelye, 1997). This country has continued not only aging ("graying") but also "browning" (racially and ethnically) at an unprecedented pace as a result of these demographic shifts (Scommegna, 2004). Both of these trends have had, and will continue to have, profound social, economic, political, and technological implications. The field of social work, as a result, will be expected to continue to play an increasingly significant role in how social services take into account linguistic and cultural factors. The label that is used to categorize the "Latino experience" in the United States says much about how this population group views itself and how others view it. The role of government (federal and state) in shaping data on Latinos plays an influential role in how this community views itself and how the country and human service organizations view it (Rodriguez, 2000).

This chapter presents the latest demographic information on Latinos and will specifically highlight key demographic trends in a variety of domains that will have direct implications for social work practice. Commentary and analysis will also be provided in an attempt to contextualize what these statistics mean from a historical and present-day perspective, in an attempt to identify key social and economic implications for the nation. In addition, a section of this chapter is devoted to looking at Latino demographics within a historical context, in order for the reader to develop an appreciation of Latinos in the United States. The reader, however, is advised that this chapter only attempts to provide a brief snapshot of a population group that is getting harder and harder to characterize through the presentation of statistics. Further, even when these statistics do a "reliable" job of reflecting the reality of this group, they are quickly becoming dated, making it arduous to capture an accurate picture even under the best of intentions and circumstances.

In an attempt to provide a comprehensive demographic snapshot of the Latino community in the United States, and to do so in a manner that does not totally overwhelm the reader in the process, this chapter is divided into three major sections: "Social Demographics and Projections"; "Educational and Economic Demographics"; and "Contact with Country of Origin and Political and Media Representation." Each of these sections can stand alone, so to speak. However, as the reader will soon discover, there will invariably be overlaps within these sections and their subsections. Life, after all, can never be relegated to sections, even though we in academia persist on making it so!

Social Demographics and Projections

Challenges in Developing an Accurate Profile

Obtaining an accurate count of the number of Latinos residing in the United States has historically been an arduous task, and the difficulty persists to this day (Alaya, 2001; Sanchez, 2002; Scott, 2003). Camarillo and Bonilla (2001, p. 120) note: "It may seem ironic to many that one of the thorniest intellectual and social-policy challenges presented by the surging number of Hispanics on the U.S. mainland today is identifying and counting them." Problems associated with the counting of Latinos have resulted in an estimated undercounting of at least 4.9 percent of this community in the 2000 U.S. census (California, *California Latino demographic databook*, 2004). This undercounting has far-reaching implications for how federal funds are distributed based upon population census. Locales where Latinos reside, as a result, have been underfunded (Fields, 2001). Undercounting, as a result, effectively translates into being invisible and underserved.

The U.S. census is arguably the most cited source for demographics, and it has serious limitations (Brahan & Bauchner, 2005; Sandelur et al., 2001; Tafoya, 2004; Williams & Jackson, 2000). The 2000 U.S. census had 126 different combinations that could be specified, unlike the 1990 census, which had six race categories. This resulted in seven million people identifying themselves as multiracial (Hodgkinson, 2004). Latinos can easily fall into multiple categories. In the 2000 U.S. census, almost half (48 percent) of Latinos considered themselves white, with 42 percent listing some other race and approximately 6 percent noting two or more races (Grieco & Cassidy, 2001). Two percent of all Latinos characterize themselves as black. Amaro and Zambrana (2000, p. 1724) raise concerns about this point from a different perspective: "In a flurry of activity to resolve challenges posed by multiple race responses, we must remember the large issue that looms in the foreground—the lack of adequate estimates of mortality and health conditions affecting Hispanics/Latinos."

Further, the large numbers of Latinos who are undocumented simply do not show up in any census tabulation, due to very realistic fears about being identified and deported back to their countries of origin (Fernandez, 2005; Rodriguez, 2001; Scott, 2001). Finally, it takes years before the U.S. Census Bureau is able to report statistics, making reflections on the present situation dubious at best. In essence, data are "dated" as soon as they appear in any public-issued report, particularly ones issued by some form of governmental agency!

Demographic Numbers and Profile

Latino demographics during the past 25 years have shown a steady trend toward significant population increases throughout the nation. It is estimated that there are over 41 million Latinos in the United States in 2004, making this group the largest "minority group" in the United States, surpassing African Americans/blacks (Caldwell, 2005; Files, 2005; Held, 2005; Pear, 2005; Saenz, 2005). The "official" point at which this occurred is 2002 (Viglucci & Henderson, 2003). Between 2000 and 2004, Latinos increased by 17 percent, the most of any ethnic and racial group in the country (Pear, 2005).

In 2004, Texas joined California to become one of the nation's two most populous states with a majority of residents being of color (Pear, 2005). Hawaii (77 percent) and New Mexico (56.5 percent) are the two other states with majority of populations of color. Latinos played important roles in these changing demographics in California, New Mexico, and Texas.

One estimate had the United States Latino population at 500,000 in 1900 (New Latino nation, 2005). Another perspective on this number is that the Latino community in the United States gives the United States the fifth largest Spanish-origin population in the world. It is estimated that by the year 2050, the United States will be the second largest Spanish-speaking country, surpassed only by Mexico (Coleman, 2003). The Latino population grew between 2003 and 2004 at a rate of 3.6 percent, or three times the rate of the total population (Files, 2005).

The Latino community in the United States is a highly diverse group consisting of 29 subgroups, as noted in figure 2.1. Updated statistics reflect how the dynamic of Latino population growth has changed the distribution of group representation: Mexicans, with 20,641,000 (58 percent), Puerto Ricans, with 3,406,000 (10 percent), Cubans, with 1,242,000 (4 percent), and Dominicans, with 965,000 (2.2 percent), account for a total of almost 26 million, or 75 percent of the entire Latino community (Marotta & Garcia, 2003). The emergence of new Latino subgroups, however, represents a dramatic departure from demographic patterns in the 1980s and before (Scott, 2003).

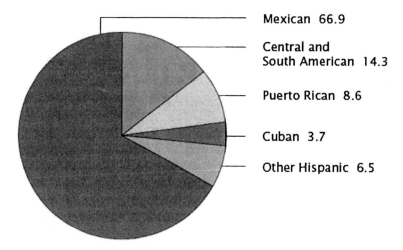

Mexican 66.9

Central and
South American 14.3

Puerto Rican 8.6

Cuban 3.7

Other Hispanic 6.5

Figure 2.1. Hispanics by origin (percentage): 2002. Source: U.S. Census Bureau, Annual Demographic Supplement to the March 2002 Current Population Survey

The "other" Latino category, consisting of 25 groups, accounted from over 10 million in the year 2000, and represented approximately 26 percent of the total Latino population in the United States, an increase from 23 percent in 1990 (Marotta & Garcia, 2003). Salvadoran (655,000), Colombian (471,000), Guatemalan (372,000), Ecuadorian (261,000), and Peruvian (234,000) represent the five largest Central and South American groups (U.S. Bureau of the Census, 2000). There were almost six million Latinos who did not provide specific information about their national origin, making these figures conservative (Hendricks, 2003).

Important demographic distinctions exist within and between Latino subgroups based upon country of origin, making generalizations impossible to do. The median age of a Latino in this country is 25.9 years, compared to 35.3 for the nation as a whole, 30.0 for African American/blacks, and 31.1 for Asians and Pacific Islanders. Mexicans, Puerto Ricans, and Central and South Americans, for example, have a median age of 24.4, 28.0, and 29.9 years, respectively. Cubans, on the other hand, have an average age of 41.4 years, making them the oldest Latino subgroup (U.S. Bureau of the Census, 2000).

As noted earlier in this chapter and in figure 2.2, Latinos in the United States are by all accounts very young and will continue to be young when compared to most other racial and ethnic groups. Approximately 33 percent of the Latino population is under the age of 18. This is similar to that of African Americans (32 percent) and Asians and Pacific Islanders, with 33 percent (U.S. Bureau of the Census, 2003, 2005).

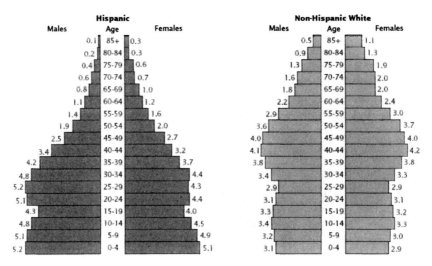

Figure 2.2. Population by Hispanic origin, age, and sex (percentage): 2002. Source: U.S. Census Bureau, Annual Demographic Supplement to the March 2002 Current Population Survey

The Latino population is increasing in age, however, and is projected to do so well into this century. Increased longevity, however, can be a blessing, as will be noted in chapter 3. If Latinos manage to live to the age of 65 years, Latinas, for example, can be expected to go on to live to age 87, and Latino males to reach 84 years, longer than any other ethnic group in this country (AFL-CIO, 2005). This longevity, as a result, has tremendous implications for Social Security, and any efforts to reform it. Further, as noted in one recent study, Alzheimer's may strike Latinos at an earlier age (67.6 years) than white non-Latinos (74.6 years), raising implications for Latinos as they increase numerically during the coming decade (Berger, 2005).

Elders enjoy a respected role in families and communities, and can be considered critical assets in the social fabric of Latino social networks (Bullock, 2005; Delgado, 1998c). Nevertheless, the effects of poverty on health carry over into old age, with Latinos having more restricted access to private pension plans than white, non-Latino retirees. And since Medicare coverage requires substantial copayments, and Social Security coverage is related to income throughout one's lifetime, low-income workers arrive at old age at a financial disadvantage, with low social security and no pensions. In 2001, an estimated 19 percent of elder Latinos 65 years or older were poor, compared to 7 percent for white, non-Latino elders. Without Social Security benefits, the Latino poverty rate would increase from 16 percent to 55 percent (Labor Council for Latin American Advancement, 2005). More significantly, elder Latinas are among the most economically impoverished older women, especially if they are unmarried, and even if they receive Social Security benefits or Supplemental

Security Income. Thus, they are subjected to triple jeopardy (female, of color, and old).

Latino elders 65 years and older, when compared to other seniors in this country, are must likely to have been employed in jobs with low wages, with a median income of $22,400, compared to $28,400 (Labor Council for Latin American Advancement, 2005). It is estimated that only 28 percent of Latino retirees have income from sources in addition to Social Security; this compares to 63 percent for white non-Latinos. One recent study, by La Raza and the Pew Charitable Trust's Retirement Security Project, found that more than half of Latinos aged 55 to 59 years had no money in retirement accounts; this compares with a median account of $10,400 for all households in that age group (O'Rourke, 2005). Not surprisingly, almost 2.3 million Latinos receive Social Security benefits, and 75 percent of them depend on it for a majority of their income (Labor Council for Latin American Advancement, 2005). Social Security keeps 32.9 percent of Latino elders out of poverty each year (Solis, 2005).

The subject of retirement has also emerged for both the undocumented and the documented Mexicans. Porter and Malkin (2005), in a topic overlooked in the gerontological literature, raise questions about Mexicans as they approach retirement; namely, where will they retire to? Will they go back to Mexico or stay in the United States? Either decision will have profound social and economic implications for the receiving nation. In 2003, California, for example, had an estimated 710,000 Mexicans over the age of 60, or 63 percent more than in 1993 (Porter & Malkin, 2005a). Projected demographic increases, as a result, can be expected to have a significant impact on all regions of that state.

As will be addressed in chapter 3, Latinos are disproportionately employed in industries that have high accident rates. Thus, not surprisingly, Latinos are 40 percent more likely to experience job-related injuries and become disabled compared to others, making them even more reliant on Social Security disability benefits (Labor Council for Latin American Advancement, 2005). Andresen and Brownson (2000) found a high rate of job-related disabilities among women of color (African American, Asian and Latina), which was two to three times that of white non-Latinas.

Foreign-Born and U.S.-Born Latinos

The distinction between Latinos born and raised in the United States and those who are foreign-born or recently arrived in this country is one that social workers and other helping professionals cannot ignore in the development of assessments and interventions. It is estimated that in 2004, one in seven workers in the United States were born overseas (One in seven U.S. workers, 2005). For example, there were 21 million workers who were foreign-born, with half having arrived since 1990. Approximately 40 percent of these foreign-born workers were from either Mexico or Central America, with 25 percent from Asia (One in seven U.S. workers, 2005).

Figure 2.3 reflects data from the 2000 U.S. census. Data from 2004, the most updated figure, show increases that have occurred since 2000. The U.S. foreign-born population totaled 34.2 million in 2004, representing a 2.3 percent increase from the previous year (Franzil, 2005). A total of 13.1 million, or 38.3 percent, obtained citizenship.

An estimated 18 million, or 53 percent, of this nation's foreign-born were Latino; Mexicans accounted for 31 percent (5.6 million) of all foreign-born, almost doubling their percent of 16 percent in 1980 (Franzil, 2005). More than 40 percent of the United States foreign-born population is Latino in origin, with 68 percent of the Latinos reporting being either immigrants themselves or the children of immigrants (Jolly, 2004). Approximately 10 percent of all Americans speak Spanish in the home.

The Pew Hispanic Center (2002c, p. 1) emphasizes the importance of second-generation Latino youth for the twenty-first century:

> If immigration fueled the Hispanic population to date, tomorrow it will be their children who drive growth. Ten million "second generation" U.S.-born children of immigrants make up 29 percent of all Hispanics. Another 11 million comprise the "third generation" (born to two native-born parents) and represent 31 percent of all Latinos.

Statistics from 2004 confirm that the newcomer population in the United States is becoming younger, creating a unique generational divide (Files, 2005).

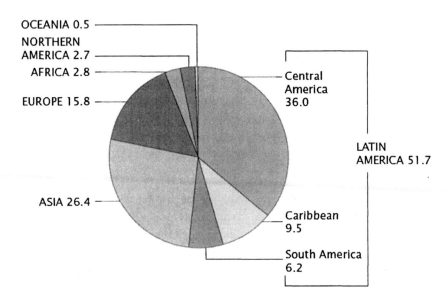

Figure 2.3. Percentage distribution of the foreign-born population by world region of birth: 2000. Source: U.S. Census Bureau, Census 2000, Summary File 3

Immigrants over the age of 40 years are largely white non-Latinos, and those under that age are most likely Latino, Asian, or from other groups of color (Files, 2005, p. A11):

> The increase in young immigrants is particularly noticeable among this nation's largest minority group, Hispanics, half of whom are under age 27. One of every five children under age 18 in the United States is Hispanic. . . . Hispanics accounted for about half of the overall population growth of 2.9 million people from 2003 to 2004.

The subject of foreign- versus U.S.-born will also be addressed from an acculturation perspective in chapter 3, and Ewing and Johnson (2003, p. 1) raise this important point for consideration when discussing Latinos in the United States:

> Latinos experience substantial socioeconomic progress across generations compared to both their immigrant forefathers and native Anglos. But this fact is lost in statistical portraits of the Latino population which don't distinguish between the large number of newcomers and those who have been in the United States for generations.

When the gap between acculturation status of children identified with American culture and parents identified with Latino culture increases, stress occurs, resulting in an increased likelihood of children engaging in risky behaviors (Elliott & Cosden, 2000).

Smith (2003) found in an economic study of Latinos in the United States that successful generations of Latinos, in this case males, experienced significantly greater improvements in income and formal education attainment when compared to white non-Latinos ("Anglos"). Jolly (2004, p. 2) makes a similar observation:

> Unfortunately, the data available through many reports and the media are based on data aggregation techniques and analyses that can lead to oversimplifying the tasks before us. Far too often, demographic reports collapse data sets across many subcategories of community, running the risk of distorting, both by overstatement and understatement, the real shifts that underlie the new demographic.

Fry (2003) also raises the importance of policymakers and practitioners being able to differentiate between foreign-born Latinos and those born in the United States in examining school dropout rates. Grogger and Trejo (2002), in examining educational and income gains between first-, second-, and third-generation Mexicans, concluded that the long-term economic prospects of U.S.-born Mexicans were considerably higher than those of their parents.

Ewing and Johnson (2003), in summarizing the literature on this topic, concluded:

> Despite the formidable obstacles confronting Latin American immigrants, Latinos are in fact experiencing a process of socioeconomic advancement across generations. Those born in the United States achieve average levels of education, income and English proficiency far greater than their immigrant parents and grandparents. However, because a large percentage of contemporary Latinos are first-generation immigrants, these advances across generations are often lost in aggregate statistics that analyze the Latino population as if it were an undifferentiated whole.

As already noted in chapter 1, Puerto Ricans are the only Latino group that has U.S. citizenship and has had this status since 1917, with the signing of the Jones Act. This Act initially gave Puerto Ricans the option of becoming United States citizens or remaining Puerto Rican citizens. Shortly after its passage, the option was rescinded, and all Puerto Ricans became citizens. Critics of this action point to the institution of the draft for Puerto Ricans to serve in World War I.

Other Latino groups, however, bring with them unique journeys that cannot be simply brushed aside (Acevedo, 2004; Hernandez, 2004; Marquez & Padilla, 2004; Zuniga, 2004). In the case of Mexicans, the Treaty of Guadalupe Hidalgo, signed in 1848, effectively transferred more than half of Mexico's territory to the United States (Arana, 2001, p. 1):

> But the document was also meant to protect the rights of those of us who had populated that land for centuries. We had not arrived on U.S. shores starry-eyed, yearning to be free. We had crossed no borders. We had settled these lands long before Pilgrims ever set foot on Plymouth Rock. The border, more accurately, had crossed us.

Borders, in essence, crossed Mexicans in the case of Texas and California; they, in turn, did not cross the border (Iglehart & Becerra, 1995). This historical fact, or consideration, is often lost in any dialogue pertaining to the presence of Mexicans in the United States, with most attention, or debate if you wish, being focused on the number of "undocumented Mexicans" residing in this country, particularly in the Southwest (Hendricks, 2002). One estimate has the number of undocumented Mexicans living in the United States surpassing that of those who are citizens and have proper legal status.

Understanding Latino history becomes an important step in better understanding the role of internal colonization in how Latinos construct their reality, perspectives on race, identity, and significant relationships (Holleran, 2003). History becomes a foundation, or set of lenses, through which Latinos, particularly youth, can find their place in this society, through affirmation rather than shame!

Portes and Rumbaul (2001), in their study of Latino newcomer youth, found that youth who become too Americanized, or highly acculturated, too fast effectively "outgrow" their parents and their influence in their lives. These youth, in turn, are more likely to engage in risky behaviors. However, those who do not acculturate, or do so at too deliberate a pace, show little or no advantage over those that acculturate too quickly in the areas of schooling and dropout rates. The subject of Latino acculturation will be addressed in much greater depth again in chapter 3.

Undocumented Latinos

Public opinions on the role and threat of undocumented newcomers in the United States indicate that this subject is bound to elicit spirited debate, if not outright hostility, depending upon who is asked and where they live (Borden, 2005; Cornelius, 2002; Hendricks, 2005a; Loera, 2004; Murdock, 1998; Seper, 2004). Like any other issue that can be considered controversial, there is no consensus on the extent of the "problem," who is to blame, and how best to address it. How the contributions of undocumented immigrants in the United States are defined and measured is such an example. Finding a "middle ground" on this subject is almost impossible in the heat of the debate on "securing our nation's borders."

Nevertheless, recent estimates of newcomers to the United States peaked in 2000. The number of legal permanent residents declined to 455,000 in 2004 from 647,000 in 2000 (Bernstein, 2005). Thus, the majority of newcomers to the United States are undocumented, with Mexicans representing a significant segment of this population.

It is important to note before proceeding, however, that the vast majority (61 percent) of immigrants to this country are permanent residents, refugees (7 percent), or temporary legal residents (3 percent), with undocumented migrants accounting for 29 percent (Hendricks, 2005b). Unfortunately, the highly charged subject of undocumented status has relegated the state of 71 percent of this country's newcomer community to a background in any discussion of immigration policies and the conditions they face upon entry into this country, particularly in the case of children (Delgado, Jones, & Rohani, 2005). Even when the immigrants are documented, their impact on state and local government, as in the case of Florida with Cubans and Haitians, can be quite significant and controversial (McNeece, Falconer, & Springer, 2002).

Critics of the undocumented argue that they used $26.3 billion in government services in 2002 but paid only $16 billion in taxes, and thereby constitute a drain on the economy (Loera, 2004). Medicaid ($2.5 billion), treatment for the uninsured ($2.2 billion), food assistance and school lunches ($1.9 billion), the federal prison and court system ($1.6 billion), and federal aid to schools ($1.4) were the major cost categories (Seper, 2004). Undocumented people are considered a threat to this nation's economy because they supposedly take jobs away from citizens and depress labor market wages, and utilize educational, health, and human services. In addition, they represent a threat to the social fabric of the country because they display no intention of adopting American values. Finally, they represent a threat to national security.

Advocates of the undocumented, however, counter that Latinos who are undocumented come to this country in search of employment and are very often recruited by businesses in the United States (Krissman, 2000, p. 277):

> I found that many labor-intensive industries in the United States have crafted personal practices to foster the proliferation of labor recruitment agents. Among other dubious activities, these agents facilitate the flow of new workers across the United States–Mexico border even as undocumented migration becomes an increasingly volatile political issue.

Wal-Mart, for example, paid an $11 million fine to settle a legal case involving independent contractors using undocumented immigrants (Cantwell, 2005). Undocumented Latinos, in turn, very often take jobs that native-born laborers refuse to take (Benson, 1999; Griffith, 1999; Marcelli, 1999). They are also in very vulnerable positions and in need of labor protection (Undocumented immigrants, 2005). Further, they do not use health care to the same extent as native-born populations (McKenna, 2005).

Cerrutti and Massey's (2001) study of female migration from Mexico to the United States found that Latino male immigrants move to this country in search of employment; wives generally do so motivated by family reasons; and daughters, in turn, generally move in search of employment. Johnson-Webb's (2000) research on recruitment of Latino immigrants for work in nontraditional areas found this group to be highly sought after by employers. Advocates also go on to note that many undocumented people pay their local, state, and federal taxes, and do not engage in criminal activity once they enter the country (Hernandez, 2003b).

A recent study by the Center for American Progress estimated that it would cost the government more than $41 billion a year to remove undocumented immigrants from the country, with the total cost amounting to $206–230 billion over the course of five years (Fears, 2005). Apprehension would cost $28 billion, followed by $6 billion for detention, $4 billion to secure the borders, $2 billion to process the immigrants, and $1.6 billion to transport them back to their country of origin.

The most recent estimates on the number of undocumented residents in this country has this group totaling approximately 11 million, or 4 percent of this nation's total population (Passel, 2005). This number and percentage represents a continued increase of the country's total population over the past decade. Between 2000 and 2004, for example, the yearly number of undocumented immigrants entering the United States averaged 485,000 (Younge,

2005). It is estimated that 1.7 million of these are children under the age of 18 years.

The likelihood of continued migration of Mexicans to the United States in the near future is considered great. Demographers project that Mexico's 11- to 40-year-old population, which is considered the prime age group for migration, will grow by 6 percent (50 million) by 2015 (Porter & Malkin, 2005b). This projection translates into approximately 400,000 Mexicans potentially entering the United States.

Although the United States has two borders, the Mexican side has received the lion's share of media and political attention. Mexico's border with the United States has facilitated the entrance of undocumented Latinos into this country. Latinos account for 81 percent of all undocumented immigrants in this country, followed by Asians (9 percent), Europeans and Canadians (6 percent) and Africans and others with 4 percent (Hendricks, 2005a). Mexicans are the most represented Latino group in this population, numbering 6 million, or 55 percent of all undocumented persons. Since the mid-1990s, a number of states with historically low numbers of foreign-born have experienced the greatest increase in undocumented residents (Younge, 2005).

Several states, following the trend established in the 1980s and 1990s, continue to be primary destinations for undocumented Latino migrants to the United States. California (which probably should not come as any great surprise to the reader) is the state with the largest number, with an estimated 2.4 million, or 24 percent of all undocumented Latinos in this country (Hendricks, 2005b). Texas (14 percent), Florida (9 percent), and New York (7 percent) follow California as the states with the greatest number of Latinos who are undocumented.

Organizations such as the Minutemen Civil Defense Corps have undertaken a highly publicized initiative to turn back undocumented Latinos crossing the Mexican border with the United States (Bernstein, 2005). Interestingly, a counter-organization called Paisanos al Rescate (Countrymen to the Rescue) has formed and seeks to limit the number of deaths occurring in border deserts (Romero, 2005).

Nonetheless, other states have started to experience unprecedented increases in the number of undocumented Latinos in the past five years, reflecting a shift in migration patterns and destinations (Martinez, 2004). North Carolina, Maryland, and Arizona, for example, are three states with large numbers of undocumented migrants. North Carolina has an estimated 300,000 undocumented Latinos, an increase from 77,000 in 1990 (Martinez, 2005). This is now considered the eighth largest undocumented Latino population in the United States (Easterbrook, 2005). Maryland's number of Latino undocumented increased from an estimated 120,000 in 2000 to 250,000 in 2004 (Brewington, 2005).

Arizona has witnessed a dramatic increase in undocumented Latinos since 2000 and now has an estimated 500,000 (5 percent of the state's total population), making it the fifth largest state with this population group (Hawley, 2005).

The popularity of Arizona as a point of entry into this country is borne out by a sad statistic, namely, the number of deaths of Latino undocumented recorded in 2003—a record during 2003–4 (Zernike & Thompson, 2003). In 2003, 135 undocumented Latinos died attempting to cross over into this country through Arizona's desert (Trial of Latino migration, 2003). During fiscal year 2005, more than 200 died, resulting in the use of a refrigerated tractor-trailer as a temporary morgue because of the record number of deaths (Deaths on border, 2005a). California, too, has not escaped this tragedy. In Holtsville, California, for example, the first 11 months of fiscal year 2004 witnessed 314 people dying while attempting to cross the United States–Mexico border (LeDuff, 2004).

Contrary to popular opinion, not every undocumented Latino who enters this country manages to succeed in staying (Brosnan, 2001; Strength in numbers, 2005). In 10 months of 2003, it was estimated that over 750,000 were apprehended and deported back to their country of origin (Trial of Latino migration, 2003). In 2004, 157,000 foreign nationals were deported from the United States, 70 percent of whom were Latinos (Llorente, 2005). The number of Latinos currently incarcerated and awaiting deportation is considerable. United States immigration prisons hold an estimated 200,000 people annually, or 23,000 on any given day (Dow, 2004).

However, this statistic does not take into account undocumented prisoners who have committed a crime and are in U.S. prisons serving their sentence. One billion dollars is the estimate of the costs associated with incarcerating the undocumented in county jails and prisons (Nelson, 2005). In 2004, San Francisco held 1,400 undocumented persons in the county jail. Arizona, in turn, held 3,600 to 4,000 in state prisons, resulting in the state billing the federal government for $118 million in unreimbursable costs associated with incarceration of this population group. In 2005, the United States Supreme Court ruled that the government cannot indefinitely incarcerate immigrants who cannot be deported back to their country of origins, in this case Cubans who have committed and served their prison sentences, because the country of origin will not accept them back (Shogran, 2005).

There is general consensus that the search for gainful employment is the primary reason for undocumented Latinos entering the United States (Berk et al., 2000). The following two social commentaries sum up the business point of view on the undocumented quite well (Source of immigration problem, 2005, p. F5):

> There are businesses all over the country paying far lower wages to illegal immigrants than they would have to pay native-born employees. They know exactly what they are doing, and they are profiting from it handsomely. . . .
> Let's not forget that, in the 18th century and the early days of the Republic, the spiritual ancestors of these businessmen felt no compunction about buying African slaves who worked hard and didn't have to be paid at all. The result was a bloody civil war, and a tragic social division that echoes into our times.

The Virginia's General Assembly's Joint Legislative Audit and Review Commission reported in 2004 that

> foreign immigrants were an economic boon that more than offset their costs. Hispanic workers were crucial to tourism and other service industries and to agriculture. . . . Economists also typically agree that [there is a] net benefit, citing the boost immigrants give the aging U.S. labor force, the taxes they funnel in Social Security and Medicare, their purchasing power and the revitalization that often accompanies their move into declining urban areas. (Turning immigrants into Virginians, 2005, p. B6)

The *New York Times* published a series of articles on social class in the United States in 2005; one article was specifically devoted to the plight of Mexican undocumented immigrants in New York City (DePalma, 2005a). The author comments on how the influx of Mexican undocumented workers has affected Latinos in the labor market, an impact that has often been overlooked in press and government reports (p. A16):

> That is not to suggest that the nearly five million Mexicans who . . . are living in the United States illegally will never emerge from the shadows. But the sheer size of the influx—over 400,000 a year, with no end in sight—creates a problem all of its own. It means that there is an ever-growing pool of interchangeable roles [*sic*], many of them shunting from one low-paying job to another. If one moves on, another one—or maybe two or three—is there to take his place.

DePalma (2005b, p. A20) goes on to provide another vivid description of how Mexican undocumented workers have helped transform labor sectors in New York City:

> In a complex, constantly changing city, niche businesses keep things humming. Fifteen years ago Mr. Kazanis [employment agency] sent men from Bangladesh and China to fill the back-of-the-house positions in restaurant kitchens. But the population of Mexicans in the city tripled during the 1990's, making Mexicans one of the fastest-growing groups in New York. Now he specializes in sending Mexican workers to Greek restaurants and diners. "They are very good quality workers . . . If these illegals leave New York City, New York will die. I know."

The exploitation of undocumented Latinos is a crime that rarely gets prosecuted, and when it does, it sheds light on the excessiveness of the abuse, as in the following case in Silver Spring, Maryland (Castaneda, 2005, p. B2):

> A Prince George's County judge ordered a Silver Spring subcontractor to pay $21,000 in restitution to a dozen Latino immigrant workers when he

admitted to cheating them out of wages. . . . Eight of the workers attended Sandoval's sentencing. . . . Jose Flores, 39, was among them. At the time that Sandoval failed to pay him, Flores said, his newborn son in his native Honduras was gravely ill with a fever. "I didn't have money to send for medicine or for the doctor," Flores said. The infant died.

The role the Latino undocumented will play in the development of New Orleans in the aftermath of Hurricane Katrina has yet to be fully understood or written about. However, early indications are that undocumented Latino immigrants will play a significant role in helping New Orleans to be rebuilt. Most of these Latino workers are coming from Texas (Varney, 2005). However, the their illegal status and limited English proficiency will highlight how this group will lead to their being further exploited (Pogrebin, 2005; Katrina's next expose, 2005).

The subjects of social security and taxes paid, however, have rarely been examined from the point of view of the undocumented (Fry, Kochhar, Passel, & Suro, 2005a; Gerson, 2005). An opinion piece by the *San Diego Union-Tribune* (Social Security tab, 2005, p. B10) on the often overlooked contributions of the undocumented, notes:

> The myth endures that illegal immigrants in the United States don't pay taxes. You hear it all the time, accompanied by complaints about how illegal immigrants are bankrupting the country and don't contribute to society. This is widely untrue. It's simple. If you live in the United States, the government will find a way to tax you. Illegal immigrants pay sales tax every time they buy a shirt at a store or a gallon of gas for the car. They pay property taxes when they rent an apartment or buy a home . . . Illegal immigrants also fork over a fortune in payroll taxes each year.

When Social Security and Medicare payments are withheld from payrolls, in cases where undocumented persons provide false Social Security numbers to employers, they are officially labeled as "inaccurate" by the government. These funds, in turn, go into an "earning suspense file" at the Social Security Administration. One estimate of the amount of this file is $189 billion (Porter, 2005a). In the current decade, this file has grown by over $50 billion a year, resulting in generating $7 billion in Social Security tax revenue and almost $1.5 billion in Medicare taxes. Another estimate of the importance of the undocumented contributions to Social Security notes that if this group were to stop existing, the loss to the Trust Fund would be $30 billion (Dinan, 2005). This amount accounts for 10 percent of the 2004 surplus (the difference between what the system receives in payments and taxes and what it pays out in pension benefits), which is a considerable sum (Porter, 2005a).

Officials believe that undocumented workers are largely responsible for this increase. A study of tax forms of businesses that employ high numbers of individuals who eventually fall into the "earning suspense file" shows that undocumented workers are generally employed in one of three industries (Arizona Republic, 2005): (1) restaurants (17 percent); (2) construction (10 percent); and farming (7 percent). An Urban Institute study of New York City estimated that undocumented immigrants contributed $1 billion to Social Security in 1995 (Passel & Clark, 1998).

The need for Latino undocumented to obtain a Social Security card has, not surprisingly, led to some inventive ways of getting one without falsifying a card. Undocumented Latinos, for example, have been able to "rent" the Social Security numbers of Latinos who have obtained legal residence in this country and now reside outside of the United States (Porter, 2005b). The "renting" of the numbers benefits those who legally own the numbers because it enhances their pensions and unemployment benefits.

Navarrette (2005a, p. G3), in a political assessment of the undocumented contributions to Social Security, raises questions about the nexus between immigration reform and taxes:

> The hard currency is the Social Security taxes that illegal immigrants and their employers pay on those earnings. This brings in about $7 billion a year. Which is why you don't hear the Social Security Administration raising a fuss over illegal immigration. And to the degree that this arm of the U.S. government has friends in Congress, it could explain why you don't see many pieces of legislation calling for mass deportations of illegal immigrants. I mean, why kill the golden goose?

Factors Influencing Demographic Growth

As noted in chapter 1, the dramatic increase in growth in the Latino population, first witnessed in the 1980s and continuing in the present, has been the result of an interplay of three demographic factors: low mortality rates, high birth rates, and high immigration rates (Sheehan & Cardenas, 2005). Each of these factors has a considerable amount of influence on the growth of the Latino community in this country. However, there is no denying that high birth rates and high net migration to this country stand out in influence.

Mortality Rates

The extent to which deaths exceed gains by births or immigration influences net gain. However, death as a factor has generally not received a great deal of attention, with the possible exception of deaths due to homicide, particularly when they involve urban youth (Main & Sweeney, 2005; Phillips, 2002). Infant mortality rates, too, receive considerable national attention (Borenstein, 2004;

McCormick & Holding, 2004). In fact, this statistic is often widely used as a key indicator of a community's overall health (Infant mortality rates, 2005).

Overall, Latinos have a lower mortality rate when compared to white non-Latinos. Heron and Morales (2002, pp. 2–3) note that statistics mask important variations among Latino subgroups of different national origins: "For example, in 1995 the overall age-adjusted mortality rate was lowest among Mexicans (362.4 per 100,000), followed by Cubans (387.4 per 100,000) and Puerto Ricans (582.9 percent per 100,000)."

Abraido-Lanza, Chao, and Florez (2005) suggest the use of an acculturation construct as an important element in better understanding the Latino mortality paradox. Latino longevity and health status, as will be addressed in chapter 3, is such that as a group, Latinos live longer and healthier lives. The term "Hispanic paradox" has been coined to help capture this phenomenon (Morin, 2004). Demographers have calculated the adult mortality rate for Latinos to be anywhere from 30 to 50 percent lower than for white non-Latinos. This translates into an additional five to eight years of life expectancy at age 45 for Latinos in the United States, when compared to comparable white, non-Latino samples.

Recent speculation as to this phenomenon has led to the use of the term "salmon effect," or "salmon bias," to help explain this disparity among Mexicans, who have the lowest age-adjusted mortality rate of any Latino group (Morin, 2004, p. B05):

> One clue came when they [demographers] saw the mortality gap was particularly large among men and women born in Mexico who lived in states closest to the Mexican border. Digging deeper into the data, they found the answer: The ill and infirm apparently returned home to die and thus didn't appear in U.S. vital statistics data, while healthy Mexican immigrants remained in the United States. It's called the "salmon effect."

Palloni and Arias (2004), however, caution against placing too much credence on this effect because it does not account for the mortality advantage found among other foreign-born Latino groups. The "salmon effect" phenomenon, I believe, can also be found in other Caribbean Latino groups such as Puerto Ricans and Dominicans, helping to explain why other Latino groups have a mortality advantage. The yearning to return to the homeland is quite strong and very often provides many Latinos with the hope that is necessary to circumvent life's challenges, and is operative when the time comes to die.

However, this is not uniformly so across all categories and Latino subgroups, or causes of deaths. For example, although the infant mortality rate for Latino infants is less than that of white non-Latinos, this is not the case for Puerto Ricans. This group has an infant death rate from sudden infant death syndrome (SIDS) that is 1.5 times greater than that of white non-Latinos. It is still lower than that of African Americans, who have a rate of 2.2 times that of white non-Latinos (Department of Health and Human Services [DHHS], 2004). Zsemik and Fennell (2005) concluded that racial/ethnic comparative health research, as a result, must eschew reference to "pan-ethnic" groups, and seek to recognize between- and within-group distinctiveness.

A recent study conducted by the Centers for Disease Control and Prevention and reported by the American Automobile Association (AAA) found that motor vehicle crashes are the leading cause of death in the United States for Latino males age 1 to 44, and Latino children age 5 to 12 are 72 percent more likely to die as a result of a crash compared to white non-Latinos of the same age (AAA, 2004). Latino youth are considered to be less likely (11 percent) than their white, non-Latino (14 percent), African American (7 percent), and Asian counterparts to drink and drive, but they are more likely to engage in behaviors that are risky, such as driving in cars with someone who has been drinking (Latino youths take more risks with drinking and driving, 2003).

Latino drivers are also more likely to ignore the use of child restraints. One study of Latino preschool aged children in west Dallas, Texas, found significantly lower use of child restraints (19 percent), compared to 62 percent for preschool children of all races in the rest of the city (Istre et al., 2002). Lee, Fitzgerald, and Ebel (2003) concluded in their study that Latino children are more likely to be unrestrained passengers in motor vehicles because their parents do not own a booster seat and are misinformed about recommended guidelines for booster seat use.

Accidents are the third leading cause of death for Latinos in the age 1 to 44 grouping. Death rates from drugs and from poisonings and falls increased 23 percent and 3 percent, respectively, between 1990 and 1998 (Mallonee, 2003). Gaps in data gathering and published research on injuries exist, making it difficult to better understand why such incidents result in a disproportionate number of Latino mortalities.

Suicide rates for Latinos are considerably lower (5.6 per 100,000) than the national rate (10.7 per 100,000). The age-adjusted rate for Latino males was 5.9 times the rate for Latinas (Centers for Disease Control and Prevention [CDC], 2004c). Latino males accounted for 85 percent of all Latino suicides. Although suicide rates are highest among those aged 85 years or older, youth and young adults (aged 10 to 34 years) accounted for 50 percent of all Latino suicides during the 1997–2001 period, and suicide was the third leading cause of death among those aged 10 to 24. Among 25- to 44-year-olds, Latino mortality rates are higher than those of their white, non-Latino counterparts (Pew Hispanic Center, 2002a).

Mexicans accounted for the majority of Latino suicides (56 percent), followed by those of "other or unknown Latino origin" (14 percent), Central and South Americans (9 and 10 percent, respectively), Puerto Ricans (11 percent), and Cubans (8 percent) (CDC, 2004c). These statistics are generally proportional to the Latino subgroup distribution in the United States. Nevertheless, it is necessary to contextualize the settings, circumstances, characteristics of Latino suicides and attempted suicides in order to better prevent and help those who survive attempts (Zayas et al., 2000).

Reliance on national mortality data, although serving the purpose of setting a context and facilitating comparisons, will not highlight how these rates will vary for Latinos across geographical areas. California is considered to have one of the nation's lowest rates of infant mortality, with pockets within cities such as San Francisco and Los Angeles with high infant mortality rates (McCormick & Holding, 2004). In Central Valley and other rural areas with high concentrations of Latinos, infant mortality rates for this group are unusually high. Pesticides may be responsible for this difference in infant mortality rates. In Washington, D.C., infant mortality increased from 10.6 deaths per 1,000 in 2001 to 11.5 deaths in 2002, with the Latino infant death rising from 4 per 1,000 to 9 per 1,000 during this period (Goldstein, 2004).

Birth Rates

The frequency with which Latinas give births is an important factor in helping to project the types of services and educational resources that are needed, and helps shape policy decisions in these arenas. Increased Latino birth rates can be viewed from a variety of perspectives. Latina adolescents' birth rates for those 15 to 19 years of age, for example, are higher than those for all other racial and ethnic population groups in the United States (CDC, 2004b). These high rates are usually associated with poorer health outcomes over the life of the child.

As noted in the introductory chapter, the birth rates of Latinos in California passed a major threshold in 2001, when Latino births accounted for a majority of the births in that state (Jablon, 2003). In 2000, in California and Texas, for example, "Jose" was the most popular name for newborn boys (Revolutionary Worker, 2000). In California, the Latino birth rate has declined since the 1990 U.S. census, when it was 3.41 babies on average, to 2.6 babies in 2000 (Kelley, 2004). This decrease in birth rates has necessitated a drop in projected demographic growth for the state, and accounts for almost half of the projected reduction (Kelley, 2004). Nevertheless, California's projected increase for the year 2040 is still largely fueled by an increase in the Latino population.

Latino birth rates are not uniformly high across all sectors of the United States. In California, for example, the birth rate varies according to region. Santa Clarita, San Gabriel Valley, and San Joaquin Valley, for example, are experiencing record high Latino birth rates (Aidem, 2004; Milbourn, 2004; Tanaka, 2005). Los Angeles County and Ventura County, however, have experienced a slowing down of birth rates (Sheppard, 2005). Texas (Magers, 2004), Georgia (Pascual, 2004), and Washington (Ganus, 2004), in turn, are experiencing increased numbers of Latino births, and so are states that historically have not been destinations for Latinos.

Immigration Rates

Immigration rates, particularly those focused on the undocumented, have without question received the lion's share of attention in the popular media, and will probably continue to do so as long as there is political and public attention on this nation's "porous borders" with Mexico (Carter, 2005). Virtually any news coverage or public forum devoted to newcomers is focused almost exclusively on "illegals" and how they are changing the national social fabric and economic structure—for the worse, I might add. Thus, the following statistics are provided with great trepidation because their "accuracy" is subject to debate. Yet any failure to report these data would be irresponsible.

As already noted earlier in this chapter, this nation's rate of population increase would be minimal or nonexistent without the influx of immigrant newcomers to this country in the past decade or so, with Latinos playing a significant role in these increases. The estimated annual immigration of approximately 125,000 people, largely Mexicans, who either "illegally" cross the borders into this country or overstay their visas has shaped the increase in the size of the Latino community. The period from 2000 to 2004 witnessed an estimated 500,000 undocumented people entering or staying in this country without legal status (Associated Press, 2005d). It is important to note, however, the presence in this group of those who are "other than Mexicans," or "OTM, " a classification used by the Border Patrol. This group consists primarily of Brazilians and Central Americans (Axtman, 2005).

As a result, both "legal" and "illegal" immigrants have contributed to dramatic changes in the racial, ethnic, and cultural composition of the entire country, with very few geographical areas not experiencing these changes. These changes will affect the country in many unanticipated ways, because the composition of the population of Latino newcomers is unlike any this nation experienced in the eighteenth- and nineteenth-century immigration periods.

Geographic Distribution

The Latino community, as already indicated in chapter 1, is no longer restricted to living on either coast of this country, although these geographic areas are home to millions of Latinos (Logan, 2001). Falcon (2001, p. 1) addresses the complexity of Latino dispersal across the United States in the following assessment.

> Latinos are highly concentrated in urban centers; nearly half live in central city areas. . . . At the same time, Latinos are scattered across the United States in a way that is different from prior immigrants. . . . They have moved to urban centers away from their original settlement. . . . There is also movement to small urban areas, away from the pressures of central city living, propelled by the search for employment and better living standards.

St. Paul, Minnesota, is such an example. This city has experienced a dramatic increase from 3,500 predominantly Mexicans in 1990 to over 41,000 in 2000. The Latino community has established roots with 22 churches offering Spanish services, 9 Spanish-language newspapers, 2 tortilla makers and nine soccer languages (Porter & Malkin, 2005b).

As shown in figure 2.4, Latinos tend to be concentrated in certain regions of the country. Nevertheless, Latinos have started to disperse across the United States and in the process have brought with them assets as well as challenges for the host communities (Vigeland, 2004). The South, Southeast, and Midwest have experienced the largest percentage increases in numbers of Latinos between 1990 and 2000, although the Latinos are still concentrated in the West and Southwest and in New York and Florida (Risen, 2005). The Pew Hispanic Center notes that the Latino migration to the South will have distinct impacts on public policy, and that those impacts have only just started to be recognized (Kochhar, Suro, & Tafoya, 2005).

The Southeastern region of the United States has experienced one of the most dramatic increases in Latino influx since 1990, particularly involving Mexicans (Maas, 2004). Appalachia, West Virginia, for example, has seen its Latino population increase substantially since 1990 with Latinos accounting for almost 20 percent of the population increase during this period (V. Smith, 2005). Latinos entering the Southeast do not fit the usual profile of a migrant worker (Mass, 2004, p. 1):

> The largest employers in South Carolina, for example, tend to be aggregated in construction (including roofing, road, and demolition work), poultry and meat packing, plastic products, textiles, and produce packaging and handling. Though these industries generally offer year-long, full-time jobs, the work frequently is dangerous.

Increases, however, can also be found in states normally not associated with having large Latino populations, such as Iowa. Iowa witnessed an increase of almost 26 percent between 2000 and 2004, reaching 104,000 (Sociologist, 2005). More specifically, in Ottumwa County, the Latino population has increased 170 percent in the past two years, making this county one of fastest growing with Latinos in the country (Shipman, 2005).

Contrary to popular opinion, Latinos generally reside in neighborhoods where they do not constitute a majority of the residents. It is estimated that almost 20 million Latinos, or 57 percent of this population group, live in neighborhoods where they make up less than 50 percent of the population. This statistic differs from that of African Americans, with 52 percent (Weisberg, 2005). Latinos now outnumber African Americans/blacks in six of this nation's largest cities, and in 18 of the 25 most populous counties in the United States (Coleman, 2003).

Table 2.1 reflects how Latino foreign born are highly concentrated in several states and urban localities. The top 10 places with a population of 100,000 or

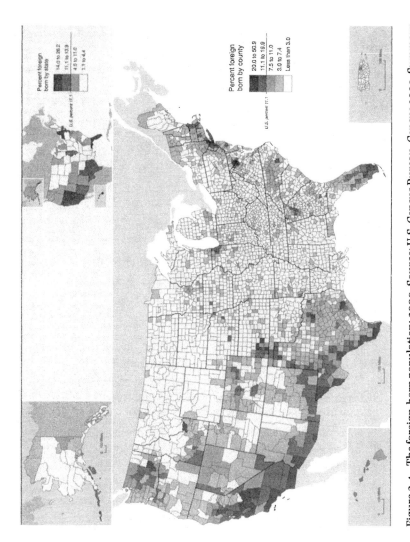

Figure 2.4. The foreign-born population: 2000. Source: U.S. Census Bureau, Census 2000, Summary File 3. American Factfinder, at factfinder.census.gov, provides census data and mapping tools.

TABLE 2.1. Ten Places of 100,000 or More Population with the Highest
Percentage Foreign Born: 2000

| Place and state | Total population | Foreign born | | |
		Number	% of total population	90-percent confidence interval on percent
United States	281,421,906	31,107,889	11.1	11.09–11.11
Hialeah, Florida	226,419	163,256	72.1	71.5–72.7
Miami, Florida	362,410	216,739	59.5	59.0– 60.0
Glendale, California	194,973	106,119	54.4	53.7–55.1
Santa Ana, California	337,977	179,933	53.2	52.8–53.8
Daly City. California	103,621	54,213	52.3	51.4–53.2
El Monte, California	115,965	59,589	51.4	50.5–52.3
East Los Angeles, California[a]	124,283	60,605	48.8	48.0–49.6
Elizabeth, New Jersey	120,568	52,975	43.9	43.0–44.8
Garden Grove, California	165,196	71,351	43.2	42.5–43.9
Los Angeles, California	3,694,820	1,512,720	40.9	40.7–41.1

(Data based on sample. For information on confidentiality protection, sampling error, nonsampling error, and definitions, see www.census.gov/prod(cen2000/doc/sf3.pdf).

Although the point estimates shown appear to differ, no statistical difference exists between the percentages foreign born in Glendale and Santa Ana, Santa Ana and Daly City, Daly City and El Monte and Elizabeth and Garden Grove

[a]East Los Angeles, California is a census designated place and is not legally incorporated.

Source: U.S. Census Bureau, Census 2000, Summary File 1 and Summary File 3.

more with the highest percent of Latinos in 2000 were located in three states:
California (East Los Angeles, San Ana, El Monte, and Oxnard), Texas (Laredo,
Brownsville, McAllen, and El Paso), and Florida (Hialeah and Miami). East Los
Angeles, California, had the highest concentration of Latinos in the United States,
with 96.8 percent of the population (High Beam Research, 2005).

These concentrations have resulted in Latinos creating unprecedented demand for businesses to meet their needs (Colon, 2004; McTaggart, 2004; Nurse,
2005). Income for Latinos is expected to grow by 43 percent by 2010 and account
for $700 billion, although other estimates are less conservative and calculate a
sum closer to $1 trillion (White, 2004). The relative youthfulness of this popu-
lation group means that Latinos have not reached their earning potential, making them that much more attractive to marketers.

Urban/Rural Distribution

As noted in the previous section but worthy of further attention, Latinos overwhelmingly tend to reside in cities. Latinos have accounted for 81 percent of the
nation's population growth in this country's 100 largest cities (United States

Hispanic Leadership, 2004). Thus, contrary to popular opinion, Latinos are generally urban-based in this country, and for many this represents a dramatically new experience and challenge in adjusting to life in this country. This is particularly the case with Latinos migrating directly from rural sectors of their countries of origin to urban centers in the United States

Nevertheless, it is necessary to point out that demographic changes are occurring, and they bring with them a set of challenges. The continued dispersal of Latinos throughout geographical sectors of the country that have historically not had Latinos brings with it challenges of serving this population group that have generally been restricted to big urban areas of the country. Decatur, Alabama, is such an example. Decatur experienced an outbreak of syphilis among Latinos, and this was traced to an outbreak of crack cocaine use and increased prostitution near a Latino community (Paz-Bailey et al., 2004). The "Decaturs" of the United States have raised questions about how to modify outreach and service delivery to Latinos that reside outside of the typical urban/rural nexus. Small cities and towns, as a result, will have to learn from what the literature and research shows, but also be willing to modify strategies and tactics to take into account local circumstances. In California, for example, 28 cities and towns accounted for 90 percent of the states' Latino population (California, 2004).

Lourdes Rodriguez's (2005, p. 1) description of how Latinos are changing Houston's African American communities illustrates the impact of Latinos moving to urban areas of the country:

> A small Pentecostal church tucked away on a gritty corner of Martin Luther King Boulevard holds Spanish services for its Latino congregation. On the MyKanas Highway side of the same South Park community, strategically placed across from a Fiesta supermarket, a Kruger billboard gamely competes in Spanish. A growing Latino presence marks a quiet but escalating demographic shift that promises to transform Houston's historically black neighborhoods in the coming decades.

In 1950, Los Angeles was considered the "whitest" major United States city (78 percent), and Houston (73 percent) was close behind. In 2000, Los Angeles became the most of-color major city (71 percent), and again Houston (69 percent) was a close second (Meyerson, 2004). Racial and ethnic composition of major cities reflects the influx of Latinos over the past half-century. Los Angeles is composed of 47 percent Latinos, and Houston of 37 percent.

Approximately 91 percent of the Latino community lives in urban areas, with the remaining 9 percent residing in rural America (Marotta & Garcia, 2003). According to the U.S. Census Bureau, the top five cities in the United States based upon numerical representation of Latinos in 2000 were: New York (2.16 million), Los Angeles (1.72 million), Chicago (753,000), Houston (731,000), and San Antonio (671,000). Almost 20 percent of this nation's Latino population resided in eight cities. Riverside, California, stands as a case in point. Between 2000 and 2004, its Latino population grew by 7 percent, while its non-Latino white population decreased by 8 percent during this period, making Latinos half of the population of this city (Haberman, 2005).

Urban living translates into assuming an urban lifestyle. Use of public transportation is a case in point. Latino immigrants, for example, use public transportation seven times more frequently than any other group (Latino immigrants, 2005). Nevertheless, there is an increasing trend of Latinos moving out of cities into the suburbs. In 2005, Latinos living in suburban Chicago outnumbered those living in the city for the first time (St. Clair, 2005).

Over 90 percent of all Latino groups tend to reside in urban areas. However, there are slight differences between groups (Pew Hispanic Center, 2002c). Puerto Ricans are the most likely to live in cities, followed by Cubans, Mexicans, and other Latino groups. The high percentage of Puerto Ricans in urban areas may reflect the urbanization and industrialization that has occurred in the island since the 1950s, making migration to urban areas in the United States relatively easier than it is for Latinos counterparts from other countries with a more agricultural/rural background, since the majority of Puerto Ricans in Puerto Rico live in major metropolitan areas of the island.

Projected Demographic Trends

Prior to examining demographic projections for the next 45 years, it is important to pause and make note that demographic projections, particularly those looking well into the future, may not actually transpire as predicted. These projections can best be described as educated guesses based upon current available knowledge. Demographic projections are based upon certain assumptions that may be altered in the course of unanticipated events, such as natural disasters, wars, epidemics, and economic upheavals. Adjustments, as a result, should be expected. Nevertheless, there is still a place for demographic projections because they raise important considerations in the strategic planning of social work services, as here.

Although this chapter and book are specifically focused on Latinos, the reader should know that the Asian community, like its Latino counterpart, is expected to triple in size (11 million to 33 million) by the year 2050 (Scommegna, 2004). The African American/black community, in turn, is expected to increase to 61 million, or 15 percent. These three groups are expected to account for almost 50 percent of the total population growth for this country by the year 2050 (Census Bureau projects, 2004).

As noted in table 2.2, projected population growth in the United States is expected to continue at a steady pace until the year 2050, when the population will number an estimated 420 million, or a 49 percent increase from 2000

TABLE 2.2. Projected Population of the United States, by Race and Hispanic Origin: 2000 to 2050

Population or percentage and race of Hispanic origin	2000	2010	2020	2030	2040	2050
Population						
Total	282,125	308,936	335,605	363,584	391,946	419,854
White alone	228,548	244,995	260,829	275,731	289,690	302,626
Black alone	35,818	40,454	45,365	50,442	55,876	61,361
Asian alone	10,684	14,241	17,988	22,580	27,992	33,430
All other races[a]	7,075	9,246	11,822	14,831	18,388	22,437
Hispanic (of any race)	35,622	47,756	59,756	73,055	87,585	102,560
White alone, not Hispanic	195,729	201,112	205,936	209,176	210,331	210,283
Percentage of total population						
Total	100.0	100.0	100.0	100.0	100.0	100.0
White alone	81.0	79.3	77.6	758	73.9	72.1
Black alone	12.7	13.1	13.5	13.9	14.3	14.6
Asian alone	3.8	4.6	5.4	6.2	7.1	8.0
All other races[a]	2.5	3.0	3.5	4.1	4.7	5.3
Hispanic (of any race)	12.6	15.5	17.8	20.1	22.3	24.4
White alone, not Hispanic	69.4	65.1	61.3	57.5	53.7	50.1

In thousands except as indicated, as of July 1, 2004, resident population.
[a]Includes American Indian and Alaska Native alone, Native Hawaiian and other Pacific Islander alone, and two or more races

Source: U.S. Census Bureau, 2004, "U.S. Interim Projections by Age, Sex, Race, and Hispanic Origin," <http://www.census.goy/lpc/www/usinterimproj/>
Internet Release Date: March 18, 2004

(Scommegna, 2004). The Latino population, in turn, will increase during this period from 36 million to 103 million or, as already noted, almost tripling in size and representing 24 percent of this country's total population.

California, for example, is expected to gain 21 million new residents between 2000 and 2050, with 18 million being Latinos (El Nasser, 2005; Kelley, 2004; Purdum, 2000). By 2015, Latinos will be 40 percent of that state's population (California, 2004). Not surprisingly, Latinos are expected to achieve majority status in California by 2040 (El Nasser, 2005). Latinos are expected to be the majority group in Los Angeles County by 2014 and in California by 2040, when they are expected to number 25.9 million out of 51.5 million (Barrett, 2004). It is probably no mistake that California, Texas, and Florida are expected to account for 25 percent of this nation's total population by 2030, and also happen to have a significant share of the country's Latino population (Murphy, 2005). Other states not normally associated with having large Latino populations, too, will witness dramatic increases. In Nebraska, for example, 5 percent of the population was Latino in 2000, and this is expected to increase to 15 percent by 2030 (Sociologist, 2005).

Although increases in Latino numerical representation are attractive from a social, economic, and political standpoint, there are less attractive aspects, too. The number of Latino elders in California is expected to increase dramatically between 2005 and 2040. By 2040, Latino seniors will equal the number of white non-Latinos. White non-Latinos accounted for 65 percent of all seniors in 2005, with California being a case in point (Teichert, 2005). Incidentally, as Latinos enter senior status, ailments associated with the aging process will also increase within the Latino community. The prevalence of arthritis (Al Snih et al., 2000; Al Snih et al., 2001) and hypertension (Arnada & Vazquez, 2004), for example, will increase, and these will interact with other illnesses to create challenges for service delivery to this age group.

The number of Latinos with Alzheimer's and other forms of dementia can be expected to increase more than 600 percent (200,000 to 1.3 million) nationally by the year 2050 (Novak & Riggs, 2004). Although education is considered a protective factor against Alzheimer's, unfortunately, Latino elders will not benefit because they have the lowest level of formal educational attainment (over 50 percent have eight years of schooling or less) of any group in the country. This, combined with high rates of vascular disease risk factors, particularly diabetes and poor health care, all point toward Latino elders being at a disproportionate risk for Alzheimer's (Elliott, 2001).

One study that was specifically focused on examining the early onset of Alzheimer's disease symptoms among Latinos found that after adjusting for treatment center, sex, and years of education, they had a mean age at symptom onset that was 6.8 years earlier than that of white, non-Latino patients (Clark et al., 2005). Subjects such as end-of-life care, too, will increase in importance, and bioethical issues and concerns will be raised as Latino cultural values and beliefs intersect with health care decisionmaking (Bade, Murphy, & Sullivan, 1999; Phipps, True, & Murray, 2003). Cultural values and beliefs heavily influence how grieving is addressed in these situations for Latinos (Gelfand et al., 2001; Munet-Villaro, 1998).

In another aspect, efforts to reform Social Security, as noted in the following quotations, will have a disproportionate impact on the Latino community from a variety of perspectives (Wasow, 2002, p. 3):

> Since in the next half-century we can expect Latinos to be a larger share of taxpayers than retirees, any extra burden on taxpayers will fall more heavily on Latinos than on other groups. If we add private accounts to the burden of our retirement system, Latinos will be over-represented among those who pay twice.

Educational and Economic Demographics

Educational Attainment

Academic achievement of Latinos, like that of their other ethnic and racial counterparts, is a complex matter, and one needs to take into account socioeconomic status, cultural characteristics, social reception, language proficiency, and gender (Chapa & De La Rosa, 2004; McLaughlin et al., 2002; Schmid, 2001). Ethnic markers such as religion and phenotype, too, must be added to this list to provide a broader context through which to examine the role of education in the lives of Latinos. Contreras (2004), for example, advocates for a broader spectrum through which to examine ethnic and racial diversity, and one that goes beyond white/black to ensure inclusiveness in debate and policy decisions.

Schmid (2001), in turn, analyzing the reasons that some Latinos are more successful at educational achievement and others are not, argues that these factors do not interact in the same manner for different newcomer groups. Garcia and Guerra (2004) also warn about the pervasiveness of a deficit perspective in viewing Latino students and a tendency to blame students, families, and communities. This perspective, as a result, when combined with a tendency to "lump" all Latinos together into one group, makes deconstructing statistics difficult. Thus, every effort has been made here to report educational statistics for specific Latino subgroups when available.

There is little disagreement that Latino students have the nation's highest high school dropout rate and the lowest college enrollment rate (Texeira, 2005). Latino children under the age of five are considerably less likely to be enrolled in preschool programs across the nation. They generally represent 20 percent of the children in preschool programs, compared with 44 percent for African Americans and 42 percent for white non-Latinos (ERIC Clearinghouse on Urban Education, 2001). Not surprisingly, their enrollment increases according to parental educational attainment.

Latino representation in high schools (grades 9–12) in 1999 was 13 percent of the student population. However, it is projected to increase to 23 percent by the year 2030 (ERIC Clearinghouse on Urban Education, 2001). Dropout rates for Latinos (30 percent, compared to 8.6 percent for non-Latino whites, and 12.1 percent for non-Latino African Americans) are influenced by the fact that many Latino youth never enroll in school (Schmid, 2001). Native-born Latino males aged 16 to 19 years are more likely (15 percent) to drop out of high school than their female (12 percent) counterparts (Pew Hispanic Center, 2004). Some urban areas, such as Allentown, Pennsylvania, for example, have experienced even higher dropout rates. Allentown's Latinos constitute 62 percent of all dropouts, compared to 20.4 percent for white non-Latinos and 16.8 for African Americans (L. Rodriguez, 2005).

California in 2002, another example, witnessed a statewide graduation rate of 57 percent for African Americans, 60 percent for Latinos, 78 percent for white non-Latinos, and 84 percent for Asians (Helfand, 2005). Latinos in California have the highest high school dropout rate (45 percent) and the lowest college graduation rate (8 percent). Further, this gap is over 50 years old and can be traced back to the 1940s (Rojas, 2000). In the Los Angeles Unified School District, however, the statistics were even more dismal, with 39 percent of Latinos, 47 percent of African Americans, 67 percent of white non-Latinos, and 77 percent of Asians graduating (Helfand, 2005).

Creating an "accurate" picture of the state of education in the Latino community has its set of challenges, like any other profile or condition addressed in this book. Breaking out Latino educational achievement according to country of origin provides a different perspective. Mexicans aged 16 to 19 years have the highest dropout rate of any Latino group (25 percent), followed by Puerto Ricans (17 percent), Dominicans (12 percent), and Cubans (9 percent) (Pew Hispanic Center, 2004). Among Central and South Americans, Guatemalans (35 percent), Hondurans (33 percent), and Salvadorans and Ecuadorians, each with 17 percent, have the highest dropout rates (Pew Hispanic Center, 2004). Unfortunately, the option of obtaining a general education diploma (GED) is not attractive, because Latinos who do not graduate from high school generally do not do as well as white non-Latinos on the test. It is estimated that by age 26, only 43 percent of Latino dropouts have taken and passed the GED test, compared to 50 percent of white non-Latinos (Pew Hispanic Center, 2004).

The topic of special education and Latinos is of such importance that an entire book can be devoted to it. (See chapter 3.) Racial inequality in special education, like its health and child welfare counterparts, finds Latinos at a distinct disadvantage. Latino children and other undervalued groups of color are not only more likely to be identified as needing special education when compared to white non-Latinos but also more likely to be in disability categories of mental retardation and emotional disturbance (Artiles et al., 2002; Fierros & Convoy, 2002). Further, they are also more likely to be removed from the general education program and to receive their education in a more restrictive environment (Losen & Orfield, 2002; Losen & Welner, 2002; Parrish, 2002).

Roche and Shriberg (2004), in a rare article on Latino students and "high-stakes" examinations, raise serious concerns about how educational systems are increasingly turning to these tests in making educational decisions, and how Latino students are not faring well in the process. The authors go on to note that Latino cultural values and practices contrast with those of school systems, making the educational process of these students arduous, and increasing the likelihood of their dropouts. Heubert (2002), too, raises serious concerns about how Latinos and other undervalued groups are disproportionally impacted by this emphasis on high-stakes testing. The No Child Left Behind law, argues Harvard University's Civil Rights Project, uses proficiency targets that are unreasonable and disproportionately singles out students such as Latinos (Law fails test, 2005).

In higher education, the picture of Latino attainment is also mixed. Latinos, for example, are generally enrolled in noncollege preparatory or academic programs (35 percent) when compared to African Americans (43 percent) and white non-Latinos (50 percent). However, they are three times more likely to take advanced placement (AP) examinations in a foreign language than any other group (ERIC Clearinghouse on Urban Education, 2001). Third-generation Latinos in California show important advances in college entrance and graduation rates. However, the 11 percent graduation rate of this group is still dramatically lower than that of those of the same grouping of East and South Asians (46 percent) and white non-Latinos (38 percent) (Phillips, 2005a,b).

Lack of access to financial aid information has been found to be a critical factor in preventing Latino youth from attending higher education. One study found that more than 50 percent of Latino parents and 43 percent of Latino adults could not name one source of financial aid. However, 75 percent of Latino youth currently not enrolled in higher education said that they would more inclined to attend college if they had better information on financial aid (Changing U.S. demographic, 2005). Lack of knowledge about financial aid has also translated into lower financial aid for Latinos when compared to other groups (Sidime, 2005).

Access to a higher educational experience beyond a community college represents an important step toward Latinos entering careers that are both intellectually fulfilling and financially attractive (Clemente, 2004, p. 21):

> Ponder the following question: "How many of the following individuals have a two-year degree in computer technology, refrigeration, auto mechanics, or electronics?" (a) developers of public policy in Washington; (b) university professors who shape the educational curriculum of the nation; (c) owners of the most powerful business corporations; (d) writers of great literature; (e) owners of NBA and NFL franchises; (f) writers of influential articles in the *Wall Street Journal*, the *Washington Post*, the *New York Times*, *Newsweek*, or *Time*; (h) government emissaries negotiating a peace treaty between Israel and the Palestinians or advising on the reconstruction of Iraq; and (i) artists who paint or write masterfully.

Clemente does not seek to demean the important role that two-year colleges play in marginalized communities across the nation. However, there is little disputing that a four-year university-level education opens the door for achieving the "American Dream." The role of community colleges in Latino upward mobility should not be dismissed. One study of Chicano access to doctoral degrees found that 23 percent of Chicano doctorates started their college education at a community college compared to 10 percent of overall U.S. doctorates (Whitaker, 2005).

Although 20 percent of all Latino students who enroll in community college desire to eventually transfer to a four-year institution, only 7–20 percent eventually succeed in doing so (Whitaker, 2005). This gap between goals and reality is probably the result of an interplay of several factors, such as lack of financial aid, discouragement from attending college far from home, and the need to work to support family financially, to list three possible common reasons (Sodders, 2005).

Latino enrollment in higher education is generally restricted to fewer than 200 colleges, known as Hispanic-serving institutions (HSIs). White, non-Latino youth entering community colleges are twice as likely as Latino youth to finish and eventually obtain a bachelor's degree (Fry, 2003). This disparity also occurs in nonselective colleges and universities with white, non-Latino students receiving a bachelor's degree (81 percent, compared with 51 percent for Latinos). Thus, enrolling and obtaining a college degree is still elusive for many Latinos, limiting access to entrance to professional careers.

Advocates are quick to advance a social change agenda that not only requires a reconceptualization of how schools relate to communities but also emphasizes the importance of a curriculum that reflects the operative reality of life in urban communities, to make education more attractive and meaningful (Blue-Banning, Turnbull, & Pereira, 2000; Haro, 2004).

Socioeconomic Status

The socioeconomic status of Latinos, probably more than any other subject, has received considerable national attention in both the popular and scholarly press. Generally this attention has focused, with some notable exceptions, on their low economic achievement levels, and has raised a series of questions about their future in this country, particularly those who are undocumented newcomers (Huntington, 2004). The emergence of a transnational identity in which newcomers to this country still maintain strong social, economic, and political ties to their home countries is often viewed as an impediment to assimilation.

Unfortunately, studies on this subject, as for many of the other topics covered in this chapter, have failed to disentangle data on different subgroups, and generally have lumped all Latinos together into one category. Further, most studies contrast different generations of Latinos by focusing on a single snapshot in time. Similar shortcomings can also be applied to this nation's Asian and Pacific Islander community (Hua, 2005). Thus, this methodology compares Latinos of different generations at the same age and in the same year, rather than comparing Latinos with predecessors of 10, 25, or even 50 years earlier (Smith, 2003). A longitudinal rather than cross-sectional approach is in order to better understand economic gains.

Further, socioeconomic status is often a proxy for economic success in this country, and economic success within a capitalist country such as ours equates to income and material possessions. The subject of socioeconomic success, or lack thereof, of Latinos must not be examined outside of a cultural context, as noted by Cortez (2005): "In order to understand the concept of success, whether academic, monetary, or familial, it must be studied within the context of culture." Consequently, any analysis or discussion of economic success must be tempered by the recognition of the importance of determining the criteria being used to assess this success. In this case, culture plays an instrumental role in shaping these criteria and is rarely taken into account in any serious discussion of what economic success means to Latinos and the price they must pay in achieving it (Shinnar, 2005).

The subject of Latino wealth is rarely covered in the popular and scholarly literature. However, whenever Latinos are compared to white non-Latinos, they have less than 10 cents for every dollar (Kochhar, 2004). Latino household income is two-thirds that of white non-Latinos, creating a rather sizable economic lacuna. This economic gap can be largely explained by the education gap, lack of inheritances, and lack of participation in financial markets (Suro, 2005a). Further, lack of home ownership is a key factor in the discrepancy of wealth. Latinos are less likely than their non-Latino, white counterparts to own their own homes, are relatively young in age, do not have high levels of formal education, and are generally concentrated in high-housing-cost regions such as New York and California (Kochhar, 2004). In 2001, the percentage of African Americans and Latinos with a net worth of zero or less was 30.9 percent and 35.3 percent, respectively, compared to 13.1 percent for white non-Latinos (Archip, 2005). In 2004, the average net worth of Latino households was $8,000, compared to $89,000 for white non-Latinos (Higuera, 2005).

Glenn (2004, p. A10) summarizes the two prevailing camps of argument on Latino socioeconomic status in the United States and in the process touches upon many of the themes addressed in this book:

> One camp argues that the new Latino immigrants will move up the educational ladder and intermarry with the larger population at least as fast as their European predecessors did. Other scholars propose a long list of reasons why the new cohort's trajectory might be very different: The American labor market is harder to break into today. Latino immigrants are more visibly "raced" than their European forerunners, and therefore will face more discrimination. Cheaper transportation and new laws make it easier today to maintain a strong sense of connection to one's country of origin. Many of today's immigrants are illegal, and therefore face structural barriers that were unknown to most migrants a century ago. Those four propositions are all controversial, and are all the subject of continuing studies.

The socioeconomic picture of Latinos in the United States is mixed and has been summarized by Camarillo and Bonilla (2001, p. 131) as alarming:

If one looks deeper and more critically, however, at the diverse Hispanic population, there is cause for real concern—in some cases, cause for alarm. Below the thin ranks of the Hispanic middle class lies a much larger group. They are not thriving. They are increasingly falling into the new categories of the "working poor" or, even, are seemly trapped as a class of severely impoverished people living in urban barrios. They are the Hispanic underclass.

Van Hook, Brown, and Kwenda (2004) decomposed trends in poverty among children of immigrants and concluded that the relative increase in poverty rates among immigrant children to U.S.-born children is the result of a divergence between newcomer and native families in racial and ethnic composition, parental educational level, and employment. Oropesa and Landale (2000) found that migration from Puerto Rico to the United States reduces the risk of child poverty because of the availability of better jobs; the economic benefits of migration to this country continue for the native-born.

Demographically, Latinos fit a social profile that makes them attractive targets for military recruiters. As of 2005, Latinos represented 11 percent of the United States military personnel, and 18 percent of those on the front lines in Iraq (Acevedo, 2005c). Latinos represented 40 of the first 100 soldiers and Marines from Texas killed in Iraq. Organizations such as Latinos for Peace have emerged to protest the Iraq war and to highlight how Latinos are now "cannon fodder," as they were during the Vietnam War (Uranga, 2005b). The No Child Left Behind Act of 2002 requires that school administrators provide the names, addresses, and telephone numbers of their students to military recruiters. Although parents can "opt out" of these lists for their children, many Latino parents, because of limited English proficiency, are likely not to do so because they are unaware of this legal provision.

Latinos are also a key target group for union organizers. In 2005, the American Federation of Labor-Congress of Industrial Organizers (AFL-CIO) gained more than 500,000 Latino workers (Heller, 2005). The Latino labor force is considered the fastest growing sector of the nation's labor movement and will, as a result, be the target of the AFL-CIO and others to attract them as members now and in the near future. The poultry industry in the South, an employer of many Latinos, too, has been targeted by union organizers (Greenhouse, 2005).

Another perspective on socioeconomic progress is well articulated in the following statement (Ly, 2005, p. B1):

> Ernesto Diaz of Rockville [Maryland] considers being a civic volunteer a sign that he has made it in this country. "When you come to the States, you come with the mentality of making money and succeeding. You don't think about about society," said Diaz, 55. . . . "After you are here for years, you start to think about those things."

The increased number of Latino newcomers into the country has translated into civic volunteering. The Lions Club, is one example, with the Gaithersburg Lion Club being totally Latino.

Economic Purchasing Power

It would be a serious shortcoming to only view the Latino community in the United States from a limited social and economic profile, without examining the role and potential of the economic purchasing power of this community in this and coming decades. This purchasing power of this community has only recently started to get the attention it deserves, and it permeates virtually all sectors of this nation's economy (Bulkeley, 2004; Feagans, 2004; Hopkins, 2004; Modern Latin, 2004; Murray, 2004; Pollack, 2004; Y. Rodriguez, 2004; Sifuentes, 2004; Smart, 2005; Turner, 2005). Investment firms, for example, have started to target Latino businesses for startup loans (Friedman, 2005). The Kauffman Index of Entrepreneurial Activity has found that Latinos start companies at a higher rate than white non-Latinos (Dalin, 2005). Further, there is international recognition of this market, as in the case of online Canadian pharmacies marketing to Latinos in this country (Rowland, 2004).

In 2003, Latino national economic purchasing power reached nearly $600 billion, up from $540 billion in 2002, or an 11 percent increase (Pollack, 2004). This purchasing power was only $223 billion in 1990, and it is projected to reach $926 billion, or almost $1 trillion, in 2007 (Schneider, 2002). Utah's Latino community, for example, spent $4 billion in 2003 (Burke, 2004). The undocumented Latino resident in this country also contributes significantly to the economy (Johnson, 2004).

In the San Diego, California, area, Latinos under the age of 45 are estimated to have a purchasing power of $397 billion, or $3 out of every $5 for the Latino community in general (Sifuentes, 2004). In California, the percentage of Latino-owned businesses almost doubled between 1987 (7.3 percent) and 1997 (13.0 percent) (California, 2004). In Los Angeles, this increase in Latino-owned businesses has been even more pronounced. Between 1992 and 1999, these businesses doubled (Kotkin, 2005).

The following description of a California-based Mexican butcher shop is a good illustration of this trend (Chavira, 2005, p. 1).

> The Mexican butcher shop, bakery and deli might seem misplaced in the heart of posh San Juan Capistrano, just yards from trendy boutiques and restaurants. . . . Yet, these staples of Mexican culture and commerce bustle with immigrants. It's as though a piece of the barrio has been transported to this enclave of wealth and privilege. . . . In fact, there's really nothing amiss. Between the swank hillside and beachfront homes are blocks of apartments, home to Mexicans who work in the residential repair, gardening and service industries.

In some sectors, Latinos play a prominent and influential role, as in the case of the agricultural sector in Fresno, California, where they own 93 percent of these types of businesses, and Latinos are five times more likely than non-Latinos to be workers (California, 2004). In New York City, Latino hip-hop artists have started selling their CDs in Latino bodegas (grocery stores) in an effort to reach out directly to a Latino market (Gonzalez, 2004). Frozen Latino foods enjoyed a $3 billion market in 2004, expected to exceed $3.4 billion by the year 2008, and this does not include tortillas and corn chips (Betancourt, 2004). Banks, too, have initiated aggressive drives to capture Latino customers by hiring Spanish-speaking staff and even opening or remodeling branches to make them more attractive to Latinos (Burke, 2004; Virgin, 2005).

Georgia, a state without a long tradition of attracting Latinos, has also started to notice the Latino purchasing power. Latinos make up approximately 6 percent of the state's total population. In 1990, Latinos had a purchasing power of disposable income of $1.3 billion, and it increased to $10.9 billion in 2004, an increase of over 700 percent (Y. Rodriguez, 2004). Some geographical areas of the state have experienced even greater increases. One recent estimate has their purchasing power increasing in Gwinnett County, Georgia, for example, to 4.3 billion in 2009, up from $2 billion in 2004 (Feagans, 2004).

McTaggart's (2004, p. 1) description of the ebbs and flows of demography highlights these changes and is but one example of how Latinos are helping to transform the national landscape:

> It's an ironic turn of events. During the past decade several supermarket chains had declared the urban Southern California market a dead end and pulled out, leaving behind a fallow field of empty boxes. But for a few eager local entrepreneurs, those abandoned stores looked ripe for cultivation into vibrant, community-oriented food markets, and those business owners set about figuring out how to serve the largely Hispanic populations the big guys hadn't been able to. Now some of these chains are clamoring to get back inside Los Angeles' ethnically diverse urban neighborhoods. . . . It's a tale of more than one city. Other multicultural hotbeds, including New York, Chicago, and Houston, are home to thriving independent retailers that made a commitment to Hispanic merchandising long before it became fashionable.

The emergence of new food and product lines tailored to Latinos in the United States has followed their increase in numbers (Kates & Wasserman, 2004). The creation of "Mi Bodega" products typifies how markets are created or expanded specifically tailored to this community's growing presence (Blumberg, 2004). Latinos on average visit grocery stores more frequently (18.3 times per month) than other non-Latino families (8.8), and this is probably the result of the importance placed on family meals and cooking from scratch (Learner, 2004). Latino households also spend 46 percent more than the general population on groceries (Solis, 2005b). However, as it will be noted later on, acculturation may be changing food buying and eating habits, causing serious health consequences.

Increased purchasing power of Latinos can be found among those who are citizens, documented, and undocumented. For example, it is estimated that undocumented Latinos can be a potential source for $44 billion in home mortgages, if provided with access to those funds (Dymi, 2004; Ordonez, 2005). Acosta (2004, p. 11) notes: "Undocumented Latinos are an invisible element in our economy today. Until now, no one has attempted to quantify the positive impact these consumers can have on our nation." An active outreach to this group is not unusual, as noted in the following example (Gorman, 2005, p.1).

> Each week Pedro Moriet knocks on doors in the Bay Area, looking for illegal immigrants. Moriet isn't an immigration agent. He's a real estate agent, and he's scouting for business. "Do you want a house, work and pay taxes but don't have a Social Security number?" reads his flier, written in Spanish and tailored to his potential consumers. "We can help you LEGALLY!"

In June 2004, almost one-third of California's house buyers were Latino (El Nasser, 2005). One estimate has the Latino first-time homebuyers representing 40 percent of this market by 2012 (Temple, 2005a,b). First-time Latino homebuyers in southern California, for example, are considered the fastest growing sector of the home-buying market (Wedner, 2005). The number of Latino homebuyers almost doubled in the last decade (from 17.6 percent in 1994 to 35.3 percent in 2004). Thus, there is no segment of the Latino population that does not have a significant economic impact on the communities where they reside.

The increased number of Latino-owned businesses reflects the growing presence of Latinos and their purchasing power. The case of St. Lucie, Florida, captures what is happening across the country regarding Latino businesses (Lane & Quigley, 2005, p. 1A):

> St. Lucie County's Hispanic population swelled by 59 percent during the past four years . . . giving birth to a whole new culture of businesses aimed at serving the lucrative Latino market[,] from a Spanish-language radio station and newspapers to a newly formed Treasure Coast Latino Chamber of Commerce.

There are approximately two million Latino-owned businesses in the United States, generating $300 billion in business (Martinez, 2004). In 2003, the 500 largest Latino-owned businesses generated revenues of $26 billion, an increase of 14 percent from the previous year (Martinez, 2004). Latino-owned businesses can be found throughout the United States (Cline, 2005; Gonzalez, 2005; Jardine, 2005; Onimura, 2004). In 2005, the first multiplex theater (Maya Cinemas) opened in Salinas, California, with one or two screens devoted to Spanish-language films to meet the increased demand of Latino moviegoers (Bernstein, 2005). In 2005, Wells Fargo surpassed its goal of lending $3 billion to Latino businesses and announced an expansion of this goal to $5 billion by 2010 (PR Newswire Association, 2005, September 15).

Latino-owned and -operated businesses that cater to the Latino community bring a perspective to the marketplace that is either not understood or appreciated by the host society, with implications for how non-Latino businesses can make significant inroads into this market (Levitt, 1995, pp. 134–135):

> In the early days of the . . . community, small businesses doubled as impromptu social centers where people came to exchange news, gossip, or simply pass time together. This is still true today. . . . "People who come frequently, it is like a social visit. Sometimes people come and say, oh, I came to say hello. They tell their problems and ask advice. They ask for help and emotional support." Some owners generally felt it was their job to help customers and that it contributed to their success, often stating, "It is the role of the businessperson to give back a little of what they have received from the community" . . . fulfilling his responsibility to the collective good.

The following description of why Panaderia (bakery) Flores, Salt Lake City, Utah, is so popular is another example of the multifaceted role Latino establishments play in their community (Sanchez, 2005, p. B1):

> Customers said they come to Panaderia Florez . . . because it reminds them of their homeland. They also come for the good customer service and their favorite Mexican treats, from flan, a custard dish, to pastel de tres leches, a cake made with three kinds of milk. They enjoy hanging out in the store's parking lot, catching up with friends they run into, and buying Spanish-music CDs from a man selling them out of his trunk. Here, they are proud of their culture and feel comfortable, not embarrassed, about speaking Spanish. "They treat you right like friends. . . . This place is like Mexico. I feel good here."

Latinos residing in this country are also a market for products from their country of origin—often, but not only, Puerto Rico (Brown, 2004, p. A20):

> While in the United States there has been a major discovery of a large Latino market by American businesses, corporations in Puerto Rico need to view the stateside Puerto Rican market in the same terms. . . . Particularly given the strong cultural nationalism of stateside Puerto Ricans, they represent a large potential market for specifically Puerto Rican products and services that has not been cultivated in any significant way.

Beeson (2004) reports on a Latino-owned business that caters to urban Latinos by selling Homie dolls, two-inch figurines that resemble Latinos wearing baggy pants, bandanas, and big white shirts, and "low-rider" model cars. Over 130 million Homies have been sold since 1999.

Unfortunately, the increased marketing attention on Latinos has also resulted in industries such as alcohol and tobacco targeting the community (Daykin, 2004; Erwin, 2004; Portugal et al., 2004; Wang, 2003). This specific interest, however, is not recent (Maxwell & Jacobson, 1989). The period between 1997 and 2002 witnessed a doubling of advertising dollars from $1.4 billion to over $3 billion (Wang, 2003). The tobacco industry recently created three Latino-immigrant specific marketing strategies. These strategies were geographically bound, segmented based on immigrants' assimilation level and their country of origin (Acevedo-Garcia et al., 2004). The tobacco industry, for example, has targeted African Americans and Latinos with menthol cigarette ads, and has slanted other ads toward women (Landrine et al., 2005).

Wineries expended a 31 percent increase in advertising dollars targeting Latinos, compared to 11 percent for white non-Latinos, between 1998 and 2003 (Wang, 2003). Increased advertising budgets are also apparent in the beer industry. Miller Brewing Company, for example, allocated $100 million (in 2004–7) for beer advertising targeting Latinos (Daykin, 2004). On a different note, one study of advertising in lay magazines catering to Latinas and African American women found that these publications published four times fewer advertisements for healthy products, and twice as many ads for health-damaging products such as alcohol and junk food, when compared to those aimed at white non-Latinas (Duerksen et al., 2005).

Not surprisingly, the appeal of cosmetic plastic surgery has also increased among Latinos. Latinos accounted for 6 percent of all cosmetic surgery performed in 2004, making them the largest group of color to use this service (American Society of Plastic Surgeons, 2005). The most commonly done procedures were augmentation, nose reshaping, and liposuction. Among the least invasive cosmetic procedures, Botox, injectable wrinkle fillers, microdemabrasion, and chemical peels were the most frequently requested services.

The role of the Internet in and its impact on the Latino community has only recently started to get national attention. The number of Latinos online was estimated to be 12.6 million in 2004, an increase of 43 percent from 2003 (Sowers, 2004). One national study of Latinos who go online found that a majority of them have incomes above $50,000, with 14 percent making $100,000 or more (Grillo, 2004). In Arizona, for example, 68 percent of the Latino community owned computers in 2003, an increase of almost 40 percent in five years, with 73 percent of this group connected to the Internet. Overall, Latinos are considered the fastest growing population group of online users in the country.

Interestingly, the emergence of an Internet job board targeting Mexican immigrants reflects how this tool is starting to be applied to Latino community needs (Milne-Tyte, 2005): "Here's how it works. Employers post job ads on LatinoHire.com. The company translates the ads into Spanish, then distributes them each week via a free newspaper to community centers in Spanish-speaking neighborhoods."

Two final ominous notes on marketing and Latinos are in order. One recent class action suit involving Federal Express highlights potential bias against Latinos and African American/blacks in evaluations and promotions (Egelko, 2005). Thus, even when they are successfully employed, Latinos are not necessarily being treated fairly. Greyhound Lines has a history spanning at least 10 years of courting Latino consumers. However, this bus carrier has recently encountered criticism from Latinos concerning its efforts to ferret out undocumented Latinos (Solis, 2005).

Between 1998 and 2001, there was a 19 percent increase in Latinos' credit card balances, compared to 10 percent for African Americans and 11 percent for white non-Latinos (Archip, 2005). An increased balance on credit cards, as the reader no doubt realizes, means excessively high interest rates, and in certain cases, a propensity to apply for predatory loans to help pay these bills. These loans, in turn, have exceedingly high interest rates, further placing these individuals in difficult economic circumstances. Major banks such as Citigroup and J.P. Morgan Chase, along with Wells Fargo, have been found to engage in this type of predatory lending with Latinos and African Americans ("Predatory lending in the Big Apple," 2005). Latinos and African Americans/blacks in one Florida study were more likely than their white, non-Latino counterparts to have disparities in either home purchases or refinancing (Bushouse, 2005). The Latino community has also become an increasingly attractive target for consumer fraud, for example, overpriced computers and credit card schemes (Torres, 2005). According to the Federal Trade Commission, Latinos are twice as likely as white non-Latinos to fall prey to illegal schemes (Grisales, 2005).

Further, a 2004 study of home loans to Latinos in Santa Clara County, California, found that they paid the highest rates for loans of any racial or ethnic group, and this pattern persisted across economic levels and size of loan (Lohse & Palmer, 2005). This pattern, as a result, raises questions about fairness and racial discrimination involving Latinos, particularly newcomers.

Contact with Country of Origin and Political and Media Representation

Contact with Country of Origin

The emergence of the term "transnational village" helps to help capture the degree and quality of interactions between newcomers to the United States and their social network in the country of origin (Levitt, 2001; Mora, 2002). This concept is operationalized by Levitt (2001) in a manner that shows people leaving their country of origin but still managing to remain active members of the community left behind. The example of Latinos sponsoring projects in their towns of origin is one way of remaining in contact and being a contributing member.

Levitt (2001, p. 11) uses the term "social remittance" to help capture one important dimension of a transnational village, and defines social remittance as

> the ideas, behaviors, and social capital that flow from receiving to sending communities. They are the tools with which ordinary individuals create global culture at the local level. They help individuals embedded in a particular context and accustomed to a particular set of identities and practices to image a new cartography . . . encouraging them to try new gender roles, experiment with new ideas about politics, and adopt new organizing strategies.

This connectedness, in turn, will be measured by the degree and frequency of contact (financial and social remittance, communication exchanges, and travel) of newcomers and viewed from a multifaceted perspective in this section.

The importance of Latino newcomers' contact with significant family and friends in their countries of origin cannot be overly emphasized, because this connectedness serves to ground, motivate, and support their existence in this country. For my purposes, there are three types of connectedness to be addressed, as follows.

Financial Remittance

Contact between Latino newcomers and their countries of origin can transpire in a variety of ways; one way is through remittance, or sending money back home to family. The term "migradollars" has been used to describe this phenomenon. The subject of remittance is one that is generally invisible in this country, yet wields a tremendous amount of influence with Caribbean and Central and South Latin American countries, and strikes at the heart of why Latino newcomers come to this country (Becker, 2004; Suro, 2003a,b).

Marcelli and Lowell (2005), for example, assert that the subject of remittance is far too important to be viewed from a one-dimensional perspective, such as the amount of funds that are transmitted between Latinos in the United States and their homeland. These authors propose three analytical categories for researching and better understanding the role and importance of remittance: research on (1) individual and social determinants of remitting behavior; (2) remittance mechanisms; and (3) how remittances affect communities. Chun and Sun (2005) found, in a study of Latino remittance in Chicago, that acculturation plays an important role in the remittance process, with those Latinos who are more acculturated limiting the frequency and amount of remittance sent to their country of origin.

There is no Latin American country that does not benefit from remittance, with some countries being more heavily dependent upon this source of income than others. It is estimated that Latinos send back home $30 billion per year (Becker, 2004). According to another estimate, approximately $123 million, or half a percent of the U.S. gross domestic product, is being sent to Central and South America on a daily basis, with about one hundred million remittances being sent per year (Morton, 2005). One study of 37 states and the District of Columbia in 2004 estimated that Latin American migrants sent a record $30 billion to their country of origin (Lahiri, 2004). Virtually no state in the country has escaped this phenomenon. Wisconsin is a case in point. Latin American immigrants in this state remitted $152 million to Latin America in 2003; this translates into an average of $1,849 per immigrant, with 69 percent of immigrants participating in this process (Lalwani, 2004).

Interestingly, one recent study found that there were no statistically significant differences between remittance receivers and the general population in terms of age, educational profile, or even income distribution, for Mexico (Suro, 2003b). Another perspective is that approximately 18 percent of all adults in Mexico, 14 percent in Ecuador, and 28 percent in El Salvador, for example, receive remittance (Suro, 2003b). In 2003, the total sum of remittance to these countries was approximately $30 billion per year (Suro, 2003b). Projected trends place the 2008 figure at $20 billion to Mexico and Central America alone (Suro, 2003a). Remittance, as a result, has shown so much growth as a market that banks in the United States, such as Wells Fargo, Bank of America, and Harris Bank, for example, have actively started initiatives to capture this largely untapped market (Orozco, 2004; Suro, 2003a). In 2005, Wells Fargo became the first major United States bank to provide consumer remittance service to El Salvador and Guatemala, in an effort to capture the $10 billion remittance market to Central America (PR Newswire Association, 2005, May 13).

Remittances, not surprisingly, have started to represent an ever-increasing segment of some Latino nations' economies, and can often surpass the foreign aid they receive from the United States. One estimate has the world's richest nations providing $54 billion in foreign aid per year (E. Becker, 2004). If the $30 billion in remittance is added to this amount, it would represent almost 56 percent of the total, an impressive amount. The Dominican Republic, for example, received approximately $1 billion in 2003 from 500,000 to 700,000 Dominicans in the New York area alone (Bernstein, 2004).

In examining individual states, California, not surprisingly, accounts for almost one-third of all remittances, with $9.61 billion annually, followed by New York ($3.56 billion), Texas (3.18 billion), Florida ($2.45 billion), and Illinois ($1.53 billion). Maryland, however, accounts for the highest average sent by a worker annually ($2,897), followed by North Carolina ($2,864), Alabama ($2,797), Georgia ($2,743), and Virginia, ($2,671) (E. Becker, 2004).

The sending of money back to the country of origin can take on other dimensions, as in the case of Mexican migrants in New York City (Lahiri, 2004, p. C13):

> When Avenamas Cruz thinks of Atopoltitlan, the little town in the Mexican state of Puebia that he left 19 years ago, he remembers the celebrations most of all. . . . "The traditions of the town, the festivals, those things I really miss," Mr. Cruz said. . . . He may never return to live in Atopoltitlan. Even so, he continues to take an active part in the life of his town, helping to raise money for festivals, a basketball court, street lights in the town center and—most recently, a clean-water system.

In New York City, it is estimated that there are about 100 groups or associations that raise money for projects back in Mexico. Organizations such as Mixteca Organization, for example, sponsor projects in Mexico and wield considerable influence on affairs back in their hometowns. Similar examples can be found across the United States involving countries other than Mexico. It is estimated that in California, for example, there are between 250,000 to 500,000 active members of hometown associations (Hecht, 2005). In the first half of 2005, these organizations provided $5 million in direct contributions toward $20 million for community projects in Mexico, under a "three for one" matching program with the Mexican government. Mr. Cruz summed up the reason for providing aid quite well when he said (Lahiri, 2004, p. C13), "The town is like one's mother—You want to offer your help."

Telephone Calls

There were days when the only means of communicating with family back home was through the mail. This, I am afraid, would be classified as ancient history, since the beginning of the century has provided numerous new ways for people to communicate across continents that previous waves of immigrants did not have at their disposal.

One such example is the use of prepaid telephone cards. As noted by Delgado, Jones, and Rohani (2005, pp. 26–27),

> phone cards are ubiquitous in newcomer communities across the United States and provide newcomers with an inexpensive way of maintaining frequent connections with close relatives and friends back home. . . . The twenty-first century has provided newcomers with instant and inexpensive connections with their homeland, something that their counterparts in the twentieth century did not have.

The advent of telecommunications and, more specifically, telephone cards, has effectively rendered written communication obsolete, at least with Latin America (Sachs, 2002). The cost and availability of telephone cards is such that this is the preferred method for contacting family back home for countless numbers of Latinos in the United States.

Return Visits

Actual visits back to one's country of origin are very difficult to achieve, particularly in the case of those who are undocumented in this country, and quite costly in the case of those who can do so "legally." Historically, Latinos' return visits to their country of origin were generally studied in relation to Puerto Ricans and in the case of Mexicans, those who lived near the border with Mexico. Dominicans have been the latest Latino group with the opportunity to visit their homeland relatively easily, although at great cost. A combination of sociopolitical and economic factors, however, play decisive roles regarding other Latino groups.

With the advent of Latinos from other countries immigrating to the United States, travel to the homeland has been less attractive: for Cubans (for political reasons), Dominicans (because of legal status in the case of those who are undocumented), and the rest of Latin America, both cost and legal status influence decisions about return visits. The emergence of new forms of communication, such as the use of telecommunication cards noted previously, has made it much easier to stay connected with families and friends. Further, for those Latinos who are sending remittances back home, the cost of trips becomes a "luxury" that few can afford economically.

Politics and Voting

The impact of Latinos on national and local elections, their voting patterns, and their level of registration has received considerable attention in the past five years (Guerra, 2005). DeSipio and Garza (2002), for example, note that Latinos can generally be counted on to be a group to be discussed in the national media during every foreseeable presidential election. The 2004 presidential election was no exception, casting the Latino vote into a national limelight. President Bush received 44 percent of the Latino vote, up nine points from that of the 2000 election (The Hispanic vote, 2004).

Although much national attention was paid to the significance of the Latino vote and its potential in future national and local elections, a closer examination of the Latino vote shows that demographic increases have not translated into corresponding increases in voter turnout. Latinos, for example, accounted for 50 percent of the nation's population growth between 2000 and 2004, but only 10 percent of new voters in 2004 (Gaouette, 2005a,b). Factors such as Latinos being too young to vote and their ineligibility because of undocumented status helped account for a major part of the discrepancy. This disparity, when put into a different perspective, is quite significant. For example, in the 2004 national election, the Latino population was greater than that of the African American community by close to five million people. However, 7.3 million more African Americans were eligible to vote, and 6.5 million more cast their votes (Wildermuth, 2005). Yet another perspective has 50 percent of white non-Latinos voting, compared to 20 percent of Latinos.

Montoya (2002), however, broadens the concept of political involvement beyond electoral participation to include mobilization and other activities, and notes that when socioeconomic status is controlled for, Latinos are as likely as white non-Latino, to engage in nonelectoral activities. A broadening of political participation to the nonelectoral process raises important considerations for social workers engaged in community practice, and for Latino participation in the governing of social service organizations.

Most recently, the election of Antonio Villaraigosa as mayor of Los Angeles represented a significant step in Latinos engaging in the electoral process, with implications beyond Los Angeles. Villaraigosa was the first Latino in 133 years to become mayor of Los Angeles, a city whose population is almost 50 percent Latino (Hendricks, 2005a; Los Angeles elects, 2005; Weinstein, 2005). The election of Mayor Villaraigosa serves to bring more attention to the Latino vote for the next national election, and raises the possibility of Villaraigosa running for national office.

Media Representation

The reader may well ask: Why a section on media representation in a chapter on demographics? The subject of the media, particularly television, generally does not appear in social work books, let alone one specifically devoted to Latinos. However, the role of the media in relation to the well-being of the Latino community is so important that one must make an effort to understand it.

The following statement by Montero-Sieburth and Villarruel (2000a, pp. 335–336) is provocative in tone and raises a perspective that has generally not been addressed regarding Latino youth:

> The impact of music and media may have a tremendous impact on Latino youth and their understanding of cultural mores. With the "crossover" to and increased marketing of music such as gangsta-rap, Latino youth are being exposed to ideologies that are culturally incongruent. Moreover, the dearth of positive role models in print and visual media minimizes the opportunities of possibility for Latino youth. In other words, negative portrayals of Latinos may result in a sense of alienation, depreciation of self, and lessening of the values related to cultural identity.

One may well find oneself in agreement or disagreement with this statement. The topic has often found its way into the national media, particularly, though not only, regarding music. Controversy generated by this subject, as a result, is to be expected when discussing Latino youth. Nevertheless, the central theme of how this nation is forming its image of the Latino community cannot simply be ignored. This section, as a result, will examine the role and impact of the media in the Latino community, and how, in this context, Latinos view themselves, as well as how others view Latinos. This subject, although of great importance, has rarely been touched upon in the social work literature, thus warranting the attention I give it here.

Latino Children and
Television Watching

The subject of television viewing and children and youth is one that has captured national attention and has been a topic of intense debate. The role and influence of television, particularly among marginalized youth of color, has added a dimension to this debate regarding the deleterious effects of negative self-images on identity development.

In a study of four inner-city middle schools (with over 90 percent of students categorized as "disadvantaged"), 77.2 percent did not participate in after-school programs, and 86.5 percent did not have extracurricular lessons of any kind. As a result, Latino children spend significant amounts of time watching television (Shann, 2001). One study showed that inner-city children spent more time watching television than engaging in any other activity, about 1.7 hours per day (Rich et al., 2005). According to Larson (2001, p. 160), "American teenagers have more discretionary time (than ever), much spent watching television or interacting with friends; (and) spending large amounts of time in these activities is related to negative developmental outcomes."

Rich and colleagues' (2005) study mirrored other findings that socioeconomic class is related to the amount of television watching. Thus, children in low-income areas watch more hours of television than those in higher income areas (Shann, 2001). Crime rates spike at 3 p.m., when school lets out, as children and adolescents are left unsupervised with nothing to do. Children are also the victims of this crime in urban areas, and may choose to remain inside as a way to escape dangers on the streets (Shann, 2001). In addition, children in single-parent homes may also watch more television, the possible result of decreased adult supervision (Lindquist, Reynolds, & Goran, 1999).

Recent studies suggest that excess television watching in childhood is associated with many harmful effects, such as childhood obesity, a lack of physical fitness, and an increased risk of smoking cigarettes, as well as elevated cholesterol in adulthood and other enduring poor health effects (Hancox, Milne, & Poulton, 2004; Pate et al., 1996). In addition, many studies show that violence on television has negative effects on children (Browne & Hamilton-Giachritsis, 2005).

If, according to the Strategy Research Corporation, as cited in Li-Vollmer (2002), 82 percent of Hispanics watch English-language television an average of four hours a day, television shows and advertisements can be a salient source of information for Latino children, providing messages about social groups, perpetuating racial biases, and stigmatizing racial and cultural groups. Often, in television shows and commercials, minorities are shown as passive, while whites are portrayed as leaders. Sometimes there is a "token" minority character, or, as is the case with Latinos, they are often not seen at all. Results from one study showed that Latinos made up only 2 percent of the characters on television, while they make up 11 percent of the total population. According to Li-Vollmer (2002), Asians, Latinos, and Native Americans make up only 5 percent of all characters on television. Thus, white non-Latinos become a visual standard. Latino children may base cognitive schemas on these conditions, which are constantly repeated. As children learn their role in this schema, they may suffer lowered self-esteem or internalize these stereotyped, racist perceptions.

In conclusion, there is usually a high concentration of Latino families in urban areas where a lack of open space, pervasive violence, and lack of adequate after-school supervision contribute to children engaging more in television watching than any other activity. This may lead to obesity, poor health effects, and a lack of physical activity, which is associated with tobacco and marijuana use. In addition, children are exposed to many themes on television that may have particular negative implications for Latino children, and Latino cultural values.

Themes Latino Children May Get from Television Watching

The amount of television watched by Latino children is significant, and the consequences evident. This section will explore some of the negative implications of Latino children watching television, and the themes promoted on television.

Lichter and Amundson (1994) give an overview of Latinos on television starting in the 1950s up to the mid-1990s. Over the years, characters of color gained more prominent (sometimes desirable, sometimes not) roles. According to Lichter and Amundson (1994), African Americans faired much better than Latinos in terms of more representation and better, higher quality roles. In addition, cultural diversity among Latinos as a group portrayed on television has been almost completely absent. Rodriquez (1997) says that the two main problems for Latinos and television are underrepresentation of Latinos and negative portrayals of Latinos, who are shown as "problem people."

While the Latino population in the United States is increasing, the number of Latinos in the media is actually shrinking (National Council of La Raza [NCLR], 2004). Latinos are objects of news stories, not subjects, and are generally portrayed as causing trouble for the host society. The problem of the generally negative images of Latinos has been compounded by the general absence of Latinos behind the scenes (Siegel, 2005). In the area of news coverage, for example, out of 140,000 stories covered by the networks since 1998, only 1,201 (0.85 percent) were about Latinos (Torres, 2005). In 2004, the percentage was 0.72; less than 1 percent of news time was devoted to Latinos, with only six Latino stories featuring Latino reporters, with four of these reporters working for Telemundo (Gonzalez, 2005).

Studies also suggest that the underrepresentation and negative portrayal of Latinos in the media may contribute to lowered self-esteem and expectations. The National Council of La Raza is working to promote the positive portrayal of Latinos on television and has succeeded with the television program *Resurrection Blvd* (Harwood & Anderson, 2002). Still, as Latinos are invisible on television and shown in a negative light, they systematically become the "other" to a white, dominant standard (Jenrette, McIntosh, & Winterberger, 1999; Berg, 2002). According to Fullerton and Kendrick's (2000) cultivation theory, television shapes reality, and people begin to accept what they see on television as real. This is true especially in the case of gender stereotyping, for example (Fullerton and Kendrick, 2000). As a result, Latinos are stuck in the role of "maid," shaping America's perception of who Latinos are (Navarro, 2002). Television has the power to dispel myths and combat stereotypes, yet the social support given to the media will most likely perpetuate the continuation of these harmful societal attitudes and beliefs (Jenrette, McIntosh, & Winterberger, 1999).

Television can also play a role in assimilation for Latinos living in America. According to dual role theory, ethnic media provides means for assimilation and helps to maintain cultural identity for third- and fourth-generation immigrants who can feel connected through news programs to their countries of origin (Jenrette et al., 1999; Subervi-Velez, 1999). Television helps to bring dominant U.S. culture, language, and customs to the homes of otherwise socially isolated families (Fullerton and Kendrick, 2000). The difficult task lies in finding a balance between the desire to assimilate and the need for U.S. society to accept the Latino culture.

Television can also be a powerful tool and serves to give a voice to historically ignored peoples (Rodriguez, 1997). Romero and Habell-Pallan (2002) discuss the Latin explosion, including everything from Taco Bell to Jennifer Lopez—the "power to define" what is popular culture and who is "Latino" (certainly not homogeneous), as noted in chapter 1. The question for social workers is how this powerful tool can be used to perpetuate positive outcomes for Latino men, women, and children, and also how social workers can take into account the significant amount of television watched by Latino children and the possible negative consequences endured. A better comprehension of television viewing habits and content, for example, can provide valuable insights into what Latino households consider to be important images in their lives.

Social Work and Demographics

The social work reader can rightfully ask: Why so much emphasis on demographics? The development of an accurate and current profile of Latinos within the community represents the cornerstone of any good social work initiative. Often practitioners believe that what they are experiencing in serving Latinos is unique to their situation. A demographic picture, however, broadens this experience and places the phenomenon being addressed within a social context. This context, in turn, helps social workers reach out across their customary boundaries and engage other social workers across communities. An embrace of demographics, as a result, facilitates intra-, inter-, and trans-community efforts.

The demographic trends regarding economic development, voting, and population increases and dispersals, for example, provide information for community organizers, policy analysts, and program planners, for example, in helping to shape how best to meet current and future needs of this community. For example, as mentioned earlier, the number of Latino babies being born in California will play a part in the shaping of major social and educational institutions as this cohort ages. The projected increase in the number of Latino elders shows the importance of Social Security reform for this population group. The demographics of remittance, too, provides important data on how money within the community is being spent, and the potential this activity has for foreign policy and aid.

The role of demographics in increased contact between different racial and ethnic groups, and the tensions that can result from this increased contact, makes these data extremely important for social work practitioners at all levels of practice. Increased racial tensions cannot but influence how "special initiatives" targeting Latinos will be perceived by a broader audience, or a specific ethnic and racial group that is threatened by the perceived "takeover" of a community by Latinos. Mind you, demographic data are have their limitations. Nevertheless, practitioners cannot ignore this source of information. The possibilities for social workers' use of the demographic data presented in this chapter are endless, and can influence direct and indirect service to Latinos.

Conclusion

The reader has hopefully developed a clearer and more in-depth understanding of the Latino community in the United States from a social-demographic perspective, and developed an appreciation of how demographics will eventually influence social policies, programs, and service delivery models. Unfortunately, reliance on demographic data often serves to blur distinctions that are very common in Latino groups and communities, for the sake of providing a profile. These types of profiles, like any other kind of profile that is dependent upon the gathering of quantifiable numbers, do not come close to capturing the immense differences that can be found between and within Latino groups. It should be noted that this limitation applies to this chapter.

The Latino community, however, is one that is increasingly occupying an important role in this society, with some regions of this country having experienced a greater impact. The view of the impact of the Latino community, however, most never be narrowed to social problems without losing sight of the incredible contributions this community makes and the challenges it faces. As this chapter has no doubt highlighted, the positive social and economic impact of this community is considerable now and will be more so in the not too distant future. This economic clout, in turn, will generate greater efforts on the part of corporations to market to this group, with positive as well as negative consequences.

Chapter 3

PROFILE OF LATINOS' HEALTH

Our results show that despite the importance of socioeconomic status in accounting for health disparities, other factors such as diet, exercise, smoking, and so on, may better explain immigrant-native or racial/ethnic disparities for some groups. Overall, the complexity of results suggest that the task of reducing or eliminating racial and ethnic disparities in health within the next few years will require a varied approach that takes race/ethnicity, immigrant status, gender and geographical location into account.

Melonie P. Heron and Leo S. Morales,
Latino Health, Nativity and Socioeconomic Status (2002)

It is impossible to discuss any form of social intervention, be it deficit or asset-driven, without a keen understanding of the multiple needs, problems, and issues confronting the Latino community in the United States. This chapter, as a result, seeks to give the reader a grounding in understanding a wide variety of health needs. No one need is emphasized, since the primary goal here is to expose the reader to a broad overview of needs; each of these "needs" easily deserves to have a book(s) devoted to it to do it justice. A health focus has been selected because it permeates all facets of the Latino community, unlike social service needs.

Determining how these problems should get conceptualized and measured is a perennial challenge in the health and human services fields. However, the Latino experience shapes how common human needs can get manifested and acted upon through a help-seeking process that is heavily influenced by the interaction of culture and environmental circumstances, otherwise referred to as context (Kaniasty & Norris, 2000; McQuiston & Flaskerud, 2003; Mendelson, 2003).

Further, interacting factors such as gender, sexual orientation, religious background and beliefs, language, and skin pigmentation, for example, also must be factored into any deliberate discussion of Latino needs and help-seeking behaviors, and of how social work and other helping professions can best anticipate and respond to these needs (Barcelona de Mendoza, 2001; Melgar-Quinoez et al., 2003).

Thus, any effort to seriously understand the challenges Latinos face in seeking and obtaining health services to meet their needs must take into account the role of several considerations: (1) rural or urban setting; (2) legal status in this country; (3) command of the English language; (4) gender; (5) social-economic status; and (6) formal educational attainment. This chapter seeks to interject these considerations as an important factor in any effort to assess needs at an individual or community level. This chapter is divided into two main sections: first, health care, and second, racism and discrimination.

Health Care

Not surprisingly, the health status, health care, and health outcomes of under-valued communities are a growing concern within this society. However, the health care issues Latinos face are many, complex, and compounded by language and cultural factors, which make them similar to those of other population groups who do not have English as their primary language. Yet some issues are quite specific to Latinos. Some of these have been identified in research and scholarly publications, despite the relative lack of data on both acute and chronic conditions that affect Latinos (Blewett et al., 2003; Documet & Sharma, 2004; Diaz, 2002; Hahn & Cella, 2003; Poon et al., 2003). McNeill and Kelley (2005) raise serious concerns about the traditional ways of disseminating knowledge about health disparities through reports, conferences, and scholarly articles, and advocate for innovative ways to involve community decisionmakers and community information brokers in getting information out to the groups who are most at risk for poor health outcomes.

Demographic data that go beyond specific health conditions can be examined within the context of the U.S. health care system to arrive at implications about the health status of Latinos (Haas et al., 2004; Ortiz, Arizmendi, & Cornelius, 2004). For example, the consequences of a lack of quality health care for Latino children, as in the case of California, can be felt across multiple social systems, including education. In the Los Angeles Unified School District, in which 70 percent of all of the students are Latino, students missed an average of 27 school days during the 2003–4 academic year (Mascaro, 2005). The costs of providing health care and health insurance are well documented. However, the costs of not doing so generally remain a mystery.

In general, the health care system reflects biased attitudes toward persons whose first language is not English, who are of color, poor, or in low-paid jobs;

who live in impoverished neighborhoods, or are recent immigrants (documented and undocumented); and who are young (Kitchen, 2005). In essence, this nation's health care system neglects to provide insurance to many people and underfunds public health prevention programs and long-term care programs. In addition, there is a dearth of services embracing cultural competence principles and strategies, although there is general agreement on the importance of this perspective in the provision of quality services (Karner & Hall, 2002). Thus, these factors and considerations create an overarching need for health care that takes into consideration cultural and environmental context (Malentacchi, Cruz, & Wolf, 2004; Management Sciences for Health, 2003b).

Further, these considerations wield a tremendous amount of influence on data gathering on Latino health status and health care. It is clear from many sources that there are difficulties in assessing the exact extent of the occurrence of many illnesses and health-impeding conditions among Latinos (Management Sciences for Health, 2003b). These difficulties go far beyond the long-standing issue of how to define Latinos raised in chapter 1 (Oppenheimer, 2001; Portillo et al., 2001). These difficulties reflect a fundamental United States policy toward health care needs assessment regarding Latinos, a traditionally undervalued and disempowered group in this country; states' policies on needs assessment mirror federal policy. Thus, attempts to elucidate the exact extent of various Latino health issues often are hampered by problems of data that are less than adequate, are complied from a variety of localities instead of nationally, or are simply missing.

Yet, despite the lack of adequate national data, a number of scholars have raised extremely important concerns through their analyses of national data that do exist, as well as through their research (quantitative and qualitative) in various localities throughout the country (Lange, 2002; Scott & Ni, 2004; Weinick et al., 2004). Homedes and Ugalde (2003), in their analysis of globalization and health at the United States–Mexico border, issue a challenge to this country. International health problems need the same political impetus that promoted international trade cooperation in the trade arena, translated into cooperation in the public health arena. Globalization is not just about trade; it brings with it social and health dimensions, too.

Overall, a disturbing national picture emerges of Latinos suffering disproportionately from poverty and lack of access to preventive health care, and known risks for a variety of illnesses and disabilities (Asamoa et al., 2004; Centers for Disease Control and Prevention, 2004a; Heron & Morales, 2002; McGavin, 2005; Morales et al., 2004; Sastry & Pebley, 2003). Descriptive data show Cubans as having the best overall health outcomes of all Latino groups, and Puerto Ricans as having the worst (Hajat, Lucas, & Kington, 2000). With the other exception of Mexicans, little is known of the other Latino groups that have witnessed dramatic numerical increases over the past decade.

A 2004 disparities report issued by the federal government identified three themes: disparities are pervasive; improvement is possible; and gaps in information exist, particularly for specific conditions and population groups such as Latinos ("Second national reports," 2005). Latinos received lower quality care than white non-Latinos, for half of the quality measures, and had worse access to care than white non-Latinos, for about 90 percent of the access measures used in the study. Research on disparities in routine physical examinations among in-school Latino adolescents has found that Mexican-origin adolescents are less likely than other Latinos to report having had a routine physical examination (Sarmiento et al., 2005).

Zambrana and Logie (2000), in a systematic review of the literature on Latino children, found four evidence-based themes related to poverty: (1) the fact that reduction in poverty will result in an increase in health coverage; (2) the need for increased funding targeting primary and preventive health care services; (3) the importance of funding to fully implement relevant health legislation; and (4) the need for improved measurement and quality of data collection. The authors concluded that unless these four recommendations are acted upon in good faith, the goals of the Department of Health and Human Services' Healthy People 2010 will essentially bypass the Latino community in this country.

One study of Latino children of migratory agricultural workers found that medical access barriers were largely not financial, including such issues as lack of transportation and lack of knowledge of where to go for care (Weathers et al., 2004). Zambrana and Carter-Pokras (2004), found that barriers such as financial, nonfinancial, and social policies hindered Latino children's access to Medicaid and state children's health insurance programs.

A Rand Corporation study (Gamboa et al., 2005) of sociodemographic determinates of Latino health found that acculturation effects are complex and very dependent upon the health problem being studied. Acculturation, for example, has a negative effect on substance abuse, dietary practices, and birth outcomes. However, it is positively associated with health care utilization and self-perceptions of health. These authors did not break down Latinos into different subgroups. Zsemik and Fennel (2005), however, do so, utilizing (1997 and 2001) data from the National Center on Health Statuses and the Center for Disease Prevention and Control.

Acevedo-Garcia, Soobader, and Berkman (2005) found, in their study of low birth weight by foreign-born status, race, ethnicity, and education, that foreign-born status does act as a protective factor, and this factor is further increased for those mothers (African American and Latina) with low formal education. Zunker, Rutt, and Cummins (2004), in turn, studied the health of older women on the United States–Mexico border and found that older women with lower socioeconomic status (SES), regardless of ethnicity, generally reported poorer health when compared to younger women with higher SES. The higher SES women, as to be expected, had greater unimpeded access to health care.

Newcomers to this country are considerably "healthier" along a wide range of social indices than their counterparts who were either born and raised in this country or have resided in this country for an extended period of time, such as 10 years (Franzini, Ribble, & Keddie, 2001; Gfoerer & Tan, 2003; Hayes-Bautista, 2002). Findings suggest that the longer newcomers stay in this country, the less healthily they become, with acculturation generally being positively associated with poor health outcomes (Brown & Yu, 2002; Lara et al., 2005).

Acculturation, in turn, is positively associated with eating disorders among second-generation Mexican American women (Chamorro & Flores-Ortiz, 2000) and high perceived barriers to use of hearing protection among workers (Rabinowitz & Duran, 2001). Acculturation has also been found to be a negative factor in promotion of healthy lifestyles among Latino adolescents (Ebin et al., 2001). High acculturation also influences the television viewing habits (higher number of hours per week) of Latino children (Kennedy, 2000).

A number of explanations have been put forth to account for this situation. Recently arrived Latino immigrants may well represent a healthy group to begin with, since the journey to this country effectively eliminates those who are not physically prepared to do so ("healthy migrant hypothesis"). In addition, although medical care for the poor and working class in Latin America may be lacking, physical activity and proper diet may help compensate for lack of access to health care.

Hayes-Bautista (2002, p. 222) coined the term "Latino epidemiological paradox" to highlight the distinctive aspects of Latino health:

> The paradox is this: although Latino populations may generally be described as low-income and low-education with little access to care, Latino health outcomes are generally far better than those of non-Hispanic whites. This paradox has been observed in so many Latino populations in so many regions over so many years that its existence cries out to be explained. Yet no currently conceptual models adequately explain its existence.

Lerman-Garber, Villa, and Caballero (2004) raise concerns about data reliability and confounding bias in the analysis of this paradox, however.

The importance of differentiating between Latino groups, and between those who are newly arrived and those either born or residing for extended periods of time in the United States, is borne out in the subject of health (Burgos et al., 2005; Flores & Brotanek, 2005). Mexicans are considered an "epidemiological paradox" among Latinos. They enter the country as the healthiest of poor immigrants. For example, Mexican mothers enjoy surprisingly favorable health outcomes (McGlade, Saha, & Dahlstrom, 2004). However, the longer they stay, the unhealthier they become. On the other hand, for Puerto Ricans, and to a lesser extent Cubans and Dominicans, the longer they reside in the United States, the healthier they become. This may be the result, in part, of increased income and greater access to health care. Cubans and Dominicans, as a result, parallel the Puerto Rican experience much more than the Mexican.

The perspective of acculturation, covered in chapter 4, has often been used to construct research on various social and health aspects of Latinos in the United States. For example, acculturation is positively associated with Latinas' having undertaken recent mammograms, but is not significant when controlling for sociodemographic factors. Acculturation did not, however, predict recent Pap smears in both adjusted and unadjusted analyses. Acculturation was associated with a greater likelihood of clinical breast examination (Abraido-Lanza, Chao, & Gates, 2005). Thus, the use of acculturation as a predictive construct is inconsistent in this sample. However, level of acculturation has been found to influence hypertension. Vaeth and Willett's (2005) study of Latinos in Dallas found that those with low levels of acculturation were significantly less likely to have hypertension than their counterparts with middle and higher levels of acculturation. Higher levels of acculturation have also been found to predict smoking. One study of Mexicans found that older age, male gender, higher level of acculturation, and younger age at migration predicted history of smoking (Wilkinson et al., 2005).

A research study of smoking behavior among Latino men and women from different countries of origin found that smoking rates did not differ significantly between men and women. However, Puerto Rican women had higher rates of smoking than other women; Central American men and women had the lowest smoking rates (Perez-Stable et al., 2001). Those who were foreign-born were less likely to smoke, and a high level of acculturation was positively associated with smoking among women. Sanchez, Meacher, and Beil (2005), in a unique study of smoking among lesbian and bisexual African Americans and Latinas, found that Latinas in the study were less likely to attempt to quit.

One Oregon study of Latinos found that it is essential for tobacco control programs to assess Latino smoking preference locally by gender and acculturation level (Maher et al., 2005). The need to develop Latino-specific interventions, particularly for young adults, has not been met (Foraker et al., 2005). Maher and colleagues (2005), however, caution that tobacco control programs should not reinforce aspects of the culture that encourage smoking, and that decreasing smoking preference in the general public might have a greater impact on Latino smoking behavior, thereby minimizing the impact of acculturation on this behavior.

Access to health services for Latinos is generally influenced or hampered by the interplay of three critical sociopolitical factors: (1) lack of health insurance coverage; (2) lack of "legal" immigrant status; and (3) difficulties in communicating in English (Betancourt et al., 2003; Casey et al., 2004; Cortez, 2005; Weinick & Krauss, 2000). Each of these factors would be quite formidable in its own right. However, when these are present and interacting with each other, and cultural values are also in play, access to quality health care becomes virtually impossible for Latinos.

Health Insurance

The impact of not having health insurance, or being underinsured, has been the focus of attention on a national level since the late 1990s (Marshall, 2003). However, there is no denying that it particularly impacts Latinos, and more specifically those who are undocumented, more than any other population group in the country (Blewett, Davers, & Rodin, 2005; Hargraves & Hadley, 2003; Rhoades, 2004). Fiscella and colleagues (2002) concluded that health disparities were significantly based upon race and ethnicity for the uninsured. Becker (2004) concurs with these findings and concludes that the absence of a "safety net" results in engagement in unhealthy practices and delays in seeking care when needed for low-income Latinos and other groups of color. Hunt, Gaba, and Lavizzo-Mourey (2005) note that racial and ethnic disparities exist regardless of the type of health plan used.

Even when Latinos have health insurance, they still face formidable barriers in receiving quality care. Nevertheless, those who are uninsured face even more formidable barriers (Betancourt et al., 2004). In early 2003, Latinos were almost twice as likely as African Americans/blacks and almost four times as likely as white non-Latinos to be uninsured (Rhoades, 2004). Roughly 20 percent of all nonelderly African Americans, Latino, and Native Americans and 10 percent of Asian Americans rely on Medicaid for health care insurance. It is estimated that Medicaid provides health insurance to 8 million Latinos, many of whom are low-income children and seniors, and people with various forms of disability (Families USA, 2005).

The lack of health insurance is probably one of the few areas where there is general consensus on the significance of this barrier for the noninstitutionalized Latino community, particularly those in rural areas (Blewett, Daven, & Rodin, 2005; Clemetson, 2002; Dvorak, 2005; Sered & Fernandopulle, 2005). Brown and Yu (2002, pp. 237–238) note:

> The access barrier created by not having health insurance coverage undoubtedly contributes to the overall disparities in health status between Latinos and non-Latino whites. Latinos are far less likely than white non-Latinos to have access to employer-based health insurance, a critical source for health insurance in this country.

Children of immigrants are considered to be more likely to have fair or poor health, lack health insurance, and suffer from the lack of a usual source of health care (Capps et al., 2004).

Another research study focused on Mexican American children found that two-thirds of first-generation Mexican American children were poor and uninsured (Burgos et al., 2005). Manos and colleagues (2001), in turn, advocate for special outreach and insurance application assistance to reach uninsured Latino children. In California, almost one-fourth of all Latino children lack any form of health insurance (Anderson, 2005). Data from the National Health and Nutrition Examination study, for example, show that 43 percent of first-generation Latino children did not receive medical care in the past year, compared to 12 percent of white, non-Latino children. In 2002, it was estimated that 46 percent of the Latino community were uninsured (Families USA, 2002). This percentage varied according to Latino group, with Central Americans (55 percent), Mexicans (49 percent), and Puerto Ricans (35 percent) being the largest Latino groups in this category (Families USA, 2002).

Carrasquillo, Carrasquillo, and Shea (2000) found that among newcomers to the United States, immigrants from Guatemala, Mexico, El Salvador, Haiti, Korea, and Vietnam were the most likely to be uninsured. For Central American newcomers, legal status played an influential role in their high uninsured rates. This may be due, in part, to less likelihood of having employer- or government-sponsored health insurance coverage, with 44 percent being uninsured.

It is estimated that 58 percent of all Latino noncitizens and 27 percent of Latino citizens are uninsured (Doty, 2003). Doty and Holmgren (2004) found that low-income Latino workers (37 percent) did not have insurance with private coverage even though they had worked all four years prior to the study. In Texas, however, almost 62 percent of the state's Latino population is uninsured, compared to 26.8 percent of white non-Latinos (Sered & Fernadopulle, 2005). In California, there are approximately 6.3 million uninsured, and Latinos account for the majority, with 54 percent (Latino Coalition for a Healthy California, 2004). The issue of access to health insurance is complex and necessitates an understanding of how factors that go beyond finances influence enrollment in insurance coverage for Latinos (Saver et al., 2003; Vitullo & Taylor, 2002).

Prescription drug access disparities, for example, have not received the attention that is warranted. A 2001 study of working-age Americans found that nearly one in five African Americans were not able to purchase all of their prescriptions because of costs; the rate for Latinos was one in six and for white non-Latinos one in ten (Reed & Margraves, 2003).

Angel, Angel, and Markides (2002), in their study of stability and change in health insurance among older Mexican-Americans, found that the uninsured tended to be younger, female, poor, and foreign-born. These individuals, not surprisingly, reported fewer health care visits, were less likely to have a stable source of care, and, because of their proximity to the Mexico border, more often received care back in Mexico.

The statistics covered so far take on greater importance in light of Latinos having high rates of employment-related deaths and injuries (Anderson, Hunting, & Welch, 2000; Dong & Platner, 2004). As noted in chapter 2, Latinos are disproportionately represented in dangerous jobs such as roofing, fruit picking, taxi driving, and construction (Greenhouse, 2001). Texas, for example, led the country in the number of Latino work-related deaths in 2003, reflecting a continued increase between 1992 (136 deaths) and 2003 (163 deaths), surpassing California (Garay, 2005). Latino employment-related deaths in Texas, like those in the nation overall, occur in riskier occupations such as manufacturing, agriculture, and construction. One study of North Carolina's poultry industry found that 60 percent of Latino workers had experienced some type of work-related injuries or illnesses in the past month (Parker, 2005).

Lack of adequate training is often the primary reason for higher death rates, according to Deborah Weinstock, an occupational safety and health specialist for the AFL-CIO. Latinos are also less likely to report hazards in the workplace because they fear being labeled as troublemakers, worry about their job security, or are not informed about their rights (Garay, 2005). The high accident rate among Latino laborers has not gone unnoticed, and demands have been made that the Occupational Safety and Health Administration enforce safety regulations (Gonzales, 2005).

A study of young Latino immigrant construction workers found that they received inadequate safety training, given the hazardous work they performed (O'Connor et al., 2005). Another study of fatal occupational injury rates in southern and nonsouthern states found fatality rates increasing for Latino men, and it was projected that they were emerging as the group with the highest unintentional fatal occupational injury rate in this region (Richardson et al., 2004).

Legal Status in the United States

Undocumented status and access to health care has become a salient topic in this country in the past five years (Bilchik, 2001; Collins, Bussarf, & Combes, 2003; Jaklevic, 2001; Kullgren, 2003). Indications are good that the subject matter will continue to take center stage in any discussion of newcomers to this country. Not surprisingly, controversies and ethical issues, particularly involving life-saving care, have emerged with greater frequency as the number of undocumented has increased numerically (Coritsidis et al., 2004; Young, Flores, & Berman, 2004).

Frates, Diringer, and Hogan (2003) note that undocumented children in California are generally underserved, are vulnerable, and have not benefited from expansion of publicly funded children's health programs. Issues regarding access have also emerged in other spheres. Bauer and colleagues' (2000) study of barriers to health care for abused Latina and Asian immigrant women, for example, found that fear of deportation for those who were undocumented was a key factor in determining access to services.

Language Barriers

There is general agreement that increasing Latino access to quality health care is very much dependent upon the health care system being able to offer services in Spanish and taking into account how cultural factors influence perceptions and expectations of treatment (Bender & Harlan, 2005; Diaz et al., 2001). Derose and Baker (2000), for example, found that limited English proficiency negatively affected Latinos' use of health care services. In focusing on language barriers, however, one cannot ignore how culture, too, plays a role in shaping language and the help-seeking process. The Spanish language is, after all, very closely connected with Latino culture (Rehm, 2003). Similar conclusions have also been made about Asians in the United States (Ngo-Metzger et al., 2003).

Suleiman (2003) addresses the need for social services to be available in Spanish as a civil rights issue because of its importance in the lives of Latinos. Dombrouski and McCahill (2004), in turn, raise a series of ethical factors and considerations pertaining to the provision of quality language services. It should not suffice that Spanish interpretation services are provided; they also have to be of a high quality. Morales and colleagues (1999) document Latino patients' dissatisfaction with their health care experiences because of language and cultural barriers. Johnson and colleagues (2004), in turn, describe feelings of cultural bias experienced by Latinos and other groups of color in seeking health care. Timmins (2002), in a content analysis of the literature (1990–2000) on language barriers to health care for Latinos, found strong evidence that language barriers do adversely affect quality of care for this population group.

Derose and Baker (2000, p. 76), in examining the relationship between limited English proficiency and Latinos' use of physicians, concluded: "The magnitude of the association between English proficiency and number of physician visits was similar to that for having poor health, no health insurance, or no regular source of care." One study found that Latino patients are at a double disadvantage when seeking health care from English-speaking physicians. They make fewer comments, and when they do make them, they are more than likely ignored (Rivadeneyra et al., 2000). Murphy and colleagues (2003), reported lack of adherence to treatment for AIDS patients who were monolingual because of language barriers, and the use of translators was not always seen as a sufficient remedy.

Provision of quality language services is but one step in the provision of quality health and social services. For example, more time conducting interviews is to be expected because of challenges associated with cultural and language differences (Kravitz et al., 2000; Tocher & Larson, 1999). Further, time must be devoted to explaining the written instructions accompanying routinely prescribed medications (Leyva, Sharif, & Ozuah, 2005). Pharmacists, too, must be prepared to overcome language and cultural barriers (Muzyk, Muzyk, & Barnett, 2004).

A number of strategies and recommendations have been advanced to address language and cultural barriers in better serving Latinos. These approaches generally fall into five categories, as follows. However, they must not be conceptualized as being mutually exclusive of each other, because the health care needs of Latinos are complex and difficult to address in a culturally competent manner by relying upon one strategy.

Provision of Trained Interpreters

Tremendous importance must be placed on having properly trained interpreters (Burbano O'Leary, Federico, & Hampers, 2003; Elderkin-Thompson, Silver, & Waitzkin, 2001; Karliner, Perez-Stable, & Gildengorin, 2004; Lee et al., 2002; Vandervort & Melkus, 2003). Jacobs and colleagues' (2004) study of the costs and benefits of interpreter services in health care found that these services are financially viable for enhancing the quality of health care for patients with limited English proficiency. Patients with interpreter services received significantly more recommended preventive services, made more office visits, and had more prescriptions written and filled. The cost per patient for interpreter services was $279 per year.

Laws and colleagues (2004) propose development of a method for evaluating the quality of medical interpretation because of the critical role interpreters play in helping Latinos achieve positive health outcomes. Use of family members, particularly children, as translators must be avoided to prevent liability problems and safety concerns resulting from errors in translating (Rollins, 2002).

Hiring Latino Bilingual and Bicultural Staff

The provision of health care by bilingual and preferably bicultural staff is one recommendation that has received attention (Fernandez et al., 2004; Manoleas et al., 2000; Sevilla Matir & Willis, 2004). Sadly, as is the case in California, even when Spanish-speaking physicians are available, the insurance status of Latinos with limited English proficiency limits their access to these physicians (Yoon, Grumbach, & Bindman, 2004). Lu and colleagues (2001), in their study of Latino and non-Latino clinicians working with Latinos, highlight the importance of being able to match practitioner's with client's ethnic background as a means of increasing communication and minimizing distances between the provider and the consumer.

This recommendation attempts to increase not only health care access for Latinos but also connectedness between institutions serving this community and the community itself. The benefits of having Latino staff, as a result, go beyond provision of quality services, and extend to good public relations and an increased likelihood of grounding services within the context of what the community believes it wants and needs.

Having Health Care Staff
Learn Spanish

If the hiring of bilingual and bicultural staff is not possible, then it is recommended that current staff learn Spanish (Barkin et al., 2003; Mazor et al., 2002; Schitai, 2004). It is acknowledged that it is preferable to hire Latino staff whenever possible as a first approach. The costs and the challenges of recruiting and keeping Latino staff in the health and social service fields are well documented. Nevertheless, there certainly is no equal substitute for the hiring of Latino staff.

Provision of professional and financial incentives, combined with in-house accessibility to language instruction, has been found to be an attractive option for increasing organizational language capacity. The investment of time and energy on the part of staff to learn Spanish, in turn, increases career options that might otherwise not be available.

Development of Culture- and
Language-Specific Assessment Tools

Any attempt to provide quality services will require that assessment tools be normed to Latinos and available in Spanish when needed. The utilization of assessment tools must take into account language and cultural considerations, thus requiring development of new or modified tools for Latinos (Blumentritt & VanVoorhis, 2004; Malgady & Zayas, 2001; Matias-Carrelo et al., 2003; Villasenor & Waitzkin, 1999).

Provision of Materials and
Sources in Spanish

The health care delivery system must be broadly conceptualized to go beyond actual face-to-face interactions between patient and health care provider. The process also includes the actions that transpire after a health care visit. The importance of follow-through on prescribed treatment is such that provisions need to be made for monolingual Latino patients to comprehend what is expected of them. Thus, follow-through on treatment necessitates provision of materials in Spanish and Internet sites that Latinos can access (Hartel & Mehling, 2002).

Lack of materials in Spanish not only affects clients and patients but also has a dramatic influence on limited English proficient staff. For example, some Latino staff at the University of North Carolina Hospitals are hindered from engaging in a grievance process because information about procedures and policies is not available in Spanish (Ferreri, 2005). This situation is not limited to this system of North Carolina.

Select Health Care Needs

The following six health conditions and emerging health care topics have been signaled out for special attention because of the prominent role they play, or are projected to play, in the well-being of the Latino community in the near future.

HIV/AIDS   It is impossible to address health care needs within the Latino community without specifically signaling out the devastating impact HIV/AIDS has had on this community (Diaezcanseco-Mallipudi, 2004). The impact of HIV/AIDS has a long and painful history within the Latino community in this country. For example, HIV/AIDS was the sixth leading cause of death among Latinos ages 25–34 in 2001 (Keiser Family Foundation, 2005). At the end of 2003, there were almost 81,000 Latinos diagnosed with AIDS, or 20 percent of all known cases in the United States (Keiser Family Foundation, 2005).

There is literally no region of the country or Latino group and subgroup that has escaped the consequences of this disease. However, there are sectors that have experienced their disproportionate share. A total of 10 states accounted for 89 percent of all known AIDS cases among Latinos in the United States (Keiser Family Foundation, 2005). The top five states were New York (20,419 cases), California (15,387 cases), Florida (7,472 cases), Texas (7,153 cases), and New Jersey (3,521) cases (Keiser Family Foundation, 2005). If Puerto Rico were included in this list, it would rank third, with 9,780 cases.

Cities have borne a disproportionate number of Latinos with HIV/AIDS. In 2001, the top four cities with the largest number of Latino males and females diagnosed with AIDS were New York (27,518 males and 9,322 females), San Juan (11,929 males and 3,455 females), Los Angeles (10,613 males and 1,023 females), and Miami (6,859 males and 866 females) (Latino AIDS Commission, 2002). New York City is one of the nation's urban areas that have witnessed a tremendous impact. However, other cities normally not associated with Latinos or HIV/AIDS have not escaped. Anchorage, Alaska, for example, has a Latino representation of 6.5 percent of its population, yet Latinos represent well over 10 percent of that city's known HIV/AIDS cases (Diaezcanseco-Mallipudi, 2004).

New York City's Latino community accounts for 9 percent of all Latinos in the United States, yet this community accounts for over 30 percent of all diagnosed AIDS cases in the nation (Declaration of an HIV/AIDS health emergency, 2001). One New York City study on AIDS found that almost 50 percent of the people of the Latino community had a friend or family member with HIV/AIDS (Declaration of an HIV/AIDS health emergency, 2001). Another research study focused on Latina prostitutes (Dominican, Mexican, and Puerto Rican) in New

York City and El Paso, Texas, although dated but still very relevant, found them to be at very high risk for drug use and HIV (Deren et al., 1997).

It is not surprising, as a result, to see signs of the impact of disease in the community landscape through memorial murals specifically noting deaths of Latino community members resulting from AIDS (Delgado, 2003). As noted in chapter 8, memorial murals present social workers with a unique vehicle for addressing bereavement issues within families and important community-wide healing after the death of a loved one.

One estimate attributes over 55 percent of all known AIDS cases among Latino males and females to sharing of contaminated needles (Declaration of an HIV/AIDS health emergency, 2001). Although the number of AIDS-related deaths has decreased since the introduction of new medicines, AIDS is still among the top six leading causes of death for Latinos (aged 20–54 years). However, more than 50 percent of these deaths are injection-related (Dogwood Center, 2002).

Approximately 40 percent of Latinas get infected by having sex with men who use intravenous drugs, making Latinas at risk for contracting AIDS through having sex with men and intravenous drug use (Declaration of an HIV/AIDS health emergency, 2001). Newcomb and Carmona (2004) found that Latinas with HIV experience additional stressors and traumatic events, further compromising their psychological adjustment and substance use. Kropp and colleagues (2005) stress the importance of Latina expectant mothers being testing during the first trimester as a means of improving counseling and testing rates for HIV transmission.

Nevertheless, although the Latino community is increasingly the subject of research, the diversity found within this group has challenged both researchers and practitioners alike in attempting to develop a comprehensive picture of how HIV/AIDS can be prevented and treated early (Campo et al., 2005; Culturally based model, 2005). The professional literature on Latinos and HIV/AIDS has started to broaden its focus to include groups that are at high risk but have generally escaped the attention of researchers and service planners. For example, although rural Latino migrant workers have been identified as a group at high risk for contracting HIV, little is known about urban-based migrant day laborers, who are also at high risk (Wong et al., 2003).

The increase in HIV infection among gay and bisexual Latinos, another high-risk group, has spurred research and resulted in targeting outreach, education, and counseling to this group (Bond, 2004; Reaching out to the down low, 2004; C. Smith, 2005). Zea, Reisen, and Diaz (2003), however, raise key methodological issues related to sexual behavior among Latino gay and bisexual men—for example, the importance of taking into account the level of acculturation and the role that social context and internalized sociocultural experiences (oppression, discrimination, racism, and homophobia) have had for nonheterosexual Latinos and Latinas.

Increased research has been focused on HIV risk behaviors among male-to-female transgendered persons of color (Nemoto et al., 2004) and bisexual and gay-identified young Latino men (Agronick et al., 2004), in an effort to better understand the interplay of culture and sexual risk-taking among these two subgroups. One study of psychosocial issues relating to gay- and non-gay-identified HIV-positive African American and Latino men having sex with men examined social domains, such as cultural and gender-bound beliefs, to draw implications for constructing group-specific interventions (Williams et al., 2004). Fernandez and colleagues (2002), in a study of how HIV testing history and future testing intentions were related to sexual risk in a community sample of Latino men, found that Latino men at highest risk (men having sex with men) were also the most likely to have undergone testing and planned future testing when compared with Latino men at low risk.

Diaz, Heckert, and Sanchez (2005) specifically examined Latino gay men using stimulants (methamphetamine and cocaine users). This research found that Latinos use stimulants for reasons they consider to be important, such as enhancement of social, emotional, work, and sexual life. One study of Latino gay men's disclosure of HIV-positive status to their social networks found that disclosure was not a generalized tendency, and is influenced by a range of factors, the target of the disclosure, and whether the target was aware of the participant's sexual orientation (Zea et al., 2004).

The increased risk of contracting HIV/AIDS that Latino youth and young adults (ages 13–29) face is shown in the statistic that they account for 40 percent of all new cases of HIV infection in the United States (Declaration of an HIV/AIDS health emergency, 2001). The relative youthfulness of the Latino community, when compared with other ethnic and racial groups, makes this population group particularly vulnerable to this form of infection (Abel & Chambers, 2004). There is no question that HIV/AIDS remains an epidemic in this community, with projections that it will continue to affect Latinos in the foreseeable future.

Hepatitis C   The emergence of hepatitis C as a significant disease in this society, and particularly in communities of color, makes it one that must be addressed within a social and health perspective. The health consequences of hepatitis C are significant for poor communities of color. The hepatitis C virus is largely responsible for the high rate of liver disease (the seventh highest cause of death) among Latinos aged 25–44, and (third highest) among those aged 45–64 (Stevenson et al., 2004).

Obesity   The medical implications of obesity among Latinos necessitates that this subject be signaled out for discussion. The so-called Fat Epidemic has certainly captured national attention. Barboza (2000), in a *New York Times* article devoted to obesity and its prevalence and impact on low-income urban communities, particularly those of color, in the United States, notes that these communities have suffered disproportionately in their members being either overweight or obese. There is a direct correlation between race, ethnicity, and income level. Hubert, Snider, and Winkleby (2005) note that Latino adults have experienced an 80 percent increase in obesity over the past decade (1995–2005). Obesity in Latino and African American communities, according to Barboza (2000), is a direct result of a lack of knowledge about proper nutrition and a lack of access to healthier foods.

Increased use of fast-food restaurants and cafeterias among highly accultur-ated Latinas was found to be a contributing factor to being overweight (Ayala et al., 2005). Lack of access to play areas that are perceived as safe has also con-tributed to overweight in this community (Rich et al., 2005). Chatterjee, Blakely, and Baron (2005), too, found that lack of safe playing areas, along with lack of time, contributed to a decrease in physical activities for Latinos.

Mazur, Marquis, and Jessen (2003) found that both acculturation and pov-erty play important roles in diets for Latino youth. One study of childhood obe-sity in California found that among low-income white, non-Latino children, 18 percent were overweight or obese, a 50 percent increase from 1994 to 2003. Among African Americans the rate was 19 percent, an increase of 46 percent during this period, and the rate was 23 percent for Latinos, a 44 percent increase (Size of California's obesity problem grows, 2004). A Los Angeles study, this one involving 14 elementary schools, found that 35 percent of the students in the sample were at risk for being overweight (Slusser et al., 2005). A study of over-weight children (two-, three-, and four-year-olds) in a New York City popula-tion in the Women, Infants, and Children program (WIC) found that Latino children were more than twice as likely to be overweight or at risk for overweight when compared to other ethnic and racial groups. The availability of "junk food" through dispensers in cafeterias has been viewed as playing an important role in schoolchildren being overweight or even obese (Nelson, Chiasson, and Ford, 2004). In this sample, two-year-olds were less likely to be overweight compared to three- and four-year-olds.

Some researchers have proposed a new framework for addressing Latino chil-dren who are overweight or obese. This framework addresses belief systems and cultural factors and identifying positive eating behaviors rather than focusing on a child's weight (Crawford et al., 2004).

A survey conducted on the United States–Mexico border found that 74 per-cent of Mexican men and 70 percent of Mexican women were either overweight or obese (Acevedo, 2005a). Sundquist and Winkleby (2000), in another study of the United States–Mexico border, concluded that country of origin and lack of acculturation to American culture, as well as sedentary lifestyle changes, explain the significant differences in abdominal obesity within Mexican Ameri-can population subgroups.

Kaplan and colleagues (2004), too, found higher risk associated with length of residence in this country, which is likely the result of unhealthy diet (high in fat and low in fruits and vegetables). Smith, Day, and Brown (2005), in turn, in their study of dietary fiber intakes in Latino mothers, found that those mothers who were older and had stronger heritage retention had higher fiber intakes. Devine and colleagues (1999) viewed consumption of fruits and vegetables from a life-course events and experiences perspective and found that among Latino households, life experiences related to liking fruits and vegetables in youth were positively associated with people's currect conception of these food items.

Latinas, when compared to African American women, consume more carbohydrates (grams) and dietary fiber (total and soluble), perceive their current body image as heavier, and reported greater body image dissatisfaction than African Americans, even when they weighed less (Sanchez-Johnsen et al., 2004). Although not studied, the question of acculturation needs to be raised, particularly in the case of Latina perception of body image. There is a strong possibility that those Latinas who are more highly acculturated may embrace a more negative body image when compared to their less acculturated counterparts.

Obesity is not a problem restricted to Latino adults, as already noted, with youth also having to contend with illnesses related to being overweight. Latino adolescents, for example, are approximately two times more likely than their white, non-Latino counterparts to be overweight (Doyle, 2004). In a Fresno, California, study it was found that for all ages, Latino youth were in the highest overweight category (27 percent), compared to 16 percent for white non-Latinos and Asian American youth (Doyle, 2004). Another study involving Latino and Asian American adolescents found that acculturation was a risk factor for obesity-related behaviors in both groups, such as decreased physical activities and an increase in fast-food consumption (Unger et al., 2004).

An interplay of various socioeconomic factors and levels of acculturation, not surprisingly, influences Latinos' diet, although it is not static in this country or in their countries of origin, as I will soon note. Diet is as much a part of culture as it is about environmental circumstances, and Latinos are no exception to this interaction. The Latino diet has historically consisted of foods that were low in fats, and generally consisting of various types of vegetables and carbohydrates that were readily available in their immediate context. A shift from a traditional diet to one emphasizing processed foods—for example, from calcium-rich corn tortillas to refined-flour tortillas, or from whole grains to white flour and rice— may have started in their country of origin and further accelerated upon their arrival in this country (Braine, 2005). According to one nutritionist, acculturation in the United States translates to the following: "fiber content decreases, intake of antioxidants and phytochemicals decreases and fat intake goes up" (Braine, 2005, p. 1).

Higher levels of acculturation result in subsequent Latino generations experiencing a greater likelihood of obesity (Vicevich, 2004). This is probably the result of a greater preference for processed foods as opposed to fresh foods, causing overweight and obesity. The benefits of this change in diet for second-generation Latinos, however, may be higher stature. The interrelationship between poor diet and a host of illnesses has been well documented in the professional literature. Winkleby and colleagues (2003), for example, emphasize the importance of health personnel knowing about the relationship between weight, diet, physical activity, alcohol, and colorectal screening among Latinos, in this case agricultural workers.

Chronic Illness   Chronic illnesses are very much a significant part of this nation's health landscape. However, certain illnesses take on added significance when addressing certain ethnic and racial groups, such as Latinos. The following illnesses have been selected because of their particular influence on Latinos in the country.

Cardiovascular illnesses. There is a general consensus in the field that there are very few published reports specifically focused on Latinos with chronic illnesses such as hypertension (Arnada et al., 2004; Artinian et al., 2004: Kountz, 2004; Perez-Stable & Salazar, 2004; Vergara et al., 2004).

Sharma and colleagues (2004) found that there are significant differences in the levels of cardiovascular disease among this nation's racial and ethnic groups, particularly when taking socioeconomic status into account. In fact, disparities in cardiovascular health are very prominent in this country (Mensah et al., 2005). Coronary heart disease mortality among Mexican Americans is equal to, or exceeds, that among white non-Latinos (Pandey et al., 2001). Lorig, Ritter, and Jacquez (2005), as a result, advocate for the expansion of community-based chronic disease self-management programs that are in Spanish and culturally based.

Kountz (2004) found that Mexican Americans have a higher prevalence of cardiovascular risk factors other than hypertension, such as hypercholesterolemia, altered glucose metabolism, type 2 diabetes mellitus, and obesity (the metabolic syndrome) when compared with white non-Latinos and African Americans. Ferdinand (2005) notes that Latinos are highly susceptible to chronic illnesses such as dyslipidemia, hypertension, obesity, and diabetes mellitus. Horowitz and colleagues (2004) found that Latinos find diets to reduce hypertension difficult to follow and expensive. Lizarzaburu and Palinkas (2002), in a rare study of Peruvians in the United States and risk factors for obesity and cardiovascular disease, found an increase for both. Latinos, for example, are twice as likely as white non-Latinos to develop kidney failure, largely as the result of the high prevalence of diabetes mellitus (Benabe & Rios, 2004).

Tuberculosis. This subject has particular significance for Latinos, particularly those living in the highly dense dwellings typically found in central cities around the United States. However, the issue is also relevant in rural areas of the country. For example, one study of prevalence and risk factors of drug-resistant tuberculosis among Latinos along the Mexico-Texas border found that among patients with a history of previous tuberculosis, being 19 years or younger was the only factor positively associated with multiple drug resistance. Further, being female, between 20 and 29 years of age, and foreign-born were risk factors for resistance among those individuals with no history of previous tuberculosis (Taylor & Suarez, 2000).

Tuberculosis prevention, not surprisingly, is closely tied to acculturation and health beliefs among Mexican Americans and, in all likelihood, other Latino groups (Rodriguez-Reimann et al., 2004). Adherence to treatment for Latinos is considered a major goal of any treatment program targeting this community (Hovell et al., 2003). This goal has necessitated the development of medical information specific to Latinos that takes into consideration language and cultural factors (Cabrera, Morisky, & Chin, 2002).

Diabetes. Diabetes is another chronic disease that has found its way into the Latino community in the United States (Gold & Acevedo-Garcia, 2005). It is estimated that direct and indirect costs of diabetes in 2002 were $132 billion, making it a major health condition in terms of costs to society (Hogan, Dall, & Nikolov, 2003). According to a recent minority health disparities report, two million Latinos (8.2 percent of the population) have diabetes, with an estimated 33 percent of Latinos being undiagnosed (DHHS, 2004). The prevalence of type 2 diabetes is 1.5 times higher in Latinos than in white non-Latinos (American Diabetes Association, 2005).

Approximately 24 percent of Mexicans, 26 percent of Puerto Ricans, and 16 percent of Cubans between the ages of 45 and 74 have diabetes (American Diabetes Association, 2005). Adams (2003), as a result, advocates that we ground our understanding of type 2 diabetes within a cultural context in order to better understand its significance, as well as that we provide guidance for developing culture-specific interventions. Developing measures on Latino health beliefs to better understand type 2 diabetes has also been advocated for in the health field (Brown et al., 2002).

Possible genetic predisposition to type 2 diabetes may be playing a significant role in its increased prevalence among Latinos (Caballero, 2005). Idrogo and Mazze (2004) identified the role of a variety of genetic, environmental, and socioeconomic factors that predispose Latinos to diabetes. Inconsistent use of diabetes medications has been associated with increased risk for kidney problems and deaths over a seven-year period for older Mexican Americans (Kuo et al., 2003). Language and cultural factors, not unexpectedly, have been identified as playing key roles in adherence to treatment. Heuer, Hess, and Klug's (2004) research on diabetes in rural Latino migrant populations found this group to be at particularly high risk for this disease and warranting specially targeted services.

The interaction of diabetes and depression, for example, has been found to be synergistic among older (65 years or greater) Mexican Americans, effectively predicting greater mortality, incidence of macro and microvascular complications, and disability in activities of daily living (Black, Markides, & Ray, 2003). Thus, high rates of diabetes among Latinos, when combined with an increasingly aging group, increase the risk of poor health outcomes. Diabetes has also been found to be a predictor of change in functional status among older Mexican Americans (Wu et al., 2003), and a risk factor for stroke incidence, in addition to mortality (Ottenbacher et al., 2004).

The prevalence of diabetes has not gone unnoticed in the Latino community; some Latino food businesses, for example, have responded to the high prevalence of diabetes in the community, and are prime community institutions that health care personnel can enlist in better reaching out to Latinos. Lynwood's MiVida–My Life Bakery in Santa Ana, California, has started to provide an alternative to baked goods that are high in sugar, carbohydrates, and fat by offering customers variations on Mexican baked goods such as spinach tortillas, sweet concha pastries, flaxseed bread, and jalapeño tortillas (Benavides, 2005). These baked goods are low in fats, sugar, and carbohydrates. Yolanda Langley's Vida Sana (Healthy Life), a store in Providence, Rhode Island, is another example of how Latino businesses can effectively work with the community to address diabetes (Grimaldi, 2005). This store, a combination grocery store and botanical shop, carries products such as homeopathic medicines and food supplements that help address unhealthy diets that lead to diabetes in the Latino community.

The presence of diabetes among African Americans and Latinos has also resulted in community and culturally tailored models for improving dietary, physical activity, and diabetes self-care behavior (Two Feathers et al., 2005).

Asthma. Health-related problems associated with asthma among marginalized groups in this country have started to receive the attention they warrant. African American/black children are at the greatest risk for childhood asthma in the United States when compared to Latino and white, non-Latino children (Smith, Hatcher-Ross, Wertheimer, & Katin, 2005). Nevertheless, it has been found that Latino children with asthma underutilize health services, when compared to other racial and ethnic groups (Berg et al., 2004).

The prevalence of asthma is higher in U.S.-born than in Mexican-born Mexican Americans (Holguin et al., 2005). Another study focused on country of birth and Mexicans found the prevalence of asthma higher in U.S.-born than in Mexican-born (Holguin et al., 2005). Ledogar and colleagues' (2000) research on asthma prevalence among Latinos of different countries of origin living on the same streets and buildings in New York City found differences between groups; prevalence was 5.3 percent among Dominicans and other Latinos but 13.2 percent among Puerto Ricans, with more recently arrived immigrants apparently better able to avoid contracting asthma. However, when examining asthma mortality, Puerto Ricans had the highest mortality rates, followed by Cuban Americans and Mexican Americans (Homa, Mannino, & Lara, 2000). One study on smoking and depressive symptoms found significant association of intentions to smoke with factors such as language use acculturation, socioeconomic status, gender, and ethnicity among Latino adolescents (Nezami et al., 2005).

Schneider, Freeman, and McGarvey (2004) found, in a study of Passaic, New Jersey, of previously diagnosed Latino children with asthma in grades 2–5, that predictors of peak flow test failure were the presence of roaches and mold in the home, pesticide use, and a family member with asthma. Follow-through on continuity of care, once asthma for Latino children has been identified, was less likely in comparison to that for other ethnic and racial groups (Brotanek et al., 2005). Zayas, Jaen, and Kane (1999) studied lay definitions of asthma among Puerto Ricans and found that expressions of illness reflected a largely symptomatic perception of asthma regardless of asthma status.

Cancer. Eschbeck, Mahnken, and Goodwin (2005) found that cancer rates among Latinos were lower than those of white non-Latinos, and that as Latinos acculturate, their lower rates dissipate. However, cancer is still the leading cause of morbidity and premature death among Latinos (National agenda, 2005).

Byrd and colleagues (2004) found "suboptimal" rates of screening for cervical cancer in a sample of young Latinas at the United States–Mexico border and raise the need for outreach efforts for this population group. Gorin and Heck's (2005) study of cancer screening among Latino subgroups in the United States found, for example, that Dominican women were 2.4 times more likely to obtain a mammogram than other Latinas; Cuban males were five times more likely to utilize prostate-specific antigen (PSA) testing. Puerto Ricans and Central and South Americans, in turn, were half as likely to have colorectal cancer screening. The authors, echoing a common theme in this book, recommend that cancer-screening programs be based upon differences among Latino subgroups and consideration of a host of sociocultural factors.

Borrayo (2004) reports on the success of a soap opera format video in Spanish to engage Latinos in regular mammography screening. Another study of barriers to breast cancer screening for low-income Mexican and Dominican women in New York City found that personal barriers (fears) rather than logistical factors represented a greater set of obstacles (Garbers et al., 2003). Fernandez-Esquer and colleagues (2003), too, raise the importance of cultural factors as barriers but also note that it is important not to lose sight of environmental factors faced by older Mexican American women.

Substance Abuse   The use and abuse of alcohol and other drugs is a serious national problem that has historically touched and currently still touches all sectors of society (Delgado, 2005; De La Rosa, Holleran, & Straussner, 2005). In the Latino community, alcohol and other drug abuse is considered a serious problem, particularly for youth. Wells and colleagues (2001) found great unmet needs for alcoholism and substance abuse treatment among Latinos. Alvarez and colleagues (2004) caution researchers and practitioners alike about socio-demographic differences between Latinos who are abusing substances and those who are in treatment.

One study of eighth-grade Latino youth, taking into account country of origin, found that Latino boys and adolescents of almost all Latino backgrounds who did not live with both parents had a higher probability of substance abuse (Delva et al., 2005). Further, drug use differed considerably depending on ethnic group, language first spoken, formal level of parental education, urban city, and geographical region. The authors, as a result, call for a more in-depth understanding of the homogeneity and heterogeneity of drug use patterns within and between Latino groups. De La Rosa (2002), in a review of acculturation and Latino adolescents' substance use, found that better understanding the effects of acculturation-related stress and accompanying mitigating factors would represent a significant conceptual leap toward preventing substance abuse in this community.

Miranda (2005), in specifically addressing the problem of alcohol abuse, which generally gets overlooked in any discussion of substance abuse, notes that its role within the Latino community has largely gone unnoticed in the field of social work. Diaz and Watts (2005), in a study of alcohol abuse among Puerto Ricans residing in the United States, found that acculturation does not play any significant role in helping to explain or predict alcoholism.

Alaniz (2000) advocates for more utilization-based community studies to help better understand the role alcohol plays within Latino communities. Cherpitel and Borges's (2001) research on Mexican American emergency room utilization in the United States and Mexico suggests a strong association between injury and alcohol drinking. The authors raise serious cautions about how drinking will have a greater impact on this Latino group as drinking patterns undergo change through acculturation.

Finally, the emergence of club-drug use among Latinos has started to get attention in the research literature because of its relationship with to sexually transmitted diseases, particularly among Latino subgroups such as gay and transgendered people (Fernandez et al., 2005). Nevertheless, the amount of research attention received by this form of drug use and abuse pales in comparison to that of heroin, cocaine, and alcohol abuse.

Mental Health   Probably more than any other topic in this book, the topic of mental health and the Latino community has enjoyed considerable attention in the professional literature since the late 1960s. Thus, it is not surprising to see a tremendous amount of literature on this need, and the challenges associated with Latinos accessing services, with researchers generally agreeing that people of color from low-income backgrounds receive fewer mental health services than comparable white, non-Latino groups (Lasser et al., 2005). Peifer, Hu, and Vega (2000) concluded that even among Mexican Americans who met diagnostic criteria for a mental illness, most simply did not use services of any kind. Rather, when seeking services, they generally went to health care or relied upon indigenous cultural resources. Fears of being labeled "crazy" were an impediment for Latinos seeking services.

It has been found that Latino underutilization of mental health services is influenced by the interplay of stigma, language, and acculturation level (Anez et al., Beiver et al., 2002; Guarnaccia, Martinez, & Acosta, 2005). Culture-specific models have the potential to positively influence and improve functional skills for Latinos with diagnosed mental illness (Berrios, 2003; Patterson et al., 2005; Vega, 2005).

Ruiz (2002), however, raises concerns about Latino access to quality mental health and health care in this country. Marin and Escobar (2001), in turn, raise a series of considerations in the use of psychopharmacological medications with Latinos. The general consensus on the subject of Latino mental health is that providers must examine mental health with consideration of an interplay between cultural and language barriers, lack of Latino professionals, high uninsured rates among Latinos, and the presence of racial prejudices and discrimination in provider systems.

One study of lifetime risk and persistence of psychiatric disorders across ethnic and racial groups in the United States found that these groups are not at an increased risk for disorders. Escobar, Hoyos, and Gara (2000), in their study of mental health and Latino (Mexican Americans) immigration, found that Mexico-born immigrants, despite considerable socioeconomic barriers, still managed to have better mental health profiles when compared to U.S.-born Mexican Americans. The authors speculate that possible reasons for this outcome could be the result of selection bias, protective effect of traditional family support networks, and a lower set of expectations of what constitutes achieving "success" in the United States.

Grant and colleagues' (2004) study of immigration and lifetime prevalence of DSM-IV psychiatric disorders among Mexican Americans and white non-Latinos found data favoring foreign-born Mexican Americans and non-Latino whites compared to U.S.-born samples. Finally, Ortega and colleagues' (2000) research on Latino acculturation and lifetime risk of psychiatric and substance abuse disorders concluded that an increase in prevalence may be attributed to increasing levels of acculturation among newly arrived immigrants from Latin America. Vega and colleagues' (2004) also conclude, based on 12-month DSM-III-R research on Mexican Americans, that greater acculturation increases psychiatric morbidity.

Posternak and Zimmerman (2005) found elevated rates of psychosis among treatment-seeking Latino patients with major depression. Laguzzi (2004) found that depression was the most common psychiatric illness among Latinos seeking mental health services in New York City. The author goes on to speculate that aside from individual and familial predisposition toward depression, the most common factors resulting in depression were poverty, a profound sense of powerlessness, and disappointment in one's life. Heilemann and colleagues (2004) studied protective factors, resources, and risks in relation to depressive symptoms among childbearing Mexican women, and found that a poor sense of mastery and dissatisfaction with life were more related to these symptoms than the childbearing experience. Lewis-Fernandez and colleagues (2005) emphasize the importance of family practitioners identifying and treating depression in their practices with Latinos.

Minsky and colleagues (2003), too, found Latinos to be more likely of being clinically diagnosed as having major depression when compared to other ethnic groups. One study that focused on maternal depressive symptoms among low-income Latinas found high levels of these symptoms. However, only half of the women identified themselves as needing mental health services (Chaudron et al., 2005).

Pole and colleagues (2005) have concluded, based upon a review of the literature and their study of Latino risks for posttraumatic stress disorder (PTSD), that Latinos are at increased risk of this disorder. Greater peritraumatic dissociation, greater wishful thinking and self-blame coping, lower social support, and greater perceived racism influence this risk. Holman, Silver, and Waitzkin (2000), in a study of traumatic life events in Latino primary care patients (involving Mexican immigrants, Central American immigrants, U.S.-born Mexicans, and U.S.-born white non-Latinos), found that Central Americans reported the highest number of traumatic life experiences. The subject of how the disaster of September 11, 2001, affected the Latino community and posttraumatic stress resulting from it is slowly being addressed, however (Galea et al., 2002; Galea et al., 2004).

Alegria and colleagues (2002) found disparities in rates of specialty mental health care for Latinos, particularly those who were poor (family income of under $15,000 per year). Gonzalez, Haan, and Hinton (2001), however, in a depression prevalence study of Mexican elders in Sacramento, California, found depression to be higher among the less acculturated and bicultural when compared to their U.S.-born and more acculturated counterparts. Schoenbaum and colleagues (2004) found that Latinos do benefit from improved care for depression when they avail themselves of it, and the cost is lower than for white, non-Latino patients.

Latino children, like their adult counterparts, have persistently lower rates of mental health service utilization. Kataoka, Zhang, and Wells (2002) found that the rate of unmet mental health needs of Latino children was greater than that for white, non-Latino children, and greater among uninsured than among publicly insured children. Another study of Latino adolescents based in San Diego found that their rates of disruptive disorders were significantly lower than those of white non-Latinos. However, when they received specialty mental health services, they did so at a later age and had made significantly fewer visits in the previous year when compared to non-Latino whites.

Ramos, Jaccard, and Guilamo-Ramos (2003), in a unique study focused on Afro-Latino adolescents, found that they exhibited higher levels of depressive symptoms than other groups, and so did older Afro-Latino males when compared to younger groups. Another study of depression among Latino and white, non-Latino, adolescents suggests the use of a measurement equivalency of an epidemiological depression scale as a means of better capturing this mental health problem among Latino adolescents (Crockett et al., 2005).

The role of caregivers has been found to wield an important influence on help-seeking for mental health services among Latino children (Alegria et al., Understanding caregivers' help-seeking, 2004; Roberts et al., 2005). Latinos, like other groups of color, are less likely, compared to white non-Latinos, to attribute etiologies consistent with biopsychosocial beliefs (Veh et al., 2004).

The importance of assessment tools that take into account language and culture, and the need for further research, are prominent recommendations in the literature. Spanish-language assessments of children and adolescents have been tested and found to be reliable as a means of better serving this age group (Bean et al., 2003). Perceived discrimination also influences delay of pharmacy prescriptions and medical tests (Van Houtven et al., 2005).

Finally, Vega and Lopez (2001) issue a call for more research on Latino mental health. Berrios (2003), too, emphasizes the importance of more research that can then form the basis for more culturally competent service providers. The National Latino and Asian American Study represents one of the latest attempts at developing national prevalence estimates in order to better understand mental health issues within these two communities (Alegria et al., 2004).

Emerging Health Care Topics The increased representation of Latinos in the United States brings with it the need to examine the health and well-being of this group from a multifaceted perspective, including subjects that have historically not been examined in any great depth among Latinos, such as: informed consent (Simon & Kodish, 2005); genetic counseling (Browner et al., 2003; Penchaszadeh, 2001); amniocentesis (Browner & Preloran, 2000); immunizations (Larson, 2003); organ donation (Alvaro et al., 2005; Frates & Garcia Bohrer, 2002); abortion (Angulo & Guendelman, 2002; Minnis & Padian, 2001); arthritis (Abraido-Lanza, Vasquez, & Echeverria, 2004); blood lead levels (Morales, Gutierrez, & Escarce, 2005); club-drug use (Fernandez et al., 2005); myocardial infraction (Fang & Alderman, 2003); osteoporosis (Yarbrough, Williams, & Allen, 2004); vision care and eye diseases (Baker et al., 2005; Hom & De Land, 2005; Unzueta et al., 2004); hospice care (Colon & Lyke, 2003; Perkins et al., 2005); immunizations (Levy et al., 2003); kidney disease (Benabe & Rios, 2004; Lopes, 2004); organ donation (Frates & Garcia Bohrer, 2002; Verble & Worth, 2003; Weiss, 2003); organ transplantation (Danovitch et al., 2005; Pietz et al., 2004; Sequist et al., 2004; Siegel, Alvaro, & Jones, 2005); dialysis (Root, 2004); oral health (Vazquez & Swan, 2003; Wall & Brown, 2004); attention-deficit hyperactivity disorder (Stevens, Harman,

& Kelleher, 2004); and workplace violence (Anderson & Parish, 2003). These topics, for example, are only recently receiving the attention they deserve regarding Latinos.

Finally, migraines, too, have generally escaped being studied among Latinos in the United States. Molgaard and colleagues' (2002) study of prevalence of migraines among Mexican Americans in San Diego found prevalence higher in women than in men, higher among low-income versus high-income groups, and decreasing with age. Further, prevalence was twice as high among Mexicans born in Mexico as among U.S.-born Mexicans.

Racism and Discrimination

Racism and discrimination and all of their insidious social and economic consequences permeate all the health needs outlined in this chapter. However, this subject is of sufficient importance to warrant a category and attention onto itself. Interestingly, the professional literature on social service utilization has generally eschewed any special attention to racism and discrimination and how it can influence the help-seeking process.

There is a paucity of information on how racial and ethnic differences influence the process of health care, too (Carpenter, 2005; Hicks et al., 2005). In-depth analysis of how this important social factor pertains to health and social disparities in this country is almost absent (Smedley, Stith, & Nelson, 2003).

Nevertheless, discrimination, as noted in a 2004 Gallup Poll conducted in June 2004 and released in July 2004 (R. Munoz, 2004, p. 1), is well recognized by Latinos and influences all of the major social arenas in their lives: "Discrimination is seen as a problem in the workplace by 75 percent, in schools by 72 percent and in housing by 66 percent." Another national opinion poll found that 31 percent of Latinos, compared to 13 percent for white non-Latinos and 46 percent for African Americans, said that either they or a family member or close friend had experienced discrimination based on their ethnic or racial background during the past five years (Dorning, 2002). Further, according to the Pew Hispanic Center survey (2002b), Latinos report that they have been subject to more subtle forms of unfair treatment because of their background, including being treated with disrespect (45 percent), receiving poorer services than others (41 percent), or being insulted or being called names (30 percent). Being Spanish-speaking (35 percent), physical appearance (24 percent), or a combination of the two (20 percent) are the primary reasons for this type of treatment.

Interestingly, in a perspective rarely addressed in national opinion polls, almost 50 percent of those surveyed noted that discrimination by Latinos toward other Latinos, on the basis of income, formal educational attainment, or country of origin, was a "major problem." As already noted in chapter 1, discrimination by Latinos on the basis of documentation status also plays an influential role in shaping these negative attitudes. From a practice perspective, this poses tremendous challenges, since social service organizations very often seek to hire Latinos to reach out to this community, and fail to take note that Latino staff from different backgrounds (religious, socioeconomic class, and country of origin) from those of the community being served may experience great difficulty in serving these communities, even though they may speak the same language and understand the role of cultural values and beliefs in service provision.

Racism and discrimination can transpire along a variety of dimensions, none of which are mutually exclusive (Fuchs, 2004; Huntington, 2004; Sommers, 2002). Having a Spanish surname, legal status, skin pigmentation, and direct or indirect efforts to prevent Spanish from being spoken within the work environment or other public places are all manifestations. Discrimination can focus on being Latino, being undocumented, or both (Earle, 1999). Proposition 227 in California, for example, specifically targeted Latinos and bilingual education for their children (Gandara, 2002; Mora, 2002). Although the courts eventually invalidated the passage of California's Proposition 187, otherwise known as "Save our State," it represented what Rosenblum (1999) calls a "watershed" in how the nation viewed undocumented immigration, and more specifically those who are Latino.

Padilla (2002, p. 3) advocates for examination of oppression and racism as a context for better understanding the Latino experiences in the United States:

> How oppression and racism influence perceptions, feelings, and behavioral expressions of Latinos is not easily dismissed in Hispanic psychology. . . . The reason that themes of oppression and racism are important in Hispanic research is that these topics emerge frequently in the accounts of Hispanics as they relate their experiences with majority institutions and individuals. Also, research bears out the fact that racism creates social barriers that pose serious obstacles for Hispanics and their experiences shape their construction of a social reality.

Ruiz (2002), too, raises the specter of racism as a key factor in Latino underutilization of health and mental health services. Szalacha and colleagues' (2003) research on discrimination and Puerto Rican children's and adolescents' mental health concluded that both the perception of discrimination and anxiety regarding discrimination effectively act as risk factors for mental health in this group.

Latinos' lack of trust in the medical system, for example, is largely based on suspicions of discrimination (disparate treatment, for example, longer waits, denial of service, and a lack of access to specialists), and it has served as a formidable impediment for them seeking and obtaining quality health care (Andrews & Elixhauser, 2000; Bliss et al., 2004; Poole, 2004; Suber et al., 2003). Not unexpectedly, Latinos with strong beliefs about having experienced discrimination in health care, for example, express a preference for the services of Latino physicians (Chen et al., 2005).

One retrospective study of African Americans/blacks and Latinos found that when compared to white non-Latinos, they were more likely to die at home and less likely to receive hospice care, raising concerns as to why physicians have not made end-of-life care options more understandable, including the availability of hospice (Enguidanos, Yip, & Wilber, 2005). Gelfand and colleagues (2004), in their study utilization of hospice care by Mexicans, found that fear of discrimination by agencies was one of the key factors (lack of knowledge of hospice services, possible costs, and language issues were others) inhibiting the use of these services. Suber and colleagues (2003) found that discrimination causes a host of health (physical and emotional) and social problems, as well as acting as a detriment to help-seeking. One study of Latina mothers with young adult children with disabilities found that they consistently found themselves confronting communication barriers and negative attitudes and treatment from providers (Shapiro et al., 2004).

Barrio et al. (2003), in a study of ethnic disparities in the use of public mental health services among patients with schizophrenia, found that Latino clients, particularly those whose primary language was Spanish, underused case management services. Although the authors speculated about the reasons for this outcome, fear of discrimination was not mentioned, even though all indications raised in this report speak of the potential influence of discrimination as a possible reason for underutilization of services. Martinez, DeGarmo, and Eddy (2004) found that Latino students, in this case in Oregon, reported higher frequency of discriminatory experiences when compared to non-Latino counterparts, increasing their likelihood of dropping out of school.

Krieger and colleagues (2005) found the "Experiences of Discrimination" measure (EOD) to be a valid and reliable short self-report instrument with African American and Latino participants, and that it can be used to better assess these experiences. It will take a concerted national effort to reduce and eventually eliminate health, educational, and social service disparities among Latinos and other groups of color (Delgado & Humm-Delgado, in press; Green, Lewis, & Bediako, 2005).

Social workers cannot afford to view Latinos' perceptions of and experiences with discrimination from a narrow perspective. Systematic effort at documenting these experiences, and institutional supports at eradicating these injustices, is the responsibility of all social workers, regardless of their method of practice. The Latino community's experiences with discrimination provide a bridge between indirect and direct social work practitioners. Macro-focused practitioners cannot "claim" this area as their own, just as direct practice social workers cannot "excuse" themselves from acting on this matter.

Conclusion

The writing of a chapter devoted to specifically identifying the most pressing health needs of Latinos is bound to upset its share of readers. If it is any consolation, it was not easy for me to write this chapter. There are so many perspectives on identifying and writing about Latino health needs. Some of these needs are well documented and benefit from a long history of attention from scholars (relatively speaking, that is), while other needs are only now receiving the attention warranted. Major methodological limitations exist in trying to put together a comprehensive picture of the Latino community in the early part of the twenty-first century. Nevertheless, a picture has emerged that raises concerns for the future of this community, given the lack of a systematic and comprehensive set of initiatives to address their needs, without losing sight of their many assets.

I am sure that there are health needs that have not received the attention they deserve in this book. I realize this, and I am prepared to accept whatever criticism will be leveled at me. However, this chapter was written from the perspective of an author who is very cognizant of the issues and challenges facing this community, but with an understanding that this community has overcome tremendous odds to arrive at this country. And, in the case of those who are of the second, third, fourth, or generation in this country, to survive and even thrive.

Nevertheless, the field of human services has historically been and, in all likelihood, will continue to be driven by a focus on deficits and pathology. This is not to say that the Latino community in the United States does not have needs or problems. After all, this chapter stands as testament to this point. However, the strengths and assets that this community possesses must be identified and incorporated into any social intervention targeting the needs addressed, and not addressed, in this chapter! The task is to understand how we as social workers can address needs without ever losing sight of assets, and how we can use assets to effectively and efficiently address needs.

Chapter 4

BEST PRACTICES WITH LATINOS

The process of deriving best social work practices is the responsibility of the entire social work profession, practitioners and scholars alike. In fact, this process can move forward only if scholars assume this task as part of their scholarly agenda. Scholars, after all, are paid to create and disseminate knowledge. This is not to say, however, that practitioners may not be undertaking innovative and highly effective practices. The profession as a whole needs to consolidate this practice wisdom and combine it with requisite research and scholarship for it to be labeled "best practices."

Melvin Delgado, Kay Jones, and Mojdeh Rohani,
*Social Work Practice with Refugee and Immigrant Youth
in the United States* (2005)

The scholarly literature on Latinos has grown dramatically in the past 15 years, reflecting the contributions of many helping professions besides social work and the continued demand for literature that arises from the pressures of demographic increases in this population. Just as important, if not more so, is the concomitant emergence of a cadre of Latino scholars writing about their own community rather than other groups doing so. This is not to say that Latino scholarship should be the exclusive domain of Latinos. However, having a significant group of Latinos undertaking research and scholarship places this group in a unique position to be role models for other Latinos to pursue this avenue as a career, and provides an insight into a population group that has been the subject of very biased research and literature in the past. The emerging scholarly literature, in turn, has also expanded to take into account the heterogeneity of this population, reflecting an important dimension that has generally been overlooked.

This chapter synthesizes for the reader the latest empirical findings, with the primary purpose of setting the foundation for explaining why a cultural assets paradigm has a prominent place in the design of programs and services targeting Latinos in the United States, and why social work is in a unique position to carry these interventions out with this population group. In addition, this chapter will also draw upon practice wisdom. Although the focus of this chapter is on best practices with Latinos, the reader is advised that research on best practices has been, and will continue to be, integrated throughout this book.

Definition of Best Practices

The appeal of best practices, as evidenced by the number of scholarly publications and professional reports issued by helping professions, signifies how important it is that social interventions be based upon the latest empirical and scholarly evidence of what constitutes the most appropriate approach toward providing services (Drake, Merrens, & Lynde, 2005; Kessler, Gira, & Poertner, 2005; Roberts & Yeager, 2004). Attention, in turn, has also slowly moved from broad-based approaches toward a better grasp of the circumstances and characteristics (profile) of those who are supposed to be the ultimate beneficiaries of the services.

Kessler, Gira, and Poertner (2005) have identified five common definitions of best practices: (1) practice wisdom; (2) emulating similar systems; (3) use of expert advice; (4) professional guidelines; and (5) evidenced-based practice. The field of social work has numerous definitions of what is a "best practice"; for my purposes here, I have selected Potocky-Tripodi's (2002, p. 123) definition as a foundation for viewing best practices with Latinos: "practice activities that are grounded in . . . [an] empirically based practice paradigm." This definition captures what I believe to be the essence of any best practice research goals. The currency of best practices is such that major conferences, journal issues, and books are ever present to help practitioners' better serve consumers. However, this new-found perspective should not be interpreted as being free of limitations, biases, and debate. Gambrill (2003, p. 3) comments on the appeal of evidence-based practice (EBP): "EBP offers practitioners and administrators a philosophy that is compatible with obligations described in our professional code of ethics and educational accreditation policies and standards . . . as well as an evolving technology for integrating evidentiary, ethical, and practical issues."

The search for best practices with Latinos, as argued by Hernandez (2004), leaves a great deal to be desired. Most of what we know about effective practices and programs with Latinos is not based upon "scientifically" conducted research using randomized control trials. In fact, there are practices and interventions that have achieved their stated goals for which the evidence base has not been fully established and documented in the scholarly literature. There rarely is any criterion that enjoys consensus of professional opinion as to what constitutes desired outcomes with Latinos, and there are differences of opinion between practitioners and consumers. Such criteria, when established, in turn, rarely enjoy any significant input from the Latino community itself, instead depending upon the educational expertise of professionals (Delgado, 2006). Lack of time and access to research findings by social workers and other helping professionals further diminishes the attractiveness of empirically based practice with Latinos (NASW, 2003a). Nevertheless, when available, research-informed findings will be emphasized in this chapter and buttressed with practice wisdom and use of expert advice.

Overview of Best Practice Themes

Any attempt to identify best practices with Latinos based upon an extensive review of the professional literature, Internet searching, attendance at professional conferences, and interviews with scholarly key informants will uncover a dearth of sources on this very important subject (Harris & Franklin, 2003). Nevertheless, there have been an increasing number of research efforts at examining various facets of social interventions focused on Latinos over the past five years.

There is little disagreement that any attempt at deriving best practices with Latinos must encompass the concept of cultural competence as an integral part of any of these practices. This, as a result, requires that special attention be paid to a host of factors and how they impinge on help-seeking behaviors and expectations of what constitutes an intervention. Best practices, in essence, span the entire spectrum of help-seeking, from outreach and engagement to termination and follow-up (Larkey et al., 2001; Perez Williams & McPherson, 2000).

Gelman (2004), in a rare article specifically focused on empirically based principles for culturally competent social work practice with Latinos, notes the importance of helping professions developing best practices for work with this ever-increasing population in this country. Cultural competence with Latinos can best be conceptualized as an evolutionary process that integrates empirical and nonempirical (experiential and intuition) based research and data. Like all forms of best practices, best practices with Latinos can best be conceptualized as evolutionary in nature, with room for improvement.

Best Practice Principles

Prior to actually reviewing a list of what constitutes best practices with Latinos, it is necessary to present a list of principles that serve as a bridge between the empirical/theoretical literature and social work practice. The following seven principles, I believe, set a stage from which to examine and better appreciate the latest information, empirical and otherwise, on reaching and serving Latinos in the United States.

1. *Latinos or those who are bilingual with requisite preparation best do delivery of services.* Language abilities in Spanish and a deep understanding and appreciation of Latino culture represent the ideal qualities for successful social work with Latinos. Thus, Latinos who are bilingual and bicultural are the preferred first choice in staffing programs targeting this community. Social workers who are bilingual and well versed on Latino cultural values represent the second choice. Monolingual social workers who are willing to learn the language and culture represent the third preference. This does not mean that each of these groups is automatically able to engage the Latino community. However, it does increase the likelihood of successfully doing so if staffing follows this recommended order.

2. *Latinos must assume decisionmaking roles in the planning, structuring, and implementation of services.* It does not suffice to hire Latino staff or those with requisite preparation if the leadership of a project or organization is not Latino. Leaders and supervisors are often called upon to provide a wide range of support within the Latino community, and their insights and role modeling is essential to help facilitate service delivery and relationship building. Thus, every effort must be made to hire Latinos for these positions.

3. *Special initiatives necessitate proper support.* It stands to reason that special initiatives at engaging the Latino community necessitate proper support throughout all levels of an organization. This support takes on added significance in the area of administrative support. Project staff, particularly in the case where they represent an organization's entire bilingual resources, should not be also expected to translate materials or to answer telephones when the caller does not speak English, or, in instances where they spend considerable time periods out in the community, to carry the same load of organizational tasks as everyone else. Special initiatives are just that, special and not "business as usual."

4. *Social workers must embrace the premise that the longer Latinos reside in this country, the greater is the likelihood that they will need support.* The process of acculturation brings with it numerous obstacles, or challenges, that cannot be ignored in any effort to reach the Latino community. Consequently, best practices focused on Latinos must take into account the presence and potential impact that acculturation brings with it. These efforts must permeate all facets of service delivery.

5. *Services must seek integration within the social fabric of the Latino community whenever possible.* Latino-focused services must actively seek to be integrated into the basic social fabric of the community. Services, for example, should be based within the community whenever possible. Project staff must be highly visible within the life of the community, through participation in community events, as community-based organization board and committee members, and in as many facets as possible. This integration helps to break down barriers between community and organization as well as to ensure that services are meeting community needs and utilizing cultural values and beliefs.

6. *It must be recognized that the Latino community is heterogeneous in composition, and "one size" does not fit all.* This principle should not come as any great surprise to the reader, given the material covered in the previous three chapters, and what follows in the remainder of this book. The diversity of the Latino community must never be taken for granted and ignored. Sociodemographic changes are constant, and any form of best practice must reflect this understanding. This understanding and willingness to entertain changes with a community must play an integral role in shaping services now and in the future.

7. *Social work practice should always focus on assets first.* The importance of always starting with Latino assets cannot be overemphasized in both practice and academic arenas. The history of social work literature and Latinos in the United States has reflected an obsession with deficits. There will always be enough interest in looking at deficits. However, the same conclusion cannot be drawn about assets. A principle based on "assets first" will pay enormous dividends for the social work profession.

The set of principles just presented will be covered again in various degrees throughout the remainder of this book and will serve to guide practitioners in the use of a cultural assets paradigm with Latinos. Although each of these principles is powerful unto itself, they become quite significant in combination with each other in presenting an affirming and unified vision of Latino best practices.

Best Practices with Latinos—Themes

Prior to addressing best practice themes involving Latinos, it is important to point out that each of the practice themes that follow must also incorporate issues related to the deleterious consequences of discrimination based upon ethnic/racial origins, as already noted in chapter 3. As shown in figure 4.1, it is impossible to separate out the role discrimination plays in influencing the issues, needs, and barriers confronting Latinos in the United States. Discrimination, as a result, permeates all facets of Latino life, with no life stage escaping its influence. Each of the following themes is firmly grounded within an ecological context, and as a consequence, they are greatly influenced by forces in the environment. Actions such as discrimination effectively impede the realization of the potential of culture as an asset, and cannot be ignored by social workers in bringing best practices to realization.

Importance of Social Relationships

The role and importance of social relationships within the Latino culture has a long tradition of recognition within the anthropological and social work literature, as I will show in chapter 6. Relationships are often considered the critical

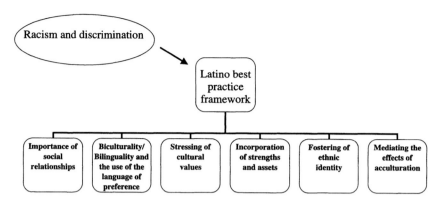

Figure 4.1. A framework for best practices in social work with Latinos

"glue" that helps bind an individual with his or her social environment. Thus, social interventions must actively seek to ground individuals within a social network that fosters positive development. Communities, too, are not exempt for this need. The term "community" often signifies how people within a geographical entity relate to each other.

In a national opinion poll conducted in 2002 among Latinos born in the United States, 82 percent agreed that relatives are far more important than friends, while 67 percent of white non-Latinos and 68 percent of African Americans/blacks agreed with this statement (Dorning, 2002). Vega (1995, pp. 13–14), in a discussion published over a decade ago and still relevant today, raised the importance of family in any effort to conceptualize cultural assets:

> Despite the provocative and dismaying array of hardships confronting Latino families . . . they are not defenseless. The existing academic and popular literatures agree that the cultural behaviors of Latinos are strongly familistic. Furthermore, from the empirical evidence thus far, the quality of social support provided by Latino family networks suggests powerful protective effects on health and emotional wellbeing.

One study of coping strategies and depression among Puerto Rican adolescents found that when they invested in family relationships and developed positive perceptions about life situations, they reduced their depression; coping strategies involving social relations were effective (Colomba, Santiago, & Rossell, 1999). Greene and Niobe's (2005) research on self-esteem trajectories among black, Asian, and Latino adolescents found that family experiences emerged as the most strongly related to self-esteem in their study sample for all groups. Farley and colleagues (2005) report the increase of Mexicans' reliance on coping mechanisms such as positive reframing, denial, and religion, rather than on substance abuse and self-distraction.

Galvan (1999), for example, in studying the sources of personal meaning among Mexican and Mexican American men with HIV/AIDS, found that those individuals who had close relationships with family and significant others, such as partners and friends; religious beliefs; and values of mutual aid and personal growth were more successful at coping than those who did not. Abraido-Lanza, Vasquez, and Echeverria (2004), in a very interesting study of Latinos with arthritis and religious and other forms of coping, found that a high level of religious coping was directly related to psychological well-being.

Gil, Wagner, and Vega (2000), in their study of acculturation and alcohol use among Latino males in South Florida, found a relationship between acculturation and acculturative stress and alcohol use, primarily as the result of a deterioration of family values, attitudes, and familistic behaviors. Finally, Root (2004), in a literature review, found that the Latino family is a significant source of support for Latino patients in dialysis.

Biculturality/Bilinguality and the Use of the Language of Preference

As the reader will soon find out, it is virtually impossible to separate the subjects of Spanish language from culture, and this is also a very politicized subject in this country. The question of whether Latinos are assimilating or are resisting assimilation has persisted over the decades and persists today. Many scholars equate the two, while others say that it is possible to be bicultural without being bilingual. Settling that argument is beyond the scope of this book. However, for my purposes, bilingual and bicultural concerns are united for the conceptualization of best practices, because these two dimensions capture the key elements necessary for social workers to be more effective practitioners.

It is important to note that "language of preference" does not automatically mean language of dominance, as was noted by Echeverria in relation to an interview he conducted on this topic (2004, p. 1):

> "I prefer speaking English in some situations, but Spanish in others. That does not mean that I dominate one language over the other . . . and if I prefer to speak 'Spanglish' (which is the case in some situations) that does not mean I am dominant in 'Spanglish' (or [any of these languages] if you ask my mom)."

Garcia's (2003, p. A03) observation of a 15-year-old New York City Dominican captures how language is determined by context: "In a span of a single city block, 15-year-old Gregory Beltre exhales words in rapid-fire Spanish, in the English drilled into him at school and in the slang on the street." One study that focused on Latino parental language during interviews and access to care for children with special health care needs found monolingual Spanish parents to be at a distinct disadvantage in accessing needed services for their children (Yu et al., 2004).

Echeverria's (2004, p. 1) comments on what constitutes a bicultural Latino describe the rewards and challenges Latinos face in this country on a daily basis:

> A "bicultural" person should at least: Understand and navigate in both cultures, which means recognizing each culture's values (e.g. family unity vs. independence), beliefs . . . and behaviors. . . . Living within both cultures has its challenges—sometimes those cultures' values are opposed to one another. . . . Understanding the inherent differences between cultures can help shed light on areas of conflict between two cultures and how [these] affect . . . a bicultural person's life.

Barlow, Taylor, and Lambert's (2000) study of women and ethnicity in the United States and the feeling of being "American" found that Cuban women reported neither feeling that they were American nor believing they were perceived as such by white non-Latinas. However, their feelings of acceptance increased with length of residence in the country.

Padilla (2004), a pioneering Latino social science researcher in the early 1970s, recently undertook a metaanalyses of the literature on biculturalism of Latino children and youth in the United States, and concluded that ethnic loyalty and biculturalism serve as important positive coping responses in a racist society. The psychological and social benefits of bicultural competence cross social domains, with implications for Latino youth and their communities. Lavender (1988), in a study of Latino given first names in five United States cities (Albuquerque, Denver, Miami, San Antonio, and Tampa), examines the relationship between ethnic identity and given names. Lavender found that Latinos had a tendency toward biculturalism, or a preference for using either Spanish names or names that can be both Spanish- and English-sounding, as opposed to names that were clearly non-Spanish in origin.

Feliciano (2001), in turn, in exploring the benefits of biculturalism among Asian and Latino youth, concluded that youth who enjoy the greatest educational success are those who embrace their cultural heritage. Bicultural youth are able to draw upon cultural capital from their own community and society, thus having two worlds to tap to help them socially navigate their way through life, unlike their English-dominant or English-limited counterparts. Bicultural youth are less likely to drop out of school when compared to English-only students. Feliciano's findings substantiate the findings of numerous other researchers in the field.

Lagana (2003), in a study of Mexican American women who were pregnant, found that those who were bicultural (balanced traditional cultural values with individualistic American cultural beliefs) were more successful at reducing stress and achieving health promotion. Chapman and Perreira (2005) raise the importance of protective factors such as cultural values (respect and familism) and biculturalism, in helping newcomer youth achieve positive well-being in the United States.

Biculturality has slowly come to be viewed as a "survival" skill and not just an asset (Koss-Chioino & Vargas, 1999; Schultz, 2005). Caravajal and colleagues (2002) found that bicultural Latino adolescents achieved more desirable mental health outcomes when compared with Latinos with less culturally based attachments and adaptations. Biculturality, in essence, provided both a protective barrier for these youth and the requisite "tools" to help them socially navigate the Latino and Anglo world. Being able to socially navigate between two worlds —one world filled with a set of values that emphasize independence, competition, individualism, and the English language and the other world valuing interdependence, cooperation, and collectivism and emphasizing Spanish as the language of choice—effectively translates into an asset that must be reinforced with any form of intervention (Coatsworth, Pantin, & Szapocznik, 2002; Delgado, Jones, & Rohani, 2005) (see chapter 6). Bicultural Latinos, in essence, serve as culture brokers between the old and the new culture (Cooper, Denner, & Lopez, 1999).

One Protestant Latino pastor, commenting on this perceived struggle, noted (Garces-Foley, 2003, p. 11): "For too long we have seen ourselves as caught between being American and Latino but instead we should see ourselves as a bridge, we are bicultural/bilingual and that is a gift." Ordonez (2005), too, reinforces the emergence of a bilingual and bicultural Latino identity that combines "Hispanic values" and "traditional-American aspirations (consumerism and upward mobility through education) to characterize this nation's Latino youth. De Leon and Carrasco (1995, p. 2) discuss the challenges of helping Latino youth achieve biculturality: "Hispanic teens struggle to accept that they are bicultural. Many think it's an either/or proposition: I'm either Latino or American. When they turn to their parents for guidance, they receive little help. Immigrants not raised in their situation are unable to relate or give proper guidance."

Easter and Refki (2004), in turn, advocate that social programs help newcomer youth develop "healthy biculturalism" that allows them to take advantage of new opportunities while maintaining the protection of cultural factors against engaging in unhealthy behaviors. Szapocznik and colleagues (1986), over 20 years ago, proposed the use of a "bicultural effectiveness training" program that emphasized helping youth broker the stressors associated with acculturation. Bilingualism, an integral part of biculturalism, is considered an asset in this quest to socially navigate two worlds (Easter & Refki, 2004, p. 1):

> The bilingualism of most immigrant youth is an enormous asset in the context of the globalizing world. Bilingual skills increase future job and leadership opportunities in our increasingly multilingual society. Youth programs

which honor bilingual skills as community and personal assets empower immigrant teens.

Schmid (2001), in a review of the literature on Latino school achievement, found that Latinos with fluency in Spanish and English had dropout rates either similar to or lower school than those of Latinos who spoke only English. Interestingly, this finding held up even when English-only families had higher socioeconomic status than parents of bilingual students. Similar findings have been reported for Vietnamese students who were bilingual in English and Vietnamese. Clearly, the implications of these findings go far beyond language and Latinos.

Bilingualism has been emphasized as a critical asset in work with Latinos of all ages, but in particular youth (Mora, 2002). A preference to communicate in Spanish does not mean that English is not valued. One national survey of Latinos found that 80 percent of them believed that all newcomers to this country need to learn English in order to succeed. Interestingly, Latinos from different countries of origin generally agreed with this statement (Pew Hispanic Center, 2002b)—Mexicans (89 percent), Puerto Ricans and Cubans (89 percent), Central Americans (94 percent), South Americans (89 percent), Salvadorians (94 percent), Dominicans (92 percent), and Colombians (88 percent). Logan, Lutz, and Stults (2002), in their research on speaking only English among grandchildren of contemporary immigrants, found that acculturation based upon language is occurring at the same pace for Asians (Chinese) as it did for Europeans. However, it is occurring at a slower pace among Latinos (Cubans and Mexicans), with home languages of third-generation children being most affected by intermarriage.

The issue of bilingualism, however, like biculturalism, is multifaceted, with generally three aspects regarding languages and Latinos, particularly among youth (Koss-Chioino & Vargas, 1999): (1) proficiency level in both languages; (2) how a decision is made as to which language to use in different situations; and (3) what language means to a particular Latino. These three aspects serve to ground, or contextualize, what it means to be bilingual. Language may well be a proxy for other cultural and identity factors that effectively serve protective roles within the lives of Latino youth. A language-specific study of English-language preference on the part of low-income Latino youth in Los Angeles found that Latinos (aged 14 to 24) expressed a preference for English when talking among themselves, reading a magazine, or channel surfing. More than 28 percent indicated a Spanish-only preference, and 14 percent selected either language (Hispanic fusion market, 2002).

Goldstein and Suro (2000, p. A01), summarizing national survey findings on bilingual, bicultural Latinos, note:

> Latinos are equally at home in Spanish or English. Yet they are not merely dangling at the midpoint of two worlds. Many Latinos in this stage live

comfortably in a bilingual, bicultural world . . . this place is more of a destination than a rest stop to full assimilation. This bicultural stage is shared by many Hispanics in the United States—slightly more than 1 in 4 Latinos surveyed.

Who are these bilingual and bicultural Latinos? They can certainly be quite varied in description, including first-generation, college-educated Latinos, Latinos who are married to non-Latinos and who have lived here for an extended period of time, or Latino newcomers' children born and raised in the United States.

The Stressing of Cultural Values

The Board of Children, Youth and Families (2004), in a review of research studies on Latino cultural differences as sources of risk and resilience, concluded that culture is a source of neither vulnerability or risk. Instead, cultural differences can become a source of risk under the following conditions: (1) when culture is considered a deficit; (2) when culture results in a mismatch between caregivers or between children themselves and members of the dominant institutions in their lives; and (3) when cultural differences result in discrimination, thereby limiting social mobility. All these situations can exist by themselves or in combination with each other.

Much can be learned about the help-seeking and the help-provision process for Latinos by examining the cultural values that appeal to them by using natural support systems. Several key elements related to Latino cultural values help account for the attractiveness of natural support systems (Delgado & Humm-Delgado, 1993): (1) "simpatia" (people are treated with honor, dignity, and respect, and not made to "lose face"); (2) cooperative helper and consumer sharing and working together; (3) reciprocity—everyone can use and give assistance; (4) action-orientation, with a focus on immediate solutions versus introspection; and (5) freedom to attend since participation is voluntary. Warda's (2000) study of Mexican Americans' perceptions of culturally competent care found a strong influence on culture, emphasizing themes of respect, caring, understanding, and patience. These values, as will be addressed in chapter 6, are critical elements among the most common Latino values.

A strong tradition of family caregiving also translates into a culture of caregiving (Ayalong, 2004; Coon et al., 2004). Valle, Yamata, and Barrio's (2004) research on help-seeking behavior of Euro-American and Latino caregivers of elders found that the effects of ethnicity on help-seeking persisted. Latino caregivers reported less formal help-seeking than other Euro-American counterparts, and thus relied more heavily on their own support systems. Weiss and colleagues' (2005) national study of informal care received by older Latinos, white non-

Latinos, and African Americans found that Latinos received significantly more hours of informal care than their two counterparts.

Stanton-Salazar (2000), in a study of urban Latino youth coping strategies, found that the term "confianza en confianza" (trusting mutual trust) was a cultural value that was a basis upon which these youth formed their interpersonal network, and must, as a result, be a part of a professional intervention if it is to succeed with Latino youth. I address these and other cultural values again in chapter 6.

Cultural assets come into play in relation to a wide variety of social needs. Low and Organista (2000) highlight dilemmas that Latinas who are victims of sexual assault face in seeking assistance. Cultural assets, if properly identified and incorporated into interventions, can wield significant positive influence on these victims. Familism serves to buffer the health (physical and emotional) consequences of this form of trauma. A study of behavioral risk factors and protective factors in Latino and non-Latino white adolescents found that Latino youth in marginalized acculturative levels formed fewer attachments and adoptions to Latino and other cultures (Carvajal et al., 2002).

A national survey of Latinos found that Latinos who hold onto their Spanish language are more likely than their English-speaking counterparts to hold onto traditional values as well (Goldstein & Suro, 2000). Gonzalez (2001, p. 17) ties language to cultural transmission for Latinos:

> Language is an essential tool for cultural transmission and for maintaining connections to our cultural heritage and traditions across generations. When these traditions are grounded in a non-English speaking community, the home language becomes a crucial link to our identity.

Traditional cultural values, in turn, help Latinos socially navigate difficult times. In essence, Latino cultural values serve as assets (see chapter 6). For example, extended family structures provide an expanded network of adults to provide instrumental, experiential, and informational support. A value of cooperation and interdependence, for example, helps buffer Latino youth against perils of materialistic goals, and collaborative decisionmaking assists youth in resolving interpersonal conflicts (Easter & Refki, 2004).

Religious cultural values and beliefs, in turn, also must be included in any social intervention that purports to reinforce Latino cultural values. Crane's (2000) study of Latino churches in the Midwest found that these institutions function as both supporters and extensions of the family for Latino youth, even though these youth may not share the same commitment as their parents to certain religious traditions and practices. Hurtig (2000), too, found a similar role for churches in Chicago's Latino community. The "family-congregation" nexus, so to speak, allows Latino youth to maintain a high level of family cohesion and linguistic-cultural continuity, by helping Latino youth socially navigate the stressful situations inherent in an acculturative process.

Incorporation of Strengths and Assets

It should come as no surprise that incorporation of Latino strengths and assets naturally falls within a best practice arena, and must ultimately form the cornerstone of any social intervention with this community, challenging as this may be for practitioners and the organizations employing them. Latino newcomers to the United States, for example, bring a well-recognized drive and hope to succeed and possess the requisite competencies and attitudes to succeed (Jacoby, 2002). Research, in turn, must actively seek to reinforce this perspective in service to the field and the communities it serves. Consequently, it becomes imperative that social work best practices identify these assets and incorporate them as central features of any form of social intervention.

Unfortunately, a 25-year retrospective examination of Latino psychology uncovered a continued preoccupation in the research with problematic behavior, rather than attention to "success or hope" (Padilla, 2002). Social workers must always walk a narrow line between identifying and addressing needs while not losing sight of and incorporating strengths and assets. Unfortunately, most human services and research are deficit driven and, as a result, present immense challenges for practitioners and academics who wish to devote time and energy to identifying and mobilizing assets. Fortunately, the field has made significant strides in the past decade, developing a practice and research agenda on strengths, resiliency, protective factors, and assets, in service to community, particularly those who are marginalized in this society (Greene, Lee, & Hoffspauir, 2005; Waites et al., 2004).

This movement, as a result, holds much promise for the creation of social intervention–focused paradigms that are founded in concepts of social and economic justice (Delgado & Staples, in press). Finn and Jacobson's (2003, pp. 57–58) challenge to the field addresses this very critical point: "A new social work paradigm is needed to confront . . . challenges, tensions, and contradictions and to address human concerns that transcend national, geographic, and cultural borders and domains of practice." The advance of a Latino cultural assets–based paradigm is one response to this challenge, and this can transpire in both rural and urban settings (Averill, 2003).

Rodriguez and Morrobel (2004), in a comprehensive review (1,010 empirical-based articles) of six youth development journals and two Latino-focused journals, found that articles were largely unguided by any specific theoretical framework and, sadly, were heavily deficit oriented, contrary to the central premises of any youth development definition that stresses youth and community assets. Further, the authors concluded that Latino youth were not considered a priority among the interests of youth development researchers. Finally, the authors go on to stress that research and practice must embrace an assets orientation when addressing Latino youth and their community. Failure to do so means that the potential of this paradigm has effectively been lost for a significant population group in this country.

Abraido-Lanza (2004) notes that among Latinos with chronic illnesses, there is a paucity of information on the role of social supports. The availability of and reliance on social supports, or natural support systems, was found by Suber (2003) to help buffer the deleterious effects of discrimination among Latinos and African Americans in New York City. One study of suicidal behavior found that Latinos appear to be protected against this behavior, with cultural constructs playing a significant buffering role (Oquendo et al., 2005).

McGlade, Saha, and Dahlstrom's (2004) study of Mexican mothers found that they enjoy good birth outcomes as a result of an informal system (family, friends, community members, and lay health workers) that serves as a protective factor. Ostir and colleagues (2003), too, found that neighborhood plays a positive role in helping Latinos, in this case older Mexican Americans with depressive symptoms. Neighborhood helps to prevent or mitigate the consequences associated with depression. De La Rosa and White (2001) advocate for collaboration between service providers and cultural social systems to increase the likelihood of achieving success in the field of substance abuse.

Farquhar, Michael, and Wiggins (2005), in their study of two communities and social capital, found that Latino and African American communities are able to mobilize indigenous resources to help identify health concerns and to create culturally appropriate responses, and are able to identify their assets and not just problems. In a another study based in the Southwest and specifically focused on older Mexican Americans, it was found that neighborhood, in this case a barrio, effectively rendered social-cultural advantages that helped outweigh the disadvantages associated with high poverty rates (Eschbach et al., 2004).

Garcia-Reid, Reid, and Peterson (2005), in turn, in a study of school engagement and success among Latino youth in an urban middle school, found that neighborhood social support (friends, parents, and family) and school support (teachers) influenced degree and nature of school engagement, a critical dimension of school achievement. The positive interplay of these two forms of social support encouraged and supported Latino youth to stay and succeed in school. Finally, Flores and colleagues' (2005) study of predictors of resilience in maltreated and nonmaltreated Latino children found that both groups of children possessed strengths. In the case of those who are maltreated, resiliency can be promoted with a greater understanding of how it gets manifested within a cultural context.

Dorrington (1995), in a study of Central American refugees in Los Angeles, found that this community possesses numerous assets such as extensive social support networks, establishment of local businesses, and strong ideological commitments, that help them adjust to life in this country. Dorrington (p. 128) notes: "The strengths of the Central American refugee community itself provide the answers to the most effective intervention strategies. The mere expansion of a purely Western model of service delivery is not the answer." Heilemann, Lee, and Kury (2002) point out that the majority of the research on depression among women of Mexican descent has focused on risk factors and totally ignored strength factors.

Freidenberg's (2000) ethnographic picture of Latino (Puerto Rican) elders living in El Barrio (Spanish Harlem) in New York City paints a picture of a group that has historically faced and currently faces innumerable challenges, yet is remarkably resilient. Barsa (1998), in turn, studied Cuban, Dominican, and Puerto Rican elder needs in New York City and found that the role and importance of informal social supports (natural) persist, although they are weakening. Burnette (1999) focused her study on custodial grandparents in Latino families in New York City, and found that the provision of caregiving by Latino elders, however, has problematic emotional and physical consequences for a caregiver. Ranney and Aranda (2001), for example, found that Latino family dementia caregivers reported moderate levels of depressive symptoms and poor health, influencing their abilities to provide the care they believed was warranted. Neary and Mahoney (2005), in a study of Latino caregivers of family members with dementia, concluded that Latino caregivers viewed family-centered home care as a culturally embedded value, and less likely to cause conflict within a family than institutional care.

The role of religion among Latinos has started to get increased attention from researchers and scholars, although practitioners have long known its importance as a social support in marginalized communities across the country. As I will address in chapter 6 in considerable detail, religious institutions have historically wielded and considerable influence within the Latino community and continue to do so.

Religious participation through attendance at religious services has served to buffer many problems common in undervalued communities such as the Latino community. Hill and colleagues (2005), in a study of religious attendance and mortality among older Mexican Americans, found that weekly attendance reduces the risk (by 32 percent) of mortality when compared to those who do not attend religious services. Religion can, as a result, be considered a community asset for parishioners.

Fostering of Ethnic Identity

As noted earlier, Latino cultural values wield a tremendous amount of influence in shaping how members of this community perceive and react to their socio-cultural experience in the United States. In no area is this as important as with the first generation of Latinos as they arrive and cope with living in a foreign country, a foreign language, and a set of foreign values (Burgos-Aponte, 2004).

The uprooting and losses associated with crossing national borders, cultures, and languages bring with them a set of dislocation traumas that severely test the endurance and resiliency of the newcomer to this or any other country, and this includes assaults on ethnic identity. The fostering of ethnic identity, however, also plays a significant role for subsequent generations of Latinos. G. Rodriguez (2005) speculates that Latinos, in this case Mexicans, will evolve in identity from that of an immigrant group to an ethnic American identity as time passes in the twenty-first century. Frequent contact with family and friends left behind in the country of origin through remittance and telephone calls, even return trips, for example, helps foster a Latino identity even though an immigrant may be thousands of miles away from home. Financially sponsoring projects in one's town of origin, as noted in chapter 2, is another way one can maintain one's identity.

In a national poll of Latinos conducted by the *Washington Post* in the fall of 2000 80 percent of those surveyed placed their ethnicity equal to or ahead of their self-description as Americans. Twenty-two percent identified themselves as Hispanic, and not "Americans." Another 25 percent consider themselves Hispanic first and American second (Rosenberg, 2005). This question, it should be noted, was framed in terms of the label "Hispanic" and did not provide an option to self-identify as a subgroup based upon country of origin. The same study, however, found that 90 percent of those surveyed believed it to be important to make necessary changes to blend in in the United States. The same percentage went on to say that it was essential to maintain their distinctive culture, however.

Umana-Taylor, Diversi, and Fine (2002), in a metaanalysis of 21 empirical studies on the relationship between self-esteem and ethnic identity among Latino adolescents, concluded that there are methodological limitations to the studies and inconsistent conceptualizations of ethnic identity and self-esteem. Nevertheless, even though formulation of ethnic identity is a complex process, there is a positive relationship between degree of ethnic identification and self-esteem. This is particularly true for Latinos who reside in areas where they are in the majority. Guinn and Vincent (2002), in their study of determinates of coping responses among Mexican American adolescents, found self-esteem to be the most effective overall coping response.

Torres's (2003) study of first-generation Latino college students concluded that Latino students do experience cultural dissonance or stress, which in turn influences how they define themselves ethnically. Greig (2003) concluded, based upon an extensive review of the literature on ethnic identity development and mental health, that Latino and African American adolescents with positive embrace of ethnic identity also show higher rates of self-esteem, and tend to have better mental health outcomes as a result. Smith and colleagues (1999) found that self-esteem and ethnic identity are distinct yet closely associated factors, and influence achievement perceptions and behaviors. Mahat, Scoloveno, and Whalen (2002), however, in their study of urban adolescents of color in school, found no relationship between self-esteem and health practices.

Stepick and Stepick (2002) note, on the basis of their research with immigrant youth, that although these youth are becoming "Americanized," they are cognizant of their differences and how society responds to them accordingly. These youth, in turn, respond with pride by defending their cultural integrity and right to be different. Thus, newcomer youth can be expected to maintain multiple identities, identifying with their homeland as well as their newly adopted country. Romero and Roberts (1998) found that Latino adolescents with a stronger sense of belonging to a group (ethnic affirmation) were positively associated with more positive attitudes toward out-groups. Negy and colleagues (2003), however, found that high levels of ethnic identity correlated significantly with high levels of ethnocentrism for white non-Latinos and Latinos, but not African Americans.

The importance of fostering positive ethnic identity among Latino youth is borne out by the tremendous amount of attention in national research focused on programmatic prevention initiatives in fields such as substance abuse. These initiatives have often explicitly utilized positive ethnic identity development as a critical aspect of any intervention activity (Delgado, 1999b; Pentz et al., 1999). These activities could entail use of folk music, art, literature, history of country of origin, drama, and the writing of short stories highlighting the ancestral heritage.

Positive ethnic pride effectively translates into a buffer helping Latino youth ward off the negative messages they receive on a daily basis in this society that can be considered racist and classist. For example, it would be rare for a local newspaper article to focus on the assets of the Latino community. Almost invariably, stories related to the Latino community focus on social problems, providing a very distorted view of this community. Further, helping youth maintain a positive ethnic identity also serves to reinforce the identity of their parents and adults in the community. Youths' pride in what they are naturally extends to their parents and elders of their community. Thus, validating or celebrating Latino youth pride easily carries over into validating and, or, celebrating community pride. Unfortunately, no one has examined the broader implications of ethnic pride and the ripple effect it has on the wider community.

Hurtado (1995, p. 60) summed up quite well the prevailing thinking on the subject of biculturality with implications for fostering a positive ethnic identity: "Cultural and language transition does occur, but it takes the form of a stable biculturalism rather than complete assimilation into the dominant mainstream." Although this statement is well over 10 years old, it has still managed to capture the sentiments of leading scholars in the early part of the twenty-first century.

Development of a positive ethnic identity can be achieved through the creation of an "integrative" identity (bicultural). This is not only possible but highly desirable if youth are to function positively in an increasingly multicultural society (Rodriguez & Morrobel, 2004). This type of identity can result in internalizing self-selecting characteristics (values and beliefs of one's own cultural group and that of the host society) that can help define one's self. It also incorporates experiences within and outside of the Latino family (Guanipa-Ho & Guanipa, 1998).

The research, although overwhelmingly positive about self-esteem and Latino identity, has not unanimously endorsed the role of Latino self-esteem and ethnic identity as protective factors. Suarez (1993), in work that is considerably dated but still relevant today, found evidence that biculturality can result in identity crises for Latino youth by making them unsure of who they are. McDonald and colleagues (2005) found no significant interaction between cultural affiliation and self-esteem among Mexican American adolescents. Barrera, Hageman, and Gonzalez (2004) found that Mexican American adolescents were no more resilient in the face of parental problem drinking and life stress than their white, non-Latino counterparts.

Mediating the Effects of Acculturation

The subject of acculturation has certainly received its share of attention in the scholarly literature on Latinos in the United States, and particularly among its youth (Gfroerer & Tan, 2003; Lara et al., 2005). The research based on this construct has proliferated in number and in arenas since the late 1970s and early 1980s, representing a significant history that spans almost a quarter of a century. This "history" is a major achievement in the social sciences and attests to the importance of this construct.

Terms such as "dietary acculturation," "acculturative stress," "dissonant acculturation," "educational acculturation," and "enculturation," for example, have emerged (Gil, Wagner, & Tubman, 2004; Martinez, DeGarmo, & Eddy, 2004; L. Rodriguez, 2004; Mora, 2002; Romero-Gwynn & Gwynn, 1997). *Enculturation* is a term that has not appeared frequently in the research and scholarly literature. Nevertheless, its popularity will increase in this decade because of its positive perspective on Latino culture as an asset. Enculturation refers to a process of learning, or relearning, as the case may be, and adopting beliefs, values, behaviors, and language pertaining to one's own culture and ethnic identity (Gonzalez, Haan, and Hinton, 2001). This perspective is premised on the belief that awareness, ownership, and pride in one's cultural heritage is a foundation from which to acquire the requisite skills and knowledge to successfully socially navigate this society.

Portes and Rumbaut (2001) have put forth the concept of "segmented assimilation" from a sociological perspective to help researchers and practitioners account for why some social norms and values are more easily adapted and others totally discarded. The concept of segmented assimilation attempts to measure

Latino health from multiple dimensions (individual, neighborhood, state, and policy levels) in an effort to better understand the Latino experience in the United States within an ecological context.

Schmid (2001), in summarizing the research and literature on acculturation and assimilation, has advanced a three-stage framework of common modes of adaptation among Latinos and other newcomer groups: (1) acculturation into the middle class; (2) assimilation into the underclass (otherwise known as dissonant acculturation); or (3) economic advancement with a distinct cultural identity (otherwise referred to as biculturality). The first and third types will be addressed in this section, as empirical studies are available. Assimilation into the underclass, or also known as dissonant acculturation, still finds itself more of an abstract concept in the literature, and in need of more depth of theoretical development and empirical testing. Thus, it will only be touched upon here. *Dissonant acculturation* refers to acculturation to inner-city subcultures rather than "mainstream" culture. The latter invariably means involvement in crime, gangs, drug abuse, and other risky behaviors that are part of a subgroup.

As already noted in chapter 3, acculturation is a complex construct that is often considered to lack breadth and methodological rigor (Chiriboga, 2004). Nevertheless, there is no denying its research and practice importance in better helping to understand Latinos in the United States as they struggle to overcome certain social problems but are able to avoid other types of problems (Gamboa et al., 2005). Adam and colleagues (2005, p. 263) sum up this importance quite well:

> The discovery of a single . . . intervention that could reduce or prevent some or all of these conditions would be hailed as one of the great accomplishments of modern medicine. . . . This is the most powerful argument for why we must gain a greater understanding of the influence of acculturation on children's health.

Acculturation is probably best defined according to Massey, Zambrana, and Bell (1995, p. 191) as

> a preference for culturally specific foods, language, social activities and English language, as well as level of education, place of birth, and number of years in the United States. In essence, this concept has served as a proxy indicator for socioeconomic status, generational status, and place of birth.

This construct has found popularity among social scientists and has been used to capture or define the interplay of the effects of culture and environment on Latinos in the United States.

Acculturation is generally viewed as being influenced by the interaction of several key sociodemographic factors (Coronado et al., 2005; Franco et al., 1998): age at arrival in the United States (youth being more able to acculturate than adults), language usage and preference, media behavior, nature and extent of ties to country of origin (visits and extent of communication), cultural value preferences (see chapter 6), length of residence (the longer the duration, the greater the exposure to the host society, leading to greater acculturation), interpersonal network composition (extent of Latinos versus non-Latinos and nature of interaction), gender (males being more adept at acculturating than females because of greater freedom to venture outside of the home), and socioeconomic status (the higher at entry, the greater the likelihood of acculturation).

Recent efforts at examining degrees of Latino acculturation have resulted in the development of the following three-stage acculturation continuum that serves a heuristic purpose in better understanding how this construct helps social workers and other helping professionals better understand this community (Three degrees of acculturation, 2005):

1. *Largely unacculturated*: this category seeks to capture those Latinos who were born outside of the United States, are largely Spanish dependent, and have been in the United States fewer than 10 years. Most undocumented Latinos would fall into this category.
2. *Partially acculturated* refers to Latinos who have spent more than 11 years in this country, are overwhelmingly bilingual (Spanish at home and English at work or in school). This category largely consists of Latinos who are permanent residents or U.S. citizens.
3. *Highly acculturated*: persons in this category are overwhelmingly U.S.-born and raised, most likely bilingual if not English dependent. They may still hold onto Latino cultural values, although they may be communicated in English rather than Spanish. This category will largely consist of Latinos with U.S. citizenship.

Ainslie (2002), however, warns scholars and practitioners alike that much of the social science literature on Latinos and acculturation, and most specifically, ethnic identity processes, have failed to look closely at how stresses are manifested at an individual level, or the role of culture in this process as an integral part of individual and family psychodynamics. Acculturation, as a result, is very often the primary, if not the only, construct that is used to explain changes in attitudes, values, and behaviors. In an effort to report research findings, aggregate data are used, and in the process of doing so, individual stories and circumstances get overlooked or minimized. Hunt, Schneider, and Comer (2004), too, have been critical of this construct because of its poor conceptual definition, and the fact that it is based more on ethnic stereotyping than on "objective representations of cultural differences."

Garcia (2004) also raises concerns about the assumption that every Latino will naturally go though a process of acculturation whereby she or he will parallel the experiences of other Latinos sharing the same socioeconomic backgrounds. This is not the case, for example, with Latinos who have various forms of disabilities, such as deafness. Deaf Latino youth do not possess auditory and linguistic capabilities possessed by their nondeaf counterparts that are requisites for being able to absorb cultural values (Cintado, 2001). Consequently, physical, emotional, and cognitive factors are often neglected in most forms of acculturation-related research. Raffaelli, Zamboanga, and Carlo (2005), in a study of Cuban American female college students, found that higher levels of sexual risk (multiple partners, less condom use, more frequent sexual intercourse, and less HIV testing) were associated with being born in the United States, more ethnically identified, older, and less religious. This brings up the importance of greater specificity in assessing the role of acculturation.

The literature on acculturative stress and Latinos generally identifies three primary sources for this stress: discrimination, legal status, and language conflict (Finch & Vega, 2003). Gil, Vega, and Dimas (1994), for example, in their research with Latino adolescent males, found that acculturative stress may be the result of any one, or combination of, communication problem(s), difference(s) in cultural values, or form(s) of discrimination. The absence of information pertaining to phenotype represents a gross oversight in the conceptualizing acculturation-related stressors, however. Discrimination, after all, may be the result of an interplay of factors, such as language accents, features, attire (which sometimes is a proxy for socioeconomic status), Spanish surname, and phenotype.

Finch and Vega (2003), in examining the effects of social support mechanisms as potential modulators and mediators of stressful acculturation experiences and self-ratings of physical health of Mexico-origin adults (aged 18–59 years) in Fresno County, California, found that overall physical health is negatively associated with acculturative stressors and positively associated with social support (peers, family members, and religion). Discrimination, not surprisingly, is associated with poorer physical health among those Latinos for whom social support is considered lacking.

Miranda and Matheny (2000), in turn, examined the sociopsychiatric predictors of acculturative stress among Latino adults and found that stress is related to the efficacy of stress-coping resources, degree of acculturation, cohesion of the family, language use, and length of residence in the United States. These variables accounted for 48 percent of the variability in the acculturative stress of Latino adults. Martinez, DeGarmo, and Eddy (2004), in their study of academic success among Latino youth, found that lower acculturation and more institutional barriers were related to less academic success for Latino youth in Oregon.

Social interventions, as a result, must embrace an explicit goal related to acculturation that was initially explicated well over one decade ago but is still relevant today: namely facilitating Latino transitions into this society in a manner that allows them to hold on to important traditional cultural values, taking into account local circumstances, but still be able to function in a "healthy" manner in the process (Vega & Amaro, 1994). This goal, needless to say, is arduous to achieve but worthy of pursuit nonetheless.

The impact acculturation has on Latinos is well acknowledged across academic disciplines, and its effects have found their way into shaping how helping professions are starting to approach Latinos, particularly those who are newly arrived in this country (Holleran et al., 2005). Elbin and colleagues (2001), not surprisingly, found that high levels of acculturation were positively associated with problems or risky behaviors of various kinds. Foreign-born Latinos were significantly less likely to engage in these types of behaviors. Gonzalez, Haan, and Hinton (2001) in their study of acculturation and the prevalence of depression in older Mexican Americans in the Sacramento, California, area, found higher prevalence rates among the least acculturated Mexican Americans when compared to white non-Latinos and African Americans. The authors speculate that this is due to cultural barriers and poorer health status. Coonrod, Bay, and Balcazar (2004) found that highly acculturated Latinas had more risk factors and adverse obstetric outcomes than low-acculturated Latinas.

Adam and colleagues (Adam et al., 2005), in a more recent study focused on Hispanic youth and early onset of sexual intercourse, made similar findings. Latino adolescents with lower levels of acculturation, who have a tendency to use Spanish as their primary language, are less likely (65 percent) than their more highly acculturated counterparts to have engaged in sexual intercourse. Highly acculturated Latino English-speaking youth, in turn, were 170 percent more likely to have had sexual intercourse when compared to their white, non-Latino counterparts. Thus, low levels of acculturation emerge as an important protective factor, even while controlling for other social and cultural factors in this study. Guilamo-Ramos and colleagues (2005), however, found that among recent immigrants, Latino youth from English-speaking homes were less likely to be sexually active than those from Spanish-speaking homes.

Rassin and colleagues (1993), in the early 1990s, found that low levels of acculturation were positively associated with breastfeeding on a research sample from the United States–Mexico border. Crespo and colleagues (2001), however, in a study of physical activity among Mexican Americans in the United States, found that low levels of acculturation were associated with less activity during leisure time, and thus a major risk factor for heart disease, diabetes, and other chronic illnesses with high prevalence rates among Latinos.

High levels of acculturation have generally been found to cause mental health problems, most notably depression and suicidal tendencies, and substance abuse problems among Latinos. Difficulties in negotiating or navigating two social worlds results in stressors related to reconciling cultural value conflicts. Lack of "success" in reconciling these conflicts results in health and emotional problems, and places Latinos in a precarious position of having to choose between conflicting values. On the one hand, if they elect to adopt the values of the host society, it marginalizes them from their family and community. On the other hand, if they elect to keep their traditional cultural values, it marginalizes them from the host

society. Being able to navigate these two worlds, in effect, allows them to succeed without alienating their family and the host society.

Conclusion

The subject of best practices with marginalized groups such as Latinos has slowly
attracted the attention it deserves in the professional literature, and all indications are that these efforts will continue to expand as the nation attempts to better
understand health disparities (Dallas & Burton, 2004). Nevertheless, there is
much territory to cover before social work or any other helping profession has a
substantial body of empirically based literature that it can draw upon to guide
the design and implementation of social interventions.

Further, an emphasis on best practices influenced by empirical research masks
very serious concerns involving research measures, methods, and research questions, so that empirically informed best practices are far from enjoying a consensus of opinions. Social research is hardly ever free of debates and controversies, and
the issue of best practices, I am afraid, is not exempt from similar conflicts. It does
not mean that we cannot encourage empirically obtained results from guiding
our interventions, however. Yet these results must always be tempered by our
understanding of how context influences research and practice. Failing to do so
is professionally irresponsible and unethical.

Best practices, as a result, must endeavor to utilize empirical findings without losing sight of or invalidating other sources of information. It takes a com-
posite picture of all these and other sources of information to create a context
upon which to build a valid intervention focused on marginalized population
groups in this society. Reliance on any one source effectively translates into a
very narrow interpretation of what is needed to reach a group. When the context is complex, as in the case of Latinos, no one source of information could
possibly do justice to the subject matter.

The subject of acculturation, it should be emphasized, must not be conceived
as having sole applicability to direct practice. Social work macro-practice, too,
can benefit from greater awareness of and inclusion in community organizing
and program development, for example. Acculturation level helps determine how
recruitment of Latino participants in community organizing and programming
can transpire and how best to undertake public education campaigns. Focusing
on acculturation level also raises for the macro-practitioner the limitations of
outreaching into Latino communities by relying on just one method, since the
community consists of Latinos with varying degrees of acculturation, necessitating various outreach and public information campaigns that take these differences into account.

As the reader saw in chapter 3, for example, concerning the medically uninsured, outreach to that group is complex, requiring consideration of a mul-

titude of social and cultural factors, not least of which is acculturation, documented status, perceptions of discrimination and racism, and language preferences and competencies. Macro-practitioners, as a result, must take into account these and other factors covered in this chapter if they are going to increase the likelihood of success in outreaching and serving Latinos in a culturally competent manner.

Part II

A Conceptual Foundation: Access, Culture, and Assets

Chapter 5

ACCESS CHALLENGES
TO SERVICE DELIVERY

It seems clear that new strategies must stress an organizing
process that enhances and builds community, and that focuses on
developing a neighborhood's own capacities to do for itself what
outsiders will or can no longer do. Taking neighborhoods seriously
in their own current condition means building social, political, and
economic structures at the local level that re-create a space for
these people to act and decide.

John McKnight, *The Careless Society* (1995)

The epigraph to this chapter implicitly challenges us to develop new
strategies for engaging communities, necessitating a clearer perspective on identifying the barriers that are typically encountered in better reaching and serving communities. As shown in chapter 4, a multitude of barriers
(individual, institutional, community, and societal) effectively render current
resources ineffective.

The question of how access to services can best be facilitated, and barriers
surmounted, has generated a considerable amount of discussion, research, professional literature, and debate in the field of social work. The concept of "access"
is complex because of the interplay of numerous individual and environmental
circumstantial factors that can be operative throughout all facets of a program's
service design and implementation.

The concept of access to services has continued to generate a fair amount of
attention in the field, particularly over the past five years or so, in an effort to
apply a cultural competence perspective, and increase effectiveness and efficiency
of services. Nonutilization, or improper utilization, of services is best viewed from
a historical, or evolutionary, perspective in order to fully grasp its meaning for

social work practice with Latinos, or any other ethnic or racial group in this country. This chapter, as a result, provides a brief overview of how service access has been conceptualized over an extended period of time, and offers a variety of frameworks from which to develop a better understanding of different ways of viewing culture ("Four Perspectives on Culture") as an important construct in the development of services. I also provide a framework ("Four Perspectives on Access") for a multifaceted perspective on access to services. These two frameworks in combination serve as theoretical and practical guides for understanding the barriers Latinos face in receiving social services, and must be utilized simultaneously to achieve their intended goals. Finally, two critical social systems with particular relevance to the issue of access will be discussed (correctional and child welfare).

Historical Overview of Access

A number of terms have emerged over the past 50 years to help explain why certain groups in the United States have not been able to benefit from services to the maximum extent of their availability. In the 1960s, the term "underutilization" emerged to describe a general avoidance of using services on the part of Latinos and other groups of color in this society. These groups were not availing themselves of a variety of services, very often mental health–related. This perspective, unfortunately, placed the burden of lack of service utilization on these groups. "Lack of sophistication" in how to use services was very often raised in a variety of ways, in terms of, for example, "an inability to plan for the future," "time as a concept was not understood," "resistance," "hostility," even "inability to communicate." All of these explanations, unfortunately, blamed the victim, as it were, for not being able to benefit from services.

The 1970s and 1980s, however, witnessed a shifting of blame from groups themselves to institutions and professions, representing an empowerment/ advocacy perspective. This shift was no doubt fueled by a "rights" perspective that emerged in the 1960s and 1970s. This "new" approach, in turn, placed the onus on practitioners to find ethnic/racial group–specific approaches to better serve people's needs. One result was an upsurge in research and scholarly publications that systematically examined institutional barriers to access for marginalized groups in this country. Barriers to community mental health services for Latinos, for example, generally fall in the socioeconomic, cultural, and psychotherapeutic realms (Kouyoumdjian, Zamboanga, & Hansen, 2003).

Since the late 1990s, the emergence of the construct of health disparities has taken this legacy to another level with the systematic gathering of data across different racial and ethnic groups for the sole purposes of measuring conditions and outcomes (Gonzalez-Ramos & Gonzalez, 2005). This represents an important step in the creation of a national picture on the status of health across all groups rather than a picture that purposefully masks regional and group-specific differences (Riolo et al., 2005; Morales et al., 2004; Zambrana et al., 2004). The work of Alvarez and colleagues (2004), for example, highlights the importance of subgroup–specific interventions, in this case in the field of substance abuse, because the heterogeneity of the Latino community is increasing significantly in this decade.

Four Perspectives on Latinos and Culture

The professional literature on specific barriers Latinos face in accessing health and social services has highlighted a variety of themes since the 1980s. However, only in the last decade has the movement just described taken shape and attempted to differentiate between Latino subgroups, rather than treating all Latinos as being alike in composition and circumstances. This represents a very crucial conceptual step forward in grounding the Latino experience in this country in the contextual manner that is needed for the effective planning and implementation of services. Strug and Mason's (2001) study of Dominican immigrants to the Washington Heights community (in New York City), for example, typifies this approach. The authors found that lack of coordinated services and limited English language skills served as major barriers to Latinos, in this case Dominicans, accessing services. Fear of deportation, in the case of those who were undocumented, was also a significant deterrent to access. The lack of availability of bilingual and, preferably, bicultural social workers is also well acknowledged in the field.

Service provision systems can emphasize one of four approaches to culture: (1) ignore culture; (2) undermine culture; (3) modify current practices; or (4) collaborate with community cultural assets. The first two are disempowering and emphasize a deficit perspective toward culture; the latter two are empowering and view culture from an assets perspective and serve as the basis for developing culturally competent practice.

Ignore Culture

An explicit, or implicit, perspective that ignores the role of culture in shaping perceptions, attitudes, and help-seeking strategies actively embraces the premise that all human beings are alike, and everyone seeking services is treated as such. This perspective is generally couched in terms of "Everyone is treated the same here!" Suleiman Gonzalez's (2004) "one-size-fits-all" categorization captures well the intent of organizations to minimize the importance of cultural background. This perspective is counter to that put forth by the National Association of Social Workers (NASW, 2003b), which stresses the importance of cultural competence guiding interventions.

"Cultural blindness" and "cultural incapacity" are other terms used to describe what is in fact the attempt, unintentional perhaps, to destroy a group's individuality and need for group, or culture-specific, interventions (Mason, 1993).

The "diversity climate" in these institutions is such that there are no formal or informal efforts to promote and sustain benefits associated with cultural diversity (Hyde & Hopkins, 2004). No special provisions are made during intakes or community needs assessments, for example, to take note of differences between groups on the basis of "distinctive characteristics" and social identities (Van Soest & Garcia, 2003). The same questions are asked of everyone regardless of persons' cultural background. The definition of "family" used by the organization is one based on the nuclear family, even though this type of family is no longer in the numerical majority in this country. The amount of space allocated on an intake or community needs assessment instrument, is no more than half an inch, with a standard deviation of a quarter of an inch. Further, there is no attempt to move from deficit-oriented questions to embracing strengths or assets.

Such organizations in serving Latinos, for example, will not make any special provisions for culture-specific supervision or training (Mizio, 1998; Ramirez, 2003). Mizio (p. 17) raised this very point quite eloquently: "Practitioners who believe that social workers can effectively work with all groups without applying cultural modifications, and those who do not recognize the commonalties in practice with all human beings irrespective of race, ethnicity, and gender, will do a disservice to their clients, negating either their humanity or uniqueness."

The organizational policy and culture that everyone is to be treated in the same manner is one that effectively renders any form of culture-specific intervention invalid, with issues raised about patriotism when someone challenges this premise! This organizational position creates communication and collaborative barriers that undermine service delivery (Rehm, 2003). These types of organizations, mind you, are not "acultural." Rather, they subscribe to a Eurocentric view of life and judge everyone accordingly.

This act of commission, when applied to Latinos who do not speak English as their primary language, for example, effectively renders their search for assistance useless. Institutions that do not make services available in Spanish, through either professional staff or interpreters, convey a total disregard for the importance of language in the help-seeking process, and in so doing, effectively limit their services to those who are able to speak English or can provide their own interpreters (Cortez, 2005; Robert Wood Johnson Foundation, 2001, Soto, 2000).

Undermine Culture

A second approach toward Latino culture is much more insidious, in that it actively seeks to systematically undermine the role of culture in the consumers' or community's search for assistance. This is unlike the previous situation, where cultural factors are systematically ignored, although, as already noted, there is an implicit embrace of one cultural view. The undermining perspective, nevertheless, is predicated on a Eurocentric view that all cultures are not created equal, and some are more attractive, or more equal, than others, so to speak. This approach embraces a deficit model that uses dominant cultural values and perspectives to measure other groups against. From this perspective, the further away people are from the established standard, the greater the deficits are that must be addressed and surmounted in order to bring the consumer up to a prescribed standard. Mason (1993) refers to this approach as "cultural destructiveness," and it is characterized by attitudes, policies, and practices that seek to destroy a cultures' viability.

The emergence of an African-centered approach, a direct response to this viewpoint, provides an alternative perspective on what qualities must be embraced (Graham, 2002). The cultural assets paradigm is similar in its goal. For example, consumers may talk about herbal medicines they have been taking, or some cultural-based rituals that they follow that they perceive may assist them with a particular ailment. One study of psychiatric medication, for example, found that 42 percent of foreign-born Latinos, compared to 8 percent U.S.-born Latinos, used herbal medications to treat their mental health problems (Marin, 2003). The provider, in turn, criticizes them for using these "outdated" methods and instead proposes Western-based medicines and treatment, without taking the necessary step of further exploring the meaning and nature of this treatment (Bharucha, Morling, & Niesenbaum, 2003). This criticism can be both explicit and implicit. The consequences, however, can be the same. There is an act of commission to undermine a culturally based approach because it is considered infinitely inferior to the one being proposed as a substitute. This approach totally disregards or refuses to question the source of any possible distrust the Latino consumer may have toward the service provider (Canles, 1996).

Modify Current Practices

A third approach is progressive and embraces the perspective of cultural competence, one that has received considerable attention in the professional literature (Colon, 1997; Shedlin & Deren, 2002; Waters et al., 2002). Mason (1993) refers to this approach as "cultural precompetence," or an organizational commitment to institute and maintain interventions that take into account cultural differences.

This approach translates into social workers, micro or macro, being prepared to modify their actions on the basis of the cultural values, beliefs, and expectations of the consumer. They must be well prepared to question the role of religion and folk healing as part of an intake or assessment (needs- or assets-focused), for example. Barron and colleagues (2004) identify the need for staff to, in effect, also go through an acculturation process of their own to better serve Latino consumers. Bean, Perry, and Bedell (2001), too, raise similar issues regarding developing culturally competent marriage and family therapists to work with Latinos. Efforts, as a result, need to be made to systematically build upon and integrate cultural values and beliefs into intervention strategies when they significantly help those seeking services to do so in a manner that is self-affirming and holds meaning for them. Social interventions that are "meaningless" are often interventions that have eschewed integrating culture.

Graham (2002) outlines the following four-pronged African-centered approach to combat racism toward Africans in an effort to overcome the deleterious effects of a Eurocentric approach. This approach has applicability to other groups of color such as Latinos. (1) Systemically expose hidden sources of oppression found within social work knowledge; (2) embrace critical theory as a means of combating complacency of conventional social work knowledge; (3) design and promote models that actively seek to strengthen community building; and (4) rely on "cultural resource knowledge" to create social interventions. These four approaches, or strategies, provide a mechanism through which undervalued people of color can reclaim their culture and history, and use it as a basis from which to address social and economic issues related to their race and ethnicity, and in the planning of services to this population group.

The use of cultural icons such as Frida Kahlo, a well-known Mexican artist, is yet another example of how culture can be utilized to influence how services, in this case group therapy, can be delivered. One New York City group of 11 Latinas meets weekly (13 sessions), in addition to taking medication, to get help with depression (Allam, 2005). The group leader uses pictures painted by Kahlo. A total of 12 paintings are used over the course that the group meets, with each painting serving as a discussion focal point to elicit group member reactions. This method effectively helps members talk about highly emotional matters related to their families or traumas they have experienced that they normally would be too embarrassed to share with others.

Organizational efforts at creative outreach to newcomer populations serve as an excellent case example of how established strategies and procedures can be modified to take into account cultural values and beliefs. Outreach efforts to new immigrants who do not speak English as their primary language in New York City, for example, necessitates development of creative ways to reach them, for example, through the use of such items as powder compacts or giving children coloring books as an incentive for attendance at community events. Such activities are excellent examples of how practices can be modified to take into account local circumstances (Melwani, 2004).

Averill (2002) reports on the use of a vignette (Magdalena's Dream) and photography to reach out to older Latino farmworkers in northeastern Colorado.

Washington (state) developed a diabetes awareness media campaign that took into account Latino media behavior and cultural factors in order to better reach this population group (Almendarez, Boysun, & Clark, 2004). Streng and colleagues (2004, p. 404) report on a creative project titled Realidad Latina (Latino Reality), based in North Carolina, that studied Latino adolescents. This project used was is called a "photovoice" method of participatory research:

> Over a one-year period, adolescents partnered with public health practitioners and researchers in: generating photo-assignments, taking photographs based on these assignments, using the photographs for photo-discussions, and deWning themes based on these photo-discussions. A photograph exhibition and community forum raised awareness among local decision-makers and community members of the issues and assets of Latino adolescents and initiated a process toward change.

Boiko and colleagues (2005), in turn, report on the success of their use of an audiotaped mental health evaluation tool for use with Latino immigrant farmworkers with a range of literacy levels, as a means of better outreaching and serving this population group. Another example would be distributing information on breast screening procedures through Latina beauty parlors (Delgado, 1999a) or providing information on HIV/AIDS in Latino botanical shops (Delgado & Santiago, 1998).

Erwin and colleagues (2005), too, in their study of Latina breast and cervical cancer education, advocate for a systematic strategy for incorporating and embracing sociocultural perspectives and constructs to appeal to a highly diverse Latino community in the development of cancer education interventions. Coughlin and Uhler (2002) underscore the importance of Latinas having access to breast and cervical cancer screening. Low English-language proficiency has also been found to be a barrier for Latinas accessing Pap smears (De Alba et al., 2004). Providing quality health care necessitates "cultural flexibility" to elicit and respond to cultural factors (Napoles-Springer et al., 2005).

Modification of practices is not limited to social workers or human services. Houses of worship in urban communities of color, as in the case of Chicago, have been enlisted to help recruit police officers to increase diversity within the police department, and better police–community relations (Ferkenhoff, 2004). Churches were selected because these institutions enjoy institutional legitimacy within their respective communities, and provide a venue for external institutions to enter the community in a positive manner.

Once the Latino community is conceptualized as consisting of caring individuals and possessing indigenous resources such as nontraditional settings, the options for reaching out to this community increase experientially, providing social work organizations with a variety of approaches toward outreach and programming. Possession of a basic trust and belief in community/cultural assets is the foundation upon which services can be modified.

Collaborate with Community
Cultural Assets

Finally, the fourth approach systematically seeks to establish collaborative relationships with community-based cultural assets as a means of providing comprehensive and culturally competent based services. Collaboration with community cultural assets offers the greatest potential for community empowerment and for the creation of highly innovative programming. This approach is typically conceptualized as "cultural competence" (Mason, 1993). Hanley (1999, p. 11) notes:

> The alternative to working towards cultural competence is to exist in a vacuum, to live with the absence of comparative information on the cultural lives of others. If we choose to live in a cultural vacuum, we will not only continue to perpetuate stereotypes we have of other people, but we will also be perpetuating the stereotypes others have of us.

The identification and mobilization of cultural assets must always be done within a collaborative context that stresses mutual respect and interdependence between organizations and communities. Collaboration not only facilitates communication between formal providers and informal providers but also serves as a vital bridge between these two communities that can be effectively used in other spheres (Rivera, 2002). Gallagher-Thompson and colleagues (2004), for example, in their study of effective recruitment strategies of dementia family caregivers (Latino and Caucasian), recommend the establishment of collaborative partnerships involving families, agencies, and community supports. The authors go on to identify the important role cultural values play in helping these collaborative partnerships succeed. This book, as a result, stresses the latter two approaches toward culture as a means of influencing practice and practice outcomes and empowerment of the Latino community.

The concept of a Latino community helper without institutional affiliation, otherwise known as a *servidor*, first appeared in the literature approximately 25 years ago (Mendoza, 1980). Although Mendoza specifically applied this term to persons who assisted elders when family could not help them due to geographical distance or other factors, it is not restricted to any one group or issue.

Servidores are individuals who are known in the community because of their skills, knowledge, and willingness to help (serve) other Latinos in need. Servidores can be male or female, young or old, and of any Latino background. Virtually any community-based asset assessment will identify a number of community residents who are well known and respected for their caregiving. These individuals usually possess specialized knowledge or skills that can help residents access human services. They tend to be bilingual and have had human service work experience, increasing the likelihood of achieving success in a helper role.

Servidores are easily reached and have willingly assumed the role of helper, thus "formalizing" the caregiving relationship.

Four Perspectives on Access

Access to culturally competent services is the cornerstone of any effective social work practice involving Latinos. Lack of access to quality services for Latinos can be broadly conceptualized from a theoretical perspective. A narrow conceptualization will invariably focus on the role and importance of language—as already noted earlier in this chapter, a key factor in successful accessing of services. However, although language is a key factor, it is not the only factor in determining successful outcome.

Accessibility must consist of four interdependent yet distinct dimensions: (1) geographical/physical; (2) psychological; (3) cultural; and (4) operational. Any one of these dimensions is important unto itself. When one or more of these factors is not operative, Latino access to culturally competent services is seriously compromised. The goal of any well-designed program or service, as a result, is to not only take into account but incorporate all four elements. Anything short of this goal will ultimately mean outright failure or improper use of valuable resources!

Geographical/Physical Access

Allard (2004), in a study of neighborhood variation in geographical access to social services in three cities (Chicago, Los Angeles, and Washington, D.C.), found that on average, low-income populations have greater access to social services than comparable groups in suburban areas. Generally, on average, social services are available within 1.5 miles of one-third of such populations in Chicago, one-fifth in Washington, D.C., and one-quarter in Los Angeles. Latinos, in turn, have the greatest access, when compared to that of African Americans and white non-Latinos with similar incomes. Having geographical access does not guarantee utilization of services, however.

Geographical accessibility is probably the most common way human service organizations and providers view service delivery barriers. Can the consumer physically get to the services without undue hindrances in the process of doing so? Physical access can relate to both geographical distances and access to buildings and offices, in the case of those consumers with various types of disabilities that necessitate accommodation.

Lack of private transportation or limited public transportation can interfere with consumers getting to organizations. Some organizations, as a result, have transportation systems of their own, such as traveling health services, or place a high value on making home visits. It is not unusual to find human service organizations, or even governmental offices (federal and state) opening outreach offices within neighborhoods or at local shopping malls to increase geographical accessibility, and in the process address other access considerations.

Psychological Access

Psychological accessibility to services is a much more difficult concept to recognize and address than geographical/physical accessibility, although practitioners as well as consumers, and communities, recognize it when they see it. It is also a form of accessibility that organizations, in general, do not wish to recognize because of how negatively the realization that consumers fear them can reflect on staff and the mission of an organization. The concept of stigma, which is the possession of negative social attitudes and cognitive beliefs, is too narrow in scope to capture the intended meaning and substance of psychological accessibility, although it can certainly be included as a possible dimension (McKay, 2002).

First, the concept of psychological accessibility does not automatically refer to a negative attitude, perception, or behavior on the part of the client community. Second, the concept of psychological accessibility can also capture questioning behavior or typical anxiety usually associated with any form of help-seeking behavior (Delgado, 1999b). This psychological perception, in turn, can be easily changed through public educational campaigns intended to demystify a service. Thus, the concept of psychological accessibility is broad in character and does not necessarily have to imply negative manifestations. Stigma, as a result, does not capture the meaning and spirit of the concept of psychological accessibility, although it can be associated with this concept.

Will the consumers feel that they have a say in determining the outcome of their visit? The question of whether the consumer feels "safe," or "comfortable," in obtaining services is at the heart of psychological accessibility. Namely, are stigma or negative consequences attached to patronizing an organization? An organization can have geographical accessibility and be located just a short walk from the community, but psychologically be inaccessible.

Cultural Accessibility

Cultural accessibility refers to the content, nature, and methods of services provided—that is, cultural competence, as this is commonly called. The acceptance and viability of cultural access are universally accepted within social work, as is attested by the National Association of Social Workers Standards for Social Work Practice and Code of Ethics, and the Council on Social Work Education. These legitimizing organizational bodies have provided the social work profession with the necessary marching orders, so to speak, to bring this important perspective into the classroom and practice arena.

A cultural access approach seeks to address key facets related to the nature of services being provided, and generally seeks to obtain answers to questions such as: Are the services in the primary language of the consumer? Do services reflect an in-depth understanding and reinforcement of key cultural values? Are staff similar in ethnic/racial background to the consumer? If not, does staff awareness of cultural belief systems translate into cultural competence? To what extent do organizational policies, procedures, and practices reinforce the language preference and cultural values of the consumers and their community?

These and other questions related to culture form the heart of the concept of cultural accessibility and the approach that seeks to contextualize services to take into account the circumstances of a community being served by the organization. Staff abilities to identify and tap Latino cultural values (see chapter 6) will ultimately dictate the degree and success of culturally based services. This necessitates that organizations place an explicit value on services being culturally informed and, as a result, seek to hire staff who are not only bilingual but bicultural whenever possible. In addition, resources are invested in providing staff with the latest information and training relating to the communities with whom they are actively engaged. Cultural access is not static; it evolves, and organizations, too, must be prepared to evolve as communities change.

Cultural access in the case of libraries is another case in point. Public libraries in communities with rapidly expanding Latino populations are now faced with the challenge of obtaining books and other materials in Spanish to meet increasing demands from this community (K. Taylor, 2004). Libraries, as a result, have now started to provide a wide range of services that historically were not considered part of a library's mission, for example, employment workshops, English classes, and activities of specific value to the Latino community, along with making efforts to recruit Latinos into the profession (Delgado, 1998b).

Operational Access

Operational, like geographical, accessibility is much easier to identify but may not be so easy to address from a service provision perspective. Operational accessibility seeks to capture a dimension of human services that is well understood in the field. Namely, are operational practices conducive to people and communities in need getting services at the time that they need these services? This question, I believe, strikes at the heart of what is meant by operational accessibility. The answer invariably is multifaceted.

One aspect of this answer must relate to finances. Can consumers, in this case Latinos, afford services if they do not have insurance? The issue of the under- and uninsured as a group (covered in chapter 3) falls into the operational accessibility category. Other questions focus on how the services are structured, for example, what are the hours and days of service delivery? The hours of an organization may be too limited, or the agency may not be open on weekends of holidays. This limitation can be quite significant in economically marginalized communities where residents cannot take time off from work to attend an appointment during the week or may have more than one job, thereby severely limiting when they can seek services.

How willing is the organization to deploy staff through outsourcing, colocation, or staff transfer, in circumstances where the Latino community is located in a part of the city or town that is either arduous for people to use public transportation or it is unavailable? These situations often necessitate creative ways of deploying staff. Thus, must consumers of services be required to go to an organization or will the organization be willing to send a social worker to their homes? Restrictions on staff mobility can be just as detrimental to quality service delivery as restrictive hours and days of operation.

Two Critical Social Systems

The following two needs, although by no means the only social needs affecting the Latino community, are two that can best be appreciated within the context of this chapter with its focus on access. These two needs are: (1) correctional supervision and (2) child welfare. I have selected these two for different reasons, although the two arenas are integrally related.

The subject of correctional supervision, although touching upon all aspects of the Latino community, has generally escaped the attention it deserves from the field of social work, even though social work played a prominent role in social reform in this arena at the genesis of the profession (Delgado, 2001). I have selected child welfare, in turn, because of the high number of Latino children and youth in this system and the fact that Latino children represent such a significant percentage of the Latino community, as noted in chapter 2, and they are, in essence, the "future" of Latinos in this country. Both of these systems, however, particularly undermine the social fabric of Latino families and the community, and an examination of them highlights many of the issues of access across a multitude of dimensions.

Correctional Supervision

This topic (including incarceration, probation, and parole) is one that permeates virtually all aspects of social work practice to one degree or another. The child welfare system, for example, is integrally related with the criminal justice system because of the percentage of inmates who also happen to be parents of children. Latinos have been caught in this nation's tendency to incarcerate people of color (Delgado, 2001; Pabon, 2005). Latinos are incarcerated three times as often and detained for trial almost twice as often as their white, non-Latino counterparts (National Council of La Raza, 2004). The important role of the Latino family, as was noted in great detail in chapter 6, is undermined when one or both parents are incarcerated, for example.

Incarceration not only directly affects the persons in prison; for example, it also has devastating impact on their children, in the case of parenthood; their significant others; their families; and the communities they reside in (Garcia, 2005). Barreras, Drucker, and Rosenthal (2005) found that out of a total of 105 families with histories of criminal justice involvement, 88 percent also had a history of substance abuse. It is not unusual to find urban families with multiple family members in some form of correctional supervision. The stigma associated with having family members incarcerated, particularly in cases where Latino mothers are in prison, makes it extremely arduous for families to seek assistance.

Child Welfare

Social work has historically played a very prominent role in the child welfare system in this country. The use of a disparities perspective is not relegated to health care and has also found its way into the field of child welfare (Roberts, 2002; Snowden, Cuellar, & Libby, 2003). Ortega (2000) and Roberts (2002), among countless other researchers, have concluded that the child welfare system in this country can be characterized as having "pronounced and disturbing" racial disparities, with profound social implications for these families and their communities.

When children of color receive services, they tend to be poor quality. Further (Roberts, 2002, p. 3),

> they are more likely to be removed from their parents and placed in foster care, they stay in foster care for longer periods of time, and they are less likely to be either returned home or adopted. In addition to their numerical disproportionality, children of color are disadvantaged by child protection services that are not culturally competent, such as the insufficiency of Spanish-speaking caseworkers and foster parents to serve Latino children or the paucity of Asian–Pacific Islander providers of child welfare services.

Lane and colleagues (2002) found that children of color had a higher likelihood of being evaluated and reported for suspected abuse, even after controlling for the likelihood of abusive injury.

Ortega's (2000, p. 10) assessment of the importance of Latino culture–specific child welfare services emphasizes the need to understand within and between group differences: "Generalizing services without recognizing differences among and between Latinos will add nothing to improving their current status nor in understanding their needs." Rivera (2002) strongly advocates for the creation of collaborative initiatives between child welfare systems and the Latino community in search of developing culturally competent services.

The social and psychological consequences of childhood sexual and physical abuse can be quite profound among low-income Latinos when this occurs.

Childhood trauma is considered a general risk factor for women, regardless of race or ethnicity (Wyatt et al., 2002). Newcomb, Locke, and Goodyear (2003), for example, found a relationship between childhood abuse and risky sexual behaviors (multiple partners, less condom use, more frequent sexual intercourse, and less HIV testing) among Latinas in southern California.

Shaw and colleagues (2001) studied a comparison of Latino and African American sexually abused girls and their families and concluded that Latino girls experienced greater emotional and behavioral problems than their African American counterparts, and that these girls and their mothers/caretakers perceived their families as more disturbed and dysfunctional. Record and Rice (2002), however, found that having had a history of abuse did not impair abused Hispanic women's ability to have a positive response to a baby.

The child welfare system in the United States, like its correctional counterpart, will wield a prodigious amount of influence on the fabric of the Latino family and community. The failure of the child welfare system to operationalize a culturally competent agenda across all sectors of the system ultimately spells doom for any Latino child or family caught up within this system.

Conclusion

How barriers can be manifested in provision of social work services is complex to understand in depth, yet the issue can be quite simple, too, and not requiring researchers and scholars to identify it. In the case of Latinos in the United States, these barriers cannot be artificially examined outside of a context of also looking at racism and discrimination, as already noted. This is a highly charged context, and one that, as social workers, we are well prepared to recognize and address in an affirmative fashion. However, it is not a context free of controversy and can be considered a "political minefield."

The various approaches to better understanding how access must be conceptualized is a step in the direction of setting a foundation for the use of a social paradigm, in this case one that is culturally assets–driven. Such a paradigm effectively addresses the multifaceted dimensions of access and takes into account the ecological dynamics inherent in any social construction of service delivery. In essence, it does justice to grounding the experience of Latinos within this society. Certain systems, such as criminal justice and child welfare, however, present social workers with incredible challenges to making them accessible from a cultural assets perspective.

Chapter 6

LATINO CULTURAL VALUES
AND BELIEFS

It has been said that every personality is like all other personalities in various respects, like some other personalities in further respects, and like no other personalities in still further respects. This generalization is not only true of the typical Puerto Rican citizen; it is also true of the values of his culture. We may assume, in other words, that certain values in Puerto Rico are entirely similar to human values everywhere in the world; others are similar to the values only of certain parts in the world; and some are unique to the Island alone.

Theodore Brameld, *The Remaking of a Culture* (1959)

The epigraph to this chapter, from a book published almost 50 years ago about Puerto Ricans, and applicable to other Latino groups, raised caution about generalizing on cultural values. Cultural values bring with them a set of factors, issues, considerations that ground them within a social context, with all of its foibles and fortes. This chapter, as a result, wrestles with Brameld's central argument, and does so in a manner, I hope, that will give the reader useful guidance without minimizing the potential pitfalls inherent in giving meaning to values that can best be characterized as "moving" as we speak.

The reader, I believe, would agree that cultural values and beliefs represent the "essence" of being a Latino in the United States, as they do for all other ethnic and racial groups. I like to think of the role of culture in a metaphorical way. Culture, I believe, functions like an anchor on a ship. It provides stability during turbulent seas, or provides a sense of security because it is readily available if needed. Culture as represented through values and beliefs, as a result, is as much a part of life as an anchor is part of a boat's equipment. No experienced sailor would think twice about casting off without an anchor; no human being can expect to navigate his or her way through life without a firm embrace of culture in all of its manifestations.

The cultural values and beliefs Latinos embrace are by no means unique to this population group. However, how these values and beliefs have withstood the pressures of acculturation addressed in chapter 4, or responded with necessary changes to take into account ecological factors and considerations of life in the United States, such as the language of Spanglish (a combination of Spanish and English), are the core elements that must be identified and integrated into any community assessment prior to a social intervention.

Further, some of these values and beliefs are counter to those of the dominant society, or host, and as a result are controversial and when reinforced in an intervention will create tensions, if not outright conflict within organizations. These values and beliefs will, as a result, make it necessary for social work practitioners, educators, and other human service academics alike to examine their own values and beliefs and note where they overlap or diverge, and what this means for services focused on Latinos (Egger-Pierola, 2005).

The reader may argue that being a Latino would facilitate the use of cultural values and beliefs. To a certain extent I would agree with this point. However, not being a Latino provides a social worker with a position of questioning these values and beliefs without appearing confrontational. Seeking "clarification" as to how a cultural value is viewed and practiced is a natural point of inquiry for a non-Latino social worker. A Latino social worker is supposed to know this and may be felt that if they were "truly Latino," they would not have to ask.

However, any efforts at capturing the meaning and significance of cultural values and beliefs, in this case those of a highly heterogeneous Latino population, can boarder very closely on stereotyping. Cultural values and beliefs are not static entities that have historically remained stagnant in appearance and content. In fact, the metaphor of a cloud best captures my view of cultural values. Clouds represent an integral part of our environment, with their presence or absence rarely going unnoticed. They take on different shapes and characteristics depending upon a whole host of weather factors, and the eye of the beholder. We can see clouds, describe them in great detail, and even track them across the sky. Any attempt to hold them in our hands, assuming that we could go up that far in the sky, would prove fruitless. They exist; they take on different meanings to different people; and they escape our physical grasp.

Culture is a dynamic construct, as noted in chapter 1, that historically has evolved to help groups adjust to changing circumstances while maintaining an anchor to their past. The cultural values and beliefs addressed in this chapter are changing, and the reader is well advised to read this material with a keen sense of determining how these values and beliefs have changed since this book went to press! Any scholarly publication that presents cultural values and beliefs as if they were stagnant, or "cookbook"-like, does a serious disfavor to the group being reported, and is the antithesis of cultural competence!

Latino cultural values can be classified in a variety of ways. Velazquez (2003) identified four commonly used clusters: (1) loyalty and identification with the family, with the community, and as an ethnic group; (2) personalization of interpersonal relationships; (3) a highly defined status within the family and community; and (4) identification with Catholic ideology.

I have used a different classification system for presenting in this chapter what I consider to be the most salient and important Latino cultural values and beliefs ("spiritual beliefs" and "cultural values"). My decisionmaking process in arriving at these, however, was not undertaken without considerable thought, deliberation, and debate, to be quite honest. The set of cultural values and beliefs addressed in this chapter, I believe, forms a core that either directly or indirectly influences numerous other values, which in turn influence behaviors. This chapter will also include personal experiences, or stories, of how cultural values and beliefs got manifested in social work practice at the micro and macro levels. The planning of any social intervention at the micro or macro level will necessitate that these Latino values and beliefs be seriously considered.

The cultural factors addressed in this chapter have profound implications for all methods of social work practice. Historically, any discussion of Latino cultural values was generally relegated to direct practice interventions, and it would be misleading to leave this impression. Macro practice interventions cannot ignore these values, since doing so will ultimately undermine any effort at engaging Latino communities. Latino cultural values form the heart and soul of interventions embracing cultural assets. These assets, as I will show in subsequent chapters, represent the crucial "missing link" in interventions that are deficit-driven—namely, situations in which Latino communities are in need of services and bring "nothing to the table" in helping to craft the interventions, nor is the community in a position to either inform these interventions or play a leading decisionmaking role in their creation.

The profession has historically struggled in bringing the multitude of methods social workers use into a unifying mission and approach. The embrace of cultural values as cultural assets is one means of effectively bridging the gap between direct and indirect practice, and doing so in a way that is affirming, empowering, and participatory. Although this chapter and book focus on Latinos, a similar perspective on other socially and economically marginalized groups in this country can go a long way toward bridging intergroup gaps, too.

Finally, cultural and spiritual values and beliefs, not surprisingly, are highly interconnected and reinforcing of each other. Among Latinos, it is impossible to separate *familismo* from collectivism, for example, with changes in one cultural value creating changes in others, as it will be become evident in this chapter. This observation will prove very challenging and probably troubling to practitioners.

Consequently, the values and beliefs presented here can only be fully appreciated and understood when viewed from a broad perspective. In this "big picture," however, one must not lose sight of how each value and belief system has its unique perspective and makes its unique contribution to Latino culture.

Spiritual Beliefs

The role and importance of spiritual beliefs, whether they are based in organized religion or involve belief in the metaphysical intervention of spirits, will have significant shaping influence on social work practice with Latinos. These beliefs, probably more than other cultural values covered in this chapter, will prove very troubling for any social work practice, regardless of the level of intervention. The subject of spirituality and its various manifestations, with some notable exceptions, has not enjoyed the attention it deserves in professional social work educational programs across the country. However, as noted by Canda and Furman (1999, p. xv), it is the foundation of social intervention: "Spirituality is the heart of helping. It is the heart of empathy and care, the pulse of compassion, the vital flow of practice wisdom, and the driving force for service." Spirituality, among Latinos, is a topic that cannot be ignored (Dingfelder, 2005c). And spirituality can be manifested through religion as well as folk beliefs and practices.

Religion

Latino religious affiliation and religiosity warrant special attention because they impact virtually all aspects of community life (Stevens-Arroyo & Diaz-Stevens, 1993, p. 245):

> The rumors of the demise of religion have been greatly exaggerated. Certainly among Latinos, one of the salient characteristics of the barrios from Boston to San Diego is the omnipresence of religion. Whether in stately stone churches, ebullient storefront Pentecostal chapels, or the mysterious botanicas filled with incense and African amulets, the Latino people of the United States surround themselves with vehicles of religious expression.

This statement, made over a decade ago, still holds true (MacGregor, 2005).

Latinos are usually considered Catholic in this country, since almost 70 percent (25 million) of them identify themselves as such (Murray, 2005), and according to the United States Conference of Catholic Bishops, they represent almost a third of this country's Catholics (Murray & Banerjee, 2005). In 2002, there were approximately 3,500 Catholic parishes across the United States that celebrated mass in Spanish (Jenkins, 2002). These parishes were larger in comparison with other religious denominations, with more than one-third having more than 1,000 Latino members, and only 1 percent of other denominations claiming this distinction (Brooklyn College, 2005).

The 80 percent increase in Catholics in the United States occurred in the six states where the Latino population increased the most between 1990 and 2000 (G. Rodriguez, 2002). In Los Angeles, for example, home of the largest archdiocese in the country, two-thirds of all Catholics are Latino, mostly Mexican (G. Rodriguez, 2002). Nationally, between 1970 and 2000, the number of Latino Catholics increased by over 18 million, or 264 percent, accounting for 86 percent of the growth in the Catholic Church in the United States during this period (*Latino Catholics*, 2005). Projections to 2050 have Latino Catholics at almost half of the total Catholic population in the country.

The example of Our Lady of Guadalupe, Omaha, Nebraska, reflects this increase. This church, considered the "anchor" of the South Omaha Latino community for 50 years, was forced to close for construction and then reopen in an expanded facility as a result of an increase of Latino newcomers, mostly Mexicans from Mexican states such as Campeche, Chiapas, and Oaxaca (Gonzalez, 2005).

Levitt (2002) comments that the Catholic Church plays an active role in helping Latino newcomers transition to this country through the use of extensive social networks that connect their countries of origin with the United States, facilitating passage between the two worlds, so to speak. The United States Conference of Catholic Bishops' Committee on Migration conducts a campaign called "Justice for Immigrants," which focuses on antiimmigrant sentiments and works for immigration reforms, is another example of how the Catholic Church is trying to meet Latino needs (Kitto, 2005). This campaign seeks to educate the public, including the nation's Catholic community, about Church teachings on immigrants and the contributions they make to the nation. Further, it generates political support for new immigration laws, legalization of undocumented immigrants, the creation of a temporary-worker program, and facilitation of family-reunification visas (Fisher, 2005).

Nevertheless, we need to assess to what degree Latinos actively follow Catholic Church doctrines and rituals. Walsh (2003), for example, says that it is necessary to differentiate between being Catholic in a "cultural" sense and being Catholic in a "devout" sense. The former involves celebration of holidays and significant Church rituals such as baptism and weddings, for example, and the latter refers to active church attendance and participation in rituals such as confession and communion. One estimate says that 12 percent of Latinos attend church on a weekly basis and 50 percent are religiously inactive, or "Catholic" in name alone (Walsh, 2003).

Why is the level of religiosity among Latino Catholics important to consider? The influence of the Catholic Church in Latin America has been the subject of debate, and one needs a historical understanding to appreciate its present-day significance. The Catholic Church was an integral part of the colonization of the

"New World," and was viewed with suspicion, if not outright dislike, by native peoples. The Catholic Church, for example, was active in importing slaves and condoning slavery in the Americas, but did have great hesitation in enslaving native people, since they were often viewed as "noble savages" who did not have the benefit of being exposed to the Catholic Church. The Church did not, however, have this viewpoint when enslaving Africans, probably because of a sense of retribution owing to Spain's occupation by the Moors over a seven-hundred-year period that ended shortly after Columbus sailed to the Americas and colonization commenced (Lewis, 1982; Viscidi, 2003).

Flores (2001) notes that 90 percent of the estimated 10 million African slaves transported during the slave trade eventually ended up in Mexico, Central and South America, and the Caribbean. Vaughn (2001), in turn, specifically focused on the impact of people of African descent in Mexico, a topic that has generally escaped scholarly interest. This history helps explain why almost 250,000 Mexican Americans defined themselves as black in the 2000 U.S. census, which allowed the selection of multiple races of origin (Hernandez, 2003a). East Coast Puerto Ricans and Dominicans, however, make up the vast majority of Latinos who also selected black.

The influence of African slavery in this hemisphere has been extensive, with the Catholic Church playing an active role in this form of economy. One critic of the Catholic Church (Viscidi, 2003, p. 56) notes that "in their own countries Hispanics did not see the Church supporting the rights of the poor. Rather it sided with the rich and influential. It can be difficult to make a distinction between the Church or clergy and the religion itself."

The number of Catholic priests in Latin America has not been as significant as has been commonly thought. Lakshmanan (2005, p. A8) notes: "From Mexico to Argentina, a single priest is expected to serve between 5,000 and 10,000 Catholics on average, in comparison with one priest per 1,000 congregants in the United States." A participant in a workshop I gave in a New England city shared a story with me that highlights this point. When I noted the general absence of the Catholic Church in rural sectors of Latin American countries, this participant laughed. She went on to say that her parents were not able to be "officially" married by a Catholic priest for 10 years because she lived in a very rural area of Puerto Rico, and the priest only visited once every 10 years.

Ortiz's (1973, p. 183) description of the role of the Catholic Church in a rural town in Puerto Rico strikes a similar, though not as extreme, note regarding the presence and influence of the Catholic Church:

> The church in Esperanza is in a very similar position to that of the government, being heavily centralized and directed from the outside. There is no resident priest and during the week . . . the church is closed. It is only on Sunday and on special occasions that the priest comes over from a nearby area.

The paucity of Spanish-speaking Church personnel is not restricted to priests. For example, in Seattle, there are not enough Spanish-speaking staff or nuns to teach religious classes. Some Seattle Catholic churches have brought nuns from Mexico City to attend to Latinos or pay a stipend for a visiting priest to hold masses in Spanish (Tu, 2005).

G. Rodriguez (2002, p. 11) raises an important perspective on the relationship between the Catholic Church and the Latino (Mexican) community in the United States, and how changes will occur on both sides:

> Acculturation is always a two-way street. Even as Mexicans wield greater influence in the American Catholic Church, America is changing them, too. South of the border, only a small percentage of Catholics attend Mass every Sunday, in part because Mexico has long suffered from a shortage of priests. Immigrants attend church more regularly as they acculturate into U.S. life. And just as latter-generation Mexican Americans are more likely to slip into mainline Protestant faiths than are immigrants, many more will be seduced by the power of secular logic. . . . The brand of Catholicism that rural Mexicans bring with them to the United States calls for different leaps of faith and allows for greater possibilities for miracles and the unexplainable.

Although the Catholic Church still wields tremendous influence among Latinos, other religious groups are reaching out to this community. In 2002, eight million Latinos in the United States, or 23 percent of this community, identified themselves as Protestant (Murray, 2005). Almost 85 percent, or 6.2 million, of all U.S. Latino Protestants classify themselves as evangelicals (Murray, 2005). Latinos are the fastest growing sector of U.S. Protestantism (Garces-Foley, 2003). In 2004, the Seventh-Day Adventist Church, for example, announced the launching of Latino-specific television programming in an effort to reach out to this growing community (J. C. Munoz, 2004).

One estimate has 20 percent of U.S. Latinos converting to evangelism between 1994 and 2004 (Uranga, 2004). Evangelicalism can encompass many different types of religion, and among Latinos, it generally involves a sect such as Pentecostalism (Uranga, 2002). Other sects, such as Seventh-Day Adventists and Jehovah's Witnesses, are also prominent in recruiting Latino members to their congregations. Unfortunately, very little is known about their success. However, from my observations, they are making significant inroads into this community.

Increased membership in evangelical religious organizations has caused tensions, however. The Seventh-Day Adventist Church hospitals, for example, have been accused by Latino immigrants of either turning people away because they lack health insurance or of "price gouging"—charging the uninsured full price or, often, three times what they charge insured customers (Connolly, 2005). Latinos say that this policy is counter to what is taught in the religion and has effectively singled them out. Catholic hospitals, also, have not escaped this accusation (Consejo de Latinos Unidos holds a news conference, 2005). It is estimated that the top seven Catholic hospital systems in the country earned over $2 billion in profits in 2004, have over $20 billion in cash and investments, and continue to "gouge" uninsured Latinos, who are predominantly Catholic (Latinos decry Catholic bishops' silence, 2005). Catholic Healthcare West, California's largest nonprofit hospital chain, for example, has been served with a class action suit alleging similar treatment of Latinos and other groups (Lin, 2005).

A number of factors may explain the high rate of Latino conversion (Uranga, 2004, p. N1):

> Many Latinos who converted from Catholicism say the strict moral code demanded by evangelical preachers is the main attraction. Others say they began to view Catholic priests, their vestments and elaborate ceremonies, as too formal and out of touch with modern life—one in which many struggle to make ends meet and try to keep their children from joining gangs.

Another explanation focuses on the backgrounds of evangelical ministers, who generally are from poor or working-class backgrounds, have limited formal education, and are from countries of origin similar to those of their congregations. Catholic priests and nuns, on the other hand, often do not share the social class and ethnic/racial backgrounds of their parishioners, making it difficult for them to relate to and communicate with their parishioners, or to be trusted.

Stevens-Arroyo and Stevens-Diaz (1993, p. 244) put forward a series of other factors to explain the attraction of non-Catholic religious groups:

> The difficulties placed in the way of the practice of Catholicism by prejudiced clergy or parishioners often rendered it more attractive to the Spanish-speaking in urban centers to join Pentecostal and Evangelical churches. Less burdened by institutional interests, open to a married clergy, and able to adapt quickly to social conditions . . . usually close-knit groups consisting of a few extended families, such churches offered Latinos an intensity of religious experience that was hard to come by in a segregated Catholicism.

Wedam (2000) cites the general absence of Spanish masses as an example of Church resistance to meeting the needs of Latino parishioners, and associates this resistance with the question of who ultimately holds cultural power within these institutions—newcomers or those who have been there for generations.

Protestants have started initiatives focused on Latinos, particularly in cities (Campo-Flores, 2005; Deck, 2004; Wiederholt, 2005). Garces-Foley (2003, p. 3), however, cautions that Anglo Protestants have historically not taken the Latinos seriously, and have much to overcome to make inroads into this community:

> Protestant churches and organizations have been slow to translate materials into Spanish, to welcome Latinos as members, and to take on political is-

sues affecting Latinos. . . . Many Latinos feel discriminated against by other Christians who perceive their style of Christianity as too emotional, unsophisticated and uneducated.

Latinos, as a result, have sought to create their own churches, as have African Americans, instead of being a part of Anglo-dominated houses of worship. One study of Hispanic churches found that 74 percent of those surveyed believed their churches should aid undocumented immigrants, even when this intervention is considered illegal (Sellers, 2003).

Federal "faith-based initiatives" have facilitated evangelical groups receiving funds for various types of social services, thus further increasing their ability to do outreach to Latinos (DeParle, 2005). The Catholic Church, in turn, has introduced innovations such as incorporating music and instruments into the mass and encouraging spontaneous expressions of "praise and thanksgiving" from the congregation (Chou, 2002; Jenkins, 2002).

It is estimated that 23 percent of Latinos in the United States are Pentecostals (Robertson, 2005), with more Latino Pentecostals than Jews, Muslims, Episcopalians, and Presbyterians combined (Espinosa, Elizando, & Miranda, 2003). Houston's Lakewood Church stands as a testament to the appeal of Pentecostalism, and is considered to have the nation's largest Latino congregation, with approximately 4,000 members, having tripled in size over a three year period (Leland, 2005; Moscoso, 2005). Estimates put the number of U.S. Latino Pentecostals or charismatics at 9.2 million (Miller, 2004).

Pentecostalism's appeal to Latinos is multifaceted (Robertson, 2005, p. A19):

> Many of these churches are storefronts . . . and they don't ask you whether you've been through sacrament. They accept you as you are. . . . Often they are lay people and they speak the language. They provide music and social service right away, so they are quick to respond. They work to make you feel part of the community right immediately.

Livezey (2000) observes that these churches create a cultural enclave that effectively buffers many of the stressors Latinos encounter in this society. Pentecostalism appears to increase with the length of time persons have been in the United States, with one study finding that although Latinos are primarily Catholic in the first generation (72 percent), by the third generation, this percentage decreases to 52 percent (Campo-Flores, 2005).

According to Cox (1995, p. 175), fundamentalists have had success appealing to Latinos:

> It was at this luncheon that I first heard some of the startling statistics that have become more widely known in the past few years. . . . If things continued to go this way, commented the Catholic priest with three decades of experience in Latin America, within thirty or forty years the Roman Catholic

Church would be reduced to serving a largely ornamental function ("like the Church of England," he added ruefully) while the real religious life of the vast majority of the people would be lived in Pentecostal congregations.

Latinos are also turning to Islam, although their numbers are relatively small, with estimates ranging from 25,000 to 70,000 (Amario, 2004; Pluralism Project, 2003; Watkin, 2002). It has been estimated that 20,000 Latinos convert to Islam every year (Rozemberg, 2005). Latino Muslims generally tend to be prominent in places such as New York, Chicago, and southern California, or cities where both Latinos and Muslims are heavily represented. Nevertheless, their presence can also be found in places such as San Antonio, for example, which has an estimated 5,000 Latino Muslims (Rozemberg, 2005). Islam's appeal cuts across genders, with anecdotal evidence that its appeal is quite strong among Latinas (Cabrera, 2005; A. White, 2005).

Amario (2004, p. 11) specifically comments on the appeal of Islam for Latinas:

Many of the Latina converts say that their belief that women are treated better in Islam was a major factor in converting. Critics may protest that wearing the veil marks a woman as property, but some Latina converts say they welcome the fact that they are no longer whistled at walking down a street. "People have an innate response that I'm a religious person, and they give [me] more respect. . . . You're not judged if you're in fashion or out of fashion." Other Latina Muslims say they also like the religion's emphasis on fidelity to one's spouse and family.

The Alianza Islamica, founded in New York City in 1975, is considered one of the oldest Latino Muslim groups in the United States, and indicative of the growth of this religious group. Its appeal is increased for Latinos who have been casualties of life in this society (Watkin, 2002, p. 1):

For many Hispanics, turning to Islam is also a way of countering feelings of being downtrodden. Islam historically has always started with slaves and moved up to kings. . . . In New York, you find a similar phenomenon. Islam is entering America through the streets, through the inner city, the ghetto, the prisons.

The number of Mormons, too, has increased among Latinos in the past two decades, with estimates of Latino Mormons quadrupling from 49,000 to 200,000 during this period (Gonzalez, 2005). Active outreach involving missionaries fluent in Spanish going door-to-door in the community is largely responsible for this growth (Niebuhr, 1999). The Mormon emphasis on family, hard work, and humility taps into deep Latino cultural values, making conversion easier to accomplish. The eventual development of Spanish-language stakes will facilitate further outreach (Gonzalez, 2005).

Not surprisingly, the rise in the number of Latinos in the United States has transformed religious institutions (Dai, 2005; Jones, 2005). Communities that have historically been non-Latino, for example, are finding that shifts in populations have resulted in religious congregations having to decide whether and how they can reach the Latino residents, as in the case of Arizona (Belles, 2004, p. 1): "Neighborhoods across the Phoenix area are going through similar demographics changes, and churches are left deciding whether to put out the welcome mat, close down or turn over the keys to those with the skills to minister to the areas."

Latino religion and spirituality can be viewed from a variety of perspectives (Franzini, Ribble, & Wingfield, 2004). It has slowly found its way into the scholarly literature on subjects as diverse as formal education, birth outcomes, sexual behavior patterns, substance abuse, and gang membership. Sikkink and Hernandez (2003) found that Latino students who actively attend church or view faith as important in their lives achieve higher grades in school and are less likely to engage in problematic behavior than Latino students who do not share similar religious behavior and attitudes. Latino students who share religiosity, in turn, are also more likely than those who do not to have postsecondary school expectations. Latino religiosity wields influence in areas usually not thought of. For example, Clark (1995), in what is probably one of the earliest attempts at studying religiosity among Latinos in the United States and its impact on health care, found religiosity playing a positive role in birth outcomes for Mexican American populations.

It is important to end this section on religion by noting that although religion is significant within the Latino community, there is also a growing sector who have turned away from organized religion. Kornblum (2003) notes that the percentage of Latinos who had no religion more than doubled between 1990 and 2000. In 1990, 926,000 Latinos, or 6 percent of all Latinos, identified themselves as not having a religion. In 2000, it increased to 2.9 million, or 13 percent. Thus, social workers must never assume that just because Latinos are predominantly Catholic, other religious groups are not present in the community; and an increasing proportion of Latinos have no religion at all.

Folk Beliefs

These beliefs can easily be included in the category of religion, particularly in the case of Espiritismo (Spiritism) and Santeria (Saintism). These can also coexist and intermingle with other religions, such as Catholicism. However, it is artificial to separate folk beliefs from folk healing, since these two subjects are highly interrelated. Folk healing beliefs, for example, can exist as their own entity without regard to religion. I have chosen to separate out this topic from religion because of the unique aspects of folk beliefs and folk healing and how they ultimately affect delivery of human and health services. In addition, the subject of folk beliefs lends itself very well to both micro and macro practice perspectives, because it facilitates service provision at the individual level and at the program development level. Folk beliefs and healing, of course, are not unique to Latinos (Kilgannon, 2005).

The social work profession recognized the importance of Latino folk beliefs and their implications for health and mental practice well over 35 ago (Delgado, 1977, 1979). Initially, this approach focused on identifying and incorporating, or collaborating in, the work Latino folk healers, to better serve consumers. More recently, there has been a shift in focused to utilizing nontraditional settings, for example, botanical shops making referrals to health clinics for HIV screening (Delgado & Santiago, 1998). Any ethnographic effort to document the important institutions in the Latino community will invariably uncover numerous types of botanical shops, or botanicas. These institutions are business entities that generally have as their product and service the health of their communities (Gomez-Beloz & Chavez, 2001; Macgregor, 2005).

According to Becerra and Iglehart (1995, pp. 37–38), folk medicine has a variety of definitions, depending upon the context within which it is used:

> The term "folk medicine" has a variety of definitions in its modern context. It can refer to: (1) specific practices of ethnic group members . . . (2) the use of medical practitioners outside the Western medical establishment; (3) "good" remedies—those drawn from earlier, superior traditions; or (4) "bad" remedies—those with which primitive societies treat themselves in lieu of trained medical care.

The last definition assigns a pejorative connotation to this term and, unfortunately, captures the general attitude of the medical establishment to this worldview of health and healing.

Latino belief in folk healing has its share of controversy. For example, there has been debate over the practices of folk healers, and how they may prevent Latino believers from challenging the status quo. Their belief that the circumstances they find themselves in are the result of being cursed or hexed effectively prevents them from undertaking social action (De La Cancela & Zavalas, 1983).

One study of herbal use by Latino surgical patients found that herbal products are highly prevalent in Latino patients on both sides of the Mexico-Texas border (Rivera et al., 2005). Loera and colleagues (2001) found herbal medication common among older Mexican Americans, particularly those with chronic medical conditions. Another study of hypertension and Puerto Ricans found that herbal medication correlated positively with patients' primary language of Spanish.

Dobkin de Rios (2002) notes that there are congruences between folk techniques and psychotherapeutic techniques such as hypnosis, behavior modification, and cognitive restructuring. Murguia, Peterson, and Zea (2003), on the basis of their research with Central Americans in Washington, D.C., emphasize the importance of providers recognizing, and where possible, integrating cultural and spiritual influences in service delivery. Failure to do so will result in a missed opportunity to engage and serve a growing population group.

Zapata and Shippee-Rice (1999) found that the use of folk healing and folk healers often coincides with the use of mainstream health care. The value Latinos placed on cultural folk medicine was sufficiently strong that participants were willing to try conventional medicine, but not at the expense of folk medicine. Luna (2003) describes the role of nurse-curandera as an emerging group of health care providers in the Latino community. Nurse-curanderas integrate folk healing and conventional medical care as a means of minimizing conflicts between these two healing systems.

Flores and colleagues (2002), in their study of cultural and linguistic issues in the emergency care of Latino children, found that the first clinical contact might be with folk healers. Poss and Jezewski (2002) in their study (in El Paso, Texas) of the role and meaning of *susto* (the changing of the bodily state resulting in a person being vulnerable to the onset of diabetes), found that health care personnel needed to be aware of how folk etiologies may be used to explain type 2 diabetes.

Duggleby (2003), in turn, stresses that the role of folk healing beliefs, along with other cultural values, is too great to ignore in better understanding how Latinos manage their pain in their homes and communities. Hunt, Arar, and Akana (2000), in their study of herbs, prayer, and insulin among a group of Mexican American diabetes patients, found this group to rely more heavily on medical treatment than alternative treatments. Traditional cultural beliefs pertaining to folk healing did not present a barrier to conventional medical care.

A number of culture-specific physical and emotional conditions can be found within Latino population groups. *Nervios*, or problems with nervousness, is one example. The issue of how service providers are to respond to these culture-specific conditions throws the importance of cultural competence into sharp relief. Pavlik and colleagues (2004), for example, found that "nervios," a "culturally bound" syndrome, is common among Latinos with symptoms of cardiac disease.

The subject of *nervios* (nerves) and *ataque de nervios* (attack of nerves) has received considerable attention in the health and anthropological literature. Pavlik and colleagues (2004), in turn, found an association between *nervios* and cardiac disease. Guarnaccia, Lewis-Fernandez, and Marano (2003) studied the role of *nervios* and *ataque de nervios* among Puerto Ricans, and developed a classification system that can be used by health care providers to better understand cultural responses to sources of suffering.

Another study of *ataque de nervios* found a relationship between anxiety or affective disorder and *ataque* among those who have been victims of physical or sexual abuse or who have had a substance-abusing caretaker with a history of psychiatric disorders (Schechter et al., 2000). The authors concluded that *ataque de nervious* represents a "culturally sanctioned expression of extreme affect dys-regulation associated with childhood trauma." Lewis-Fernandez and colleagues (2003), in a study of Latino childhood trauma and *ataque de nervios,* found that childhood trauma did not account for *ataque* status among Latina outpatients. Another study concluded that *nervios* is a much broader illness than *susto,* and more related to continual stress (Baer et al., 2003). Baez and Hernandez (2001) propose a model that actively views Latino spiritual beliefs as complementary to psychotherapeutic practices.

Cultural Values

The subject of cultural values, I believe, gets addressed in a very superficial man-ner in the professional literature on Latinos. In many ways, the subject matter comes to function similarly to a backdrop to discussion of more "pressing" con-cerns and issues. Yet it represents the "glue" of what it means to be Latino and serves to unite a heterogeneous group. Cultural values, in essence, are gener-ally those identified and embraced by members of a specific cultural group (Brown, 2002).

An extensive review of the literature on Latino cultural values and cultural orientations necessitates reliance on literature that can easily be considered "dated" by most scholars and practitioners. Interestingly, with the general ex-ception of some passing observations and comments, usually no more than two or three sentences in length, the literature on Latinos in the past decade has generally eschewed depth on the subject matter. It is difficult to explain this phenomenon, but it bears noting nevertheless. The importance of the subject warrants more careful attention and detail. This section, as a result, represents an attempt to provide more depth, while acknowledging the paucity of recent research and articles on the subject matter.

The following classification of Latino cultural values helps practitioners bet-ter understand the unique features inherent in each cultural value, but also helps to develop an appreciation of how each category and the cultural variations within them, relate to each other. Further, as found by Perez and Padilla (2000) —in their study of three Latino adolescent generations (those born outside of the United States, those born in the United States but whose parents were foreign born, and those born to parents who were also born in this country) in Los An-geles (sample was predominantly Mexican)—acculturation plays an influential role in the maintenance or disregarding of cultural values, including the wan-ing of familism between the second and third generations.

Consequently, any serious effort at capturing the meaning of cultural values in the lives of Latinos can best be thought of as an attempt to "capture a moving target." This reality does not take away from observations and conclusions on the subject. It does mean, however, that the paucity of empirical research and scholarship limits the conclusions that can be drawn for practice with Latinos in the early part of the twenty-first century.

Gender Relations (Machismo and Marianismo)

As noted in chapter 1, the subject of gender-role values and expectations, and their influence on interrelations within the Latino culture, has generated considerable discussion, or debate, in academic and practice arenas. Germany (2000) and Mayo (1997), in discussing the core values found in machismo, note that the values of *dignidad* (dignity), *respecto* (respect), and *personalismo* (personalism) closely parallel key social work principles, such as the importance of self-determination, respect for others, and the importance of empowerment. The subject of machismo is generally discussed in isolation from these other values in a manner that invariably brings out its deleterious effects upon both Latinas and Latino males.

Marianismo, in turn, is a concept that does not enjoy the recognition of its machismo counterpart, although it, too, is well recognized in the professional literature and in the practice arena (Child Welfare League of America, 2003, p. 1):

> Marianismo is a concept, based in Catholicism, that Latino women represent virginity, spirit virtue, and obedience. Women are spiritually superior to men and endure more emotional and physical pain for their families. Their sexuality is defined and controlled by men. Sex is for procreation, not pleasure, and there only valid when a woman is married. Motherhood, however, is highly valued and respected in the Latino community.

Adherence to a subservient position places Latinas in a compromised position, and at risk for contracting HIV, intimate partner violence, and depression, for example (Russell, Alexander, & Carbo, 2000). Lack of awareness of resources impeded Latina newcomers from seeking assistance in one rural North Carolina study, raising the importance of providing information in Spanish to educate them about the seriousness of intimate partner violence and the options they have for leaving such partners (Moracco et al., 2005).

As is the case with many different concepts used in the social sciences, *machismo* has served to capture attitudes and behaviors that covered a wide spectrum, without any meaningful effort to differentiate between different "positive" or "negative" types. One study of traditional Latino families and male-female relationships found that machismo and patriarchal authority characterized the male role in these families (Galanti, 2003). Heavy drinking, domestic violence, and pursuit of high-risk activities were among the most negative manifestations of machismo. *Personalismo*, as will be addressed later on in this chapter, emerged as a critical component in assisting these families.

Mirande (1988), however, was one of the first social scientists to differentiate between different types of manifestations related to machismo. The creation of "false" and "authentic" forms of machismo seeks to emphasize and capture different social meanings and behaviors. The former is meant to capture excessive demonstrations of machismo, such as fixation on sexual powers or sexual conquests. The latter, in turn, seeks to capture strengths under adverse circumstances and uncompromising positions in situations requiring a firm decision. It would not be unusual to find terms such as *trabajador* (hard worker), *noble* (honorable), *responsable* (responsible), *un hombre de palabra* (a man of his word) to describe the positive elements of machismo (National Latino Alliance for the Elimination of Domestic Violence, 2001).

Achievement of fatherhood is a key factor in any definition of machismo. Foster's (2004) research on the meaning of children among Puerto Rican partners of adolescent mothers found that fathers embraced an opportunity to consider possible positive alternatives in their lives as a result of fatherhood. Thus, fatherhood had the potential of becoming a life-altering event that provided fathers with an opportunity to reflect on their lives and plan for a more positive future.

Torres, Solberg, and Carlstrom (2002), too, attempted to examine the construct of machismo and conceptualized it as multidimensional in composition. They found that only about 10 percent of their sample of Latino men (average age of 36 years, primarily Mexican American and Puerto Rican) could be classified as falling into the "traditional" category. These categories consisted of authoritarianism, emotionally restrictive, and controlling. The authors developed a five-part typology for categorizing machismo: (1) contemporary masculinity, (2) machismo, (3) traditional machismo, (4) conflicted/compassionate machismo, and (5) contemporary machismo.

As with machismo, there are numerous elements with Marianismo that can be considered desirable. The negative elements related to subservient positions to men, however, have received the greatest attention. Comas-Diaz (1987), Falicov (1998), and Santiago (2004) point out some of these positive qualities: an ability to maintain strong traditions of familismo, generosity, increased self-esteem manifested in one's ability to be giving of expressive and instrumental support, and communication styles that stress harmony. Exaggerating, or heavily emphasizing, any one aspect, however, can become counterproductive within this society.

As the acculturative process takes hold, Marianismo's emphasis on a position subservient to males and sex for the sole purposes of procreation is either minimized or discarded. One example of how acculturation influences the way the concept of Marianismo gets carried out in this society is the subject hysterectomy. One study of hysterectomy prevalence among Latinas, found that overall, Latinas undergo fewer hysterectomies than their white, non-Latina counterparts. However, hysterectomies are positively associated with increased acculturation, with country of origin having minimal influence (Brett & Higgins, 2003).

Harris, Firestone, and Vega's (2005) research findings on country of origin, acculturation, and gender role ideology in relation to wife abuse concluded that Latinas, in this case Mexicans, with more traditional value orientations (meaning less acculturated) are less likely to report abuse. Mattson and Rodriguez (1999) found that Mexican women in rural Arizona with the highest incidence of abuse also had the highest levels of acculturation. In one study of Latino youth acculturation, gender stereotypes, and attitudes about dating violence, Latino youth with low acculturation reported less knowledge about abuse and lower endorsement of nonviolent attitudes.

Sanderson and colleagues (2004), too, found greater prevalence of dating violence among ninth-grade Latino students with greater acculturation. Garcia, Huritz, and Kraus (2005), in turn, found that highly acculturated Latinas living in Los Angeles were more likely to report intimate partner abuse than moderately and minimally acculturated Latinas. Lown and Vega (2001) found that Mexican American women who had experienced intimate partner physical or sexual violence also reported poorer self-assessed health and many health symptoms, when compared with counterparts who had not experienced intimate partner violence.

A shift in attitudes toward gender roles may be occurring in succeeding generations of Latinos. A 1999 national survey found that foreign-born Latinos who say they believe that husbands are expected to have the final say on family decisions was almost twice as high as that of children and grandchildren of immigrants (Goldstein & Suro, 2000). Almost 90 percent of the respondents, however, said that it was important to maintain their culture.

It is important to point out, before ending this section on gender roles, that culturally competent services to Latinos will necessitate taking into account both gender roles and culture (Schifter & Madrigal, 2000). Andrade and Estrada (2003), for example, studied the roles of gender and culture in the lives of Latino injection drug users (IDUs), particularly how Latina IDUs experience greater pressures to fulfilling stereotyped gender and cultural roles. This type of research will become more common this decade as the awareness of Latino within- and between-group differences comes into play in conducting research and provision of services.

Familismo

The importance of the family within Latino culture has enjoyed a long tradition of research attention, particularly the role and importance of the extended family. Recent researchers have stressed that the Latino family is undergoing major changes as a result of increasingly significant structural demands in this society. Nevertheless, it continues to be an area of support that plays an important role in any definition of Latino cultural assets. Steidel and Contreras (2003) developed a Latino familism scale that highlights the key elements usually associated with this cultural value: (1) familial support; (2) familial interconnectedness; (3) familial honor; and (4) subjugation of self for family. Each of these factors examines a different dimension of familismo and brings out how complex this construct has become for both researchers and practitioners alike.

Familismo among Latinos reflects very strong emotional and value commitments toward family life (Vega, 1995). This attachment to family has a long historical significance that was shaped by both Spanish traditions and economical necessity (Goodman & Silverstein, 2002). *Familismo* places a tremendous amount of importance, or value, upon family identification, loyalty, attachment, and solidarity between family members (Garcia et al., 2000; Romero et al., 2004).

Shinnar (2005, p. 6), in a summary of the literature on Latino *familismo*, notes:

> The familialism value is significantly different from the Anglo view, which considers the family as the environment in which the child is socialized into an individualistic society. As adults, North Americans are expected to count on themselves to get ahead based on individualism and self-sufficiency. North American values do not negate the importance of family—they simply mean that people value self-reliance and independence from the family unit. . . . Hispanics, on the other hand, are likely to place emphasis on family needs when making career related decisions. In fact, family considerations are paramount and often come before the self.

Mena (1989), in a study that is somewhat dated but still relevant, describes the importance of cultural sensitivity in working with Latino adolescent fathers, and the strength and influence of familial orientation in helping families.

Familismo, nevertheless, has its challenges because of its emphasis on involving extended families and the keeping of privacy within the family. Baer, Prince, and Velez (2004), in their study of Mexican American adolescents, also raise a series of concerns about how the concept of fusion has been applied to Latino families. More specifically, they raise concerns about (1) the need for better measurement testing; (2) the need to revisit what the concept of autonomy signifies as a universal task during adolescent development; and (3) caution about the use of clinical concepts such as fusion and independence when discussing Mexican adolescents and their families. The term "enmeshment" has also been applied to Latino families to describe "overinvolvement, dependence, discouragement of self-differentiation" within families. These negative terms applied to Latino families are very much shaped by this society's emphasis on the nuclear family. It is ironic that this family type is no longer the norm in this society yet still wields a prodigious amount of influence in shaping public thought on what constitutes a "real" or "American" family.

Rios (2003, p. 59), in an interesting study of telenovelas (Spanish television soap operas) and English soap operas, concluded that the popularity of this medium rests with providing Latino audiences with an opportunity to reaffirm their cultural values such as that of familism: "Latinos use melodrama serials to keep in touch with Latino culture as well as learn more about and keep in touch with the dominant European American culture that surrounds them in their daily lives." The use of fotonovels, in this case comic books, is controversial, as in the case of Denver. The Denver Public Library was forced to remove thousands of Spanish fotonovelas from its shelves because of complaints about pornographic and violent content (Gartner, 2005).

Shinnar (2005), in another interesting study, this one focused on Mexican immigrants' career progression (in the Las Vegas hospitality industry), found that they evaluated job changes as desirable or undesirable on the basis of how their family life would be impacted. Magana's (1999) research on Puerto Rican families caring for an adult with mental retardation found that familism played an influential role in providing support to these families. The larger the social support network, the greater the satisfaction with social support.

The role and importance of the "familia" is not restricted to any one particular age group and must be viewed from a life-cycle perspective, with the family playing an influential role throughout. Hernandez, Siles, and Rochin (2000, p. 24), however, particularly single out the family in the lives of Latino youth:

> We assert that Latino youth must be examined within the context of one of the most powerful institutions that exists in their community: *la familia*. Immigration, recency of arrival, racial/ethnic diversity within the Latino community, racial definitions, and religiosity rooted customs within the Latino community all play an integral part in the formation of diverse familial structures, attitudes, and trends. However, the traditional strength and cohesion of *la familia* remains universal.

Latino families can consist of a number of individuals who can be related by blood, marriage, and cultural traditions (godparents) and close friends and neighbors who are called *como familia*, "like family." This flexibility in defining a Latino family serves to encompass new members who can be of aid to the family and reject individuals who are considered detrimental to the family's well-being. Thus, how a Latino family is defined must ultimately be determined by the response of the individual being asked. Conventional or stereotypical definitions of Latino families, as a result, do not take into account how ecological factors in society are shaping how the Latino family is defined.

The system of relationships commonly known as *compadrazo* has been referred to as a safety net or form of social security for Latino children. Ortiz (1973) notes that this system should ideally be made up of two married couples, a child, a priest and God, with one couple being the parents of the child and the other being *padrinos* (godparents) at the baptizing of a child. *Padrinos* assume the role of moral and religious supervisors of the child for life. If the parents of the child cannot take care of the child because of death, illness, or some other factor, then *padrinos* will assume responsibility for the child's well-being. The social relationship between parents and *padrinos* is now referred to as *compadres*.

Familismo gets carried out on a daily basis in a multitude of ways. Latinos, regardless of level of acculturation, generally express a desire to be in close proximity to their families. This "geographical closeness" will often mean that when children get married, they will establish homes in very close proximity to their parents. In urban areas, this can translate into moving out of their homes on the second floor, for example, and moving in to the fourth or another floor within the same building. From a community assessment perspective, this can mean that extended family members may reside in clusters in certain sectors of a geographical community. Thus, how community members' blood or marriage relates to those of other residents becomes an important point of analysis. *Familismo* will also influence household structure, often involving two, three, and, in some cases, four or more generations within the same home (Hurtado, 1995).

I could certainly share numerous stories about how *familismo* translates into behavior that can prove challenging for social work practice. The following two stories come most powerfully to mind.

1. An intake with Latinos will often require a social worker to be considerably flexible in how she or he conducts it. Conducting intakes with Latinos often means that many individual members of the family may attend the session, and it may even involve the minister from a family's congregation. I would generally start the intake by asking the person seeking services a question, and then all of a sudden I would have a member of the family party answering it. In a short period of time, anyone walking into the intake session could not discern who was the "client" by observing the degree of interaction going on between the social worker and the family, and so on, in the room. It would not be unusual to have contradictory answers to the question being posed and having the group discuss why one answer was "better" than another. The prospective client, too, would enter into this dialogue. Intakes, as a result, would rarely take the customary time period that would be the case with "typical" clients. Development of a high tolerance, or competencies (communication and interpersonal), to work in these situations becomes a necessity because of the role and influence of *familismo*.

2. *Familismo*, as in the example just cited, means that social workers must have a keen appreciation of the role of the group in helping to shape expectations and behaviors. I remember one situation when I was contracted to do a training session with emergency room personnel in a local hospital in New England that served a high proportion of Latinos, particularly after 5 p.m. I arrived early and sat in the emergency waiting room to observe interactions, climate, and so on. There were approximately 50 to 60 individuals in this emergency room. One of the physicians asked the intake nurse how many patients were there. She responded that there were nine patients. The physician was quite perplexed by this answer. The nurse responded that there were approximately

seven to eight individuals accompanying each patient. Interestingly, the physicians were only interested in the identified patient and one translator, who were taken to one of the examination rooms. Examination rooms can barely hold three of four people, because in this society illness is an individual phenomenon. In some cultures, Latino culture being one, illness often becomes a group phenomenon. The Latino patients, upon being reunited with their families in the emergency room, would then be questioned about their experiences. If their treatment met the expectations of the group as to what constituted proper treatment, then they would go home. If it did not, the plan was to go to another emergency room where their expectations could be met.

The inability, or unwillingness, of emergency room physicians to meet with the entire group meant that an important step in the development and follow-through of treatment was wasted. Hicks and colleagues (2005) found that there are significant racial and ethnic differences in patient preferences for hospital care, and recommend that time and effort be devoted to understanding and addressing Latino expectations of what constitutes treatment.

Finally, the definition of what constitutes a Latino family has undergone changes that on the surface appear slight, but can be clearly seen in recent years. Latino sexual orientation and sexuality have generally not received the attention they deserve in the professional literature, although this has started to change in the last decade or so (Reyes, 1998; Schifter & Madrigal, 2000). Within the Latino culture, the subject of homosexuality is laden with stigma, and this may be one of the primary reasons why it has historically not benefited from increased research and scholarly focus. Nevertheless, a number of researchers and scholars have drawn attention to this subject, with implications for how Latino family gets defined.

How the phenomenon of same-sex couples manifests itself within the Latino community, for example, has generally escaped any attention until just recently. One study conducted out of the University of California at Los Angeles (UCLA) found that one-third of same-sex couples in California included at least one Latino or Latina, and that there are a higher proportion of Latino same-sex couples raising children than homosexual couples of other ethnicities (Buchanan, 2005).

Interpersonal Relations between Latinos and Non-Latinos

This issue necessitates a multifaceted perspective that touches upon at least five key concepts such as *confianza, respecto, sympatia, dignidad,* and *personalismo.* Each of these cultural values forms an important dimension influencing interpersonal behavior. Although each these five concepts will be addressed independently of each other, in reality that is very artificial. For the purposes of discussion, however, it is necessary. The reader will no doubt see a tremendous overlap. Deconstructing cultural values is never like breaking down a machine!

Confianza

Velez (1980), well over 25 years ago, identified the importance of *confianza*, or confidence, as a cornerstone of any helping relationship. *Confianza* effectively translates into a construct that is learned and is an underlying condition for any meaningful interactional behavior within the Latino culture. The term *en confianza*, for example, translates into meaning that the information being shared must be kept between the two parties, and not shared with anyone else who is not entitled to know this.

Confianza taps an individual's trust and belief in the competence of the helper, in our case, a social worker. The provider will be expected to conduct himself or herself in a highly professional manner, and will abide by the contract he or she has established in the helping relationship. *Confianza*, in turn, can also involve a community perspective and establishes a bond that can exist over an extended period of time and is based on proof of positive and contributing actions proving that *confianza* exists.

Respecto

Respecto, or respect, is a normative cultural value that effectively cuts across all socioeconomic levels and translates into deferential behavior as part of any relationship, particularly one between a provider and a consumer of services (Flores & Sheehan, 2000). Usually, *respecto* is addressed from the perspective of consumers and how they show respect to authority figures. However, respect must also take place between authority figures and those considered "below" them, such as clients or consumers. Deferential behavior is influenced by social factors such as age, gender, position of authority, social position, and social-economic class (Flores, 2000).

On the surface, *respecto* may be well understood in U.S. society. However, this society is highly socially stratified on the basis of education, income, and profession. Consequently, the concept that everyone must be treated with respect is universal, in theory, but from a practical standpoint is rarely followed. Latinos use a term called *buen educador*, or "well-educated." This does not mean well educated formally with requisite credentials. It means that the individual is polite and respectful, regardless of, or in spite of, his or her formal position and level of education.

Latinos expect to be treated with respect, irrespective of their socioeconomic position in society. This value takes on greater significance when Latino experiences with discrimination have resulted in being disrespected (See chapter 3). The use of the term *usted* typifies this approach. *Usted* can be literally translated into English as "thou." Rarely used in this society, this pronoun takes a prominent place in Spanish and is a term that explicitly conveys respect (Ortiz, 1973, p. 93): "*Usted* is a term which implies either respect, distance, or formality. *Tu*

[you] is the more intimate form of address. It implies either closeness or equality when used by two or more persons addressing each other." Although non-Spanish-speaking social workers are generally not expected to know the difference between *usted* and *tu*, Spanish-speaking social workers are expected to be well versed in the usage of these terms.

The absence of *respecto*, as noted by Flores and Sheehan (2000) can result in an inaccurate history, decreased satisfaction, nonadherence to intervention, and inadequate follow-up. From a community perspective, it can translate into not allowing an organization to undertake a community assessment or a community-wide avoidance of using services provided by the organization. In effect, a lack of respect means that a poor working relationship has been established that will be very difficult to overcome for progress on a social intervention to occur.

Dignidad

This term is closely associated with *respecto* and literally translates as "dignity." Within a Latino cultural values context, it symbolizes and translates into "mutual respect." This value closely parallels that of *respecto* (Leavitt, 1974, p. 46): "The essence of the individual, his soul, is expressed by the value of *dignidad*, which is guarded from insult and invasion by *respecto*, a pattern of ceremonial politeness constantly observed by all but the closest of relatives and friends." However, *dignidad* goes beyond *respecto* and brings a dimension that embraces the total person rather than just focusing on the aspects of the individual a social worker is assisting. *Dignidad*, as a result, conveys to the broader Latino and Anglo community the totality of a person who knows how to conduct himself or herself in public, even under the most trying conditions.

Sympatia

This cultural value has not benefited from close scrutiny or numerous scholarly articles, yet it wields a tremendous amount of influence in staff/consumer relations. Sosa (2003, p. 4) captures the role of *sympatia* in social relations, noting

> many Hispanics' preference for smooth social relations based on politeness and respect, as well as avoidance of confrontation and criticism. Overt disagreement is not considered appropriate behavior. Some expect offers of gifts or food to follow a pattern of offer, refusal, insistence, and final acceptance, so receivers do not appear greedy or givers insincere.

The complexity of this cultural value is influenced by the fact that *sympatia* places an emphasis on the quality rather than the longevity of the relationship. In essence, trust and rapport between Latinos and providers is created through warm, friendly, and social relationships that stress kindness, politeness, pleasantness, and the avoidance of conflict.

Personalismo

This concept also has not been addressed in the professional literature yet it wields tremendous influence in shaping interpersonal relations between social workers and helping professionals and Latino consumers of services. The quality of the relationship is more important than the longevity (Sosa, 2003). *Personalismo* can be translated into "formal friendliness," or a warm, personal relationship that attempts to minimize professional distance. There is never any question of who is the "authority" figure in the relationship. However, there is an active effort to minimize this social distance in a manner that necessitates walking a thin line between being overly "professional" and overly "friendly" and nonprofessional. This can prove challenging, or problematic, when social workers subscribe to maintaining a professional distance between themselves and the client/community they seek to engage and work with.

Thus, *personalismo*, like *simpatia*, emphasizes the promotion of behaviors and attitudes that effectively promote pleasant demeanor and repression of anger (Shinnar, 2005). Engagement in dignified and respectful behavior under the most trying conditions is sought, though not always achieved. Cooperation, as will be addressed later on in this chapter, is preferred to competition. Competition usually results in winners and losers; the latter can harbor harsh feelings, and every effort must be made to avoid causing these feelings in others. Competition in U.S. society is about winning; the social reactions it causes are inconsequential, even if this means hurt feelings. In addition, *personalismo* translates into Latinos relating to individuals who work within organizations rather than institutions themselves.

Detachment, which is often the perception a professional is expected to convey to a client, for example, may alienate Latinos who embrace *personalismo* (Dingfelder, 2005b). There are a variety of ways of engendering *personalismo*. Some of these are more "acceptable" to social workers; others are less so. The sharing of personal information is one area that helps in establishing relationships. Most social workers learn quickly that the sharing of any personal information is taboo in our field. Sharing of this type of information sometimes raises a caution flag and questions about boundaries, countertransference, one's need to be liked, and so on. However, when this sharing is placed within a cultural context, it loses its stigma for a social worker. The type of information that is shared, as a result, is very much determined by the nature of the work we are doing with consumers and communities, and our "comfort" level in doing so.

Invitations to attend family functions is another indicator of the degree to which *personalismo* is present. I have personally been invited to attend birthdays, baptisms, weddings, and wakes, for example. An opportunity for the Latino community to see a social worker at functions like these can convey a positive relationship that can often be carried over to other facets of community life for a social worker. Attendance at family and community functions, however, often entails doing so outside of the usual confines of a workday. Meetings conducted in people's homes, be they therapeutic or information/training related, also provides social workers with opportunity to share meals and eat Latino food. A high comfort level often translates into the sharing of food during these meetings, a positive sign that the worker and the individual offering the food have a high level of trust and respect for each other.

There are numerous physical dimensions to *personalismo*. Gestures such as the shaking of hands, proximity, a hand on a shoulder, even hugging and giving a kiss on the check are expected in relationships sustained over an extended period of time. These physical aspects of *personalismo*, undoubtedly, generate a great deal of discussion or even discomfort on the part of the worker. Perceived lack of *personalismo*, however, will make it difficult to engage Latinos individually and collectively within the community.

Individualism and Interdependence/Collectivism

The emphasis placed on the value of collectivism, or interdependence, is bound to give rise to a number of significant challenges in the creation of services and programs in the effort to engage Latinos. Like the other values addressed in this chapter, the role acculturation plays among Latinos becomes very important in any assessment. Traditionally, Latinos embrace a value of interdependence. This essentially translates into the understanding that family or group needs are far more important than the individual needs.

The cultural perspectives of individualism and collectivism are considered to be at opposite ends of the spectrum (Kim et al., 1994). Western Europe, the United States, and Canada are generally believed to be at one end of the continuum (individualism), while Asian, Latin American, and African countries are at the other end (collectivism). Hofstede (1991, p. 51) provides a definition for both:

> Individualism pertains to societies in which the ties between individuals are loose: everyone is expected to look after himself or herself and his or her own immediate family. Collectivism as its opposite pertains to societies in which people from birth onwards are integrated into strong, cohesive in-groups, which throughout people's lifetime continue to protect them in exchange for unquestioning loyalty.

Acculturation as a mediating factor, as with other cultural values and beliefs, has an important role to play in the transplantation of individualism and collectivism between generations (Mishra, 1994). However, Oserman, Coon, and

Kemmelmeier, on the basis of their metaanalyses of the literature, issue a word of caution about generalizing to groups that are far from being homogeneous in composition.

Competition versus Cooperation

The embrace of a value centered on either competition or cooperation, I believe, strikes at the heart of what it means to be an "American" in this society. The importance this society places on competition (personal, academic, and professional) permeates much of how this society views success. As already noted in chapter 2, success must be examined within a cultural context to determine its meaning. There is, after all, no universal standard for measuring the meaning of success. This value, combined with individualism, effectively translates into a definition of who is a "winner" and "loser" in this society.

Latinos' embracing cooperative values means that an important emphasis is placed on feelings and relationships rather than on outcomes that result in winners and losers. Cooperation, as a result, will manifest itself in a variety of ways, such as an emphasis on how well a student is liked by the teacher rather than an obsession with grades, or a shying away from assuming supervisory positions because of the need to discipline others, for example.

Conclusion

This chapter has exposed the reader to a variety of cultural values and beliefs that can be found in the Latino community in the United States. The reader, however, has been warned, and needs to be reminded again, that these values and beliefs are not stagnant and are ever changing as the result of Latino contact with this society's dominant values and beliefs. This is particularly the case for those new to this country. The process of acculturation, addressed throughout the early part of this book, is alive and well regarding values and beliefs. Thus, the reader must be prepared to examine this content with a very critical eye toward the influence of change within the community.

However, any in-depth understanding of Latino cultural values and beliefs necessitates that one be open and willing to examine one's own cultural values and beliefs as a baseline from which to assess those of another cultural group. The process of discovery of others, as well as one's own values and beliefs, cannot be accomplished without considerable amounts of discomfort, as well as the joy of self-discovery. However, this journey is necessary if any form of service that hopes to be culturally competent can be developed and implemented at an individual and organizational level.

Chapter 7

A CULTURAL ASSETS PARADIGM:
A CONCEPTUAL FOUNDATION

Social forces such as prejudice, economic inequality, and attitudes toward violence in mainstream American culture interact with the influences of early childhood to foster the expression of violence. Not everyone affected by these forces, however, turns to violence. In some cases, for example, forces within the child's ethnic culture may serve as a buffer against adverse social circumstances. Culture builds identity, sets norms for behavior, and provides a sense of group cohesion that is vital to a child's growth and development. A promising area for intervention efforts is in identifying and strengthening the protective factors that keep the vast majority of youth from turning to violence as a response to social conditions.

American Psychological Association Commission on Violence and Youth, *Violence and Youth* (1993)

The epigraph to this chapter, although specifically focused on youth and violence, can also be applied to other age groups and social problems, and serves as an excellent starting point for this chapter on the importance of a cultural assets paradigm. The emergence of new social paradigms that view historically marginalized groups and communities from strengths and assets perspectives is very exciting for the social work profession, with tremendous potential for not only better serving these communities but also bringing different social work practice methods together in pursuit of common goals. The shift from a predominant focus on deficits and problems to one that stresses assets and empowerment accords well with the central direction of this book, which views culture as a key contributing element in shaping social work interventions. However, this shift is much more than a change in vocabulary; it represents the emergence of a distinctive view that has generally not enjoyed the support it deserves.

In the case of Latinos, an ecological or contextual perspective has facilitated the shift from problems and deficits to one that is hopeful, empowering, and systematically identifies and builds upon individual and community assets. Culture is one of the most prominent assets that can be successfully mobilized to address needs and concerns of communities in a manner that empowers and affirms in the process. The perspective of cultural assets, however, goes far beyond individual cultural values and beliefs to embrace the broad context and role of assets within communities. This is particularly important when discussing communities that can be characterized as "undervalued" within this society and that as a result have been portrayed as consisting of nothing but problems without any cultural capital to speak of, as noted in chapter 2. Embracing a Latino cultural assets paradigm, however, as the reader will find out later on in this chapter, is not without its share of challenges. On the other hand, any social work intervention focused on marginalized groups within this society should expect nothing but challenges!

Community-based assets such as houses of worship and other nontraditional settings such as beauty parlors, grocery stores, botanical shops, and public spaces used for murals and gardens, for example, all combine to create a highly dynamic and energized environment for service provision, and provide the field of social work with numerous options for developing social interventions across different methods of practice (Delgado, 1999a, 2000). These assets can also be mobilized to bring disparate community groups together.

Cultural assets–based interventions must be guided by a set of principles that, at minimum, stress affirmation of identity, empowerment, collaborative partnerships, and cultural values, and must be capacity enhancing in the process. Further, this approach thrusts social workers into positions of collaborator, learner, broker, and facilitator, rather than a conventional role of "expert," which is disempowering and further perpetuates marginalization. This shift in roles, as already addressed in the previous chapter, provides ample opportunities for staff to engage Latinos in a manner that builds upon such cultural values as *respecto, dignidad, simpatia,* and *personalismo.*

Before proceeding, I must pause and revisit a concern I had over a decade ago about reliance on any form of indigenous community assets (Delgado, 1995d, p. 19):

> It is necessary, however, to pause and examine the implications of utilizing "self-help" and "natural support systems" concepts with undervalued communities. . . . Concepts such as the aforementioned are receiving a great deal of attention at the national and local levels. Both the political "right" and "left" have stressed the importance of empowering communities as an approach for meeting social and economic needs. Nevertheless, the manner in which empowerment practices are operationalized and the meaning they have for government intervention will vary depending upon one's political perspective.

Thus, advocating for a social paradigm based on cultural assets does not, in any way, relieve federal, state, and local government, and other sectors, from their responsibilities of ensuring the well-being of this nation's people, and the responsibility of providing a safety net. It does mean, however, that these entities must endeavor to work with community assets in any formation of social policies and programs. Failure to do so will essentially result in wasted resources and further alienating communities in the process.

The Historical Roots and Evolution of the Latino Cultural Assets Approach

The evolution of the use of a cultural construct as an asset among Latinos has a long tradition within the social work profession, almost 50 years to be exact, and one needs a brief overview of its history in order to best understand and appreciate the emergence of a new paradigm such as the cultural assets paradigm.

In the 1960 and 1970s, the professional literature, including social work, focused primarily on deficits related to Latinos and generally emphasized three issues pertaining to culture and its role: (1) the importance of family and religion; (2) the importance of food and celebrations; and (3) problems and needs in adjusting to life in the United States. An occasional positive cultural attribute would be mentioned, then not pursued in any meaningful way. These perspectives, in effect, did little more than reinforce stereotypes in both general and professional circles. This deficit perspective permeated the professional literature on other socially and economically marginalized communities in this country as well. This perspective, in addition, set a tone that essentially shaped scholarship, research, and practice, when addressing marginalized groups, particularly those of color living in this nation's cities.

The 1980s, however, witnessed a dramatic shift in focus away from deficits to one valuing cultural factors, and the importance of not only recognizing these factors but also finding ways they could play a role in shaping interventions across the service delivery spectrum. In 1980, Valle and Vega published *Hispanic Natural Support Systems: Mental Health Promotion Perspectives*, representing the first mention in the professional literature of this cultural assets perspective. This publication was issued by the State of California's Department of Mental Health, in response to recommendations made by the President's Commission on Mental Health (1979). This commission report sparked national interest in the use of natural support systems. Although Valle and Vega's book was only 131 pages long, it provided an important national venue for Latino and other scholars interested in viewing the Latino community from a nondeficit perspective. Its importance to the field of Latino scholarship and the advancement of a cultural assets perspective has never fully been recognized. It played an important moral and scholarly role in shaping research in the decades to follow.

In the early 1980s, Delgado and Humm-Delgado (1982), almost in parallel fashion to Valle and Vega, further advocated a unifying framework for social work that they also called "Hispanic Natural Support Systems" as a means of bringing together various types of Latino cultural resources for the purposes of designing social work interventions on the basis of assets. This emphasis on natural support systems represented a philosophical stance, but also had very "concrete" implications for social work interventions. Delgado and Humm-Delgado broadened the construct of natural support systems. This scholarship, in turn, was also greatly influenced by the scholarship of two other social workers and the publication of *Natural Helping Networks: A Strategy for Prevention* by the NASW (Collins & Pancoast, 1976). However, unlike Valle and Vega (1980), the Delgado and Humm-Delgado conceptualizion of natural support systems included indigenous institutions that fulfilled important cultural functions.

Delgado and Humm-Delgado's (1982) definition embraced Baker's (1977, p. 139) definition of natural support systems:

> In most communities there exists a network of individuals and groups who band together to help each other in dealing with a variety of problems in living. Such groupings, which provide attachments among individuals or between individuals and groups such that adaptive competence is improved in dealing with short-term crises and life transitions, are referred . . . to as natural support systems. The word "natural" is used to differentiate such systems from the professional care-giving systems of the community. . . . Natural support systems include family and friendship groups, local informal caregivers, voluntary service groups not directed by care-giving professionals and mutual help groups.

The inclusive nature of Baker's definition facilitated the incorporation of more cultural assets into a Latino natural support systems paradigm.

The definition by Delgado and Humm-Delgado (1982) brings to the foreground five key themes relating to how health and social service organizations can use these resources in creating partnerships with the Latino community: (1) the importance of personal relationships based on mutual trust and respect; (2) the accessibility of these systems from a geographical, psychological, cultural, and operational viewpoint; (3) the role of natural support systems in helping to foster and maintain a Latino identity; (4) the importance of self-help and mutual support groups; and (5) identification of the Latino community's capacity to help itself in a variety of ways.

As illustrated in figure 7.1, Delgado and Humm-Delgado (1982) conceptualized Latino natural support systems as consisting of four basic types or categories: (1) family, extended family, and friends; (2) religion (Catholic, Seventh-Day Adventist, Pentecostal, and Jehovah's Witness); (3) folk healers (mediums,

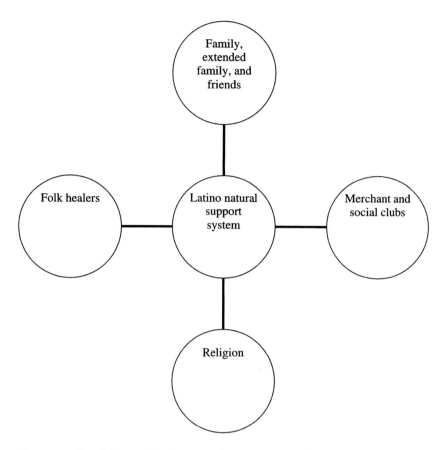

Figure 7.1. Breakdown of Latino natural support system framework

santeros, and herbalists); and (4) merchant and social (hometown) clubs, for example, grocery stores, botanical shops, and beauty parlors. These cultural support systems can be found in the Latino community in various configurations and settings; their influence on help-seeking and help-provision is very much influenced by the local context within which they appear.

The concept of "Hispanic natural support systems" has spread into many different fields and been used to address a wide range of community needs and concerns. Interest in this perspective has stemmed primarily from its promise of the ability to buffer harmful environmental effects, along with its affirmation that Latinos have brought with them cultural assets that typically have not been recognized by society in general, and social work and other helping professions in particular. The concept of natural support systems has also been incorporated into a variety of constructs, along with coping, strengths, resiliency, capacity, protective mechanisms, and, most recently, cultural assets. However, the attractiveness of the Latino natural support systems construct often lies in its ability to be subsumed under other constructs, allowing them to exist autonomously.

Each of the aforementioned factors exercises a strong influence concerning the power of natural support systems within a cultural and community context. However, when these factors are combined, it is easy to see why natural support systems have survived and even thrived over the years and why they have been transplanted to this country. Like cultural assets (a broader construct), these systems have changed in relation to the demands of the environment. Latino natural support systems can get operationalized differently according to ecological demands and circumstances. Thus, any effort to assess Latino natural support systems must be sufficiently flexible to take into account changes that have occurred in this country.

As shown in figure 7.2, Latino natural support systems can be used in various levels of intervention. The 1980s and 1990s witnessed the use of the Hispanic natural support systems approach with primary (De La Rosa, 1988; Delgado, 1995e; Vega et al., 1987), secondary (Delgado, 1995d, 1996a), and tertiary levels

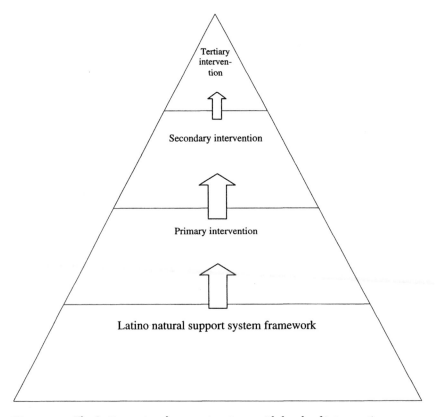

Figure 7.2. The Latino natural support system, with levels of intervention

of intervention (Delgado & Humm-Delgado, 1993; Delgado & Rivera, 1997; Gutierrez, Ortega, & Suarez, 1990). Latino natural support systems, then, can be mobilized for use at multiple intervention levels and organizational settings. This approach also provides a venue for multidisciplinary professionals to work together on behalf of Latinos and their community.

Latino natural support systems have also been applied for interventions with women (Sanchez, 1987; Sanchez-Ayendez, 1988; Vega et al., 1987), elementary-aged children and their parents (Delgado, 1995b; Delgado & Rivera, 1997), the latency-aged and adolescents (Becerra & Reece, 1993), and elders (Delgado, 1995e; Delgado & Tennstedt, 1997). A number of researchers have also used natural support systems with special populations such as newcomers (Delgado, Jones, & Rohani, 2005; Vega & Kolody, 1985) and persons with HIV/AIDS (Delgado & Santiago, 1998). Population-specific interventions bring an added appeal to this paradigm for social work and other helping professions.

The 1990s, in turn, witnessed the introduction of a strengths perspective, thus helping to fuel a broader access across all ethnic and racial groups; their cultural assets were embraced (Saleebey, 1992, 1996). Sullivan's (1992, pp. 148–149) comment on the advantages of using an assets approach highlights the appeal of this social paradigm:

> A strengths perspective . . . offers an alternative conception of the environment. This perspective promotes matching the inherent strengths of individuals with naturally occurring resources as a source of opportunities for clients, rather than an ecology of obstacles, [and so] the sheer number of helping resources we perceive expands dramatically.

An ecology of opportunities effectively replaces an ecology of problems and deficits, opening up new arenas for practice.

In the early to mid-1990s, Delgado (1994, 1995c,d, 1996b) helped spur an evolution of Latino natural support systems by developing a classification system for assessing the status of these systems for the purpose of developing collaborative cultural assets interventions, and identified three forms of assistance (expressive, instrumental, and informational) that can be provided in time of need.

The classification system presented in figure 7.3 attempts to take a dynamic perspective on Latino natural support systems by bringing into any form of assessment and intervention the interplay of cultural assets and environmental considerations. The classification system consisted of a five-stage framework, with each stage representing a unique set of circumstances in Latino natural support systems that necessitated Latinos turning to formal sources for assistance (Delgado, 1995d).

Each of the following stages requires social workers and other helping professionals planning interventions to also seek to reinvolve, or reconnect, natural support systems whenever possible, or help re-create them if necessary.

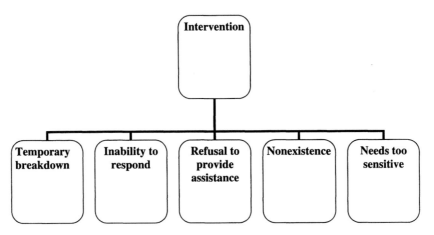

Figure 7.3. Breakdown of Latino natural support systems framework

1. *Temporary breakdown*: A Latino natural support system may be temporarily unable to respond to a request for assistance because, it, too, may be undergoing its own crisis. It would like to assist but is unable to because of its own needs at the time a request is made for help. This does not mean that it cannot do so at another point in time, however, or cannot respond to a different request for assistance. A "temporary" status means just that; it is temporary. The length of this temporary state, however, may vary.

2. *Inability to respond*: An inability to respond positively to a request for assistance differs dramatically from a temporary inability to do so. This unresponsiveness may be the result of one of two factors: (a) the support system would like to assist, but the demand for assistance is beyond its capabilities to help (e.g., financial assistance, medical care for severe injury); or (b) it has attempted to assist in the past but has been unsuccessful in achieving positive change, and therefore is unwilling to continue assisting on the presenting need or problem. In the former situation, the support system may not know how to assist in a positive manner or may lack information on informal resources within the community. In the latter situation, Latino natural support systems have limits to their abilities to aid. Lack of expertise or experiences may severely limit such a system's ability to respond. A future request for assistance, however, may be successful if conditions change. Unfortunately, to serve the current request is not possible, and that is why a client may be seeking help from formal sources.

3. *Refusal to provide assistance*: An outright refusal to provide aid is a very serious situation, since it is a conscious decision not to offer assistance. A Latino, in turn, may be very reluctant to discuss this situation because he or she may be embarrassed by this state of affairs. The refusal may be the result of any one or combination of the following reasons, and it is necessary to identify the reason from an individual or community assessment perspective: (a) lack of a solid social

relationship or social skills necessary to develop and maintain supportive relationships; (b) limited participation in social situations, thus restricting the opportunities to develop necessary ties; (c) a history of negative experiences between the parties that may have been caused by a disruptive influence of the helper; (d) the presenting problem not being perceived as a "pressing problem" compared to other issues and needs confronting the support system, and thus being considered low priority; and (e) a situation wherein the person in need has historically relied heavily upon his or her support system and either has not been able to reciprocate or has refused to do so when called to provide assistance (in essence, the relationship is one-sided, with mutuality being absent). Becker and colleagues (2003), in their study of mutual assistance and intergenerational reciprocity, found that assistance and reciprocity were important elements in a social support system. Failure to reciprocate when possible was viewed as a significant breakdown in the helping relationship.

4. *Nonexistence*: This type of condition of natural support systems represents an extremely serious state of affairs for Latinos. An individual in need cannot rely on his or her natural supports and must turn instead to formal services for assistance, even though he or she would prefer not to. This barrier can result from an interplay of the following factors: (a) a disintegration of the support system over an extended period of time, which can occur in circumstances where acculturation has effectively changed cultural values pertaining to helping; (b) a natural disaster in the process of which the support system has disappeared; or (c), as is common with many uprooted newcomer groups, the support system has been left behind and has not had sufficient time to be replaced in the new setting.

Social workers, as a result, cannot involve informal resources and must also endeavor to help re-create a natural support system by helping to broker contacts and commitments. For example, someone may have been very religious at one point in time and then stopped attending religious services altogether. One aspect of an intervention may be having the social worker help facilitate reentry into religious institutions within the community by meeting with and enlisting a religious leader in reaching out to the person in need. In effect, helping to broker the reestablishment of a relationship between these two parties.

5. *Needs too sensitive*: This perspective raises important issues concerning what types of aid Latinos feel most comfortable seeking from natural support systems. Not all forms of social needs share the same level of "stigma" in this society, for Latinos or any other ethnic or racial group. Some services are particularly stigmatizing; others are not. Thus, the level of stigma, or shame, associated with a problem or illness will wield tremendous influence on help-seeking patterns of Latinos. For example, issues related to substance abuse for women, AIDS, family violence, and child sexual abuse are very stigmatizing and not easily shared among people within families and close social networks. The social stigma and consequences associated with HIV/AIDS, for example, illustrate this breakdown in informal, or natural support.

Varas-Diaz, Serrano-Garcis, and Toro-Alfonso (2005) found in their study of Puerto Ricans living with HIV/AIDS that they experienced loss of social support, persecution, isolation, job loss, and problems accessing health services. Their diagnosis negatively influenced social interactions with family, friends, sexual partners, coworkers, and health professionals. Consequently, formal or institutional support services may very well be the only "viable" alternative for a Latino wishing to obtain assistance without close family and friends finding out about it. As a result, a Latino in this state may well have an active support system for other types of social needs that are less, or are not, stigmatizing.

By the mid-1990s, Latino natural support systems as a construct had evolved to include a broader and much more inclusive construct that incorporated natural support systems along with other indigenous resources or assets. This evolution, however, would not have transpired without the pioneering work of numerous scholars during the decade of the 1980s, as outlined earlier. In essence, any social paradigm based on indigenous cultural and community resources owes a great debt to the construct of natural support systems.

The construct of natural support systems filled a void in the field of human services and provided a much-needed conceptual foundation for the development of innovative and Latino-affirming services that followed. It served to ground individual cultural values, beliefs, and assets in a broader community context. The importance of understanding community context is borne out by numerous studies, such as a study of environmentally related diseases (developmental and respiratory) among young children in several New York City communities (Perera et al., 2002).

Principles Guiding a Cultural Assets Paradigm

I have professionally always had an affinity for principles and the role they play in guiding my practice. Principles play an important role in helping to narrow the gap between theory and practice. This function helps the practitioner better understand how theory ultimately informs practice, and has elements that are both descriptive and prescriptive. The following six important practice principles are based upon the literature and my experiences in working with Latino clients and communities across the United States.

1. *All age groups possess assets.* Assets must never be conceived as being the exclusive domain of any one age group, although youth and more specifically the very young have suffered from a perspective that views them as assetless in this society. It has only been recently that adolescents have started to get attention because of their assets and how they can help other youth as well as adults. Embracing the principle that all age groups bring with them assets effectively broadens the development of interventions that systematically seek to identify

and mobilize indigenous resources found within all age groups, and facilitates creation of intergenerational activities and services.

The importance of elders within families and their role as community resources has been recognized in the scholarly literature (Delgado, 1995e, 1998a). Latino elders are often called upon to provide a wide range of services to their families that can be categorized as instrumental and expressive in nature. Elders are also one of the primary agents for the transmission of cultural values within a community. A strong emphasis on oral traditions reinforces the important role Latino elders play in helping to shape a family's sense of their history, ties to country of origin, and values.

Latino youth, too, play influential roles as cultural brokers and interpreters in helping family members socially navigate their way through the external community (Delgado, Jones, & Rohani, 2005). Socially and economically marginalized communities in this society do not have the luxury of significant sectors of their communities not having socially meaningful roles, and the Latino community is no exception. Youth must be expected to play influential roles within the life of a community and not to wait until adulthood to do so (Delgado, 2006).

2. *Any effort to identify and engage Latino community assets will be labor intensive.* The engagement of Latino community assets must be conceptualized as a long-term project, or investment if you wish, that initially will be labor intensive, in terms of time, energy, and resources, but will more than pay for itself in the future. These cultural assets are based upon interpersonal relations, which by their very nature are time-intensive and difficult to judge as to how long it will take for them to begin providing benefits.

Communities, it should be remembered, are the lifeblood of social service organizations. Consequently, long-lasting relationships that have survived over extended and, at times, troubling times do not just happen. An investment in Latino cultural assets requires a strong commitment on the part of the organization and community. Organizational administrators, as well as funders, must recognize this important consideration. It would prove very troubling from a community standpoint if bureaucratic expediency replaces hard-earned trust.

Fisher, Marcoux, Miller, Sanchez, and Cunningham (2004, p. 3), for example, concluded, on the basis of their research of Latino farmworkers and their families in the Pacific Northwest, that indigenous resources, such as barbershops, play influential roles in helping Latino newcomers navigate their way through life in this country:

> Given the language, cultural, and economic barriers coupled with the deep extent of everyday needs associated with immigrants, especially those working in dangerous, low-tech occupations, it is consistent that they would rely heavily upon interpersonal information sources, especially close families and friends or people like themselves, finding credibility in the similarity of these populations.

Accessing this and other types of cultural resources necessitates that social workers not only venture into the field (community) but also be prepared to engage in conversation with the owners of these types of establishments; this may entail countless visits before there is a relationship sufficiently trustworthy to establish a collaborative partnership.

3. *Only those who have the proper attitudes and preparations should engage in collaboration with Latino community assets.* Collaboration with Latino community assets must be undertaken by those who are prepared attitudinally and skill-wise to engage in this type of practice. Collaboration requires patience, skills, and a willingness to share power in the guiding of interventions. These personal qualities will be tested throughout all facets of the collaborative process and stages of the Latino cultural assets framework presented in chapter 8. These personal qualities will be tested throughout all facets of a collaborative partnership process. The sharing of power in decisionmaking promises to be the greatest challenge, necessitating that social workers also be adept at diplomacy.

4. *Controversy is to be expected when engaging Latino community assets.* Social work staff must be prepared to encounter controversies when engaging Latino community assets, particularly those involving houses of worship and folk healers (De La Cancela & Zavalas, 1983; Delgado & Rosati, 2005). There is no way that avoidance of controversy can occur, and it is advisable to be better prepared to engage in dialogues to minimize these disturbances.

Involving folk healers, for example, could possibly engender an adverse response from houses of worship. These institutions may also object to the use of memorial murals, particularly in the case of deaths resulting from community violence. The possibility of a political reaction should not dissuade social workers from initiating projects. However, they cannot ignore the criticism and must be prepared to engage in ways to minimize it. If this "tension" is conceptualized as a "normal" part of the process, then it becomes much easier for social workers to identify the source of this tension, the reasons why it exists, and what strategic moves can be used to minimize its influence on the service delivery process.

5. *Interventions must seek not only to utilize cultural assets but also to enhance them in the process.* The importance of cultural assets makes attractive to identify and mobilize them in the creation of a cultural assets paradigm. However, it must be noted that utilization of cultural assets brings with it immense responsibility to ensure that they are not compromised in the process. Further, effort must be made to strengthen them whenever possible. Time and resources should be set aside to assist Latino cultural assets to be better prepared to engage with social workers in pursuit of capacity enhancement initiatives.

6. *The engagement of Latino cultural assets can not be turned on and off depending upon funding.* This principle is one that very often gets over looked in any development of community-based interventions. Very often marginalized communities

such as the Latino community are engaged when funders mandate it. However, once this funding is terminated, organizations generally feel no obligation to continue to engage the community.

Latino cultural assets cannot be conceptualized as a faucet one turns and off at will. This callous approach to community involvement will prove detrimental to an organization. The community has a very long-term memory and does not read or subscribe to the same theories that we as social workers do. Consequently, once an organization ventures out into the community to engage it, it does so for life! A decision to engage the community must be seriously thought out, particularly when organizational actions can cease once funding for a project is terminated.

Cultural Assets Framework

A framework is best thought of as a tool that can be used in the field of practice, in this case, involving Latinos, and that helps operationalize a theoretical social paradigm. Any good framework incorporates theory and interactional (political) considerations in helping practitioners use principles in guiding social work interventions. A Latino cultural assets paradigm must play a central and influential role in all phases of program design, from assessment (need as well as asset) to program design, implementation, and evaluation (process, outcome, and impact). How each of these phases gets conceptualized will influence how Latino cultural assets get identified and incorporated into program and service design.

The framework presented hereafter and in figure 7.4 lends itself to social work interventions focused on individuals and communities, thereby having relevance to all forms of interventions. This is particularly important because the profession must be prepared to address the needs of Latinos across an intervention spectrum, which may involve social workers focused on individual practice with those focused on community practice. Individual-focused interventions can be based upon this framework. On the other hand, organizations, too, can generate data and programs and services using this framework. It serves to unify all aspects of social work interventions.

As noted in figure 7.4, the Latino cultural assets framework consists of six stages, each of which has a set of analytical (theoretical) and interactional (sociopolitical) dimensions and all of which effectively work together. Each of the stages has a set of goals specific to itself, as well as goals that interact with the goals of the other stages. Thus, practitioners never have the luxury of thinking only about one stage and totally ignoring the other stages while doing so. The stage being addressed becomes foreground, and the other stages become background, with all being equally important.

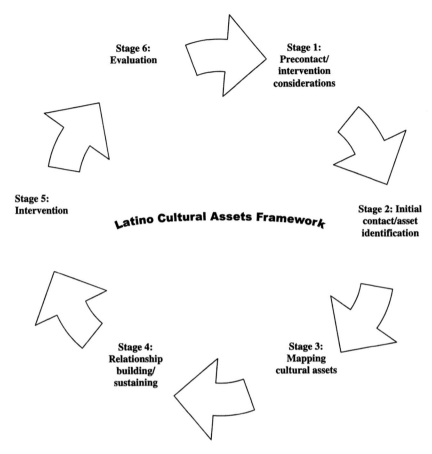

Figure 7.4. Latino cultural assets framework

Stage 1: Precontact/
Intervention Considerations

This stage represents the foundation of this framework and systematically examines the social worker, the consumer group or community, and the organization sponsoring the social intervention. Each of these arenas is assessed in order to determine the best course of actions, and the considerations that must be addressed in order to succeed. The stage, as a result, focuses on obtaining basic information on the following factors: (1) language competencies (English and Spanish); (2) knowledge of cultural values and beliefs; (3) knowledge of the community and its history; and (4) the history, nature, and reputation of organizations within the Latino community.

The initial stage, as the reader no doubt realizes, represents the foundation upon which an intervention is based. Another perspective on the importance of this stage relates to assessing legitimacy. According to Rein (1977), there are four sources of legitimacy when assessing community-focused intervention: (1) expertise of knowledge (educational and experiential); (2) institutions; (3) ethics; and (4) consumer perception. Ideally, social interventions should have all four forms of legitimacy to increase the likelihood of achieving success. Missing sources of legitimacy, as a consequence, must be addressed before a project or initiative can commence. Otherwise, the likelihood of failure increases; the more sources of legitimacy that are missing, the higher the chances of failure. Conversely, having all legitimacies present does not guarantee success. It does, however, increase the likelihood of success significantly.

The precontact/intervention stage can be simply characterized as a phase for preliminary assessment and consideration. Nothing could be further from the truth! This is an extremely complex stage that necessitates stark and candid dialogues and debate about an organization's capacity to undertake an intervention (Holley, 2003a,b). It has been my experience in working with organizations wishing to reach the Latino community that these types of discussions are rare. Even addressing this content through the material and lenses covered in chapter 3, discussions tend to be "politically sensitive." Nevertheless, regardless of the sensitivity, an honest appraisal of organizational capacity is warranted.

Stage 2: Initial Contact/ Asset Identification

Assessments fulfill many important roles in the design and implementation of social programs. However, within a Latino cultural assets paradigm, they take on significantly more importance. The importance placed on recognizing the influence of context (cultural and ecological) has resulted in an increased number of studies specifically focused on identifying how Latinos view their sociocultural circumstances, as a means for better informing program and service development.

Bishop and Sayeed (2003), for example, stress the importance of providers, in this case health personnel, being open to hear Latina perceptions of their circumstances. For example, Pearce's grounded research (1998) has focused on identifying Latina views of both pregnancy and prenatal care. Talashek and colleagues (2004) have focused their attention on identifying antecedents to unsafe sex to guide the development of HIV-prevention interventions targeting adult Latinas. Thus, an asset or need assessment must never lose sight of identifying how individuals, groups, or a community conceptualize their context and the awareness and meaning they place on circumstances. There is no substitute for this insight or input.

This stage represents the first "formal" attempt to enter the Latino community and the initial effort to identify and assess consumer and community assets (Delgado, 1999a, 2000). The availability of assets at the community level is tied to individual (client) consumer assets. An inventory of both is developed. It must be noted that identification and assessment of Latino assets is an ongoing process of discovery (Delgado, 1995a). Communities are highly dynamic, and changes are to be expected that impact community cultural assets. Thus, assessment will uncover assets that are newly arrived and assets that may no longer be there.

Reliance on data from governmental sources should not be counted upon as providing an accurate and updated picture of the Latino community, as already noted in the previous chapters. These data must be supplemented with qualitative data, particularly those gathered in a way that actively involves the community in shaping the nature of the information being gathered. Use of key informants (individuals in a propitious position to know the community and lend various types of legitimacy to the interventions) is highly recommended. Community "buy-in" into a project must commence at the start rather than as an afterthought.

Stage 3: Mapping Cultural Assets

The mapping stage represents an attempt to develop a visual and broader picture of community assets and how they can be mobilized in service to individuals and communities. Mapping within human services has historically focused on locating community problems, for example, the number and location of bars and liquor stores. From an assets perspective, mapping can be used to locate houses of worship that are playing particularly influential roles within a community or grocery stores that virtually all of the community patronize, and may be excellent locations for outreach and providing educational information on services and programs targeting the Latino community (Delgado & Rosati, 2005).

Mapping these resources can benefit social interventions focused on individual consumers as well as communities at large (Delgado, 2000). Further, mapping cultural assets can serve as a bridge between social workers focused on individuals and managers and planners interested in the "big picture" of a community. Both benefit from such mapping.

The mapping stage also represents an excellent chance to encourage and achieve participation from a wide sector of the Latino community, allowing for wide variety of input to take into account local circumstances. The visual presentation of a community's assets map also serves as an interactional (political) opportunity to involve the media—for example, showcasing the map in community fairs and events, and making it available for students to use in school-community learning assignments, for example (Delgado, 2006). So mapping fulfills a wide variety of program and organizational functions. It is necessary to remember that there are relatively few chances for the Latino community to be presented to the broader community in a positive light; the use of asset maps is one that lends itself to this goal quite well.

Stage 3 also represents a significant step in the planning of interventions. It is during this phase that social workers analyze the multitude of data gathered during the first three stages of the framework. This analysis, however, can only be as "sophisticated" as the data gathered. The greater depth and range of data gathered in the initial two stages, the more in-depth the analysis. Consequently, the emphasis placed on the initial two stages can best be thought of as an investment in a comprehensive analysis. Missing data will severely compromise the mapping stage and all of the stages that follow. This stage, not surprisingly, can require the expenditure of considerable amounts of time and resources, and may also entail having to go back into the community to gather additional data.

Stage 4: Building and Sustaining Relationships

The development of a collaborative relationship based upon mutual trust is a basic tenet of social work practice. In the case of the Latino cultural assets paradigm, it remains so and is expanded beyond one-to-one relationships to the Latino community at-large. Relationships based upon mutual trust and respect involving Latinos must also take into account language competencies of the social worker when dealing with those who have limited English proficiency. Consequently, there is a tremendous advantage when bilingual, and preferably bicultural, social workers are actively setting out to develop bridges an organization and the community.

Although relationships start from an initial contact between a social worker and a consumer of services, the goal of relationship building and sustenance is important enough to warrant its own individual phase, because it represents the bonding agent that will unite the helper with the helped. The stronger the bond, the easier it is to achieve the goals associated with any form of social intervention, at the micro or macro level.

This phase may involve holding meetings at community houses of worship to sponsor a program or service, or other places in a community that are usually not considered to be "appropriate" for meetings, such as beauty parlors or restaurants, for example. These places are selected because they meet the criteria advanced in chapter 4 (geographical, psychological, cultural, and operational accessibility). Social workers, as a result, must expand their vision of places and spaces within a community that can be enlisted in designing and implementing services. Broadening this conception will go a long way toward increasing access in the Latino community to social service organizations, and the building of bridges between the community and the organization in the process.

In the case of individually focused interventions, the social worker may, for example, meet with the head of the house of worship the consumer attends to set the stage for a the social worker and the head of the congregation to collaborate in implementing a particular service in the intervention stage of the framework. And perhaps this may also entail the creation of a project advisory committee consisting of key Latino gatekeepers in the community who can help guide the evolution of an intervention. However, regardless of how a relationship is structured, this stage of the paradigm represents the "social glue" that will serve to assist staff through good and not-so-good times in a project's implementation.

Stage 5: Intervention

This intervention stage is clearly the "bottom line" in any form of social intervention, and very often engages the greatest attention in any discussion of services to Latino communities. This stage will emphasize certain qualities, such as development of collaborative relationships between formal and community cultural assets, as well as numerous examples of different types of interventions that address both individual and community-focused intervention designs.

Latina beauty parlors are an excellent example. The use of these as settings for conducting a variety of social work practices, like their male counterparts, barbershops, represents an exciting development in the past five years. The emergence of beauty parlors as partners with health and social service organizations has started to open up new arenas for service delivery. Beauty parlors in marginalized communities are generally owned and operated by local residents. These persons, in turn, share the same language and cultural background as the residents. This facilitates communication, and acts as a facilitating factor in outreaching and assisting women, in this case Latinas, who for a variety of very good reasons may not feel comfortable accessing conventional health and social services.

As will be addressed in the following chapter, interventions based upon cultural assets can cover a range of goals, durations, resources, and staff deployments. Nevertheless, regardless of these factors, cultural assets–based interventions provide social workers with an opportunity to overcome barriers usually found between organizations and marginalized communities, and effectively integrate the worker within the social fabric of the community.

Stage 6: Evaluation

Evaluation of practice plays a central and important role in the design and implementation of any form of social intervention, particularly as the profession relies more heavily upon empirically informed practice (see chapter 5). This stage is no les important. Evaluation is usually conceptualized as consisting of both process and output objectives, and stresses identifying the strengths of an intervention and how to make it stronger. Special considerations related to the use of a Latino cultural assets paradigm, however, are required in order to make evaluation meaningful.

Evaluation based on a Latino cultural assets paradigm requires flexibility on the part of the organization and staff on how to define and measure success. Creation of methods for actively involving the ultimate beneficiaries of the services must be present in all facets of the evaluation process, including process (everything that needs to be accomplished in order to bring about a positive change), output (actual desired change), and impact (outcomes that reverberate throughout the community) objectives.

It is highly recommended that evaluation of a Latino cultural assets initiative be undertaken by a team composed of internal and external members. Although this model is both time-consuming and, therefore, financially costly, its value goes beyond the usual benefits associated with evaluation. This composition helps increase the likelihood of providing various forms of expertise to help ensure that all key aspects of the intervention are addressed. This process will invariably entail community members being trained and prepared to assume a variety of roles on the research team. Ideally, community members should be involved in all aspects of the evaluation, from the initial conceptualization to data analysis and report writing and dissemination (Delgado, 2006).

Considerations in Using a Latino Cultural Assets Paradigm

The framework I have outlined here has many qualities that will make it "attractive" for use by social workers across all spectrums of intervention, settings, and populations. This paradigm, for example, lends itself to interventions focused on individuals and families, as well as community and organizational levels. A Latino cultural assets paradigm, in addition, can be applied to youth as well as adults and work with Latino elders. This paradigm incorporates an analytical-interactional perspective that allows the practitioner to integrate the latest theoretical-empirical findings on best practices with Latinos. Further, it provides practitioners with a way to take into account sociopolitical factors and pressures that must not be ignored in the formation of any intervention. Further, this framework lends itself to developing collaborative partnerships with other human service organizations and making use of nontraditional settings (Delgado, 1999a).

The most important factor, however, is this paradigm's unique and affirming perspective on a community that is rarely viewed as possessing assets and is capable of making positive and long-lasting contributions to society. This "innovative" quality alone separates social workers who embrace cultural assets from those who take a "business as usual" perspective that is deficit driven.

No framework or paradigm, regardless of how well it is conceptualized, can be without limitations of various kinds, and the Latino cultural assets paradigm and framework proposed in this book are no exception. Special attention, as a consequence, needs to be paid to the following considerations.

1. The "newness" of the paradigm means that it has not provided academics with sufficient opportunities to evaluate its effectiveness. The emergence of any innovative social paradigm brings with it this limitation. One cannot expect any paradigm, including one based upon Latino cultural assets, to be embraced without considerable data on why it is effective, and for whom. This step, unfortunately, will require the passage of a considerable period of time.

2. The cultural assets paradigm advanced in this book is not taught in social work curricula, although parts of it are, and various aspects, such as strengths, resiliency, coping mechanisms, protective factors, and capacity enhancement, can be found in social work schools and departments throughout the country. Thus, with the exception of the readers of this book, mention of a Latino cultural assets paradigm will generally bring blank looks to most practitioners' faces.

3. The complexity of the Latino community, and the dynamic nature of demographic trends, makes obtaining an "accurate" picture of this community difficult to achieve. This makes any social paradigm that seeks to be encompassing, yet sensitive to local circumstances, difficult to grasp and bring to life in practice. There certainly is a prodigious leap between theory and practice. Although I have endeavored to narrow this gap, it would be foolish to think it does not exist.

4. Few, if any, organizations systematically gather data on assets of any group, let alone Latinos. Thus, the process of identifying cultural assets is labor intensive under the best of circumstances. I wish it were as simple as picking up a resource directory and systematically going through multiple categories of Latino cultural assets until we found the one we wanted. Then it would be as simple as picking up the telephone or emailing this resource. Nothing could be further from reality when discussing Latino cultural assets.

5. Funders of social work–related services invariably are only interested in addressing social problems and are not interested in community assets. This bias, unfortunately, permeates the use of the vast majority of resources in this society. Consequently, organizations, too, are only interested in initiating projects that meet the expectations of funders. Thus, if funders view Latino communities from a deficit perspective, funding with this bias follows, and organizations, in turn, create services along similar lines.

Any one of these five limitations is formidable in their own right. However, when present in any combination of more than one, and chances are very good that this will be the case, these limitations take on mythical proportions and can effectively dissuade social work organizations from embracing a paradigm that not only has tremendous potential to help Latino communities but also can be transformative in nature.

Conclusion

Social paradigms have historically shaped social work intervention frameworks. Some paradigms, such as the psychoanalytical, some would argue, have wielded too much influence, while others, particularly those embracing assets, have not. The Latino cultural assets paradigm covered in this chapter owes much of its existence to the scholarship originating in the 1980s and 1990s, and integrates empirically based evidence with practice wisdom achieved during a career developed in urban practice with marginalized communities of color, particularly Latinos. The past two decades have witnessed the advance of Latino culture as an asset in various manifestations, with natural support systems playing a critical role in this evolution.

The advancement of any "new" social paradigm brings with it excitement and skepticism, and that is to be expected. Ultimately, the "survivability" of any practice paradigm will rest in how "user-friendly" and "relevant" it is to the circumstances surrounding the group it is intended to help. Practitioners and consumers of services will be the ultimate judges. Academics will enter into this discussion if the paradigm has saliency. It thus becomes "survival of the most relevant" in the field of human services. Finally, it is necessary to emphasize that for practice to be effective, it must be contextualized, or grounded, to take into account local circumstances. This statement or theme, if you will, permeates much of my writings over the past three decades, and reflects my deepest belief that context shapes practice, and practice shapes context. One cannot have meaning without the other. However, the published literature on social work practice generally presents practice in a manner that conveys to the reader that techniques and approaches can be implemented as described, without taking into account how local circumstances may influence implementation. This perspective does a serious disservice to the field of practice.

Part III

A View from the Field

Chapter 8

PRACTICE APPLICATIONS
AND CONSIDERATIONS

Unfortunately, the dominance of the deficiency-oriented social
service model has led many people in low-income neighborhoods
to think in terms of local needs rather than assets. . . . The process
of identifying capacities and assets, both individual and
organizational, is the first step on the path towards community
regeneration.

John McKnight and John Kretzmann,
Mapping Community Capacity (1991)

The role and importance of social paradigms and frameworks (which
bring the paradigm to life, so to speak) is such that it is often taken
for granted in the development of social interventions. The field of social work,
as well as other helping professions, not surprisingly, is lacking in social paradigms to guide interventions. In many ways, social paradigms come and go, and
this is to be expected, and is very much driven by advances in research, degrees
of funding, the prestige of advocates, and "user-friendliness." Most take on the
trajectory of a new star in the horizon that eventually dies, with it being just a
question of time. Paradigms that enjoy a "long" lifespan, so to speak, do so because they have managed to capture the imagination of the practice world, have
proven relevant, and have been able to bear the pressures of research scrutiny.
Last, and probably most important, they have also attracted the attention of
policymakers and funders!

This chapter integrates the content covered in chapters 4–7, devoted to best
practice findings and principles, cultural values, and the Latino cultural assets
paradigm itself. The use a series of case vignettes to illustrate the applicability of
a Latino cultural assets paradigm in social work practice will be a central feature

of this chapter. Although case examples and illustrations have been integrated throughout this book, this chapter is specifically devoted to providing the reader with more in-depth examples to illustrate the various stages of a Latino cultural assets framework that brings to life the paradigm, and opens the door for creative thinking about other ways it can be utilized at the local level.

The case examples cover a wide variety of types, settings, and geographical locations throughout the country, in a concerted effort to draw national rather than regional implications. However, I must confess that these cases are heavily representative of urban practice in the northeastern part of the country, particularly New England. This "bias" is acknowledged and reflects my area of scholarly interest and practice opportunities. Nevertheless, practitioners in rural and other geographical regions of the country, I believe, can draw important implications for practice in their specific localities. Latino cultural assets, after all, are not the exclusive domains of any one geographical region of the country, and the paradigm lends itself to taking into account local circumstances to make it relevant to social work practice.

Practice Applications

I will utilize case examples to illustrate the six stages of the Latino cultural assets framework presented in chapter 7 and figure 7.2. A framework, it should be reiterated, is best conceptualized as no more than a "tool" that helps bring a social paradigm to life by providing a practitioner with a "guide" to the various elements that must be considered throughout all facets of an intervention. However, like any tool, it is only as good as the person using it. The "best" hammer in the world would be totally wasted on me, because I do not possess the requisite hand-eye coordination to effortlessly put a nail in a wall. The same hammer in the hands of a craftsperson, however, would result in a nail being hammered into the wall without any damage to the surrounding area. That would not be so in my case. I cannot blame the nail or the hammer, but must ultimately blame myself. Thus, a framework is only as good as the individual(s) who use it.

Not all practitioners, and I would include myself, are equally competent at all stages of a framework. Each stage requires not only a specific set of knowledge and competencies but also requisite attitudes that enhance the potential of the stage. Stage 1 is such a case in point. Fortunately, most social work interventions, in the case of macro or community-centered practice, involve a team of staff. The composition of this team, as a result, must be carefully thought out to ensure that members are complementary rather than duplicative in abilities. Gaps, in turn, can be filled through collaboration with other organizations, use of consultants, interns, volunteers, and so on.

The cases in this chapter will involve the following Latino cultural assets: *beauty parlors, barbershops, memorial murals, botanical shops, Pentecostal churches,* and *restaurants*. Unfortunately, space allows for only a brief snapshot of these cultural assets, with the exception of botanical shops. Some of these illustrations will specifically show social workers in practice, while others reflect the potential for social work interventions even though no social worker was involved. Nevertheless, regardless of the presence or absence of social workers, sufficient details will be provided to allow the reader to develop an appreciation of the tasks that are entailed in a particular stage of the Latino cultural assets framework.

This chapter will utilize one case example (botanical shops) throughout all six stages of the Latino cultural assets framework, and provides the reader with the benefits of one example that can be followed throughout all of the phases in the design, implementation, and evaluation. In addition, other case examples representing different types of Latino cultural assets will be presented in each of the stages to provide a different perspective, and thus enrich the readers' comprehension of how different cultural assets require modifications to achieve results.

This chapter, as a result, will be conceptualized in a manner unlike any other chapter in this book in order to highlight the importance of case illustrations. The discussion of each Latino cultural assets stage has four sections: (1) context setting; (2) case example focused on botanical shop; (3) case example involving other type(s) of Latino cultural asset; and (4) lessons learned and key considerations. Each of these sections will ground the reader in a particular aspect of the case examples. However, in order to facilitate the flow of case material on botanical shops and other cultural assets, I will first present a context for the botanical shop case.

Botanical Shop Background and Context

This section is intended to provide the reader with the background information needed for understanding the cultural asset that will be used as an example throughout the discussion—the botanical shop. The background has three facets, as follows.

1. *Geographical and Latino population profile*: As noted in chapter 2 and elsewhere in this book, the Latino community is increasing in number and diversity. Each geographical region of the country has experienced an increase in the influx of new Latino groups. In New England, Puerto Ricans have historically been the most visible Latino group. However, in Massachusetts, as well as other New England states, there has been an increase of Caribbean, Central, and South American groups in the past decade. Of these groups, Dominicans have made the most numerically significant strides, particularly in medium-sized cities in the state. Mexicans, however, have shown a dramatic increase in the last five years (2000–5), as well as along the eastern seacoast.

Lawrence, Massachusetts, located 25 miles north of Boston, and has a population of approximately 72,000, making it the fourth largest city in the state. Lawrence has a rich tradition of being a haven for newcomers going back to the Industrial Revolution. The Latino community numbers approximately 43,000, or 59.7 percent of the total population, making it the city with the highest representation of Latinos in Massachusetts. The Puerto Rican and Dominican communities are almost evenly represented; the former accounts for 15,800, or 36.8 percent of the total Latino community, and the latter numbers 13,800, or 32 percent (U.S. Bureau of the Census, 2001). The Dominican community in Lawrence represents the nation's largest proportion of Dominicans in a city, although numerically the number of Dominicans in New York City is the largest. Lawrence, as a result, is a unique city with a history on immigration that brings a rich tradition to this subject. However, the Latino community and particularly its cultural assets are not unique, and there are lessons and applicability to other sections of the country.

2. *Complementary theoretical foundation*: The Latino cultural assets paradigm expounded in this book does not exist in total isolation from a variety of other social paradigms that stress viewing people and communities from a strengths perspective, and the paradigm can be complementary in nature. The Latino cultural assets paradigm is broad in scope and can incorporate a variety of concepts and constructs that are currently used in the field of social work and human services.

The concept advocated by Portes and Sensebrenner (1993) is such an example, and lends itself well to viewing cultural assets, in this case, botanical shops. Portes and Sensebrenner (1993, p. 1329) draw upon the construct of social capital to ground their social embeddedness perspective toward the Latino community: "a more common use of social capital is the creation and consolidation of small enterprises. A solitary ethnic community represents, simultaneously, a market for culturally defined goods, a pool of reliable labor, and a potential start for start-up capital."

The greater the distance (cultural and linguistic) between the "old" country and the "new" receiving country, the greater the cultural tension and clash; this ultimately may result in a group developing their own network (bounded solidarity), with minimal contact with the host society, as a means to help ensure their safety and survival. This tension is further exacerbated if the group is largely undocumented. Bounded solidarity serves to both reinforce cultural traditions and minimize the influence of the "outside" world through the fostering of internal reliance on goods and services.

3. *Botanical shops—description and roles*: Botanical shops represent an important source of social—or what I prefer to call cultural—capital in the Latino community. In addition, botanical shops give the owners of community-owned businesses with an opportunity to assume the role of what Pfeffer (1994) calls a "social buffer." This construct fits well within Portes and Sensebrenner's (1993) bounded solidarity and the Latino cultural assets paradigm used in this book.

Social buffers are individuals within a community, in this case Latino, who assume the social role of reinforcing cultural norms and values, provide access to the external community, and thus stabilize a community. These gatekeepers, so to speak, function as brokers and standard-setters for the newcomer community.

Bounded solidarity and social buffering provides a context for botanical shops to develop and thrive, particularly in Latino communities that largely consist of newcomers, and no more so than among those who are undocumented, have limited English proficiency, and, to use a concept covered earlier and throughout, have a low level of acculturation. Botanical shops represent an important source of cultural capital in the Latino community and a culturally accepted way for achieving entrepreneurial goals, serving as a vehicle for meeting a wide range of health and social service needs for residents. These individuals may either mistrust the host society or have limited access to quality health and social service resources because of discrimination, poverty, documented status, or limited English proficiency.

The professional literature on botanical shops, as already noted in chapter 6, is very limited in scope and depth. Featherstone's (1992, p. 32) description of a New York City botanical shop, although almost 15 years old, is still very relevant today and captures the vibrancy of this establishment:

> Santos Variety is a slightly misleading name for the store, since the variety is confined to four groups of products; the greeting cards in Spanish and English on the rack at the center of the sales floor, the music on cassettes in the center case, the cotton crocheted yarn in a rack in the back, and the paraphernalia of Santeria that lines the walls and dominates the scene. This concentration is duly noted on the front window, upon which is painted, in cherry yellow and red paint, the word "Botanica."

Featherstone's description of a botanical shop holds true for botanical shops throughout the country. The size of these establishments may differ, as well as the extensiveness of their inventory. However, their role and function within Latino communities goes far beyond that of a pharmacy. These establishments also fulfill important cultural roles and help bridge life between the "old" and "new" country for countless numbers of Latinos who find themselves in need of various types of health care. The selling of products that can be considered outside of the "medicinal" realm is an attempt to expand the economic base of the business to draw in customers who normally would not have to patronize a botanical shop. The health role of Latino botanical shops is not diminished by their effort to sell "commercial" products. Community residents, as a result, may patronize a botanical shop for a variety of reasons other than seeking health-related products and services.

Well-established (historically and numerically) Latino communities will have several botanical shops of various sizes. However, in emerging Latino communities, this function may be fulfilled by bodegas (grocery stores). These grocery stores may set aside a section of the store devoted to herbs and other healing paraphernalia to meet this demand. However, once the community expands numerically, it can then financially support a botanical shop. These cultural institutions will invariably work alongside folk healers in the community, and carry out the "prescriptions" given by these healers. Thus, the presence of botanical shops is also indicative of the presence of folk healers.

In 2005, UCLA's Fowler Museum presented an exhibition, probably one of the first of its kind in the country, titled "Botanica Los Angeles: Latino Popular Religious Art in the City of Angels." This exhibition highlighted botanicas from artistic, cultural, and religious perspectives (MacGreger, 2005). The importance of these establishments will only increase among Latinos as their numbers increases. Botanical shops are the only culturally based institution that have specifically targeted health care needs as their primary purpose within the Latino community. Consequently, these establishments are in strategic positions to reach individuals who are either dissatisfied with established medical institutions or have not accessed them because of a lack of health insurance (see chapter 3).

Stage 1: Precontact/ Intervention Considerations

Context Setting

As already addressed in chapter 7, the precontact/intervention stage in a Latino cultural assets paradigm is critical, and effectively sets the stage for all of the other stages to follow. It is a foundation upon which an intervention will rest. A solid foundation is essential to help ensure that an intervention can weather all of the trials and tribulations inherent in social interventions of any kind, but particularly those addressing undervalued communities. It is never possible to anticipate all of the potential problem areas an intervention will encounter in the course of its history. However, it is possible to minimize the type and number of pitfalls through careful deliberations and planning.

The precontact/intervention stage is of sufficient importance to warrant its "official" category, and must not be taken for granted prior to initiating a project. Specifically designating it a *stage* forces social workers to set aside the time and resources necessary to address the multitude of goals associated with it. Further, this provides the "space" and "legitimacy" for candid dialogue to transpire that facilitates all parties within an organization voicing their hopes and concerns about a new initiative.

Some social workers may be particularly inclined to develop assessment and evaluation instruments, while others prefer to do actual interviews, for example. Reaching out to meaningfully involve the Latino community is another example that highlights the importance of the "right" social worker doing this. Some of us feel quite comfortable in making visits to homes, houses of worship, botanical shops, or beauty parlors, for example. However, some of us may not feel that we can do this in a manner that effectively encourages Latino participation in the design of a project. Thus, it is very important for social workers and other human service professionals to acknowledge situations as being difficult, and identify what indigenous institutions are particularly challenging for us to visit.

Botanical Shop

The engagement of Latino cultural assets such as botanical shops (see chapter 6) provides an excellent example of the types of deliberations that must transpire before moving onto the next stage. Any effort to involve Latino botanical shops in an intervention will engender both goodwill and criticism within the community. The Latino community, I am afraid, is no different. Sometimes the disagreements may reflect age-old rivalries between organizations or between Latino groups representing different countries of origin, even tensions between those born and raised in this country and newcomers. These sentiments, or "feelings," are further compounded when the initiative involves a highly stigmatizing disease such as HIV/AIDS, as in this case study.

The example of Lawrence, Massachusetts, illustrates this key consideration. Lawrence, which is almost evenly divided between Puerto Ricans and Dominicans, has a long history of tensions between these two Latino groups. These tensions are well acknowledged and have a tendency to emerge in all social spheres, including the world of social services. It is also necessary to note that differences of opinion between these two communities are not universally shared, and key stakeholders in both communities have actively searched for ways of bringing them together in pursuit of common goals.

A collaborative partnership was developed between a Latino community–based multiservice organization and me. This organization wanted to develop more community-centered services for outreaching to high-risk HIV Latinos living in the city who were at high risk for HIV infection. Involvement of botanical shops represented a natural linkage, particularly in light of the health care services provided by this cultural asset. Botanical shops are cultural variations of pharmacies in this society, and a consequence are often a critical asset in Latinos' seeking health care. These cultural assets take on prominence in cases where Latinos have Limited English Proficiency and are not highly acculturated.

An assets inventory and assessment of the community's botanical shop was thought to be the first, and least controversial, step in the creation of a collaborative project. In addition, it would provide critical information on the receptivity of individual botanical shops, along with data on how botanical shop staff and owners viewed HIV/AIDS, and the role of the medical establishment in helping Latinos infected with this disease. Once this assessment was conducted, an informed deliberation could transpire as to which botanical shops would be most amenable to engaging in a system of shops referring people to the organization for the purposes of testing high-risk Latinos, along with a better understanding of the administrative and operational logistics to be weighed in developing a training program for botanical shop owners, and an outreach and referral intervention.

Deliberations involved assessments of the following: (1) helping and hindering forces within and outside of the Latino community; (2) the qualities and availability of staff to carry out the assessment; (3) the best time period in which to venture out to engage the community; (4) where and with whom within the community it was best to start; (5) reasonable objectives to achieve; (6) how much time and resources should be deployed for each stage of the intervention; and (7) what potential of-shoots in interventions could result from a successful project.

Each of these considerations brings with it another set of subquestions that require answering, for example, how will the backgrounds of Latino staff, such as their countries of origin and gender, be received within the community? The decision to match Latino backgrounds and gender is not an easy one to arrive at because of the sensitivities involved, and the possible limited options in cases where the organization has only one or two Latinos on its staff. Nevertheless, these questions must be raised and answered in the best manner possible so as to increase the likelihood that these, and other sociopolitical points, do not serve as insurmountable barriers.

Latino staff undertaking an assessment involving botanical shops must be prepared to answer personal questions pertaining to their ethnic background, place of birth, type of work they usually do, and, most important, spiritual belief systems. Not every social worker, be they Latino or otherwise, may feel "comfortable" with this type of interaction. Further, the reader is warned that even when questions and considerations are raised and answered appropriately, issues can still emerge as in the case of botanical shops. There was one situation in which one of the field interviewers experienced great anxiety. At the conclusion of one interview, the botanical shop owner volunteered to raise key issues and concerns that she perceived the interviewer to be experiencing in her life. The interviewer concluded that these observations were very accurate, and called to mind previous experiences she had had with folk healers that were unpleasant. However, she had thought that she had dealt with these experiences well in the past, and had "moved on." Thus, not every Latino staff member who is a resident of the community will be willing to engage botanical shops. Some degree of "discomfort" with these establishments may interfere with the establishment of a working relationship based on mutual trust.

Other Latino Cultural Asset

I include discussion of two case illustrations involving memorial murals in this stage because these cultural forms of expression are ever present in Latino communities across the United States, yet there is almost a total absence of understanding of their origins and the therapeutic role they play in the lives of countless numbers of Latino families struck by various kinds of tragedy. Thus, the potential of memorial murals as a Latino cultural asset has only recently been recognized and tapped to aid Latino families in their bereavement process (Delgado, 2003). Nowhere are they as prominent as a cultural resource as in marginalized urban Latino communities (Cooper & Sciorra, 1994).

Memorial murals can be defined as artistic murals that have been commissioned by family, friends, or loved ones to help celebrate the life of someone whose life was cut short as a result of violence or illness. Invariably, these commissioned public art forms are the result of tragic acts, and therefore symbolize a lost life. Although not restricted to any age or gender group, the vast majority of memorial murals involve the death of someone who is young and male. The memorial mural can best be conceptualized as a mural genre. These murals differ from their more conventional counterparts because of the tragic circumstances surrounding their existence and purpose. They are usually painted near or at the spot where an individual lost his or her life and his or her soul departed this earth.

Latino culture has a long and distinguished history of embracing murals as windows into the life and soul of a community. Conventional Latino murals can depict a variety of themes that can be celebratory, historical, and embracing of a sociopolitical stance on life in the United States for the Latino community (Delgado, 2000). Memorial murals, however, always provide a voice for the family and friends of the deceased, as well as the broader community.

Two memorial mural projects will be discussed here. One represents the typical commissioning process of a family member dedicating a mural to a deceased member. The second involves a human service organization commissioning the mural. Both murals, however, involve the New York City police—one from a critical standpoint and the other from a positive one. Both situations entailed serious dialogue between interested parties before the murals were painted.

The memorial mural commissioned by Mr. and Mrs. Rosado (Bronx, New York City) highlights the sociopolitical existence of Latinos in this country, and particularly the generally contentious relationship between the community and the police. The second memorial mural (Brooklyn, New York City), in turn, presents a different experience involving police-community relations, and was commissioned by a youth agency (Crown Heights Youth Collaborative) to celebrate the life of a police officer killed in the line of duty. Both of these memorial mural case examples illustrate the importance of stage 1, and the deliberations, or dialogue, that must be undertaken before initiating a Latino cultural assets intervention.

The memorial mural commissioned by Mr. and Mrs. Rosado was intended to celebrate the lives of their child and nephew, who were killed by the police in a shootout. The mural, however, went beyond the more conventional story depicted in memorial murals and explicitly took on a sociopolitical issue, namely, police brutality. The mural, in addition, maintains a listing of individuals killed in police shootouts across the country and raises important issues pertaining to racism. Mrs. Rosado met with a memorial mural painting crew (TATS CRU) to paint the mural. She initially wanted the artists to show that these Puerto Rican youth were assassinated by the police. However, the artists raised concerns about their own safety if they granted this request. In fact, one of the artists' parents called Mrs. Rosado and asked if she would not put her son in danger with the police. Mrs. Rosado agreed, and suggested a compromise.

The painting of the memorial mural was done on the side of the Rosado home, which they owned. Community reactions covered the gamut from very positive, with statements being made about the importance of the mural and the bravery of the Rosados to negative, for example, asking why put the police department in such negative light and why bring such a mural to a residential community that is trying to forget the tragedy?

The Crown Heights Youth Initiative sponsored memorial mural of a 29-year-old patrolman, Jeff B. Herman, is unique in two regards. First, it is one of a very few memorial murals commissioned by a human services organization. This organization has sponsored several neighborhood memorial murals in the past. Second, there are also very few memorial murals commissioned by communities to honor the life and service of patrolmen in this country. This memorial consisted of four key images: (1) Patrolman Herman's patrol car; (2) a picture of the emblem of the Police Department of the City of New York; (3) a picture of Patrolman Herman; and (4) an "elegy" to a police officer.

The sponsoring organization solicited and obtained extensive community input into this intervention, including input on the size and location of the mural. The following elegy was created and provides insight into how the community struggled with the untimely death of Patrolman Herman (Cooper & Sciorra, 1994, p. 45).

> On a fateful day, with kindness, and courage and respect in his heart, was called to the test; one of the best; a-peace officer, protector, peaceful warrior, kind-spirit, proud father, husband, good man & friend—new york's finest, peace officer, bearer of love, truth, justice, order & strength; faith, fairness, trust & kindness. He ran to a citizen in distress, to his ultimate fate without a slight hesitate or debate sought to save a citizen from another's hate; our best to relate, a peace officer, on that ill-feeling day, he went on his way, as a peace officer, the ultimate to pay—in celebration of the life of officer Jeff b. Herman, (pop 71st, born; May 1, 1964—who give his life—. . . . June 2, 1989. . . .

Public art, by its very nature, tends to create controversy and dialogue. If properly anticipated and planned for, much good can result from it. In Latino communities, murals are a cultural manifestation that can be found in all Latin American countries and serve as a unifying mechanism for providing disenfranchised communities with a voice in articulating their passions, fears, and hopes, for the future. The use of memorial murals to help the bereavement process for the families of the deceased and their communities offers tremendous potential for social workers working with death and dying. However, as already noted, use of Latino cultural assets in interventions will not be without critics, and this necessitates that the conversations taking place in stage 1 be deliberate and candid. Otherwise, when the controversies emerge, social workers and the organizations that sponsor memorial murals can find themselves caught off guard, with disastrous consequences. I do not say this to dissuade social workers from embracing public art as a vehicle for creating positive community change. It simply means that we must try and anticipate potential reactions.

I remember one situation where a family commissioned a memorial mural and the local Catholic priest, at a mass, raised public concerns about this form of art work and why it was detrimental to the community. The controversy that ensued effectively alienated various sectors of the community from each other. Stage 1 is meant to anticipate and minimize adverse reactions from within the Latino community.

Lessons Learned and Key Considerations

This stage reflects all of the hopes and tensions involved in reaching out to a newcomer community, such as that represented by Latinos. There are so many different perspectives on how best to serve this community, and with a multitude of views come tensions and insecurities. The creation of an atmosphere that understands and encourages different perspectives is essential to make this stage of the framework live up to its potential, and to minimize unforeseen circumstances. *Minimize*, not totally avoid, the unexpected! Even when potential controversial issues and considerations are raised, and it is believed they have been successfully addressed, as in the case of botanical shops, this does not mean that "uncomfortable" situations will not emerge.

The case examples of botanical shops and memorial murals reflect two dramatically different views of a Latino cultural asset that are unified by a view of the community that encourages community members to explore their strengths, even in moments of sadness. Both of these examples highlight the importance of team members being open to dialogue and debate, and being encouraged to broaden their horizons in perceiving what constitutes a "legitimate" intervention. Partnerships involving botanical shops and the commissioning of memorial

murals are generally not thought of as being social work interventions. However, when using a Latino cultural assets paradigm, they certainly enter the
sphere of social interventions.

This stage, in addition, sets the foundation and should not be minimized for
the sake of fast-tracking a project or withholding the time and resources that
should be devoted to this stage. Nevertheless, finding the right blend between
serious thought and finding an excuse for not acting is not easy, and there is no
magic formula that can be used to help social workers decide when there has been
enough considerations, and when it is time to move onto the next stage.

Stage 2: Initial Contact
and Assets Identification

Context Setting

Most social paradigms and frameworks generally start with this stage of an
intervention, and essentially take for granted the first stage addressed earlier.
However, to do this would be foolhardy in the case of the Latino cultural assets
paradigm, because the time and effort devoted to precontact considerations actually informs and ultimately shapes how stage 2 gets conceptualized and implemented, and represents a considerable amount of planning.

The initial contact in an effort to assess Latino community assets is an propitious moment to accomplish the following goals: (1) actually documenting an
asset; (2) establishing a relationship; (3) helping to overcome stereotypes that
each party has of the other; (4) providing the community with an opportunity
to "buy in" and shape the intervention from the beginning of the planning process; (5) assessing potential for future projects; and (6) identifying potential areas
of conflict or differences of opinion that can prove problematic later in the life of
a project. These six goals are just a few examples of the benefits that can be
achieved if this stage gets planned and implemented in a deliberate manner, with
the guidance of a set of philosophical principles that stress participation, empowerment, and partnership with cultural assets.

This stage necessitates a considerable amount of fieldwork in the community
because of the general absence of data on cultural assets. For example, there are
no "resource directories" I am familiar with that specifically focus on providing
information on Latino cultural assets, as one would typically find in "formal"
resource directories. Consequently, staff must be prepared to spend extended
periods of time in the community, and possibly time outside of the "usual" work
hours, because a nine-to-five or Monday-to-Friday timeframe does not regulate
community life. This operational access dimension often proves quite challenging when staff view their responsibilities as falling within a highly prescribed time
period. Flexibility in how work responsibilities get carried out, rather than a rigid

focus on time period, is essential to better understanding the Latino community, and for the community to better get to know and understand a social worker.

The undertaking of a Latino cultural assets assessment represents a critical step in the development of an intervention, be it outreach, educational, or referral driven, for example. The process of conducting such an assessment, as noted in chapter 7, is usually conceptualized as a two-step process (Delgado, 1999a, 2000). The initial step is one of identifying and obtaining pertinent information on the establishment, such as location, days and hours of operation, and key contact person (usually the owner, in the case of a business). The second step involves actually interviewing key personnel and assessing their receptivity to engaging in collaborative endeavors with an organization.

These interviews, needless to say, are extremely important because they represent the first organized attempt at establishing a collaborative partnership. These interviews provide the owner of the establishment with a chance to express his or her concerns, as well as hopes, about a partnership. It is important to remember that these individuals have rarely been approached to engage in partnerships with social workers and other helping professionals. Consequently, much time and effort will need to be devoted to answering numerous questions that typically would not be a part of a process involving other professionals. It is best to conceptualize this process of assessment as also a process of relationship building, and setting the stage for collaborative partnership. Doing this makes the expenditure of time and energy on this stage more meaningful and easier to substantiate for administrators and funders.

Botanical Shop

The presence of botanical shops in Latino communities has generally not been considered a cultural asset by the broader health and social service community. These indigenous institutions, although not as ubiquitous as grocery stores (bodegas) and restaurants, are still very prominent, and are invariably situated within the commercial district of the Latino community, and therefore are easily geographically accessible, not to mention the other dimensions of accessibility addressed in chapter 4.

A 15-block area of Lawrence was selected, because of its high density of Latino residents, commercial establishments, and botanical shops, and all eight botanical shops in this area were interviewed. This stage consisted of two distinct phases. The identification phase located botanical shops and obtained information on the following: (1) name of shop; (2) address; (3) telephone number if easily available; (4) type of botanical shop (three types, with each type representing different organizational levels); and (5) comments and observations of the field interviewer. The latter category specifically focused on geographical proximity to other Latino establishments and the external physical condition of the shop.

The second phase entailed a detailed interview with the owner of the botani-cal shop or his or her designee, which lasted between 10 to 40 minutes, depend-ing upon the degree of cooperation, and sought information on the following items: (1) identifying information on the shop; (2) characteristics of the owner; (3) types of services provided; (4) willingness of the owner to participate in fu-ture interventions; (5) description of the shop; and (6) commentary and ob-servations of the interviewer. Each of these areas of information allowed the interviewer and interviewee to exchange perspectives, thoughts, and personal information. The qualitative nature of this stage also facilitates the development of a social relationship between the botanical shop owner and the interviewer, thus setting the stage for a possible collaborative partnership.

A total of eight botanical shops were located, and five agreed to be interviewed. The three shops that refused to be interviewed expressed serious reservations about the process, for example, concern about how the information obtained would be used, and the lack of time for interviews, although no time period was considerable suitable. The high percentage of refusals (39 percent) is similar to that reported by Delgado and Rosati (2005) in their study of Puerto Rican Pen-tecostal churches, when 7 out of 18 churches (39 percent) refused to participate in their study.

Other Latino Cultural Asset

Another Latino cultural asset in Lawrence, Massachusetts, was Latina beauty parlors in generally the same geographical area of the botanical shop assessment. This assessment sought to develop a better understanding of the role these es-tablishments play within the Latino community, and more specifically with Latinas. A total of seven beauty parlors owned by Latinas were identified and interviewed. These establishments, unlike their botanical counterparts, drew upon a broader client base that went beyond the Latina community; in the case of some of the beauty parlors, up to 25 percent of their customers were non-Latina in origin, with the low being 10 percent.

In similar fashion to their botanical shop counterparts, none of these estab-lishments had ever been approached by a human service agency to collaborate on a community-centered project. When asked about the extent of collabora-tion, all said they would be willing to distribute pamphlets. However, only two were willing to show public health–related videos in their shops; four out of the eight said that they would sponsor lectures or discussion groups; six were will-ing to offer counseling or advice as needed; and three were willing to make re-ferrals. Only two, however, were willing to do all of these activities. Thus, careful strategizing for involving this Latino cultural asset can provide human service organizations with increased options in seeking and obtaining community par-ticipation in initiatives that meet community needs.

Although it will not be addressed again in any of the subsequent stages, this effort at identifying and assessing Latina beauty parlors is generally not different from the efforts to do so for the other Latino cultural assets covered in this chapter. Gender, as in the case of Latino barber shops, however, becomes a critical element and effectively taps the interest (humanitarian as well as financial) of Latina beauty parlor owners, because of their concerns about the community in general but also because of their customer base. Gender, as a result, serves to allow all of the stages to focus on this demographic factor. Latino cultural assets can thus be viewed from either a multifaceted perspective that is inclusive or one that is exclusive, as the case in point with Latinas and beauty parlors.

Lessons Learned/ Key Considerations

The initial contact stage effectively grounds the social worker within a community context, facilitates the initiation of a relationship, helps inform the following stages, and represents the first "formal" and concrete effort to venture out of the agency and into the community. The exact amount of time needed to conduct interviews is very difficult to judge, since it depends upon the willingness and availability of the interviewee and the competencies of the interviewer, the number of distractions (as in the case of commercial establishments), and the depth of the questions being asked and degree of "sharing" of the interviewer. Nevertheless, this stage generates a wealth of information that will play a critical role in dictating program design, potential helping and hindering forces, and the extent to which Latino cultural assets can be counted upon to enter partnerships.

Stage 3: Mapping Cultural Assets

Context Setting

The creation of a Latino cultural assets map signifies an important step for both the community and the organization sponsoring the effort. Maps, it should be emphasized, have historically been created by society's elites to serve the goals and purposes that they have identified. Communities, particularly those that have been socially marginalized in this society, generally are not provided with an opportunity to identify what kind of maps would be beneficial to them. Consequently, the development of a map, in this case one identifying assets, will be a totally new and, I would argue, empowering experience, and one that should be used whenever possible by social workers.

Sufficient time must be set aside to orient participants to the role maps can play in helping to shape Latino cultural assets interventions. Mapping is as much about group process as it is about analysis. Both must be present to make this stage successful. Ultimately, the greater the participant involvement in the analysis and decisions, the greater the "ownership" of the project and outcomes. This point takes on greater significance when the evaluation stage is discussed.

Botanical Shop

The mapping stage, as noted in chapter 7, is the stage during which not only are data "mapped" but specific cultural and contextual factors are analyzed and interventions fine-tuned. The mapping of the botanical shops involved a two-step process, as already outlined in the previous chapter: (1) obtaining a map of the geographical area being assessed and enlarging it to six or more times its normal size (this facilitates group dialogue), and (2) locating the botanical shops on the map and using pins of different colors to designate the number of years in operation (red symbolized 5 years or longer, yellow covered 1.1 to 4.11 years, and blue 1 year or less).

Not surprisingly, as shown in table 8.1, the botanical shop ("D") with the oldest owner is also the shop with the greatest longevity. Two of the five botanical shops participating in the assessment had been open for less than one year, and one shop for one year. This upsurge in the number of botanical shops may be typical or untypical. Not having longitudinal data did not allow for an in-depth assessment of whether this upsurge was cyclical or represented a dramatic development within the Latino community. All of the establishments were opened Monday through Saturday, and generally shared the same operating hours.

Table 8.2 provides pertinent information related to the owners, and represents a rare effort to actually develop a profile of the individuals behind this Latino establishment. The high level of formal education of shop owners (four out of five were high school graduates), combined with very limited previous full-time employment history, limited their potential employment in the health field in the country. Further, only one individual ("B") indicated that she had had previous work experience in botanical shops prior to owning this business. Consequently, ownership of a botanical shop may be one of the few avenues for Latinos to enter a helping profession in the health field in the United States, and it is a venue that may not require previous work experience in the area.

TABLE 8.1. Characteristics of Botanical Shops

Botanical shop	No. of years open	Days open	Hours of operation
"A"	4	Mon.–Sat.	9:30–6:00
"B"	0	Mon.–Sat.	9:00–6:00
"C"	0	Mon.–Sat.	10:00–6:00
"D"	12	Mon.–Sat.	9:00–6:00
"E"	1	Mon.–Sat.	8:00–8:00

TABLE 8.2. Characteristics of Botanical Shop Owners

Botanical shop	Said they possess "special" healing powers	Ethnic background of owner	Gender	Current age	Formal education level	Previous experience working in botanical shops	No. of previous (nonbotanical shop) full-time jobs
"A"	Yes	Dominican	Female	32	12	No	None
"B"	Yes	Puerto Rico	Female	23	12	Yes	None
"C"	Yes	Dominican	Female	36	12	No	None
"D"	Yes	Cuban	Female	51	12	No	None
"E"	Yes	Dominican	Female	41	7	No	None

Table 8.2 also shows the diversity of owners' countries of origins, with three being born in the Dominican Republic, another in Cuba, and another in Puerto Rico. None of the owners had had previous full-time work outside of the home prior to establishing or purchasing the business, and only one said that she had previously worked in a botanical shop prior to her current ownership. All of the owners said that they had "special healing powers" and that this was definitely an asset in their business. All of the owners indicated that this power was a gift from God and that it has always been a part of their lives. All of the shops were owned by Latinas ; these women's average age was 35. There are few businesses (other than beauty parlors) that lend themselves to ownership by Latinas. Healing establishments, such as centros (spiritist centers) and botanical shops, are probably the only types of businesses that are open to Latinas, both as healers and entrepreneurs.

Table 8.3 gives information on the types of social services provided by botanical shops. Latino botanical shops, unlike other establishments such as bodegas (grocery stores), restaurants, and religious institutions, do not offer an extensive range of social services. Studies conducted in other cities in Massachusetts involving food establishments (grocery stores and restaurants), for example, showed that they provided an average of 3.4 types of social services. Pentecostal churches provided an average of 7.3 types. Others—beauty parlors and clothing, dry goods, and appliance repair businesses, for example—provided an average of 2.83 services. Nevertheless, botanical shops averaged 3.4, services with a high range of 5 and a low of 2, with the oldest botanical shop ("D") providing the highest number of services.

Other Latino Cultural Asset

Latino barbershops have not received the same level of attention as their female counterparts , even though they fulfill many of the same roles within the community. Intrabartola (2002) notes that barbers and their customers develop a strong bond, and that this bond can cut across generational levels, race and ethnicity, and country of origin. The mapping of barbershops took place in Worcester, Massachusetts.

Worcester, like Lawrence, is a city with a long history of attracting immigrants to work in its industry, in this case the shoe industry. Worcester is the third largest city in Massachusetts, and is located approximately 40 miles west of Boston. Its Latino community has historically been predominantly Puerto Rican, although other Latino groups have started to enter the city in the past decade. A section of the downtown area of Worcester (Main Street South) was selected for an assessment and mapping of Latino barber shops because of its high concentration of Latinos, its geographical accessibility, and the relationship between the community-based organization and the Latino community in that area, thus facilitating the tapping of this Latino cultural asset.

TABLE 8.3. Social Services Provided by Botanical Shops

Botanical shop	Consider themselves as providing a community service	Willing to collaborate	Financial assistance	Information and referral	Assistance in locating housing	Assistance in locating food	Counseling for personal problems	Number of services
"A"	Yes	Yes	No	Yes	No	No	Yes	2
"B"	Yes	Yes	Yes	Yes	No	No	Yes	3
"C"	Yes	Yes	No	Yes	Yes	Yes	Yes	4
"D"	Yes	Yes	Yes	Yes	Yes	Yes	Yes	5
"E"	Yes	Yes	Yes	No	No	Yes	Yes	3
Number of total responses	5	5	3	4	2	3	5	X3.4

The mapping of Latino barbershops in Worcester only identified two Latino barber shops in the area, many fewer than the botanical shops that were mapped in Lawrence. Nevertheless, the low number of Latino-owned barber shops did not discourage movement forward with an intervention; in this case, one of distributing information on social services available in the geographical area. The geographical area was experiencing a rapid and quite dramatic increase in newcomers, who may not have been familiar with local resources.

A map is a powerful piece of paper that lends itself to travel, input, and sharing with other human service organizations. Although only two barbershops were located, the process followed was similar to the Lawrence process. Both of the barber shop owners willingly shared information on the shops' history, their ownership, and the services they provided. This information, in turn, was easily mapped. Participants, in turn, were provided with copies of the maps to share with family, neighbors, and friends, to allow their input and insights.

Lessons Learned and
Key Considerations

There is a tremendous amount of flexibility in how the mapping stage can be used within a Latino cultural assets paradigm. Its flexibility can accommodate a wide range in budgets and levels of data analysis, and most important, provides a tool for encouraging community participation. Mapping, in effect, becomes an empowering tool that is within the grasp of any community, regardless of how marginalized it is within this society. Further, it opens the door for communities to use maps to meet their own needs rather than allowing elites to dictate how maps are constructed. The mapping stage, in addition, takes on added significance when used within a group format because it encourages all members to view the same item and to participate in sharing reactions and thoughts. Social workers in these situations effectively become facilitators of a dynamic group process that can be quite powerful in laying the foundation for the other stages to follow.

This stage of the Latino cultural assets framework is probably best carried out by staff who have solid group work skills, since the group method is the preferred method of practice. As noted in chapter 7, participants need to play an active role in helping to analyze data gathered during stage 2, and in the process of doing so, in helping to develop, or modify, potential interventions. Community input represents a critical element of this stage, as evidenced in both the botanical and beauty parlor shop assessments. The insights created during the process of analyzing the distribution of Latino cultural assets are best accomplished in staff partnership with community participants. They have a true sense of history surrounding these assets, and also possess insights into why they may be located in certain geographical regions of the community, and the profile of who patronizes these establishments.

Holders of Latino cultural assets have the right to refuse participation in any form of partnership with social service organizations, social-work-staffed or otherwise. However, not asking them represents a serious breach of respect for the Latino community. These establishments may initially say no, but can change their minds at some future point, as I will note later on. Either way, the Worcester and Lawrence examples illustrate the value of mapping as a tool for increasing participation and empowerment.

Stage 4: Building and Sustaining Relationships

Context Setting

The reader may well be puzzled by the presence of a stage specifically devoted to the goals of building and sustaining relationships. This facet of an intervention is of such critical importance that it not only warrants its own stage but also must permeate all stages. Thus, I find it necessary to set aside time and resources devoted to the goals of this stage. This stage provides the practitioner with an opportunity to reexamine the extent and success of the relationship building that has occurred during the previous three stages. It is only then that a specific relationship-sustaining agenda can be developed.

This stage can involve one-on-one meetings, group meetings, community-wide meetings, or all or any combination of these. Beauty parlors in Pawtucket, Rhode Island, are a good example of how interventions, if successful, can create a demand for collaboration between social service organizations and Latino cultural assets. This stage is best characterized by face-to-face contact, sharing of oneself (see chapter 6), discussion of concerns that holders of Latino cultural assets may have about involvement with social service organizations, and the development of procedures to safeguard against outcomes about which concerns have been voiced.

In the case of Latina beauty parlors, these concerns have touch upon fears that beauty shop personnel might be overwhelmed by opening up avenues for customers to share their personal problems, developing reputations (lack of confidentiality) that can scare away customers, doing the "wrong thing" in response to customer problems and making matters worse, devoting time to helping customers that may cut into business profits, open up the "flood gates" to other social service organizations requesting more of their time and services.

Botanical Shop

On the basis of an analysis of data mapped in stage 3, a decision was made to hold a meeting of the five botanical shops that had agreed to participate in the assessment for possible collaboration in an HIV intervention that would involve them in outreach and referral of Latinos who were at high risk for HIV infection. Three out of the five botanical shops agreed to participate in this meeting. Botanical shops A, B, and D attended a meeting during which the project was described (see stage 5) and questions and concerns addressed.

The meeting provided important information on how best to plan and implement an intervention. Botanical shops can best be thought of as small businesses that are generally owned and staffed by one person. Thus, any effort at enlisting their support through targeted training, that is, relating to HIV/AIDS, requires that this training take place outside of the usual work week, preferably on Sundays when the shops are closed. Further, social service institutions must consider paying botanical shop owners for the time they spend in training. These individuals generally do not have the time and money to close their businesses or hire personnel in order to participate in collaborative activities.

Further, it was found that these owners do not have an extensive support network that can be mobilized to help then in handling crises. Consequently, Latino customers presenting issues of HIV/AIDS, alcohol and other drug abuse, depression, and, can prove an enormous burden to owners. Provision of consultation, special hotline telephone numbers, or contact persons can help alleviate the burden often associated with caregiving. Training can also help owners refine their helping skills and increase their knowledge of particular issues and problems such as HIV/AIDS.

Other Latino Cultural Asset

One cultural assets initiative in Pawtucket, Rhode Island, focused on Latina beauty parlors distributing materials in Spanish on HIV/AIDS prevention to customers. These beauty parlors were visited by staff from a local Latino social service organization and asked to participate in an HIV/AIDS partnership. Approximately half of the shops contacted agreed to participate during the assessment stage. A meeting was then held to finalize details, and all shops were invited to attend, even those that initially declined. The hope was that they may have a change of heart.

This stage provided project staff with an opportunity to go over expectations, possible concerns not expressed in the assessment stage, and determine the best time to start the initiative. In addition, there was a discussion about why the other beauty parlors were reluctant to take part in the initiative. The intervention proved immensely successful—so much so that the amount of business increased significantly for those beauty parlors participating in the project. It created goodwill within the community, and this translated into a concerted effort to patronize these establishments. During the second year of the initiative, an invitation was sent out to all Latina beauty parlors, even those who decided not to participate during the initial year. Surprisingly, the second year witnessed

100 percent participation. The beauty parlors that had "passed" on the initial venture, it turned out, had lost business to those establishments that offered information and material on HIV/AIDS.

Lessons Learned and
Key Considerations

Any effort on the part of holders of Latino cultural assets to assist human service organizations brings with it concerns about how this relationship will alter one's business, as in the cases of beauty parlors and botanical shops. The Pawtucket, Rhode Island, beauty parlors that initially refused to participate in the HIV/AIDS project, did so because of concerns about losing customers. Not participating when other shops elected to do so, however, proved detrimental their business. Collaborative partnerships between agencies are never easy to achieve, even under the best of circumstances. Holders of Latino cultural assets, however, do not share the same vocabulary as social workers, nor do they subscribe to the same theories of etiology, interventions, and so on. Consequently, stage 4 brings added challenges pertaining to communication and trust not present in conventional collaborative partnerships between social agencies.

Fears of how the Latino community will view participation are quite natural and should be explored, even if the Latino establishment is reluctant to raise them. "Normalizing" these fears is a critical step in relationship building and conveying to the establishment that the proposed initiative has been well thought out, including potential obstacles.

There is no set number or configuration of meetings that can be expected during this stage. Interviews and meetings can take place during typical working hours and in the establishments themselves; they may also occur outside of working hours and in "neutral" places. Social workers must, as a result, be comfortable conducting interviews and meetings in homes, community establishments, and wherever Latinos feel most comfortable. It would be ill advised to "shortcut" these sessions in the interest of moving a proposed project forward. "Relationship building and sustaining" is an apt name for a stage that is all about developing trust and comfort between all participating parties, regardless of how long it takes. It is certainly time that can be considered well invested.

The communication and relationship building that are so critical to developing and sustaining partnerships with Latino cultural assets such as botanical shops or barbershops can best, if not only, be accomplished in face-to-face encounters. Telephone, mail, email, faxes, and so on cannot substitute for *personalismo*. This effectively translates into time outside of the office and travel time to the sites. It is important that project staff be supported in expending this type of time, and—since almost all of this work is done in the community and not in the organization—that other staff not involved in these types of projects recognize that "work" is talking place, even though it is not in the physical setting of the organization, and that this work may look very different from that accomplished by other staff.

Stage 5: Intervention

Context Setting

The stage at which an intervention is actually carried out represents the culmination of much hard work and expenditure of resources. However, it would be unwise to think of the other stages in this framework as being "non-intervention-related." In fact, intervention occurs throughout all facets of a framework, just like it does during the intake for a one-on-one intervention. An improperly conducted intake effectively undermines all the important work that follows. If an intake is carried in a professional and highly engaging manner, it not only results in a wealth of information but also sets the stage for a relationship based upon mutual trust and respect, key elements in work with Latinos.

On the basis of the results of the assessment conducted in stages 3 and 4, it was concluded that botanical shop owners can be engaged in any of the following six activities: (1) consulting, either on special instances or on an ongoing, contractual basis; (2) providing assistance in orienting new staff to the Latino community, like what transpires when new staff visit other agencies to develop a better understanding of the services that are provided; (3) serving as trainers for in-service activities involving folk medicine; (4) serving as key informants for future community asset assessments related to health matters (physical as well as emotional); (5) educating the community; and (6) acting as referral agents. Each of these activities lends itself to a range of goals, resources, and timetables, and they may be used any combination or permutation needed as an adaptation to organizational capacity and local circumstances.

Botanical Shop

Initially, the botanical shop project was limited to primarily developing a referral system between the owners and the community-based organization testing for HIV/AIDS. However, the initial stages revealed that the intervention that was originally planned (training and referral system) could be expanded to include the other dimensions outlined in the preceding section, as follows.

Training

The structure and content of the training was explored during stage 4. The training was conducted on a Sunday, because this did not disrupt the operation of the botanical shops, which were open Monday to Saturday (see table 8.1). The training took place from 8 a.m. to 5 p.m. and included a one-hour lunch break that allowed for informal interaction between the trainer and the participants. Social breaks were also taken when either the trainer or participants felt they were needed. These breaks were important, because they facilitated informal conversation and, as a result, relationship building.

The training content covered six topics: (1) the cause of HIV/AIDS, including common myths; (2) the ways the disease is spread; (3) types of symptoms; (4) the length of time before symptoms appeared; (5) testing procedures; and (6) treatment procedures. Materials developed by the Massachusetts Department of Public Health served as the basis for the information used in the training session. The nature of the epidemic and how it particularly impacts the Latino community in general, and Lawrence in particular, permeated the entire training. Case examples and illustrations of Latinos in Lawrence were presented to contextualize the meaning of HIV/AIDS in the community. Training methods used were didactic techniques, exercises, discussion, and question and answer. The training was multifaceted, as had been recommended during earlier contact with the participants, and was conducted in Spanish. Further, participants were encouraged to share their perspectives on HIV/AIDS, based upon their knowledge of the community and the requests they had received for medications to help alleviate symptoms related to the disease.

The payment of money for participating in a training session may be viewed with suspicion by some social service organizations. However, if "expertise," which is usually the criteria applied in determining the payment of funds, is defined from a cultural perspective, then botanical shop owners can be considered "experts" who possess "cultural and local knowledge." This form of knowledge cannot be obtained from a university or a textbook; nevertheless, it is essential in the crafting of community-based social initiatives of any kind (Delgado, 2006).

In the case of Lawrence, participants were paid $250 for attending the training and their willingness to engage in a social intervention on HIV/AIDS. Interestingly, the two botanical shop owners initially did not want to be compensated, saying that it was their duty to serve their community. However, as noted in chapter 6, the values of *respecto* and *personalismo* won out. Their time and knowledge of the community was such that they were "worthy" of being paid for their time; we certainly were being paid for our services! Their willingness to participate free of charge was acknowledged by project personnel. However, funds were available to pay them, and they were convinced that such payment was "professional," and in order.

Referral System

The establishment of formal referrals between Latino cultural assets, such as botanical shops and human service organizations, is a goal that not only addresses immediate needs but also can serve as a foundation for future partnership activities.

On the surface, this appears as a rather easy goal to achieve. However, as the reader has no doubt noticed, it is not.

The development of a referral system between participating botanical shops and the community-based social service agency represented the central goal of the Lawrence project. Such a system would not only serve to increase service delivery to Latinos, particularly those reluctant to access services, but also act as a bridge between this cultural asset and HIV/AIDS services. Botanical shop owners were provided with a profile of a Latino(a) who was at high risk for HIV/AIDS. The trust (community legitimacy) that these owners enjoyed within the community and the knowledge base they had acquired in the training combined to make them significant referral agents. They would help dispel myths customers might have about HIV/AIDS, testing, and services for those who tested positive.

Latino customers who were to be referred for testing would be provided with an individual contact person at the agency, and whenever feasible, the botanical shop owner would call the contact staff member while the customer was still in the shop. Then the customer would be given the telephone to talk with the contact person. The value of *personalismo*, as already noted, represents the critical "glue" between the botanical shop and the agency. Latino botanical shop owners, in turn, were provided with a variety of ways that the subject could be raised and a referral made without stigmatizing the customer. Fortunately, their interpersonal skills and knowledge of the community made this aspect of the project relatively easy to carry out.

During the three-month trial period, a total of nine persons were referred for testing, all of whom tested negative. A meeting was held with the participating botanical shop owner, and it was determined that no changes needed to be made with the referral service at that point in time. Further, any fears about "turning off" customers were not realized. This was a credit to the owner and the time and attention given to making sure the customers were respected and informed of their options. The period of one year was established for the gathering of detailed data on the program, and the streamlining of the referral process. A total of 38 persons were referred during the one-year period of operation, of whom four tested positive.

Community Education

The community education component of the project consisted of making pamphlets available for consumers. Nevertheless, both participants and staff felt that these shops had the capacity for much more general education based upon the needs of the community. Availability of videos in Spanish, particularly in the telenovela format discussed earlier, for example, was identified as having great potential. The Massachusetts Department of Public Health provided Spanish material. It was recognized that botanical shops also had the potential to provide time and space where health personnel could be stationed to meet customers and answer questions they might have. It was decided, however, that it would be prudent to start "small" on community education and systematically build upon this effort, rather than start too ambitious and run the risk of failure and alienating the botanical shop owners.

Other Latino Cultural Asset

The involvement of Latino establishments, as in the case of Holyoke, Massachusetts, in recruiting Latino foster parents has generally not been utilized, although the potential for doing so continues to be strong. In Holyoke (100 miles west of Boston), the owner of a local, well-respected restaurant and his spouse were enlisted not only to distribute information on foster parenting, but also enlisted to become foster parents themselves.

Their high visibility and respect within the community also served to aid in the recruitment of other foster parents. Their restaurant, in turn, became a central place within the community where social work activities such as trainings, meetings, and outreach could be held. These activities were held in the rear of the restaurant during time periods when it was not too busy and disruption of the business could be minimal. One activity, if successful, then leads to the potential for other activities, therefore increasing the options social service organizations have to broaden outreach, public education, referral, and other initiatives.

Lessons Learned and
Key Considerations

With the proper foundation laid out in the previous stages, Latino cultural assets can then be involved in a variety of social work community-centered initiatives (Delgado, 2004). Bodegas, for example, can distribute information pertaining to nutrition programs; beauty parlors can provide information on women-related health screenings; barbershops can target males on male-related health issues; houses of worship can provide space for trainings and help their congregations with information on contact people within social service organizations; bars and liquor stores can help identify customers in need of counseling. In essence, social initiatives can take various forms and do not necessitate long-term commitments.

The establishment of low-labor-intensive initiatives—such as consultation or participation in future key informant assessments, for example—facilitates the continuation of contact with social workers, even when projects are completed and lose their funding as a result. Continual contact, however, does not have to be labor intensive, and relationship building can continue. Latino cultural asset establishments, in turn, can participate in initiatives that do not require the expenditure of huge resources, or require making long-term commitments. These cultural resources can participate in social initiatives by acting as a point for distribution of public education materials, as in the case in Lawrence. Posters, too, can be placed in windows, and materials can be made easily accessible for customers to take with them and share with family and neighbors.

Both the Lawrence and Holyoke cases illustrate how initiatives can lead to unanticipated benefits in reaching and serving the Latino community. The restaurant foster parents' initiative was originally considered low-labor-intensive but ultimately resulted in a wide range of activities in many different social spheres. Both cases, however, highlight the importance of personal and sustained contact between social workers and key Latino stakeholders. These stakeholders, however, did not fit the conventional view of an influential stakeholder —someone holding an "official" position of decisionmaking within the community. Thus, broadening the concept of stakeholder to include individuals who are cognizant of cultural values makes outreach into the community more feasible.

Stage 6: Evaluation

Context Setting

Every stage of the Latino cultural assets framework brings with it its own set of challenges and rewards, and the evaluation stage is no different. The rewards of actually documenting the positive changes achieved through the use of this paradigm can be quite satisfying. The challenges of documenting the changes themselves can cause great headaches, too. Nevertheless, evaluation, even when compromised, must move forward. One of the key challenges of this stage is figuring out how community input and decisionmaking are going to be accomplished. Community ownership of outcomes (benefits) permeates all stages and must be continued in this stage. Input and decisionmaking may entail considerable time and the devotion of other resources to supporting community participation.

This stage, not surprisingly, lends itself to qualitative methods and flexibility in measure design and methods, and must take advantage of the local and cultural knowledge possessed by the cultural assets. These themes, as a result, place tremendous pressures upon staff and evaluators because of the "unconventionality" of the approach to evaluation. But evaluation of a Latino cultural assets paradigm can not be expected to be conventional in nature!

Botanical Shop

The evaluation stage involved both rewards and challenges, with the data that were gathered serving an important role in helping to design future interventions involving this Latino cultural asset. Only one of the two botanical shops that participated in the interventions was able to honor its commitments.

Botanical shops, like other Latino establishments, must be viewed developmentally, regarding provision of services that can be considered beyond the usual types associated with these establishments, as well as being able to enter into collaborative partnerships with social service organizations and social workers. Botanical shops that have only been opened a relatively short period of time (one year or less) may not have enough in-depth understanding of the demands consumers will place upon them or of the human services system within their geographical area to make necessary referrals. In addition, the economic processes of opening and maintaining a business may make it too difficult for owners to provide services that are not related to the "products" or "services" they are selling.

Data on the number of referrals, their demographic profile, and people's expectations and motivations, for example, can be obtained relatively easily in the process of scheduling and conducting tests for HIV/AIDS. Botanical shop owners' experiences and recommendations for changes, too, lend themselves to process evaluation objectives, with minimal disruption in their businesses. Conducting evaluation involving these owners, however, must accommodate their schedules.

Other Latino Cultural Asset

As already shown, a memorial mural can play an important role in helping bereaved families and communities mourn and recover in a manner that is culturally based and affirming, and make active use of their environment. The case of I.B.A. (Emergency Tenants Council), Boston, and their sponsorship of a memorial mural dedicated to Jorge Ramos, a slain youth worker, reflects how process and output objectives can be developed to measure the success of this cultural asset. The number of community members participating in the creation of the mural, the duration of time the mural has survived intact (no tagging), the number of participants at the dedication ceremony, the reactions of family members to the mural, the number of other Latino and non-Latino agencies cosponsoring the mural, the extent to which youth participants in the agency programs have knowledge of why the mural was painted, and the extent to which the community is aware of the mural and its purpose represent a significant set of objectives that actively involve the community.

Ultimately, memorial murals such as the one sponsored by I.B.A. must rely on output objectives that specifically focus on the grieving family and, whenever possible, from a longitudinal standpoint. Their sentiments and reactions as well as their input into the sponsoring and painting of a memorial mural represent the "bottom line" on the value of this type of Latino cultural asset. Its community-wide impact (impact objective) involves a different purpose, and one that requires active outreach to other organizations, in this case those involving youth, to measure how their services have been influenced by events leading up to, and including, the creation of the memorial mural itself.

Lessons Learned and
Key Considerations

Both the botanical shop and the memorial mural cases highlight the rewards and challenges associated with evaluation, not unlike their conventional social agency counterparts. The ultimate measures of success can only be developed through the active participation of the ultimate beneficiaries of the interventions. Thus, the development of measures must reflect local circumstances—for example, the methods must be qualitative, and must reflect language preference (Spanish, English, Spanglish). Further, evaluation efforts must endeavor to maximize community participation in obtaining data on the interventions.

Participants—for example, those involved in memorial murals—have an understanding of why it is important to evaluate an intervention. The ability to develop evaluation questions that are respectful (*respecto*), culturally attuned, and not "overly intrusive" is important. Funders, in turn, must view evaluation involving Latino cultural asset interventions as evolutionary. As Latino cultural asset interventions increase in number, so will the knowledge base of how best to evaluate these efforts. No one is saying that evaluation is not feasible. However, evaluation cannot be "business as usual" when venturing into the realm of cultural assets. Further, it will require input from all sectors of the endeavor, particularly cultural assets and the ultimate beneficiaries of the intervention, the Latino community itself.

Conclusion

I hope these case examples show how a Latino cultural assets paradigm can significantly alter the lives of Latinos in the United States. The case examples used in this chapter represent but a small number of Latino cultural assets that can be found in various manifestations and representations in Latino communities across the country. The case study of Latino botanical shops and the other case examples illustrate the potential benefits of a university-community partnership. As McCartt Hess and Mullen (1995, p. 5) have commented: "To collaborate is to labor together. . . . When practitioner and researcher work as coinvestigator, they accept equal responsibility for the process and the product." In the Latino botanical shop case example, it also involved the community in a three-part partnership!

This Latino cultural assets project could not have been possible without any of the three partners. The university-based researcher did not have direct access to the Latino community; the community-based agency, in turn, did not have access to the necessary resources and time needed for developing the project; finally, the botanical shop owners played a hugely influential role in shaping how the project got designed and implemented because of their knowledge of the community, and of the art of healing within a cultural context.

The other case examples have illustrated the power of a Latino Cultural Asset, but do not do justice to all of the details and considerations involved in "real" life practice. Nevertheless, this chapter, I hope, has captured the essence of practice embracing a Latino cultural assets paradigm, and provided a range of case examples on how the theoretical material covered in the previous chapters gets modified to take into account local circumstances.

Social workers and other helping professionals must continually ask the question "Where are the Latino assets?" rather than "Are there any Latino assets?" The former question symbolizes the cornerstone of a Latino cultural assets paradigm and provides the "stance" social workers must take if they are to provide the necessary impetus to not only serve but also engage the Latino community in this country.

Chapter 9

EPILOGUE

> The social world is a complicated place, and unless you have a clear
> and accurate understanding of how it works, forceful interventions
> for change are as likely to do harm as good. Activist[s] . . . seeking
> to remake the world need to bear in mind that hackneyed but
> nonetheless true saying that the road to hell is paved with good
> intentions.
>
> Douglas S. Massey, "From Social Sameness,
> a Fascination with Differences" (2005)

The reader has every right to ask what lessons are learned in planning and implementing a cultural assets paradigm with Latinos.
This chapter gives me an opportunity to identify overarching themes related to
the use of this paradigm. The content will be drawn from the case studies presented in chapter 8, along with theoretical matters covered in the literature. This
epilogue presents key factors, issues, and considerations that emerged through
the writing of this book, with implications for future social work practice. These
factors, however, reflect one person's perspective; the reader, no doubt, will be
able to identify others. Further, some of the perspective offered in this epilogue
will be eagerly embraced, while others will no doubt prove quite controversial,
and difficult to implement.

A topic like that of this book will undoubtedly have its share of advocates
and critics; to be quite honest, to have it otherwise would prove very disappoint-
ing to me. It is not my nature or intent to provoke controversy. However, social issues, by their very nature, are controversial. My hope is that the raising
of these issues will help provide the impetus for the establishment of a dialogue
involving both social work academics and providers that can set the tone and

direction for engagement in a broader context. Seven "talking points," so to speak, follow. Their sequencing reflects their "birth-order" rather than their significance.

Complexity Is the Name of the Game

"Social work practice is complex." I wonder how many of us have heard that saying? As I entered the profession, I was warned, and quickly realized, that "good" social work practice was complex and challenging, requiring an ever-questioning mind and a willingness to work hard. To give any less than 100 percent in this endeavor would prove ineffective and unsatisfying. Nevertheless, to say that practice has gotten more complex would be a serious understatement, and just when you think it cannot get any more complex, it does! The proliferation of scholarly journals devoted to social work practice has been nothing short of incredible. The number of social workers actively engaged in a research agenda, too, has shown tremendous growth over this time period. Finally, the nation as a whole has gotten very diverse.

I attended social work school in New York City in the early 1970s. The racial and ethnic composition of the city was always diverse. However, New York and other cities across the country have gotten even more diverse, if that is possible. My social work education did not, to the best of my ability to recall, address issues related to the undocumented. It was as if this group simply did not exist. Or if they did exist, either their numerical representation was too minimal to devote curriculum to them or the issues confronting this group were not seen as those that social workers would be concerned with. Regardless of the answer, I was not prepared to address the issues associated with undocumented, Latino or otherwise. Life was artificially less complex back then!

The process of writing this book has been a daunting experience! It proved very challenging, if not taxing, to address in this book the complexity of how social work can best reach and serve Latinos in the United States. I endeavored to do justice to the multiplicity of terms and perspectives, and in some cases, they only received a cursory glance in this book. I was impressed by the amount of literature, both professional and popular, that has emerged regarding Latinos in the past decade. All indications are that this trend will only increase in the next decade.

I also witnessed a shift, although ever so slight, away from deficits to assets. This slight shift, unfortunately, did not surprise me. Deficit models are still alive and well, and can count on a steady stream of funding to ensure that their popularity continues. There are a cadre of researchers and scholars, and many in training, who will focus their expertise and attention on social problems. Of course this work is important, because no community exists without various social problems, some more obvious than others. However, I sincerely believe that social work has a tremendous amount of potential for identifying community assets, and we must endeavor to do so even if viewing marginalized communities from a deficit perspective continues to be very "popular"!

Latino Cultural Values as a Moving Target

Any serious and sustained effort at better understanding the importance of cultural values for Latinos will encounter numerous obvious, and not-so-obvious, challenges. Cultural values are best understood when there is a comparison set of values (baseline) to measure them against. However, what happens when that set of values is also changing, as is happening in the United States? Cultural values become relative and lose their "absolute" meaning, making any effort to compare them with another group of limited value at best. Let us not forget that cultural values have existed and will continue to exist when they play an instrumental role in helping a group not only survive but also thrive by adapting to changing ecological circumstances.

The Latino cultural assets addressed in this book represent some of the most obvious ones. However, numerous other values were only touched upon, as in the case of same-sex unions. The role of acculturation and how it either erodes or transforms, depending upon the political perspective taken, will increase the difficulty social workers will encounter in trying to make sense of how a Latino cultural assets paradigm gets manifested on a daily basis in practice. The term "moving target" best captures this challenge for the profession.

What's in a Name?

By what name will Latinos from throughout Latin America and the Caribbean, and those born and raised in this country, call ourselves? Is it important to arrive at a common name that is easily embraced by Latinos from all geographical corners and backgrounds? I believe it is, and the time and effort devoted to this goal is time and effort well spent. Nevertheless, I would be fooling the reader and myself to think that a goal of arriving at a consensus definition would be reachable within the foreseeable future. We Latinos, unlike African Americans, do not have someone of the stature of the Reverend Jesse Jackson who can get up before a national public audience and say "We are to be referred to as "'African Americans,'" as he did over a decade ago. Since being "Latino" is not a racial category, and we share African (Yoruba and Bantu, in the case of Caribbean Latinos), Native People, and European heritages, with the combination of these strands differing depending upon geographic origins on the Latino map.

The history of racism and slavery in this country makes color a key variable in any kind of assessment of acculturation and assimilation. The Latino community can expect to be compared to their European counterparts who entered this country over the past century and a half. However, it would be irresponsible to neglect the role of phenotype in who becomes "successful" in achieving the American Dream. After all, the European counterparts were all white.

Understanding the historical sociopolitical context influencing the events that shaped our past is critical to our understanding of how events shape our present context. This, in turn, shapes how we view our march into the future. This is a future that, incidentally, increasingly will find us in the numerical majority in various geographical regions of this country. Our language and cultural values will be transformed from a "minority status," or "paradoxical perspective," to norm or standard setting. In essence, we will not be the ones with an accent.

A Century Named after Us?
How about a City?

I still have very vivid images of the late 1970s and the decade of the 1980s, which was supposed to be the "Hispanic Decade." My initial hopes of witnessing the positive outcomes resulting from this national attention slowly, and quite profoundly, shifted to grave concerns about the response to this attention. The "Decade of Hispanics" simply meant that from a numerical viewpoint, we were significant enough to be considered a threat, but not large enough to wield significant political and economic power in shaping our existence in this country. A better label would have been "Hispanic Menace" because it best captures the negative reactions of the decade. Will the advent of the twenty-first century witness similar national attention, with the same consequences? I certainly hope not.

Simply put, having an era named after an ethnic or racial group means that you have the "privilege" of having a bull's-eye placed on the back of your group, making it an attractive target for scapegoating at a national level. Numerical strength does not automatically translate into social, economic, and political power. Women have numerical strength, yet the Equal Rights Amendment is still not the law of the land. African Americans have numerical strength, yet they, too, find themselves seeking social and economic justice, and faced with the prospect that national media attention has moved onto the "newest" majority group of color in the country. Latinos' ability to build bridges with the African American and other communities of color will play an influential role in shaping the national landscape of this country in the early part of the millennium.

The next 50 years will give new meaning to cities with Latino names such as Los Angeles, San Francisco, San Antonio, Santa Barbara, El Paso, Santa Fe, and Las Vegas. Los Angeles, Wichita, and San Antonio now have mayors who are Latino. Boston (Miller, 2005), New York City (Murr, 2005), and others have experienced politics that bring together communities of color, African American and Latino in particular, to establish new leadership. Latinos must not be satisfied to be labeled as a group along the lines of "Soccer Moms" and "NASCAR Dads" every four years, when a presidential election is in the offing. Clarifying Latino positions on local, national, and international issues will require a more "sophisticated" level of analysis; anything less would be detrimental to this country's well-being. A unified position, however, is simply not possible now or in the future.

An Embrace of Assets as Evolutionary or Revolutionary in Social Work

The attraction of an assets paradigm, regardless of how it gets conceptualized and operationalized in research, scholarship, and practice, has remained a central passion for me, particularly one that serves as a bridge between micro and macro social work practice. I am under no illusion, however, that deficits "rule," so to speak. There is plenty of financing, services, and research, not to mention social work educational programs, that signifies the embrace of deficits.

To embrace an assets paradigm, particularly one based on culture, does not mean denying that individuals and communities have needs, issues, or problems. However, any social intervention that seeks to reach and help Latinos, or any other marginalized group in this society, must first start with assets. These assets must be identified, measured, and incorporated as a central feature of any social intervention. Human service organizations must put as much effort and zeal into collecting data on assets as they do collecting data on deficits. These data, in turn, must not sit on a shelf or in a computer file but must lead to programming and services.

Collection of asset data will make it necessary for social agencies to actively venture forth into the community, because these types of data are never stagnant. The embrace of a community-centered approach involving assets will serve to strengthen not only communities but the profession as well. In essence, all parties win when discussing assets. Marginalized communities can no longer be viewed as "asset-less." The profession, in turn, can play a pivotal role in shaping services to Latinos and other groups who are unvalued in an increasingly multicultural country and world.

Los Estados Unidos de Latino America, or "We All Speak Spanish Here!"

The emergence of the term "the Hispanicization of America" is slowly finding its way into all sectors of this country (Gomez, 2005). However, there are few subjects that can cause an instant debate in this country, but language is one of the few that, I believe, is guaranteed to get everyone to provide an opinion! People, particularly non-Latino whites, may not have an opinion on who we as a country are at war with, or balance-of-trade deficits, tax reform, and so on, but they certainly have an opinion on why "English" is the official language, and why Spanish should be outlawed in all public places outside of the home. Mind you, there is no Latino leader (politically elected or otherwise) who has publicly advocated a position of not having English as the primary language for undertaking business (public and private) in this country. Yet those who embrace English as the official language have great difficulty letting go of this position, even when a global economy necessitates that countries embrace multiple languages to advance commerce (New nationwide Hispanic education initiative, 2005).

Ironically, as this nation embraces the concept of a global economy, and there is a realization that the educational system in this country is not preparing our youth to compete in a global sphere, so to speak, with lack of competencies in foreign languages and understanding of other cultures being two primary reasons for this, there will be a call to action to make our country more competitive at a global level. There is no mistake that Miami, for example, has played a tremendous role in the globalization process involving Latin America.

The city of Miami, for all intents and purposes, is a bilingual and bicultural city. Virtually no professional social worker, or any other helping professional, for that matter, can expect to be successful there, personally and in service to community, without being bilingual, and preferably, bicultural. If Miami is to be considered a "multicultural city," or the "city of the twenty-first century," it will also be necessary to recognize the tensions (economic, political, and social) that go with this designation. Economic displacement of a labor force that is not bilingual, as in the case of African Americans, is bound to cause tension. Miami, I am afraid, has witnessed these tensions between communities of color (riots), and between Latinos and the dominant society, as in the case of Dade County versus Miami! Much needs to be learned about how the Latino community has been successful, or unsuccessful, in reaching out to other ethnic and racial groups, because if demographic trends continue, there will be countless Miamis across this nation in the next 30 to 40 years.

As noted in chapter 1, any concerted or national effort to enhance Latino self-confidence (Latino pride) can be expected to raise serious backlashes because of the sensitivity of the subject matter. Having Latino pride does not diminish those who are Italian having "Italian pride," or those who are Irish having "Irish pride," and so on. Having pride in one's racial and ethnic background must never be conceptualized as a zero sum. Namely, having pride in one's background does not mean that other groups cannot be proud of their own! Generally, ethnic and racial pride in this country has been conceptualized as a "zero-sum" proposition. If one group gains pride, it must be at the expense of other groups! Given this nation's history of immigration, there certainly is enough pride to go around without taking away from any other groups.

Practice Is All about Context

This point has been addressed in various ways—explicitly, as in chapter 7, and implicitly throughout this book. I never tire of having to explain the importance of context in influencing practice. If I am talking about developing social work interventions involving Latino seasonal workers in a rural county in North Carolina, the context is significantly different from addressing the needs of newly arrived Latino seasonal workers in the South Bronx, New York City, South Central Los Angeles, or Little Havana, Miami. True, there may be some universal points that transcend geography. However, living arrangements, availability of services, transportation systems, weather, and so on will influence how I plan and deliver an outreach or public education program.

Although this book attempts to provide a balanced (urban/rural) picture of the Latino community in the United States, it is clearly slanted toward urban-based practice with this community. As mentioned in chapter 2, 90 percent of the Latinos in the United States live in cities. This is not to take way from the experiences of the remaining 10 percent who do not. No section has specifically been devoted to the rural experience of Latinos. However, careful reading of this book will find numerous references and examples related to the rural experience, which brings with it a unique set of rewards and challenges for social work practice with Latinos. Even when Latinos live in urban areas, there is certainly a very high percentage of them who have rural experiences in their backgrounds, either prior to arriving in this country or shortly after arriving here, before eventually finding their way to cities.

How Do Social Workers
Get on Board?

There is no question that "learning curve" is an appropriate term to use regarding learning about Latinos in the United States. Social work education, particularly at those institutions that have embraced an urban mission, must launch educational initiatives such as Spanish-language acquisition programs, courses on social work with Latinos, field placements within Latino communities, and efforts to recruit and maintain Latino faculty.

The demographics profile and trends addressed in this book are quite clear about what the present and future hold for this country. My experience in the field is that social workers who are bilingual and bicultural are in great demand for social work jibs. Social workers who are bilingual, too, find themselves in a propitious position regarding employment options. The social work profession, as a result, is in a favorable position to provide qualified staff for countless numbers of programs and service across the country attempting to serve Latinos.

The profession must actively sponsor conferences and workshops at the national and local levels to help inform practitioners. These training opportunities also provide social workers in the field with an opportunity to network and share their experiences in meeting the increasing demands brought by the Latino demographic explosion. There is no sector of the profession that can "exempt" itself from this challenge. It will take a concerted and sustained effort for social work to play a meaningful role in shaping how human services are conceptualized, planned, and implemented with Latinos as a population in mind.

Development of an "accurate" and current picture of Latinos is difficult because of the dynamic changes this community is experiencing. Thus, any presentation of information about this community, particularly when based upon official reports and scholarly material, can be considered dated when it appears in print. This limitation, however, gives conferences and workshops greater importance in the field of social work.

Research: Can't Live with It, Can't Live without It

It would be irresponsible for me to end this epilogue without specifically mentioning the role research can and must play in helping to shape social work practice with Latinos. It has become painfully obvious to the reader that Latino-focused research is challenging at best. Nevertheless, what is the alternative?

Researchers who have a keen understanding of the community they are trying to reach do social research best. Multidisciplinary research that embraces multiple methods has tremendous promise for shaping scholarship. Social work research must go beyond federal mandates to include "minorities," "women," and "children" in research endeavors. My experiences sitting on federal reviews of research has been quite frustrating. The inclusion of these groups in research, unfortunately, has not translated into analyzing findings with these groups as central figures in the research. Simply to include them, as a result, is seen as being enough.

Social work research must embrace models that are participatory and capacity-enhancing in the process (Delgado, 2006). Our value base necessitates that all of our actions, practice as well as research, must actively seek to bring about social and economic justice for marginalized and undervalued groups, and Latinos certainly fall into this categorization. Social work research, as a result, must not focus exclusively on the generation of scholarly materials that few in the Latino community ever get to read, let alone see immediate significant changes resulting from. Thus, research endeavors must embrace models that seek to engage the Latino community in decisionmaking roles as well as to enhance their competencies in the process. Actively hiring and training community residents to be a part of a research team is but one simple example of this perspective.

The continued popularity of evidenced-based social work practice, as evidenced by the number of workshops, conferences, and scholarly publications, and the endorsement of major national social work organizations, holds much promise for social work interventions with Latinos and other marginalized groups in this society. However, the issue of best practices with Latinos brings with it a host of positive and challenging factors that will undoubtedly complicate an already controversial topic, namely, whose evidence will be used to determine outcomes? To what extent will Latino culture be considered an asset in these deliberations? These questions, although specifically directed toward Latinos, are also applicable to all other marginalized groups in this society, and strike at the heart of what is intended by best practice evidence. I believe that this is a healthy discussion topic for both academics as well as practitioners, not to mention Latino consumers.

There is no question that social work practice with Latinos must be included in any serious discussion of evidence-based practice; otherwise this perspective would be relegated to an insignificant status regarding this population group. An alternative response would be that this population group is not worthy of best practices. Increased research and scholarly attention will increase the quality of services Latinos can be expected to experience when engaging social workers. Nevertheless, how this form of research is defined regarding Latinos and defining who is benefiting is no small feat to accomplish. However, as already noted earlier in this book, the literature on best practices with Latinos is very limited, at best. The level of specificity regarding Latinos will need to be increased significantly. For example, the reader has been exposed to a multitude of factors that need to be considered in defining a sample population. The days when it was sufficient to say "Latino" or "Puerto Rican" in the sample description have long passed. This increased level of attention to how Latinos are defined "complicates" the research process, but is nevertheless necessary if findings are to be generalizable to comparable population groups.

Further, the increased presence of undocumented Latinos makes this group worthy of more focused attention. Access to undocumented Latinos, however, is quite challenging, making them an "undesirable" group to include in research. Sponsors as well as institutions entrusted to carry out research must be prepared to develop new methods for enlisting this group in social research. Just the fact that it is difficult not to does not make it acceptable to ignore a group such as the undocumented. There is so much to be learned about this group—their resiliency and competencies in making what is a dangerous journey to this country, and their ability to both survive and even thrive under less than ideal conditions once they arrive here. Their stories of success have not found their way into mainstream media, and they should. At a minimum, these stories must find their way into social work education.

Factors such as skin pigmentation, English-language proficiency, self-identification, documented status, degree of religiosity and spirituality, and being bilingual and bicultural, to list but a few, must be carefully considered and defined. Being "Latino" has become a lot more challenging to define in any serious effort at arriving at best practices with this group. Further, embracing participatory decisionmaking makes it essential for the social work field to develop research methods that actively place this population group in a central role in defining "benefits." What roles will Latino consumers play in deciding what constitutes best practice?

Finally, best practices must not be restricted to direct practice, as it has been, with some exceptions, up to this point in time. Macro practice, too, must enter into the discussion concerning best practices. Unfortunately, macro practice seems to have escaped the focus of best practice research. Any comprehensive review of the literature on this subject highlights the disparities in attention between direct and indirect practice. Bringing the Latino community into the discussion on macro practice, as a result, will influence the shaping of important policy, community organizing, and programming decisions.

I am afraid that this book has only touched on the surface of the challenges facing social work practice that is informed by scholarship. The emerging new and ever more participatory methods of research that are qualitatively based will need to be considered in any determination of what is Latino best practice. The success of these, and any other forms or methods, will ultimately depend upon the competencies of the researcher and scholar. In essence, to what degree are researchers, too, bilingual and bicultural? Their insights into the construction of research questions and, ultimately, the analysis will play an increasingly important role in shaping social work education, practice, and research and scholarship in the early part of this century.

Conclusion

There is little question that the seven points presented in this epilogue are bound to get a reaction out of social workers and the organizations employing them, not to mention the general public. Each of these concerns can be expected to test all facets of the profession in the early part of this millennium. Although each of the topics covered here was treated as if it existed in isolation from the others, they are all highly integrated, making the finding of "solutions" challenging, to say the least. Nevertheless, it would be unwise for the social work profession, or the nation, to engage in denial of any of the points raised in this epilogue.

The Latino community will not go away. We are entering an era in this nation that, I believe, is unprecedented. The Latino community will continue to expand numerically and to diversify in composition. There is nothing that I or anyone else can say to stem this tide; a tide that will result in a golden age for the country!

REFERENCES

Abel, E., and Chambers, K. (2004). Factors that influence vulnerability to STDs and HIV/AIDS among Hispanic women. *Health Care Women International*, 25, pp. 761–780.

Abrahams, D. (2005, July 13). Immigration battles begin in Congress. *Gannett News Service*. Available at: http://web.lexis-nexis.com/universe/document?_m= f5df021elefe207. Accessed 7/27/05.

Abraido-Lanza, A. F. (2004). Social support and psychological adjustment among Latinas with arthritis: A test of a theoretical model. *Annuals of Behavioral Medicine*, 27, pp. 162–171.

Abraido-Lanza, A. F. (2005). *The Latino mortality paradox revisited: Is acculturation bad for your health?* New York: Columbia University, Mailman School of Public Health.

Abraido-Lanza, A. F., Chao, M. T., and Gates, C. Y. (2005). Acculturation and cancer screening among Latinas: Results from the National Health Interview Survey. *Annals of Behavioral Medicine*, 29, pp. 22–28.

Abraido-Lanza, A. F., Chao, M. T., and Flores, K. R. (2005). Do healthy behaviors decline with greater acculturation? Implications for the Latino mortality paradox. Social Science Medicine, 61, pp. 1243–1255.

Abraido-Lanza, A. F., Vasquez, E., and Echeverria, S. E. (2004). En las manos de Dios [in God's hands]: Religious and other forms of coping among Latinos with arthritis. *Journal of Consulting and Clinical Psychology*, 72, pp. 91–102.

Acevedo, E. B. (2005a, April 8). Hispanics and obesity. Scripps Howard News Service. Available at: http://web.lexis-nexis.com/universe/document?_m= 2e4b8a55b5ad15. Accessed 5/20/05.

Acevedo, E. B. (2005b, July 27). Latino community an appealing target for military recruiters. Scripps Howard News Service. Available at: http://web.lexis-nexis .com/universe/document?_m=fdc62efbd6401dd. Accessed 8/2/05.

Acevedo, E. B. (2005c, July 29). Sending a Latino to do America's job. Washington, D.C.: Hispanic Link News Service.

Acevedo, G. (2004). Neither here not there: Puerto Rican circular migration. In D. Drachman and A. Paulino (Eds.), *Immigrants and social work: Thinking beyond the borders of the United States* (pp. 69–85). New York: Haworth Press.

Acevedo-Garcia, D., Soobader, M. J, and Berkman, L. F. (2005). The differential effect of foreign-born status on low birth weight by race/ethnicity and education. *Pediatrics*, 115, pp. e20–30.

Acosta, G. (2004, October 10). Undocumented and out of the market. *Los Ángeles Times*, p. K11.

Adam, M. B., McGuire, J. K., Walsh, M., Bosta, J., and LeCroy, C. (2005). Acculturationas a predictor of the onset of sexual intercourse among Hispanic and white teens. *Archives of Pediatrics and Adolescent Medicine*, 159, pp. 261–265.

Adams, C. R. (2003). Lessons learned from urban Latinas with type 2 diabetes mellitus. *Journal of Transcultural Nursing*, 14, pp. 255–265.

AFL-CIO. (2005). *What Social Security privatization would mean for Latinos.* Washington, D.C.: Author.

Agronick, G., O'Dinnell, L., Stueve, A., Doval, A. S., Duran, R., and Vargo, S. (2004). Sexual behaviors and risks among bisexually and gay-identified young Latino men. *AIDS Behavior*, 8, pp. 185–197.

Aidem, P. F. (2004, December 26). SCV birth rate hits new high. *Daily News of Los Angeles*, p. SC1.

Ainslie, R. C. (2002). The plasticity of culture and psychodynamic and psychosocial Processes in Latino immigrant families. In M. M. Surarez-Orozco and M. M. Paez (Eds.), *Latinos remaking America* (pp. 289–301). Los Angeles: University of California Press.

Alaniz, M. L. (2000). Community-identified alcohol issues in the Mexican American community: Research design and utilization. *Substance Use and Misuse*, 35, pp. 157–169.

Alaya, A. M. (2001, August 17). Yes, they're Hispanic, and much, much more. *Newark Star-Ledger* (New Jersey), p. 1.

Alba, R., Logan, J., Lutz, A., and Stults, B. (2002). Only English by the third generation? Loss and preservation of the mother tongue among the grandchildren of contemporary immigrants. *Demography*, 39, pp. 467–484.

Alegria, M., Canino, G., Lai, S., Ramirez, R. R., Chavez, L., Rusch, D., and Shrout, P. E. (2004). Understanding caregivers' help-seeking for Latino children's mental health care use. *Medical Care*, 42, pp. 447–455.

Alegria, M., Canino, G., Rios, R., Vera, M., Calderon, J., Rusch, D., and Ortega, A. N. (2002). Mental health care for Latinos: Inequalities in use of specialty mental health services among Latinos, African Americans, and non-Latino whites. *Psychiatric Services*, 53, pp. 1547–1555.

Alegria, M., Takeuchi, D., Canino, G., Duan, N., Shrout, P., Meng, X. L., Vega, W. A., Zane, N., Vila, D., Woo, M., Vera, M., Guarnaccia, P., Aguilar-Gaxiola, S., Sue, S., Escobar, J., Lin, K. M., and Gong, F. (2004). Considering context, place and culture: The National Latino and Asian American Study. *International Journal of Methods and Psychiatric Research*, 13, pp. 208–220.

Allam, A. (2005, July 14). When art imitates pain: Therapy group for Hispanic women uses Kahlo as a starting point. *New York Times*, p. A22.

Allard, S. W. (2004). *Access to social services: The changing urban geography of poverty and service provision.* Washington, D.C.: Brookings Institute.

Almendarez, I. S., Boysun, M., and Clark, K. (2004). Thunder and lightning and rain: A Latino/Hispanic diabetes media awareness campaign. *Family and Community Health*, 27, pp. 114–122.

Alonso-Zaldivar, R. (2004, December 6). What's in a racial identity? American Latinos all over the map. *Los Angeles Times*, p. 17.

Al Snih, S., Markides, K. S., Ostir, G. V., and Goodwin, J. S. (2001). Impact of arthritis on disability among older Mexican Americans. *Ethnicity and Disease*, 11, pp. 19–23.

Al Snih, S., Markides, K. S., Ray, L., Freeman, J. L., and Goodwin, J. S. (2000). Prevalence of arthritis in older Mexicans. *Arthritis Care and Research*, 13, pp. 409–416.

Alvarado, B. (2005). Spanish-speaking Latina migrant mothers' experiences and strategies in linking to social institutions in the United States. Ph.D. diss. prospectus, Boston University School of Social Work.

Alvarez, J., Olson, B. D., Jason, L. A., Davis, M. I., and Ferrari, J. R. (2004). Heterogeneity among Latinas and Latinos entering substance abuse treatment: Findings from a national database. *Journal of Substance Abuse Treatment*, 26, pp. 277–284.

Alvaro, E. M., Jones, S. P., Robles, A. S., and Siegel, J. T. (2005). Predictors of organ donation behavior among Hispanic Americans. *Progressive Transplant*, 15, pp. 149–156.

Amario, C. (2004, December 27). US Latinas seek answers in Islam. *Christian Science Monitor*, p. 11.

Amaro, H., and Zambrana, R. E. (2000). Crillo, mestizo, mulato, LatiNegro, indígena, white, of black? The US Hispanic/Latino population and multiple responses in the 2000 census. *American Journal of Public Health*, 90, pp. 1724–1727.

American Automobile Association. (2004, March 31). AAA calls for in-depth research on Latino seat belt use. Washington, D.C.: Author.

American Diabetes Association. (2005). *Diabetes statistics for Latinos.* Washington, D.C.: Author.

American Psychological Association Commission on Violence and Youth. (1993). *Violence and youth: Psychology's response.* Vol. 1. *Summary report of the American Psychological Association Commission on Violence and Youth.* Washington, D.C.: American Psychological Association.

American Public Health Association. (2003). The obesity epidemic in U.S. minority communities. *APHA Issue Brief*, 1, pp. 1–23.

American Society of Plastic Surgeons. (2005, March 21). Cosmetic plastic surgery procedures for Hispanics up in 2004. Available at: www.plasticsurgery.org. Accessed 7/7/05.

Anderson, B. (2005, April 27). Latino health issues studied. *Fresno (Calif.) Bee*, p. B1.

Anderson, C., and Parish, M. (2003). Report of workplace violence by Hispanic nurses. *Journal of Transcultural Nursing*, 14, pp. 237–243.

Anderson, J. T., Hunting, K. L., and Welch, L. S. (2000). Injury and employment patterns among Hispanic construction workers. *Journal of Occupational and Environmental Medicine*, 42, pp. 176–186.

Andrade, R., and Estrada, A. L. (2003). Are Hispana IDUs tecatas? Reconsidering gender and culture in Hispana injection drug use. *Substance Use and Misuse*, 38, pp. 1133–1158.

Andresen, E. M., and Brownson, R. C. (2000). Disability and health status: Ethnic differences among women in the United States. *Journal of Epidemiology and Community Health*, 54, pp. 200–206.

Andrews, R. M., and Elixhauser, A. (2000). Use of major therapeutic procedures: Are Hispanics treated differently than non-Hispanic whites? *Ethnicity and Diseases*, 10, pp. 384–394.

Anez, I. M., Paris, M., Bedregal, L. E., Davidson, L., and Grilo, C. M. (2005). Application of cultural constructs in the care of first-generation Latino clients in a community mental health setting. *Journal of Psychiatric Practice*, 11, pp. 221–230.

Angel, R. J., Angel, J. L., and Markides, K. S. (2002). Stability and change in health insurance among older Mexican Americans: Longitudinal evidence from the Hispanic Established Populations for Epidemiologic Study of the Elderly. *American Journal of Public Health*, 92, pp. 1264–1271.

Angulo, V., and Guendelman, S. (2002). Crossing the border for abortion services: The Tijuana–San Diego connection. *Health Care for Women*, 23, pp. 642–653.

Arana, M. (2001). *The elusive Hispanic/Latino identity*. Washington, D.C.: National Association of Hispanic Journalists.

Aranda, M. P., and Knight, B. G. (1997). The influence of ethnicity and culture on the care- giver stress and coping process: A sociocultural review and analysis. *Gerontologist*, 17, pp. 342–354.

Arcevedo-Garcia, D., Barbeau, E., Bishop, J. A., Pan, J., and Emmons, K. M. (2004). Undoing an epidemiological paradox: The tobacco industry's targeting of U.S. immigrants. *American Journal of Public Health*, 94, pp. 2188–2193.

Archip, A. (2005, May 12). Credit card debt increasing among African Americans, Latinos. *Ascribe Newswire*. Available at: http://web.lexis-nexis.com/universe/document?_m=9c09dale8349501. Accessed 5/20/05.

Arcia, F., Skinner, M., Bailey, D., and Correa, V. (2001). Models of acculturation and health behaviors among Latino immigrants to the US. *Social Science Medicine*, 53, pp. 41–53.

Arnada, J. M., Marquez, J., Oreasita-Ng, J. A., and Lupu, V. (2004). Treatment of hypertension in the Hispanic community: Cultural case studies. *Clinical Cornerstone*, 6, pp. 71–75.

Arnada, J. M., and Vazquez, R. (2004). Awareness of hypertension and diabetes in the Hispanic community. *Clinical Cornerstone*, 6, pp. 14–15.

Arredondo, P. (2002). Mujeres latinas—Santas y marquesas. *Cultural Diversity and Ethnic Minority Psychology*, 8, pp. 308–319.

Artiles, A., Ruesda, R., Salazar, J. J., and Higareda, J. P. (2002). In Daniel J. Losen and G. Orfield (Eds.), *Racial inequity in special education* (pp. 117–136). Cambridge, Mass.: Harvard University Press.

Artinian, N. T., Nies, M. A., Myers, S. S., Vander Wal, J. S., and Keves-Foster, M. K. (2004). Hypertension and diabetes in Detroit Hispanics. *Applied Nursing Research*, 17, pp. 158–167.

Asamoa, K., Rodriguez, M., Gines, V., Varela, R., Dominguez, K., Mills, C. G., Sotomayor, G., and Beck-Sague, C. M. (2004). Report from the CDC. Use of preventive health services by Hispanic/Latino women in two urban communities: Atlanta, Georgia and Miami, Florida, 2000 and 2001. *Journal of Women's Health*, 13, pp. 654–661.

Avalos, G. (2005, May 3). Latinos' median wage falls. *Contra Costa Times* (Walnut Creek, Calif.), p. 1.

Averill, J. B. (2003). Keys to the puzzle: Recognizing strengths in a rural community. *Public Health Nursing*, 20, pp. 449–455.

Averill, J. B. (2002). A portrait: Magdelena's dream. *Public Health Nursing*, 19, pp. 156–160.

Axtman, K. (2005, July 26). Illegal entry by non-Mexicans rises. *Christian Science Monitor*, p. 1.

Ayala, G. X., Mueller, K., Lopez-Madurga, E., Campbell, N. R., and Elder, J. P. (2005). Restaurant and food shopping selections among Latino women in Southern California. *Journal of the American Dietary Association*, 105, pp. 38–45.

Ayalong, L. (2004). Cultural variants of caregiving or the culture of caregiving. *Journal of Cultural Diversity*, 11, pp. 131–138.

Bacallao, M. L., and Smokowski, P. R. (2005, August 10–13). Entre dos mundos: Cultural identity formation in Latino adolescents. Paper presented at the annual meeting of the Society for Social Work Research, Miami.

Bade, K. R., Murphy, J., and Sullivan, M. C. (1999). Lessons from the field: health care experiences and preferences in a Latino community. *Bioethics Forum*, 15, pp. 33–42.

Baer, J. C., Prince, J. D., and Velez, J. (2004). Fusion or familialism: A construct problem in studies of Mexican American adolescents. *Hispanic Journal of Behavioral Sciences*, 26, pp. 263–273.

Baer, R. D., Weller, S. C., De Alba Garcia, J. G., Glazer, M., Trotter, R., Pachter, L., and Klein, R. E. (2003). A cross-cultural approach to the study of the folk illness nervios. *Culture, Medicine and Psychiatry*, 27, pp. 315–337.

Baez, A. (2005). Alcohol use among Dominican-Americans: An exploration. In M. Delgado (Ed.), *Latinos and alcohol use/abuse revisited: Advances and challenges for prevention and treatment programs* (pp. 53–65). New York: Haworth Press.

Baez, A., and Hernandez, D. (2001). Complementary spiritual beliefs in the Latino community: The interface with psychotherapy. *American Journal of Orthopsychiatry*, 71, pp. 408–415.

Baird, J., and Guidos, R. (2004, September 30). Utah on a fast track for ethnic change: lots of Latinos. *Salt Lake (Utah) Tribune*, p. A1.

Baker, F. (1977). The interface between professional and natural support systems. *Clinical Social Work Journal*, 5, pp. 139–148.

Baker, R. S., Bazargan, M., Bazargan-Hejazi, S., and Calderon, J. L. (2005). Access to vision care in an urban low-income multiethnic population. *Opthalmic Epidemiology*, 12, pp. 1–12.

Baldassare, M. (2000). *California in the new millennium: The changing social and political landscape.* Berkeley: Public Policy Institute of California. Barboza, D. (2000, December 26). Rampant obesity, a debilitating reality for the urban poor. *New York Times,* p. D1.

Barcelona de Mendoza, V. B. (2001). Culturally appropriate care for pregnant Latina women who are victims of domestic violence. *Journal of Obstetrics, Gynecological and Neonatal Nursing,* 30, pp. 579–588.

Barkin, S., Balkrishnan, R., Manuel, J., and Hall, M. A. (2003). Effect of language immersion on communication with Latino patients. *North Carolina Medical Journal,* 64, pp. 258–262.

Barlow, K. M., Taylor, D. M., and Lambert, W. E. (2000). Ethnicity in America and feeling "American." *Journal of Psychology,* 134, pp. 581–600.

Barrera, M., Hageman, D. N., and Gonzalez, N. A. (2004). Revisiting Hispanic adolescents' resilience to the effects of parental problem drinking and life stress. *American Journal of Community Psychology,* 34, pp. 83–94.

Barreras, R. E., Drucker, E. M., and Rosenthal, D. (2005). The concentration of substance use, criminal justice involvement, and HIV/AIDS in the families of drug offenders. *Journal of Urban Health,* 82, pp. 162–170.

Barrett, B. (2004, May 20). Latinos to shed minority status. *Daily News of Los Angeles,* p. N1.

Barrio, C., Yamada, A. M., Hough, R. L., Hawthorne, W., Garcia, P., and Jeste, D. V. (2003). Ethnic disparities in use of public mental health case management services among patients with schizophrenia. *Psychiatric Services,* 54, pp. 1264–1270.

Barron, F., Hunter, A., Mayo, R., and Willoughby, D. (2004). Acculturation and adherence: Issues for health care providers working with clients of Mexican origin. *Journal of Transcultural Nursing,* 15, pp. 331–317.

Barsa, B. R. N. (1998). *The independence of urban Hispanic elderly.* New York: Garland.

Bauer, H. M., Rodríguez, M. A., Quiroga, S. S., and Flores-Ortiz, V. G. (2000). Barriers to health care for abused Latina and Asian immigrant women. *Journal of Health Care for the Poor and Underserved,* 11, pp. 33–44.

Bean, D. L., Rotheram-Borus, M. J., Leibowitz, A., Horwitz, S. M., and Weidmer, B. (2003). Spanish-language services assessment for children and adolescents (SACA): Reliability of parent and adolescent reports. *Journal of the American Academy of Child Adolescent Psychiatry,* 42, pp. 881–888.

Bean, F. D., Lee, J., Batalova, J., and Leach, M. (2005). *Immigration and fading color in America.* Washington, D.C.: Population Reference Bureau.

Bean, R. A., Perry, B. J., and Bedell, T. M. (2001). Developing culturally competent marriage and family therapists: Guidelines for working with Hispanic families. *Journal of Marriage and Family Therapy,* 27, pp. 43–54.

Becerra, M., and Reese, F. (1993). Natural support systems and Hispanic substance abuse. In R. S. Mayers, B. L. Kail, and T. D. Watts (Eds.), *Hispanic substance abuse* (pp. 115–130). Springfield, Ill.: Charles C. Thomas.

Becerra, R. M., and Iglehart, A. P. (1995). Folk medicine use: Diverse populations in a metropolitan area. *Social Work in Health Care,* 21, pp. 37–58.

Becerra, R. M., Karno, M., and Escobar, J. I. (Eds.). (1982). *Mental health and Hispanic Americans: Clinical perspectives.* New York: Grune and Stratton.

Beck, E., Williams, I., Hope, L., and Park, W. (2001). An intersectional model: Exploring Gender and ethnic and cultural diversity. *Journal of Ethnic and Cultural Diversity in Social Work*, 10, pp. 63–80.

Becker, E. (2004, May 18). Latino migrants to U.S. send billions home. *New York Times*, p. C4.

Becker, G. (2004). Deadly inequality in the health care "safety net": Uninsured ethnic minorities' struggle to live with life-threatening illnesses. *Medical Anthropological Quarterly*, 18, pp. 258–275.

Becker, G., Beyene, Y., Newsom, E., and Mayen, N. (2003). Creating continuity through mutual assistance: Intergenerational reciprocity in four ethnic groups. *Journal of Gerontology*, 58, pp. S151–S159.

Beeson, B. (2004, December 12). Toys in the "hood": Ken and Barbie they're not; homies, low-rider dolls are hot. *Herald News* (Passaic County, N.J.), p. C1.

Beiver, J. L., Castano, M. T., de las Funetes, C., Gonzalez, C., Servin-Lopez, S., Sprowls, C., and Trip, C. G. (2002). The role of language in training psychologists to work with Hispanic clients. *Professional Psychology: Research and Practice*, 33, pp. 330–336.

Belles, M. (2004, December 26). Demographics shifts stir older congregations. Associated Press State and Local Wire, p. 1.

Benabe, J. E., and Rios, E. V. (2004). Kidney disease in the Hispanic population: Facing the growing challenge. *Journal of the National Medical Association*, 96, pp. 789– 798.

Benavides, D. (2005, August 3). Living la Vida Buena. *Orange County (Calif.) Register*, p. 1.

Bender, D. E., and Harlan, C. (2005). Increasing Latino access to quality health care: Spanish language training for health professionals. *Journal of Public Health Management Practice*, 11, pp. 46–49.

Benson, J. E. (1999). Undocumented immigrants and the meatpacking industry in the Midwest. In M. Foner, R. G. Rumbaut, and S. J. Gold (Eds.), *Immigration research for a new century: Multidisciplinary perspectives* (pp. 172–192). New York: Russell Sage Foundation.

Berg, C. R. (2002), *Latino images in film: Stereotypes, subversion and resistance.* Austin: University of Texas Press.

Berg, J., Wahlgren, D. R., Hofstetter, C. R., Meltzer, S. B., Meltzer, E. O., Matt, G. E., Martinez-Donate, A., and Hovell, M. F. (2004). Latino children with asthma: Rates and risks for medical care utilization. *Journal of Asthma*, 41, pp. 147–157.

Berger, E. (2005, May 10). Study shows Alzheimer's may strike Latinos at an earlier age. *Houston Chronicle*, p. 08.

Berk, M. L., Schur, C. L., Chanez, L. R., and Frankel, M. (2000). Healthcare use among undocumented Latino immigrants. *Health Affairs*, July/August, pp. 1–14.

Bermudez-Millan, A., Perez-Escamilla, R., Damio, G., Gonzalez, A., and Segura-Perez, S. (2004). Food safety knowledge, attitudes, and behaviors among Puerto Rican caretakers living in Hartford, Connecticut. *Journal of Food Protection*, 67, pp. 512–516.

Bernstein, D. (2005, August 1). A new multiplex is aiming to capture a bilingual audience. *New York Times*, p. 4.

Bernstein, L. (2005, July 15). Latino groups denounce Campo patrol; Border watchers gather tomorrow. *San Diego Union-Tribune*, pp. B2–7, B3–6.

Bernstein, N. (2005, September 28). Decline is seen in immigration: Study finds arrivals in U.S. peaked in 2000. *New York Times*, pp. A1, C19.

Bernstein, N. (2004, December 5). Dominican president visits, reaching out to diaspora. *New York Times*, p. 45.

Berrios, C. (2003). Culturally competent mental health care for Puerto Rican children. *Journal of Child and Adolescent Psychiatric Nursing*, 16, pp. 112–122.

Bertera, E. M., Bertera, R. L., and Shankar, S. (2003). Acculturation, socioeconomic factors and obesity among immigrants from El Salvador living in the Washington D.C. area. *Journal of Ethnic and Cultural Diversity in Social Work*, 12, pp. 43–59.

Betancourt, E. (2005, November 8). Increasing numbers, diversity distinguish Latino voters. *Intelligencer Journal* (Lancaster, Pa.), p. 5.

Betancourt, E. (2004, September 29). Taste of Latino foods catching on with retailers, restaurateurs. *Intelligencer Journal* (Lancaster, Pa.), p. B6.

Betancourt, J. R., Carrillo, J. E., Green, A. R., and Maina, A. (2004). Barriers to health promotion and disease prevention in the Latino population. *Clinical Cornerstone*, 6, pp. 27–29.

Betancourt, J. R., Green, A. R., Carrillo, J. E., Ananch-Firepong, O. (2003). Defining cultural competence: A practical framework for addressing racial/ethnic disparities in health and health care. *Public Health Reports*, 118, pp. 293–302.

Bharucha, D. X, Morling, B. A., and Niesenbaum, R. A. (2003). Use and definition of herbal medicine differ by ethnicity. *Annals of Pharmacotherapy*, 37, pp. 1409–1413.

Bilchik, G. S. (2001). No easy answers. *Hospital Health Network*, 75, pp. 58–60.

Birman, D. (1998). Biculturalism and perceived competence of Latino immigrant adolescents. *American Journal of Community Psychology*, 26, pp. 335–354.

Bishop, R. A., and Sayeed, P. (2003). Te contaria mi vida: I would tell you my life, if only you would ask. *Health Care for Women International*, 24, pp. 723–737.

Black, S. A., Markides, K. S., and Ray, L. A. (2003). Depression predicts increased incidence of adverse health outcomes in older Mexican Americans with type 2 diabetes. *Diabetes Care*, 26, pp. 2822–2828.

Blea, I. I. (1988). *Toward a Chicano social science*. Westport, Conn.: Praeger Press.

Blewett, L. A., Davern, M., and Rodin, H. (2005). Employment and health insurance coverage for rural Latino populations. *Journal of Community Health*, 30, pp. 181–195.

Blewett, L. A., Smaida, S. A., Fuentes, C., and Zuehlke, E. U. (2003). Health care needs of the growing Latino population in rural America: Focus group findings in one midwestern state. *Journal of Rural Health*, 19, pp. 33–41.

Bliss, E. B., Meyers, D. S., Phillips, R. L., Fryer, G. E., Dovey, S. M., and Green, L. A. (2004). Variation in participation in health care settings associated with race and ethnicity. *Journal of General Internal Medicine*, 19, pp. 831–836.

Blue-Banning, M. J., Turnbull, A. P., and Pereira, L. (2000). Group action planning as a support strategy for Hispanic families: Parent and professional perspectives. *Mental Retardation*, 38, pp. 262–275.

Blum, R. W., Beuhring, T., Shew, M. L., Bearinger, L. H., Sieving, R. E., and Resnick, M. D. (2000). The effects of race/ethnicity, income, and family structure on adolescent risk behaviors. *American Journal of Public Health*, 90, pp. 1878–1884.

Blumentritt, T. L., and VanVoorhis, C. R. (2004). The million adolescent clinical inventory: Is it valid and reliable for Mexican American youth? *Journal of Personality Assessment*, 83, pp. 64–74.

Blumberg, D. L. (2004, December 21). New competition: A battle for bodega big bucks; company hopes to find a niche in the expanding market for foods and products with a Latino flavor. *Newsday*, p. A21.

Board of Children, Youth and Families. (2004). *Children's health, the nation's wealth: Assessing and improving child health.* Washington, D.C.: National Academies Press.

Boiko, P., Katon, W., Guerra, J. C., and Mazzoni, S. (2005). An audiotaped mental health evaluation tool for Hispanic immigrants with a range of literacy levels. *Journal of Immigrant Health*, 7, pp. 33–36.

Bond, L. (2004, November 18). A grim prognosis: HIV infection is soaring in the Latino population. Can El Futuro slow it down? *Denver Westword*, p. 1.

Borak, J., Fiellin, M., and Chemerynski, S. (2004). Who is Hispanic? Implications for epidemiologic research in the United States. *Epidemiology*, 15, pp. 240–244.

Borden, T. (2005, March 21). Study analyzes data on illegal immigrants. Cox News Service. Available at: http://web.lexis-nexis.com/universe/document?_m=2bde751df5f9b1. Accessed 9/14/05.

Borenstein, S. (2004, February 12). Infant mortality rate rises for first time since 1950s. Knight Ridder/Tribune Service. Available at: http://web.lexis-nexis.com/universe/document?_m=e739c0a22cabb7. Accessed 5/12/05.

Borrayo, E. A. (2004). Where's Maria? A video to increase awareness about breast cancer and mammography screening among low-literacy Latinas. *Preventive Medicine*, 39, pp. 99–110.

Borrell, L. N. (2005). Racial identity among Hispanics: Implications for health and well-being. *American Journal of Public Health*, 95, pp. 379–381.

Brahan, D., and Bauchner, H. (2005). Changes in reporting of race/ethnicity, socioeconomic status, gender, and age over ten years. *Pediatrics*, 115, pp. 163–166.

Braine, T. (2005, April 25). Latino diet changes deemed health crisis. Associated Press Online. Available at: http://web.lexis-nexis.com/universe/document?_m=ae966967b2a99b. Accessed 5/16/05.

Brameld, T. (1959). *The remaking of a culture: Life and education in Puerto Rico.* New York: Wiley.

Brent-Goodley, T. B. (2005). An African-centered approach to domestic violence. *Families in Society*, 86, pp. 197–206.

Breslau, J., Kendler, K. S., Su, M., Gaxiola-Aguilar, S., and Kessler, R. C. (2005). Lifetime risk and prevalence of psychiatric disorders across ethnic groups in the United States. *Psychological Medicine*, 35, pp. 317–327.

Brett, K. M., and Higgins, J. A. (2003). Hysterectomy prevalence by Hispanic ethnicity: Evidence from a national survey. *American Journal of Public Health*, 93, pp. 307–312.

Brewington, K. (2005, March 22). Number of illegal migrants increases. *Baltimore Sun*, p. 1.

Brook, D. W., Brook, J. S., Rosen, Z., De La Rosa, M., Montoya, I. D., and Whiteman, M. (2003). Early risk factors for violence in Colombian adolescents. *American Journal of Psychiatry*, 160, pp. 1470–1478.

Brooks, D. (2005, August 14). Two steps toward a sensible immigration policy. *New York Times*, p. 12.

Brosnahan, J., Steffen, L. M., Lytle, L., Patterson, J., and Boostrom, A. (2004). The relation between physical activity and mental health among Hispanic and non-Hispanic white adolescents. *Archives of Pediatric and Adolescent Medicine*, 158, pp. 818–823.

Brosnan, G. (2001, August 7). U.S. migrants face a harrowing journey. *Metro* (Boston), p. 13.

Brotanek, J. M., Halterman, J., Avinger, P., and Weitzman, M. (2005). Inadequate access to care among children with asthma from Spanish-speaking parents. *Journal of Health Care for the Poor and Underserved*, 16, pp. 63–73.

Brown, D. (2002). The role of work and cultural values in occupational choice, satisfaction, and success: A theoretical statement. *Journal of Counseling and Development*, 80, pp. 48–56.

Brown, E. R., and Yu, H. (2002). Latinos' access to employment-based health insurance. In M. M. Suarez-Orozco and M. M. Paez (Eds.), *Latinos remaking America* (pp. 236–253). Los Angeles: University of California Press.

Brown, H. B. (2004, December 26). Companies are tapping into Latino market; natives seeking a taste of homeland. *Herald News* (Passaic County, N.J.), p. A20.

Brown, S. A., Becker, H. A., Garcia, A. A., Barton, S. A., and Hanis, C. L. (2002). Measuring health beliefs in Spanish-speaking Mexican Americans with type 2 diabetes: adapting an existing instrument. *Research and Nursing Health*, 25, pp. 145–158.

Browne, K. D., and Hamilton-Giachritsis, C. (2005). The influence of violent media on children and adolescents: A public health approach. *Lancet*, 365, pp. 702–710.

Browner, C. H., and Preloran, H. M. (2000). Latinas, amniocentesis and the discourse of choice. *Culture, Medicine and Psychiatry*, 24, pp. 353–375.

Browner, C. H., Preloran, H. M., Casado, M. C., Bass, H. N., and Walker, A. P. (2003). Genetic counseling gone awry: Miscommunication between prenatal genetic service providers and Mexican-origin clients. *Social Science Medicine*, 56, pp. 1933–1946.

Buchanan, W. (2005, July 14). Latino same-sex couples as parents; UCLA study shows higher proportion than other ethnics. *San Francisco Chronicle*, p. B1.

Bulkeley, D. (2004, August 29). Entrepreneurs tapping into Latino market. *Deseret Morning News* (Salt Lake City), p. 1.

Bullock, K. (2005). Ahora le voy a cuidar mis nietos: Rural Latino grandparents raising grandchildren of alcohol and other drug abusing parents. In M. Delgado (Ed.), *Latinos and alcohol use/abuse revisited: Advances and challenges for prevention and treatment programs* (pp. 107–129). New York: Haworth Press.

Burbano O'Leary, S. C., Federico, S., and Hampers, L. C. (2003). The truth about language barriers: One residency program's experience. *Pediatrics*, 111, pp. e569–e573.

Burgos, A. E., Schetzina, K. E., Dixon, L. B., and Mendoza, F. S. (2005). Importance of generational status in examining access to and utilization of health services by Mexican American children. *Pediatrics*, 115, e322–e330.

Burgos-Aponte, G. D. (2004). Ethnic identity and self-esteem among high school students. Master's thesis, Central Connecticut State University, New Britain.

Burke, J. (2004, November 30). Banks focus more on accommodating Latino customers: Some are gearing whole branches specifically to Spanish-speaking people. *Salt Lake (Utah) Tribune*, p. E1.

Burnette, D. (1999). Custodial grandparents in Latino families: Patterns of service use and predictors of unmet needs. *Social Work*, 44, pp. 22–34.

Bushouse, K. (2005, September 30). Report finds minorities more likely to receive high- interest mortgage loans. *South Florida Sun-Sentinel*, p. 1.

Byrd, T. L., Peterson, S. K., Chavez, R., and Heckert, A. (2004). Cervical cancer screening beliefs among young Hispanic women. *Preventive Medicine*, 38, pp. 192–197.

Caballero, A. E. (2005). Diabetes in the Hispanic or Latino population: Genes, environment, culture, and more. *Current Diabetes Report*, 5, pp. 217–225.

Cabassa, L. J. (2003). Measuring acculturation: Where we are and where we need to go. *Hispanic Journal of Behavioral Sciences*, 25, pp. 127–146.

Cabrera, C. (2005, March 30). Latinas embrace Islam. *Tampa Tribune*, p. 1.

Cabrera, D. M., Morisky, D. E., and Chin, S. (2002). Development of a tuberculosis education booklet for Latino immigrant patients. *Patient Education Counseling*, 46, pp. 117–124.

Cafferty, P. S. J., and Engstrom, D. W. (Eds.). (1999). *Hispanics in the United States: An agenda for the twenty-first century*. New York: Transaction.

Caldwell, A. A. (2005, August 12). Non-white now majority in Texas. *Boston Globe*, p. A25.

California, State of. (2004). *California Latino demographic databook*. 3rd ed. Sacramento: Author.

Camarillo, A. M., and Bonilla, F. (2001). Hispanics in a multicultural society: A new American dilemma? In N. J. Smelser, W. J. Wilson, and F. Mitchell (Eds.), *America becoming: Racial trends and their consequences* (vol. 1, pp. 103– 134). Washington, D.C.: National Academy Press.

Campo, R. E., Alvarez, D., Santos, G., and Latorre, J. (2005). Antiretroviral treatment considerations in Latino patients. *AIDS Patient Care STDS*, 19, pp. 366–374.

Campo-Flores, A. (2005, March 21). Pentecostal churches are using savvy marketing to attract traditionally Catholic Hispanics: A holy struggle in Chicago. *Newsweek*, p. 50.

Campo-Flores, A., and Fineman, H. (2005, May 30). A Latin power surge. *Newsweek*, pp. 25–27, 30–31.

Canda, E. R. & Furman, L. D. (1999). *Spiritual diversity in social work practice*. New York: Free Press.

Canles, L. (1996). Issues of health care mistrust in East Harlem. *Mount Sinia*, 66, p. 257.

Cantwell, S. (2005, April 8). Forum about immigration issues dispels popular myths. *Star News* (Wilmington, N.C.), p. 1B.

Capps, R., Fix, M., Ost, J., Reardon-Anderson, J., and Passel, J. S. (2004). *The health and well-being of young children of immigrants*. Washington, D.C.: Urban Institute.

Carlson, K. (2004, September 30). Latino wages lagging gains made over decade. *Modesto (Calif.) Bee*, p. A1.

Carpenter, T. (2005, April 14). Racial, ethnic disparities found in Kansas. *Topeka (Kansas) Capital-Journal*, p. A1.

Carrasquillo, O., Carrasquillo, A. I., and Shea, S. (2000). Health insurance coverage of immigrants living in the United States: Differences by citizenship status and country of origin. *American Journal of Public Health*, 90, pp. 917–923.

Carter, S. A. (2005, September 28). Economists' conference throws light on growing Latino market. *InLand Valley Daily Bulletin* (Ontario, Canada), p. 1.

Carvajal, S. C., Hanson, C. E., Romero, A. J., and Coyle, K. K. (2002). Behavioral risk factors and protective factors in adolescents: A comparison of Latino and non-Latino whites. *Ethnicity and Health*, 7, pp. 181–193.

Casey, M. M., Casey, M. S., Blewett, L. A., and Call, K. T. (2004). Providing health care to Latino immigrants: Community based efforts in the rural midwest. *American Journal of Public Health*, 94, pp. 1709–1711.

Castaneda, R. (2005, August 12). Subcontractor ordered to pay laborers' wages. *Washington Post*, p. B2.

Castel, L. D., Timbie, J. W., Senderky, V., Curtis, L. H., Feathers, K. A., and Schulman, K. A. (2003). Toward estimating the impact of changes in immigrants' insurance eligibility on hospital expenditures for uncompensated care. *BMC Health Services Research*, 10, pp. 1.

Castillo, J. (2004, May 23). Degree of uncertainty. *Austin (Texas) American-Statesman*, p. A1.

Cauce, A. M. (2002). Examining culture within a quantitative-empirical research framework. *Human Development*, 45, pp. 294–298.

Census Bureau projects surge in Hispanic and Asian Populations. (2004, April 20). *American Perspective Report*. Available at: www.amperspective.com/htm/demographic-projections.html. Accessed 4/29/05.

Centers for Disease Control and Prevention. (2004a). Access to health-care and preventive services among Hispanic and non-Hispanics—United States, 2001–2002. *Morbidity and Mortality Weekly Report*, 53, pp. 937–941.

Centers for Disease Control and Prevention. (2004b, October 14). *Hispanic teen birth rates remain the highest of any racial or ethnic groups in the United States*. Atlanta: Author.

Centers for Disease Control and Prevention. (2004c, June 11). Suicide among Hispanics—United States, 1997–2001. *MMWR Weekly*, 53, pp. 478–481.

Centers for Disease Control and Prevention. (2002). *A demographic and health snapshot of the U.S. Hispanic/Latino population: 2002 National Hispanic Health Leadership Summit*. Atlanta: Author.

Cerrutti, M., and Massey, D. S. (2001). On the auspices of female migration from Mexico to the United States. *Demography*, 38, pp. 187–200.

Chamorro, R., and Flores-Ortiz, Y. (2000). Acculturation and disordered eating patterns among Mexican American women. *International Journal of Eating Disorders*, 28, pp. 125–129.

Changing U.S. demographic creates critical need for more Latinos to pursue higher education. (2005, July 27). PR Newswire US. Available at: http://web.lexis-nexis.com/universe/document?_m=fdc62efbd6401dd . . . Accessed 8/2/05.

Chapa, J., and De La Rosa, B. (2004). Latino population growth, socioeconomic and demographic characteristics, and implications for educational attainment. *Education and Urban Society*, 36, pp. 130–149.

Chapman, M. V., and Perrerira, K. M. (2005). The well-being of immigrant Latino youth: A framework to inform practice. *Families in Society*, 86, pp. 104–111.

Chatterjee, N., Blakely, D. E., and Barton, C. (2005). Perspectives on obesity and barriers to control from workers at a community center serving low-income Hispanic children and families. *Journal of Community Health Nursing*, 22, pp. 23–36.

Chaudron, L. H., Kitzman, H. J., Peifer, K. L., Morrow, S., Perez, L. M., and Newman, M. C. (2005). Prevalence of maternal depressive symptoms in low-income Hispanic women. *Journal of Clinical Psychiatry*, 66, pp. 418–423.

Chavira, R. (2005, March 18). In California, general racial balance and surprising harmony. Scripps Howard News Service. Available at: http://web.lexis-nexis .com/universe/document?_m=ae966967b2a99b. Accessed 5/16/05.

Chen, F. M., Fryer, G. E., Phillips, R. L., Wilson, E., and Pathman, D. E. (2005). Patients' beliefs about racism, preferences for physician race, and satisfaction with care. *Annals of Family Medicine*, 3, pp. 138–143.

Cherpitel, C. J., and Borges, G. (2001). A comparison of substance use and injury among Mexican American emergency room patients in the United States and Mexicans in Mexico. *Alcohol: Clinical and Experimental Research*, 25, pp. 1174–1180.

Child Welfare League of America. (2003). *Preventing Latin teen pregnancy*. Washington, D.C.: Author.

Chiriboga, D. A. (2004). Some thoughts on the measurement of acculturation among Mexican American elders. Hispanic Journal of Behavioral Sciences, 26, pp. 274–292.

Cho, D. (2002, December 7). Latinos spur charismatic resurgence. *Washington Post*, p. 1.

Chun, S., and Sun, W. (2005, May 25). *Remittance behavior, acculturation, and socio-cultural-economic factors: A case study of Latinos in the Chicago Metropolitan area.* Paper presented at the Annual Meeting of the Population Association of America, Philadelphia.

Cintado, A. (2001). Educational aspects of deaf Hispanic children. Kent State University. Available at: http://monster.educ.kent.edu/deafed/010123a.htm. Accessed 5/23/05.

Clark, C. M., DeCarli, C., Mungas, D., Chui, H. I., Higdon, R., Nunez, J., Fernandez, H., Negron, M., Manly, J., Ferris, S., Perez, A., Torres, M., Ewbank, D., Glosser, G., and Van Belle, G. (2005). Earlier onset of Alzheimer disease symptoms in Latino individuals compared with Anglo individuals. *Archives of Neurology*, 62, pp. 774–778.

Clark, M. A. (1995). Examining a paradox: Does religiosity contribute to positive birth outcomes in Mexican American populations? *Health Education Quarterly*, 22, pp. 96–109.

Clark, S. T. (n.d). *"Machismo": Friend or foe?* California State University at San Marcos. Available at: http://public.csusm.edu/public/selark/machpap.html. Accessed 5/25/05.

Clemente, R. (2004, July 12). In search of Latino intellectuals; transforming a new generation. *Hispanic Outlook in Higher Education*, pp. 1–5.

Clemetson, L. (2002, October 6). A neighborhood clinic helps fill the gap for Latinos without health care. *New York Times*, p. A12.

Clemmons, J. C., DiLillo, D., Martinez, I. G., DeGue, S., and Jeffcott, M. (2003). Co-occurring forms of child maltreatment and adult adjustment reported by Latina college students. *Child Abuse and Neglect, 27*, pp. 751–767.

Cline, S. (2005, March 4). Surveys indicate minority businesses should de well in Colorado in 2005. *Colorado Springs Business Journal*, p. 1.

Coatsworth, J. D., Pantin, H., and Szapocznik, J. (2002). Familias Unidas: A family-centered ecodevelopmental intervention to reduce risk for problem behavior among Hispanic adolescents. *Clinical Child and Family Psychological Review, 5*, pp. 113–132.

Cohn, L. M. (1999). Maintaining and reunifying families: Two case studies of shifting legal status. In D. W. Haines and K. E. Rosenblum (Eds.), *Illegal immigration in America: A reference book* (pp. 383–395). Westport, Conn.: Praeger.

Coleman, J. A. (2003, August 26). A changing landscape? Si. *America*, p. 5.

Collins, A. H., and Pancoast, D. L. (1976). *Natural helping networks: A strategy for prevention.* Washington, D.C.: NASW Press.

Collins, M., Bussard, P. A., and Combes, J. R. (2003). The worsening Medicaid fiscal crisis: implications for hospitals. *Journal of Ambulatory Care Management, 26*, pp. 349–354.

Colomba, M. V., Santiago, E. S., and Rossello, J. (1999). Coping strategies and depression in Puerto Rican adolescents: An exploratory study. *Cultural Diversity and Ethnic Minority Psychology, 5*, pp. 65–75.

Colon, E. (1997). Program design and planning strategies in the delivery of culturally competent health and mental health prevention and treatment services in Latino communities. *Journal of Multicultural Social Work, 4*, pp. 49–66.

Colon, M., and Lyke, J. (2003). Comparison of hospice use and demographics among European Americans, African Americans, and Latinos. *American Journal of Palliative Care, 20*, p. 182–190.

Colon, V. (2004, May 5). America drinks up all things Hispanic: Consumer culture falls in love with Latino influence. *Fresno (Calif.) Bee*, p. A1.

Comas-Diaz, L. (2001). Hispanics, Latinos, or Americanos: The evolution of identity. *Cultural Diversity and Ethnic Minority Psychology, 7*, pp. 115–120.

Comas-Diaz, L. (1987). Cross-cultural mental health. In L. Comas-Diaz and E. E. H. Griffith (Eds.), *Clinical guidelines in cross-cultural mental health* (pp. 337–381). Washington, D.C.: Society for International Education Training and Research.

Connolly, C. (2005, August 28). Religion-linked hospitals accused of price gouging uninsured. *Boston Globe*, p. A6.

Consejo de Latinos Unidos holds a newsconference to release a report on the "scandalous profits and abuses by Catholic non-profit hospitals" and will comment on the "absolute silence and stillness from Catholic bishops." (2005, November 15). Washington Day Book. Available at: http://web.lexis.com/universe/document?_m=a9604c8f484383. Accessed 11/15/05.

Contreras, A. R. (2004). Epilogue: Latinos at the portal of the twenty-first century. *Education and Urban Society*, 36, pp. 223–234.

Coon, D. W., Rubert, M., Solano, N., Mausbach, B., Kraemer, H., Arguelles, T., Haley, W. E., Thompson, L. W., and Gallagher-Thompson, D. (2004). Well-being, appraisal, and coping in Latina and Caucasian female dementia caregivers: Findings from the REACH study. *Aging and Mental Health*, 8, pp. 330–345.

Coonrod, D. V., Bay, R. C., and Balcazar, H. (2004). Ethnicity, acculturation and obstetric outcomes. Different risk factor profiles in low- and high-acculturation Hispanics and in white non-Hispanics. *Journal of Reproductive Medicine*, 49, pp. 17–22.

Cooper, C. R., Denner, J., and Lopez, E. M. (1999). Cultural brokering: Helping Latino children on pathways towards success. *The Future/Children*, 9, pp. 51–57.

Cooper, M., and Sciorra, J. (1994). *Memorial wall art*. New York: Holt.

Coritsidis, G. N., Khamash, H., Ahmed, S. I., Attia, A. M., Rodriguez, P., Kiroycheva, M. K., and Ansari, N. (2004). The initiation of dialysis in undocumented aliens: The impact on a public hospital system. *American Journal of Kidney Diseases*, 43, pp. 424–432.

Cornelius, W. A. (2002). Ambivalent reception: Mass public responses to the "new" Latino immigration to the United States. In M. M. Suarez-Orozco and M. M. Paez (Eds.), *Latinos remaking America* (pp.165–189). Los Angeles: University of California Press.

Coronado, G. D., Thompson, B., McLerran, D., Schwartz, S. M., and Koepsell, T. D. (2005). A short acculturation scale for Mexican-American population. *Ethnic Disabilities*, 15, pp. 53–62.

Cortez, C. (2005). *Latino perceptions of success: Success as a cultural construct*. California State University, Santa Barbara. Available at: http://webpages.csusb.edu/-menair/Raymond.html. Accessed 5/29/05.

Cortez, G. (2005, February 17). Many Hispanics lack health access: Language barrier, often contributes. *Times-Picayune* (New Orleans), p. 8.

Coughlin, S. S., and Uhler, R. J. (2002). Breast and cervical cancer screening practices among Hispanic women in the United States and Puerto Rico, 1998–1999. *Preventive Medicine*, 34, pp. 242–251.

Coutin, S. B. (2003). *Legalizing moves: Salvadoran immigrants' struggle for U.S. residency*. Ann Arbor: University of Michigan Press.

Cox, H. (1995). *Fire from heaven: The rise of Pentecostal spirituality and the reshaping of religion in the twenty-first century*. Reading, MA: Addison-Wesley.

Crane, K. R. (2000). *Latino churches: Faith, family, and ethnicity in the second generation*. New York: LFB Scholarly.

Crawford, P. B., Gosliner, W., Anderson, C., Strode, P., Becerra-Jones, Y., Samuels, S., Carroll, A. M., and Ritchie, L. D. (2004). Counseling Latina mothers of preschool children about weight issues: Suggestions for a new framework. *Journal of the American Dietary Association*, 104, pp. 387–394.

Crespo, C. J., Smitt, E., Carter-Pokas, O., and Andersen, R. (2001). Acculturation and leisure-time physical activity in Mexican American adults: Results from

NHANES III, 1988–1994. *American Journal of Public Health*, 91, pp. 1254–1257.

Crockett, L. J., Randall, B. A., Shen, Y. L., Russell, S. T., and Driscoll, A. K. (2005). Measurement equivalence of the center for epidemiological studies depression scale for Latino and Anglo adolescents: A national study. *Journal of Consulting and Clinical Psychology*, 73, pp. 47–58.

Crowder, E. J. (2005, September 29). Hispanic hiring practices queried in Connecticut. *Connecticut Post* (Bridgeport), p. 1.

Crunkilton, D., Paz, J. J., and Boyle, D. P. (2005). Culturally competent intervention with families of Latino youth at risk for drug abuse. In M. De La Rosa, L. Holleran, and L. A. Straussner (Eds.), *Substance abusing Latinos: Current research on epidemiology and treatment* (pp. 113–131). New York: Haworth Press.

Cullen, F. (2005, July 20). On immigration policy, conservatives can learn a lesson from President Bush. *Union Leader* (Manchester, N.H.), p. A8.

Culturally based model designed to reduce Latino adolescent HIV sexual risk. (2005, June 26). *Health Insurance Week*, p. 149.

Dai, I. (2005, March 14). Changing demographics imperil churches. *San Gabriel Valley (Calif.) Tribune*, p. 1.

Dalin, S. (2005, September 28). Higher percentage of Latinos starting companies, study says. *Tribune* (Port St. Lucie/Fort Pierce, Fla.), p. 1.

Dallas, C., and Burton, L. (2004). Health disparities among men from racial and ethnic minority populations. *Annual Review of Nursing Research*, 22, pp. 77–100.

Danovitch, G. M., Cohen, D. J., Weir, M. R., Stock, P. G., Bennett, W. M., Christensen, L. L., and Sung, R. S. (2005). Current status of kidney and pancreas transplantation in the United States, 1994–2003. *American Journal of Transplants*, 5, pp. 904–915.

Davila, A. (2001). *Latinos Inc.: The marketing and making of a people*. Berkeley: University of California Press.

Daykin, T. (2004, October 9). Miller pours on the sales pitch to Latinos. *Milwaukee (Wisc.) Journal Sentinel*, p. 1.

De Alba, I., Sweningson, J. M., Chandy, C., and Hubbell, F. A. (2004). Impact of English language proficiency on receipt of pap smears among Hispanics. *Journal of General Internal Medicine*, 19, pp. 985–986.

Deaths on border of Arizona strain morgues capacity. (2005, September 4). Associated Press. *New York Times*, p. 11.

Deck, A. F. (2004). A Latino practical theology: Mapping the road ahead. *Theological Studies*, 65, pp. 275–297.

De Genova, N., and Ramos-Zayas, A. Y. (2003). *Latino crossings: Mexicans, Puerto Ricans, and the politics of race and citizenship*. New York: Routledge.

Deison, J. (2005, August 14). Latinos work to shore up border. *Los Angeles Times*, p. B1.

De La Cancela, V., and Zavalas, I. (1983). An analysis of culturalism in Latino mental health: Folk medicine as a case in point. *Hispanic Journal of Behavioral Sciences*, 5, pp. 251–274.

De La Rosa, M. (2002). Acculturation and Latino adolescents' substance use: A research agenda for the future. *Substance Use and Misuse*, 37, pp. 429–456.

De La Rosa, M. (1988). Natural support systems of Hispanic Americans: A key dimension of wellbeing. Health and Social Work, 13, pp. 181–190.

De La Rosa, M., Holleran, L., Rugh, D., and MacMaster, S. A. (2005). Substance abuse among U.S. Latinos: A review of the literature. In M. De La Rosa, L. Holleran, and L. A. Straussner (Eds.), *Substance abusing Latinos: Current research on epidemiology and treatment* (pp. 1–20). New York: Haworth Press.

De La Rosa, M., Holleran, L., and Straussner, S. L. A. (Eds.). (2005). *Substance abuse and Latinos: Current research on epidemiology, prevention, and treatment.* New York: Haworth Press.

De La Rosa, M., and Rugh, D. (2005). Onset of alcohol and other drug use among Latino gang members: Preliminary analysis. In M. Delgado (Ed.), *Latinos and alcohol use/abuse revisited: Advances and challenges for prevention and treatment programs* (pp. 67–85). New York: Haworth Press.

De La Rosa, M., and White, M. S. (2001). A review of the role of social support systems in the drug use behavior of Hispanics. *Journal of Psychoactive Drugs, 33,* pp. 233–240.

De Leon, D., and Carrasco, R. (1995). Two language, two cultures: Fact, not fiction, for Hispanic churches of the future. *Hispanic Association of Bilingual Bicultural Ministries Newsletter,* February, pp. 1–3.

Delgado, M. (2006). *Designs and methods for youth-led research.* Thousand Oaks, Calif.: Sage.

Delgado, M. (2003). *Death at an early age and the urban scene: The case for memorial murals and community healing.* Westport, Conn.: Praeger.

Delgado, M. (2001). *Where are all of the young men and women of color? Capacity enhancement practice and the criminal justice system.* New York: Columbia University Press.

Delgado, M. (2000). *Social work practice within an urban context: The potential of a community capacity enhancement perspective.* New York: Oxford University Press.

Delgado, M. (1999a). *Social work practice in nontraditional urban settings.* New York: Oxford University Press.

Delgado, M. (1999b). A state of the art review of Latinos and substance abuse. In S. B. Kar (Ed.), *Substance abuse prevention: A multicultural perspective* (pp. 155–170). Amityville, N.Y.: Baywood.

Delgado, M. (1998a). Puerto Rican elders and merchant establishments: Natural caregiving systems or simply businesses? *Journal of Gerontological Social Work,* 30, pp. 33–45.

Delgado, M. (1998b). *Social services in Latino communities: Research and strategies.* New York: Haworth Press.

Delgado, M. (1996a). Implementing a natural support system AOD project: Administrative considerations and recommendations. *Alcoholism Treatment Quarterly,* 14, pp. 1–14.

Delgado, M. (1996b). Puerto Rican food establishments as social service organizations: Results of an asset assessment. *Journal of Community Practice,* 3, pp. 57–70.

Delgado, M. (1995a). Community asset assessment and substance abuse prevention: A case study involving the Puerto Rican community. *Journal of Adolescent and Substance Abuse Prevention,* 4, pp. 57–77.

Delgado, M. (1995b). A guide for school-based personnel collaborating with Puerto Rican natural support systems. *New Schools, New Communities*, 12, pp. 38–42.

Delgado, M. (1995c). Hispanic natural support systems and alcohol and other drug services: Challenges and rewards for practice. *Alcoholism Treatment Quarterly*, 13, pp. 17–31.

Delgado, M. (1995d). Natural support systems and AOD services to communities of color: A California case example. *Alcoholism Treatment Quarterly*, 13, pp. 13–24.

Delgado, M. (1995e). Puerto Rican elders and natural support systems: Implications for human services. *Journal of Gerontological Social Work*, 24, pp. 115–129.

Delgado, M. (1994). Hispanic natural support systems and the AODA field: A developmental framework for collaboration. *Journal of Multicultural Social Work*, 3, pp. 11–37.

Delgado, M. (1979). Herbal medicine in the Puerto Rican community. *Health and Social Work*, 4, pp. 24–40.

Delgado, M. (1977). Puerto Rican spiritualism and the social work profession. *Social Casework*, 58, pp. 451–458.

Delgado, M. (Ed.). (2005). *Latinos and alcohol use/abuse revisited: Advances and challenges for prevention and treatment programs*. New York: Haworth Press.

Delgado, M. (Ed.). (1998c). *Alcohol use/abuse among Latinos: Issues and examples of culturally competent services*. New York: Haworth Press.

Delgado, M. (Ed.). (1998d). *Latino elders and the twenty-first century: Issues and challenges for culturally competent research and practice*. New York: Haworth Press.

Delgado, M., and Humm-Delgado, D. (In press). *Health and health care in prisons: Issues, challenges, and policies*. Westport, Conn.: Praeger.

Delgado, M., and Humm-Delgado, D. (1993). Chemical dependence, self-help groups, and the Hispanic community. In R. S. Mayers, B. L. Kail, and T. D. Watts (Eds.), *Hispanic substance abuse* (pp. 145–156). Springfield, Ill.: Charles C. Thomas.

Delgado, M., and Humm-Delgado, D. (1982). Natural support systems: A source of strength in Hispanic communities. *Social Work*, 27, pp. 83–89.

Delgado, M., Jones, K., and Rohani, M. (2005). *Social work practice with refugee and immigrant youth in the United States*. Boston: Allyn and Bacon.

Delgado, M., and Rivera, H. (1997). Puerto Rican natural support systems: Impact on families, communities, and schools. *Urban Education*, 32, pp. 81–95.

Delgado, M., and Rosati, M. (2005). Pentecostal religion, asset assessment and alcohol and other drug abuse: A case study of a Puerto Rican community in Massachusetts. In M. Delgado (Ed.), *Latinos and alcohol use/abuse revisited: Advances and challenges for prevention and treatment programs* (pp. 185–202). New York: Haworth Press.

Delgado, M., and Santiago, J. (1998). Botanical shops in a Puerto Rican/Dominican community in New England: Implications for health and human services. *Social Work*, 43, pp. 183–186.

Delgado, M., and Staples, L. (In press). *Youth-led community organizing*. New York: Oxford University Press.

Delgado, M., and Tennstedt, S. (1997). Making the case for culturally appropriate community services: Puerto Rican elders and their caregivers. *Health and Social Work*, 22, pp. 246–255.

Del Olmo, F. (2001). *Hispanic, Latino or Chicanos? A historical review*. Washington, D.C.: National Association of Hispanic Journalists.

Delva, J., Wallace, J. M., O'Malley, P. M., Bachman, J. G., Johnston, L. D., and Schulenberg, J. E. (2005). The epidemiology of alcohol, marijuana, and cocaine use among Mexican American, Puerto Rican, Cuban American, and other Latin American eighth-grade students in the United States: 1991–2002. *American Journal of Public Health*, 95, pp. 696–702.

DePalma, A. (2005a, May 26). Fifteen years on the bottom rung: Mexican immigrants and the specter of an enduring underclass. *New York Times*, pp. A1, A16.

DePalma, A. (2005b, May 27). Who has work? He who finds busboys: Employment agency heeds the call for Mexican kitchen help in New York. *New York Times*, p. A20.

Deparle, J. (2005, May 3). Hispanic group thrives on faith and federal aid. *New York Times*, pp. A1, A16.

Deren, S., Shedlin, M., Davis, W. R., Clatts, M. C., Balcorta, S., Beardsley, M. M., Sanchez, J., and Des Jarlais, D. (1997). Dominican, Mexican, and Puerto Rican prostitutes: Drug use and sexual behaviors. *Hispanic Journal of Behavioral Sciences*, 19, pp. 202–213.

Derose, K. P., and Baker, D. W. (2000). Limited English proficiency and Latinos' use of physician services. *Medical Care Research Review*, 57, pp. 76–91.

DeSipio, L., and Garza, R. O. de la. (2002). Forever seen as new Latino participation in American elections. In M. M. Suarez-Orozco and M. M. Paez (Eds.), *Latinos remaking America* (pp. 398–409). Los Angeles: University of California Press.

DeSipio, L., and Henson, J. R. (1997). Cuban Americans, Latinos, and the print media. *Harvard International Journal of Press/Politics*, 2, pp. 52–70.

Devine, C. M., Wolf, W. S., Frongillo, E. A., and Bisogni, C. A. (1999). Life-course events and experiences: Association with fruit and vegetable consumption in three ethnic groups. *Journal of the American Dietary Association*, 99, pp. 309–314.

Diaezcanseco-Mallipudi, C. (2004, October 15). Latinos react today to high AIDS rate. *Anchorage (Alaska) Daily News*, p. B-12.

Diaz, E., Prigerson, H., Desai, R., and Rosenheck, R. (2001). Perceived needs and service use of Spanish-speaking monolingual patients followed at a Hispanic clinic. *Community Mental Health Journal*, 37, pp. 335–346.

Diaz, H. L., and Watts, T. D. (2005). *Alcohol abuse among Puerto Ricans in the United States: An exploratory study*. Lewiston, N.Y.: Edwin Mellen Press.

Diaz, R. M., Heckert, A. L., and Sanchez, J. (2005). Reasons for stimulant use among Latino gay men in San Francisco: A comparison between methamphetamine and cocaine users. *Journal of Urban Health*, 82, pp. 171–178.

Diaz, V. A. (2002). Cultural factors in preventive care: Latinos. *Primary Care*, 29, pp. 503–517.

Dinan, S. (2005, February 17). Legal immigrants will help Social Security, study says. *Washington Times*, p. A09.

Dingfelder, S. F. (2005a). Closing the gap for Latino patients. *APA Monitor on Psychology*, 36, p. 58.

Dingfelder, S. F. (2005b). Cultural considerations. *APA Monitor on Psychology*, 36, p. 59.

Dingfelder, S. F. (2005c). Latino psychology takes center stage. *APA Monitor on Psychology*, 36, p. 62.

Diviney, A. (2005, January 28). Keeping the faith. *Evening Sun* (Hanover, Pa.), p. 1.

Dobkin de Rios, M. (2002). What we can learn from shamanic healing: Brief psychotherapy with Latino immigrant clients. *American Journal of Public Health*, 93, pp. 1576–1581.

Documet, P. I., and Sharma, R. K. (2004). Latinos' health care access: Financial and cultural barriers. *Journal of Immigrant Health*, 6, pp. 5–13.

Dogwood Center. (2002). Health emergency: The spread of drug-related AIDS among Latinos. Princeton, NJ: Author.

Dombrouski, J., and McCahill, C. (2004). Practical ethics. Hable usted Espanol? *Hospital Health Network*, 78, p. 35.

Dong, X., and Platner, J. W. (2004). Occupational fatalities of Hispanic construction workers from 1992–2000. *American Journal of Industrial Medicine*, 45, pp. 45–54.

Dorning, M. (2002, December 18). Hispanic immigrants cite importance of English proficiency in poll. *Chicago-Tribune*, p. 1.'

Dorrington, C. (1995). Central American refugees in Los Angeles. In R. E. Zambrana (Ed.), *Understanding Latino families: Scholarship, policy, and practice* (pp. 107–129). Thousand Oaks, Calif.: Sage.

Doty, M. (2003). *Hispanic patients' double burden: Lack of health insurance and limited English. Findings from the Commonwealth Fund 2001 Health Care Quality Survey.* The Commonwealth Fund, New York. Available at: http://www.smwf.org/usr_docdoty_hispanicdoubleburden_592.pdf. Accessed 6/3/05.

Doty, M., and Holmgren, A. L. (2004). Unequal access: Insurance instability among low- income workers and minorities. *Issue Brief* (Commonwealth Fund), 729, pp. 1–6.

Dow, M. (2004). *American Gulag: Inside U. S. immigration prisons.* Berkeley, Ca.: University of California Press.

Doyle, M. (2004, March 22). Obese Latino youth at risk: Valley researchers find group's teens more likely to be overweight and face diabetes, other illnesses. *Modesto (Calif.) Bee*, p. B1.

Drachman, D., and Paulino, A. (Eds). (2004). *Immigrants and social work: Thinking beyond the borders of the United States.* New York: Haworth Press.

Drake, R. E., Merrens, M. R., and Lynde, D. W. (Eds.). (2005). *Evidence-based mental health practice.* New York: Norton.

Duerksen, S. C., Mikail, A., Tom, L., Patton, A., Lopez, J., Amador, X., Vargas, R., Victorio, M., Kustin, B., and Sadler, G. R. (2005). Health disparities and advertising content of women's magazine's: A cross-sectional study. *BMC Public Health*, 5, p. 85.

Duggleby, W. (2003). Helping Hispanic/Latino home health patients manage their pain. *Home Healthcare Nurse*, 21, pp. 174–179.

Dvorak, P. (2005, August 3). Plight of uninsured children underscored; many youngsters see no doctor for a year, study finds. *Washington Post*, p. B3.

Dymi, A. (2004, November). Undocumented Latino immigrants seen as potential sources of $44 billion in home mortgages. *American Banker-Bond Buyer*, 14, p. 17.

Earle, D. M. (1999). Border crossings, border control: Illegalized migrants from the other side. In D. W. Haines and K. E. Rosenblum (Eds.), *Illegal immigration in America: A reference book* (pp. 396–411). Westport, Conn.: Praeger.

Easter, M., and Refki, D. (2004). Creating successful programs for immigrant youth. *Practice Matters* (Cornell University), December, pp. 1–4.

Easterbrook, M. (2005, March 22). Study: three hundred thousand living illegally in North Carolina; population may be eighth-largest in U.S. *News and Observer* (Raleigh, N.C.), p. B5.

Echeverria, C. C. (2004, September 30). Are you bicultural and/or bilingual? Available at: http://juantornoe.blogs.com/hispanictrending/2004/10/are_you_biculu .html. Accessed 5/23/05. Educating the largest minority group. (2003, November 28). *Chronicle of Higher Education*, p. 6.

Egan, T. (2005a, May 30). A battle raging against illegal workers in Idaho has unlikely driving force. *New York Times*, p. A11.

Egan, T. (2005b, March 24). Vibrant cities find one thing missing: Children. *New York Times*, p. 1.

Egelko, B. (2005, September 29). FedEx minority workers get OK for class action; Blacks, Latinos in firm's West region allege job bias. *San Francisco Chronicle*, p. B4.

Egger-Pierole, C. (2005). *Connections and commitments: Reflecting Latino values in early childhood programs*. Portsmouth, N.H.: Heinemann.

Elbin, V. J., Sneed, C. D., Morisky, D. E., Rotheram-Borus, M. J., Magnusson, A. M., and Malotte, C. K. (2001). Acculturation and interrelationships between problem and health-promoting behaviors among Latino adolescents. *Journal of Adolescent Health*, 28, pp. 62–72.

Elderkin-Thompson, V., Silver, R. C., and Waitzkin, H. (2001). When nurses double as interpreters: A study of Spanish-speaking patients in a US primary care setting. *Social Science Medicine*, 52, pp. 1343–1358.

Ellington, B. (2005, April 17). Hard working immigrants vital to economic growth. *State Hornet* (California State University, Sacramento), p. 1.

Elliott, K., and Cosden, M. (2000). Acculturation, family stress and school performance of Latino children. Santa Barbara: University of California, Santa Barbara. Available at: http://lmri.ucsb.edu/profdev/2/Imri_conference/98_conf/ 98elliot.htm. Accessed 5/19/05.

Elliott, S. (2004, November 15). Beer brewers scuffle their accounts in an effort to capture bigger shares of the Hispanic market. *New York Times*, p. 10.

Elliott, V. S. (2001, August 6). Cultural competency critical in elder care. *AMNews*. Available at: http://www.ama-assn.org/amednews/2001/08/06/hll20806 .htm. Accessed 5/18/05.

El Nasser, H. (2005, February 15). "New urbanism" embraces Latinos. *USA Today*, p. 1.

Enguidanos, S., Yip, J., and Wilber, K. (2005). Ethnic variation in site of death of older adults dually eligible for medicaid and medicare. *Journal of the American Geriatric Society*, 53, pp. 1411–1416.

ERIC Clearinghouse on Urban Education. (2001). *Latinos in school: Some facts and findings*. ERIC Digest Number 162. New York: Author.

Erut, S., Szalacha, L. A., Coll, C. G., and Alarcon, O. (2000). Puerto Rican early adolescents' self-esteem patterns. *Journal of Research on Adolescence*, 10, pp. 339–
364.

Erwin, D. G. (2004, May 11). Latins fight for identity beyond beer billboards' stereotyped façade. *Sacramento Bee*, p. B1.

Erwin, D. O., Johnson, V. A., Feliciano-Libid, L., Zamora, D., and Jandorf, L. (2005).
Incorporating cultural constructs and demographic diversity in the research
and development of a Latina breast and cervical cancer education programs.
Journal of Cancer Education, 20, pp. 39–44.

Eschbach, K., Mahnken, J. D., and Goodwin, J. S. (2005). Neighborhood composition and incidence of cancer among Hispanics in the United States. *Cancer*, 103,
pp. 1036–1044.

Eschbach, K., Ostir, G. V., Patel, K. V., Markides, K. S., and Goodwin, J. S. (2004).
Neighborhood context and mortality among older Mexican Americans: Is there
a barrio advantage? *American Journal of Public Health*, 94, pp. 1807–1812.

Escobar, J. L., Hoyos, N. C., and Gara, M. A. (2000). Immigration and mental health:
Mexican Americans in the United States. *Harvard Review of Psychiatry*, 8,
pp. 64–72.

Espinosa, G., Elizondo, V., and Miranda, J. (2003). *Hispanic churches in American public
life: Summary of findings*. Terra Haute, Ind.: University of Notre Dame Press.

Ewing, W. A., and Johnson, B. (2003). *Immigrant success or stagnation? Confronting
the claim of Latino non-advancement*. Washington, D.C.: American Immigration
Law Foundation.

Falcon, L. M. (2001, March 25). Does a Latino community exist? *Boston Globe*, p. 1.

Falicov, C. J. (1998). *Latino families in therapy: A guide to multicultural practice*. New
York: Guilford Press.

Families USA. (2005, February 9). *Cut Medicaid: Increase health disparities*. Washington, D.C.: Author.

Families USA. (2002, December). *Health coverage in Latino communities*. Washington, D.C.: Author.

Fang, J., and Alderman, M. H. (2003). Is geography destiny for patients in New York
with myocardial infarction? *American Journal of Medicine*, 115, pp. 448–453.

Farley, T., Galves, A., Dickinson, L. M., and Perez, M. J. (2005). Stress, coping, and
health: A comparison of Mexican immigrants, Mexican-Americans, and non-
Hispanic whites. *Journal of Immigrant Health*, 7, pp. 213–220.

Farquhar, S. A., Michael, Y. L., and Wiggins, N. (2005). Building on leadership and
social capital to create change in two urban communities. *American Journal of
Public Health*, 95, pp. 596–601.

Farrakhan: Fox was right on Backs, jobs. (2005, August 15). Associated Press. Available at: http://web.lexis-nexis.com/universe/document?_m=c51ecee04222a2.
Accessed 9/1/05.

Feagans, B. (2004, September 23). Hispanics' economic clout: Got dinero? *Atlanta
Journal-Constitution*, p. 1J.

Fears, D. (2005, July 27). Cost of illegal-immigrant returns put at $41 billion. *Bos-
ton Globe*, p. A7.

Fears, D. (2003, July 14). Race divides Hispanics, report says. *Washington Post*, p. A3.

Fears, H. (2002, December 29). Some Hispanic immigrants are perceived as black in U.S. *Tampa Tribune*, p. 20.

Featherstone, D. (1992, August 17). Shop where business is a religion. *Newsday*, p. 33.

Feliciano, C. (2001). The benefits of biculturalism: Exposure to immigrant culture and dropping out of school among Asian and Latino youth. *Social Science Quarterly*, 82, pp. 865–879.

Ferdinand, K. C. (2005). Managing cardiovascular risk in minority patients. *Journal of the National Medical Association*, 97, pp. 459–466.

Ferkenhoff, E. (2004, October 18). Chicago turns to minority clergy to recruit police: Black, Latino officers are sought to improve community relations. *Boston Globe*, p. A2.

Fernandez, A., Schillinger, D., Grumbach, K., Rosenthal, A., Stewart, A. L., Wang, F., and Perez-Stable, E. J. (2004). Physician language ability and cultural competence. An exploratory study of communication with Spanish-speaking patients. *Journal of General Internal Medicine*, 19, pp. 167–174.

Fernandez, M. I., Perrino, T., Collazo, J. B., Varga, L. M., Marsh, D., Hernandez, N., Rehbein, A., and Bowen, G. S. (2005). Surfing new territory: Club-drug use and risky sex among Hispanic men who have sex with men recruited on the Internet. *Journal of Urban Health*, 82, pp. 179–188.

Fernandez, M. I., Perrino, T., Royal, S., Ghany, D., and Bowen, G. S. (2002). To test or not to test: Are Hispanic men at highest risk for HIV getting tested? *AIDS Care*, 14, pp. 375–384.

Fernandez, T. (2005, January 10). Growing city counts on head count; population increase brings federal funds, but newcomers slip by unnoticed. *Crains New York Business*, p. 12.

Fernandez-Esquer, M. E., Espinoza, P., Torres, I., Ramirez, A. G., and McAlister, A. L. (2003). A su salud: A quasi-experimental study among Mexican American women. *American Journal of Health Behavior*, 27, 536–545.

Ferreri, E. (2005, January 22). Workers decry lack of policies in Spanish: Employee claims harassment after meeting on work conditions. *Durham (N.C.) Herald*, p. 1.

Feuer, A. (2003, September 6). Ethnic chasm in El Barrio: Changes pit Mexicans against Puerto Ricans. *New York Times*, p. A10.

Field, C. A., and Caetano, R. (2003). Longitudinal model predicting partner violence among white, black, and Hispanic couples in the United States. *Alcohol: Clinical and Experimental Research*, 27, pp. 1451–1458.

Fields, R. (2001, August 10). Decline of Latino groups in census. *Los Angeles Times*, p. 11.

Fierros, E. G., and Conroy, J. W. (2002). Double jeopardy: An exploration of restrictiveness and race in special education. In Daniel J. Losen and G. Orfield (Eds.), *Racial inequity in special education* (pp. 39–70). Cambridge, Mass.: Harvard University Press.

Files, J. (2005, June 10). Report describes immigrants as younger and more diverse. *New York Times*, p. A11.

Finch, B. K., and Vega, W. A. (2003). Acculturation stress, social support, and self-rated health among Latinos in California. *Journal of Immigrant Health*, 5, pp. 109–117.

Finn, J. L., and Jacobson, M. (2003). Just practice: Steps toward a new social work paradigm. *Journal of Social Work Education*, 39, pp. 57–78.

Fiscella, K., Franks, P., Doescher, M. P., and Saver, B. G. (2002). Disparities in health care by race, ethnicity, and language among the uninsured: Findings from a national sample. *Medical Care*, 40, pp. 52–59.

Fisher, K. E., Marcoux, E., Miller, L. S., Sanchez, A., and Cunningham, E. R. (2004). Information behaviour of migrant Hispanic farm workers and their families in the Pacific Northwest. *Information Research*, 10, pp. 1–20.

Fisher, M. (2005, July 8). California bishop defends bid to help immigrants. Scripps Howard News Service. Available at: http://web.lex-nexis.com/universe/document?_m=f141dbc51c34f0f. Accessed 7/27/05.

Flores, C. (2001, Winter/Spring). Race discrimination within the Latino community. *Dialogo*. Available at: http://condor.depaul. edu/-dialogo/back_issues/issue_5/race_discrimination.htm. Accessed 6/6/05.

Flores, E., Ciechetti, D., and Rogosch, F. A. (2005). Predictors of resilience in maltreated and nonmaltreated Lation children. *Developmental Psychology*, 41, pp. 338–351.

Flores, G. (2000). Culture and the patient-physician relationship: Achieving cultural competency in health care. *Journal of Pediatrics*, 136, pp. 14–23.

Flores, G., and Brotanek, J. (2005). The healthy immigrant effect: A greater understanding might help us improve the health of all children. *Archives of Pediatric Adolescent Medicine*, 159, pp. 261–265.

Flores, G., and Sheehan, P. (2000). Curbside consultation: Dealing with adolescent Latino patients. *American Family Physician*, 63, pp. 1–6.

Flores, G., Rabke-Verani, J., Pine, W., and Sabharwal, A. (2002). The importance of cultural and linguistic issues in the emergency care of children. *Pediatric Emergency Care*, 18, pp. 271–284.

Flores, J. (2000). *From bomba to hip-hop: Puerto Rican culture and Latino identity*. New York: Columbia University Press.

Fong, R. (Ed.). (2004). *Culturally competent practice with immigrant and refugee children and families*. New York: Guilford Press.

Fong, R., and Furuto, S. (Eds.). (2001). *Culturally competent practice: Skills, interventions, and evaluations*. Boston: Allyn and Bacon.

Foraker, R. E., Patten, C. A., Lopez, K. N., Croghan, I. T., and Thomas, J. L. (2005). Beliefs and attitudes regarding smoking among young adult Latinos: A pilot study. *Preventive Medicine*, 41, pp. 126–133.

Foster, J. (2004). Fatherhood and the meaning of children: An ethnographic study among Puerto Rican partners of adolescent mothers. *Journal of Midwifery and Womens Health*, 49, pp. 118–125.

Franco, F., Cuadra, A., Tobol, C. E., Zea, M. C., and Peterson, R. A. (1998). Factors affecting acculturation level for Latin American immigrants. *Journal of Multicultural Nursing and Health*, Fall, pp. 22–31.

Franzil, J. L. (2005, February 23). U.S. foreign-born population on the rise. UPI. Available at: http://web.lexis-nexis.com/universe/document?_m=9c09dale8349501. Accessed 5/20/05.

Franzini, L., Ribble, J. C., and Keddie, A. M. (2001). Understanding the Hispanic paradox. *Ethnic Disparities*, 11, pp. 496–518.

Franzini, L., Ribble, J., and Wingfield, K. (2004, November 6–10). Relationships between social factors, religion, and self-reported health in white, black, and Hispanic low income individuals. Paper presented at the annual meeting of the American Public Health Association, Washington, D.C.

Frates, J., Diringer, J., and Hogan, L. (2003). Models and momentum for insuring low-income undocumented immigrant children in California. *Health Affairs*, 22, pp. 259–263.

Frates, J., and Garcia Bohrer, G. (2002). Hispanic perceptions of organ donation. *Progressive Transplant* 12, pp. 169–175.

Freidenberg, J. N. (2000). *Growing old in El Barrio*. New York: New York University Press.

Friedman, J. (2005, September 26). Investment firms focusing on Latinos' purchasing power. *Los Angeles Times*, p. C1.

Fry, R. (2003). *Hispanic youth dropping out of U.S. schools: Measuring the challenge.* Washington, D.C.: Pew Hispanic Center.

Fry, R., Kochhar, R., Passel, J., and Suro, R. (2005). *Hispanics and the Social Security debate.* Washington, D.C.: Pew Hispanic Center.

Fuchs, L. H. (2004). Mr. Huntington's nightmare. *American Prospect*, August, p. 70.

Fullerton, J. A., and Kendrick, A. (2000). Portrayal of U.S. men and women in U.S. Spanish-language television commercials. *Journalism and Mass Communication Quarterly*, 77, pp. 128–142.

Galanti, G. A. (2003). The Hispanic family and male-female relationships: An overview. *Journal of Transcultural Nursing*, 14, pp. 180–185.

Galea, S., Ahern, J., Resnick, H., Kilpatrick, D., Bucuvalas, M., Gold, J., and Vlahov, D. (2002). Psychological sequelae of the September 11 terrorist attacks in New York City. *New England Journal of Medicine*, 346, pp. 982–987.

Galea, S., Vlahov, D., Tracy, M., Hoover, D. R., Resnick, H., and Kilpatrick, D. (2004). Hispanic ethnicity and post-traumatic stress disorder after a disaster: Evidence from a general population survey after September 11, 2001. *Annals of Epidemiology*, 14, pp. 520–531.

Gallagher-Thompson, D., Singer, L. S., Depp, C., Mausbach, B. T., Cardenas, V., and Coon, D. W. (2004). Effective recruitment strategies for Latino and Caucasian dementia family caregivers in intervention research. *American Journal of Geriatric Psychiatry*, 12, pp. 484–490.

Galvan, F. H. (1999). Sources of personal meaning among Mexican and Mexican American men with HIV/AIDS. *Journal of Multicultural Social Work*, 7, pp. 45–67.

Gamboa, C. L. M., Kahramanian, M. I., Morales, L. S., Hayes Bautista, D. E. (2005). Acculturation and Latino health in the United States: A review of the literature and its sociopolitical context. *Annual Review of Public Health*, 26, pp. 367–397.

Gambrill, E. D. (2003). Evidence-based practice: Sea change of the emperor's new clothes? *Journal of Social Work Education*, 39, pp. 3–23.

Gamst, G., Dana, R. H., Der-Karabetian, A., Aragon, M., Arellano, L. M., and Kramer, T. (2002). Effects of Latino acculturation and ethnic identity on mental health outcomes. *Hispanic Journal of Behavioral Sciences*, 24, pp. 479–504.

Gandara, P. (2002). Learning English in California: Guidepoints for the nation. In M. M. Suarez-Orozco and M. M. Paez (Eds.), *Latinos remaking America* (pp. 339–374). Berkeley: University of California Press.

Ganus, S. (2004, June 17). Analysis: Hispanic, Asian growth continues. United Press International. Available at: http://web.lexis-nexis.com/universe/document?_m=8defbbas5714c2. Accessed 5/10/05.

Gaona, E. (2004, April 15). Illegal immigrants paying taxes as example of good citizenship. *San Diego Union-Tribune*, p. A1.

Gaona, E., and Graham, D. (2005, August 12). Immigration confrontation contained; Carlsbad forum draws protesters—and 150 law officers. *San Diego Union-Tribune*, p. B1.

Gaouette, N. (2005a, July 3). Hispanic voters are still staying away in droves. *Boston Globe*, p. A18.

Gaouette, N. (2005b, June 28). Latino clout at polls lagging. *Los Angeles Times*, p. 14.

Garay, A. (2005, April 26). Study finds immigrant and Latino worker deaths increased in Texas. Associated Press State and Local Wire. Available at: http://web.lexis-nexis.com/univrse/document?_m=3d41aadf07ea9d. Accessed 5/6/05.

Garbers, S., Jessop, D. J., Foti, H., Uribelarrea, M., and Chiasson, M. A. (2003). Barriers to breast cancer screening for low-income Mexican and Dominican women in New York City. *Journal of Urban Health*, 80, pp. 81–91.

Garces-Foley, K. (2003, May 9). The public voice of Latino Protestantism. Paper presented at the conference entitled "Religious Pluralism in Southern California," University of Santa Barbara.

Garcia, B. (2005). Incarcerated Latinas and alcohol: Assessment and intervention considerations. In M. Delgado (Ed.), *Latinos and alcohol use/abuse revisited: Advances and challenges for prevention and treatment programs* (pp. 87–106) New York: Haworth Press.

Garcia, H. A. V., Coll, C. G., Erkut, S., Alarcon, O., and Tropp, L. R. (2000). Family values of Latino adolescents. In M. Montero-Sieburth and F. A. Villarruel (Eds.), *Making invisible Latino adolescents visible: A critical approach to Latino diversity* (pp. 239–264). New York: Palmer Press.

Garcia, J. E. (1999). *Hispanic/Latino identity: A philosophical perspective*. New York: Oxford University Press.

Garcia, L., Hurwitz, E. L., and Kraus, J. F. (2005). Acculturation and reported intimate partner violence among Latinas in Los Angeles. *Journal of Interpersonal Violence*, 28, pp. 569–590.

Garcia, M. (2003, December 25). Latino youth find their own tongue: Growing community development lively voice. *Washington Post*, p. A03.

Garcia, S. B., and Guerra, P. L. (2004). Deconstructing deficit thinking: Working with educators to create more equitable learning environments. *Education and Urban Society*, 36, pp. 150–168.

Garcia, T. (2004). La promesa de un tesoro: The promise of a treasure. Available at: http://www.df.org. Accessed 5/23/05.

Garcia-Reid, P., Reid, R. J., and Peterson, N. A. (2005). School engagement among Latino youth in an urban middle school context: Valuing the role of social support. *Education and Urban Society*, 36, pp. 257–275.

Gartner, E. (2005, August 11). Denver library yanks Spanish-language books after pornography complaints. *Associated Press*. Available at: http://web.lexis-nexis.com/universe/document?_m=cd658817e90771. Accessed 8/15/05.

Gelfand, D. E., Balcazar, H., Parzuchowski, J., and Lenox, S. (2004). Issues in hospice utilization by Mexicans. *Journal of Applied Gerontology*, 23, pp. 3–19.

Gelfand, D. E., Balcazar, H., Parzuchowski, J., and Lenox, S. (2001). Mexicans and care for the terminally ill: Family, hospice, and the church. *American Journal of Palliative Care*, 18, pp. 391–396.

Gelman, C. R. (2004). Empirically based principles for culturally competent practice with Latinos. *Journal of Ethnic and Cultural Diversity in Social Work*, 13, pp. 83–108.

Germany, A. M. (2000). *Cultural competency with Latinos*. University of Georgia School of Social Work. Available at: http://www.ssw.uga.edu/mexico/cultcomp1.html. Accessed 3/11/05.

Gerson, D. (2005, April 15). Immigrants in U.S. illegally file taxes, too. *New York Sun*, p. 1.

Gfoerer, J. C., and Tan, L. L. (2003). Substance use among foreign-born youths in the United States: Does the length of residence matter? *American Journal of Public Health*, 93, pp. 1892–1895.

Gibbs, J. T., and Bankhead, T. (2001). *Preserving privilege: California politics, propositions, and people of color*. Westport, Conn.: Praeger.

Gil, A. G., Vega, W. A., and Dimas, J. M. (1994). Stress and personal adjustment among Hispanic adolescent boys. *Journal of Community Psychology*, 22, pp. 43–54.

Gil, A. G., Wagner, E. F., and Tubman, J. G. (2004). Culturally sensitive substance abuse intervention for Hispanic and African American adolescents: Empirical examples from the Alcohol Treatment Targeting Adolescents in Need (ATTAIN) Project. *Addiction*, 99, pp. 140–150.

Gil, A. G., Wagner, E. F., and Vega, W. A. (2000). Acculturation, familism, and alcohol use among Latino adolescent males: Longitudinal relations. *Journal of Community Psychology*, 28, pp. 443–458.

Gittelsohn, J., McCormick, L. K., Allen, P., Grieser, M., Crawford, M., and Davis, S. (1999). Inter-ethnic differences in youth tobacco language and cigarette brand preferences. *Ethnicity and Health*, 4, pp. 285–303.

Glenn, D. (2004, February 13). Scholars cook up a new melting pot: Questioning old models of assimilation, social scientists examine the experience of recent Latin American immigrants. *Chronicle of Higher Education*, p. A10.

Gold, D. R., and Acevedo-Garcia, D. (2005). Immigration to the United Status and acculturation as risk factors for asthma and allergy. *Journal of Allergy and Clinical Immunology*, 116, pp. 38–41.

Goldstein, A. (2004, June 25). D.C. infant mortality rate up, but number drops for

Blacks; slight increase overall rise in white, Latino baby deaths. *Washington Post*, p. B02.

Goldstein, A., and Suro, R. (2000, January 16). A journey in stages: Assimilation's pull is still strong, but its pace varies. *Washington Post*, p. A01.

Gomez, F. (2005, July 5). Diversity, acceptance make America beautiful. Scripps Howard News Service. Available at: http://web.lexis-nexis.com/universe/document?_m=d197ffdbf91ac49. Accessed 7/20/05.

Gomez, L. M. (2004, December 13). Hispanics differ on cultural identity. *San Antonio Express-News*, p. 3B.

Gomez-Beloz, A., and Chavez, N. (2001). The botanicas as a culturally appropriate health care option for Latinos. *Journal of Alternative and Complementary Medicine*, 7, pp. 537–546.

Gonzalez, C. (2005a, September 10). A growing faith: New generations of Latino immigrants drive Our Lady of Guadalupe's expansion plans. *Omaha (Nebraska) World-Herald*, p. 1E.

Gonzalez, C. (2005b, April 18). Latino businesses forming chamber tailored for newer immigrants. *Omaha (Nebraska) World-Herald*, p. 1D.

Gonzalez, D. (2004, May 19). Hip-hop between the cold cuts: Bypassing record stores to sell CD's at bodegas. *New York Times*, p. A22.

Gonzalez, H. M., Haan, M. N., and Hinton, L. (2001). Acculturation and the prevalence of depression in older Mexican Americans: Baseline results of the Sacramento area Latino study on aging. *Journal of the American Geriatrics Society*, 49, pp. 948–953.

Gonzalez, J. (2001, March 9). Latinos now major players. *Daily News* (New York City), p. 17.

Gonzalez, J. M. (2003, July 15). The Hispanic color divide: Some align more with blacks. *Newsday*, p. 8.

Gonzalez, M. (2005, March 8). Mormon church attracts increasing number of Latinos. Scripps Howard News Service, p. 1.

Gonzalez, N. A., Knight, G. P., Birman, D., and Sirolli, A. (2001). Acculturation and enacculturation among Hispanic youths. In C. Schellench, K. Maton, B. Leadbetter, and A. Solarz (Eds.), *Investing in children, families, and communities: Strengths-based research and policies* (pp. 481–511). Washington, D.C.: American Psychological Association.

Gonzales, R. J. (2005a, September 7). Latinos doing dangerous jobs need safe conditions. *Fort Worth Star-Telegram*, p. 1.

Gonzalez, R. J. (2005b). Latinos seek more realistic portrayal of their presence. *Fort Worth Star-Telegram*, p. 2.

Gonzalez-Ramos, G., and Gonzalez, M. (2005). Health disparities in the Hispanic population: An overview. In M. J. Gonzalez and G. Gonzalez-Ramos (Eds.), *Mental health care for new Hispanic immigrants: Innovative approaches in contemporary clinical practice* (pp. 1–19). New York: Haworth Press.

Goodman, C., and Silverstein, M. (2002). Grandmothers raising grandchildren: Family structure and well-being in culturally diverse families. *Gerontologist*, 42, pp. 676–689.

Gorin, S. S., and Heck, J. E. (2005). Cancer screening among Latino subgroups in the United States. *Preventive Medicine*, 40, pp. 515–526.

Gorman, A. (2005, August 9). Despite illegal status, buyers get home loans. Mortgage lenders are designing programs aimed at undocumented immigrants. Real estate agents also see a huge untapped market. *Los Ángeles Times*, p. A1.

Goto, S. (2005, January 10). Latino money transfer battle heats up. *United Press International*, p. 1.

Graham, M. (2002). *Social work and African-centered world views*. Birmingham, England: Venture Press.

Grant, B. F., Stinson, F. S., Hasin, D. S., Dawson, D. A., Chou, S. P., and Anderson, K. (2004). Immigration and lifetime prevalence of DSM-IV psychiatric disorders among Mexican Americans and non-Hispanic whites in the United States: Results from the National Epidemiologic Survey of Alcohol and Related Conditions. *Archives of General Psychiatry*, 61, pp. 1226–1233.

Green, B. L., Lewis, R. K., and Bediako, S. M. (2005). Reducing and eliminating health disparities: A targeted approach. *Journal of the National Medical Association*, 97, pp. 25–30.

Green, G., Lee, M. Y., and Hoffpauir, S. (2005). The language of empowerment and strengths in clinical social work: A constructivist perspective. *Families in Society*, pp. 267–277.

Greene, M. L., and Niobe, W. (2005). Self-esteem trajectories among ethnic minority adolescents: A growth curve analysis of the patterns and predictors. *Journal of Research on Adolescence*, 15, pp. 151–178.

Greene, R. R., and Barnes, G. (1998). The ecological perspective, diversity, and culturally competent social work practice. In R. R. Greene and M. Watkins (Eds.), *Serving diverse constituencies: Applying the ecological perspective* (pp. 63–112). New York: de Gruyter.

Greene, R. R., Watkins, M., McNutt, J., and Lopez, L. (1998). Diversity defined. In R. R. Greene and M. Watkins (Eds.), *Serving diverse constituencies: Applying the ecological perspective* (pp. 29–61). New York: de Gruyter.

Greenhouse, S. (2005, September 6). Union organizers at poultry plants in South find newly sympathetic ears. *New York Times*, p. A15.

Greenhouse, S. (2001, July 16). Hispanic workers die at higher rate. *New York Times*, A11.

Greig, R. (2003). Ethnic identity development: Implications for mental health in African-American and Hispanic adolescents. *Issues in Mental Health Nursing*, 24, pp. 317–331.

Grieco, E. M., and Cassidy, R. C. (2001). *Overview of race and Hispanic origin*. Washington, D.C.: U.S. Bureau of the Census.

Griffin, K. W., Scheier, L. M., Botvin, G. J., and Diaz, T. (2000). Ethnic and gender differences in psychosocial risk protection, and adolescent alcohol use. *Prevention Science*, 1, pp. 199–212.

Griffith, D. (1999). Social and cultural bases for undocumented immigration into the U.S. poultry industry. In D. W. Haines and K. E. Rosenblum (Eds.), *Illegal immigration in America: A reference book* (pp. 157–192). Westport, Conn.: Praeger.

Griggs, S., and Dunn, R. (1999). Cultural values of Hispanic Americans. *Brown Quarterly*, 3, pp. 1–2.

Grillo, J. B. (2004, December 8). Culture of a million facets: Research is shedding new insights into many aspects of Latino consumers. *Multichannel News*, p. 1A.

Grimaldi, P. (2005, September 4). Pulling together: Latino merchants are finding a home in Rhode Island's business community. *Providence Journal*, p. F1.

Grisales, C. (2005, September 16). Fighting scams that take aim at Hispanics in Austin: 175 officials from Mexico, U.S. learn about schemes, how to stop them. *Austin American-Statesman*, p. D1.

Grogger, J., and Trejo, S. J. (2002). *Falling behind or moving up? The intergenerational progress of Mexican Americans*. San Francisco: Public Policy Institute of California.

Grow, B., Carter, A., Crockett, R. O., and Smith, G. (2005, July 18). Embracing illegals: Companies are getting hooked on the buying power of eleven million undocumented immigrants. *Business Week*, p. 56.

Guanipa-Ho, C., and Guanipa, J. A. (1998). *Ethnic identity and adolescence*. Available at: http://edweb.sdsu.edu/people/cguanipa/ethnic.htm. Accessed 5/29/05.

Guarnaccia, P. J., Lewis-Fernandez, R., and Marano, M. R. (2003). Toward a Puerto Rican popular noslogy: Nervios and ataque de nervios. *Culture, Medicine and Psychiatry*, 27, pp. 339–366.

Guarnaccia, P. J., Martinez, I., and Acosta, H. (2005). Mental health in the Hispanic Immigrant community: An overview. In M. J. Gonzalez and G. Gonzalez-Ramos (Eds.), *Mental health care for new Hispanic immigrants: Innovative approaches in contemporary clinical practice* (pp. 21–46). New York: Haworth Press.

Guerra, F. J. (2005, May 3). The browning of U.S. politics. *Los Angeles Times*, p. 1.

Guilamo-Ramos, V., Jaccard, J., Pena, J., and Goldberg, V. (2005). Acculturation-related variables, sexual initiation, and subsequent sexual behavior among Puerto Rican, Mexican, and Cuban youth. *Health Psychology*, 24, pp. 88–95.

Guinn, B., and Vincent, V. (2002). Determinants of coping responses among Mexican-American adolescents. *Journal of School Health*, 72, pp. 152–156.

Gutierrez, L., Ortega, R. M., and Suarez, Z. (1990). Self-help and the Latino community. In T. J. Powell (Ed.), *Working with self-help* (pp. 218–236). Silver Springs, Md.: NASW Press.

Gutierrez, L., Yeakley, A., and Ortega, R. (2000). Educating students for social work with Latinos: Issues for the new millenium. *Journal of Social Work Education*, 36, pp. 511–557.

Haas, J. S., Phillips, K. A., Sonneborn, D., McCulloch, C. F., Baker, L. C., Kaplan, C. P., Perez-Stable, E. J., and Liang, S. Y. (2004). Variation in access to health care for different racial/ethnic groups by the racial/ethnic composition of an individual's county of residence. *Medical Care*, 42, pp. 707–714.

Haberman, D. (2005, October 1). City's Latino count climbs. *Press Enterprise* (Riverside, Calif.), p. B1.

Hagan, J., and Rodriguez, N. (2002). Resurrecting exclusion: The effects of 1996 U.S. immigration reform on communities and families in Texas, El Salvador, and Mexico. In M. M. Suarez-Orozco and M. M. Paez (Eds.), *Latinos remaking America* (pp. 190–201). Berkeley: University of California Press.

Hahn, E. A., and Cella, D. (2003). Health outcomes assessment in vulnerable populations: measurement challenges and recommendations. *Archives of Physical Medicine and Rehabilitation*, 84, pp. S35–S42.

Hajat, A., Lucas, J., and Kington, R. (2000). *Health outcomes among Hispanic subgroups: United States, 1992–1995. Advance data from vital and health statistics: No. 310.* Hyattsville, Md.: National Center for Health Statistics.

Hancox, R. J., Milne, B. J., and Poulton, R. (2004). Association between child and adolescent television viewing and adult health: A longitudinal birth cohort study. *Lancet*, 364, pp. 257–62.

Hanley, J. (1999). Beyond the tip of the iceberg: Five stages toward cultural competence. *Reaching Today's Youth*, 3, pp. 9–12.

Hargraves, J. L., and Hadley, J. (2003). The contribution of insurance coverage and community resources to reducing racial/ethnic disparities in access to care. *Health Services Research*, 38, pp. 809–829.

Haro, R. (2004). Programs and strategies to increase Latino students' educational attainment. *Education and Urban Society*, 36, pp. 205–222.

Harris, M. B., and Franklin, C. G. (2003). Effects of a cognitive-behavioral school-based, group intervention with Mexican American pregnant and parenting adolescents. *Social Work Research*, 27, pp. 71–83.

Harris, R. J., Firestone, J. M., and Vega, W. A. (2005). The interaction of country of origin, acculturation and gender role ideology on wife abuse. *Social Science Quarterly*, 86, pp. 463–483.

Hartel, L. J., and Mehling, R. (2002). Consumer health services and collections for Hispanics: An introduction. *Medical References Services Quarterly*, 21, pp. 35–52.

Harwood, J., and Anderson, K. (2002). The presence and portrayal of social groups on prime-time television. *Communication Reports*, 15, pp. 81–97.

Hawley, C. (2005, March 22). Undocumented migrants coming to stay. *Arizona Republic*, p. 1.

Hayes-Bautista, D. E. (2002). The Latino health research agenda for the twenty-first century. In M. M. Suarez-Orozco and M. M. Paez (Eds.), *Latinos remaking America* (pp. 213–235). Los Angeles: University of California Press.

Hayes-Bautista, D. E., Schink, W. O., and Chapa, J. (1988). *The burden of support: Young Latinos in an aging society.* Stanford, Calif.: Stanford University Press.

Hecht, P. (2005, August 29). A drive for clout: Community groups representing Mexican immigrants form a confederation to influence public policy in California. *Sacramento Bee*, p. A1.

Hielemann, M. V., Frutos, L., Lee, K., and Kury, F. S. (2004). Protective strength factors, resources, and risks in relation to depressive symptoms among child-rearing women of Mexican descent. *Health Care Women International*, 25, pp. 88–106.

Hielemann, M. V., Lee, K. A., and Kury, F. S. (2002). Strengths and vulnerabilities of women of Mexican descent in relation to depressive symptoms. *Nursing Research*, 51, pp. 175–182.

Held, T. (2005, August 11). Latino numbers booming. *Milwaukee Journal Sentinel*, p. 1.

Helfand, D. (2005, March 24). Nearly half of Blacks, Latinos drop out, school study shows. *Los Angeles Times*, p. I.

Heller, M. (2005, August 12). Unions fight to attract Latino workers. Scripps Howard News Service. Available at: http://web.lexis-nexis.com/universe/document?_m=0ce2e1407223a7f. Accessed 8/17/05.

Hendricks, T. (2005a, May 10). L.A. mayor race seen as win for all Latinos. *San Francisco Chronicle*, p. A1.

Hendricks, T. (2005b, March 22). 10.3 million immigrants in U.S. illegally, researcher on Latinos says. *San Francisco Chronicle*, p. A4.

Hendricks, T. (2004, August 26). Group's study says illegals not paying their way. *San Francisco Chronicle*, p. A4.

Hendricks, T. (2003, May 6). Census refines state's Hispanic tally. No change in total, just a better idea of who has roots where. *San Francisco Chronicle*, p. A5.

Hendricks, T. (2002, May 3). Upbeat findings on Latinos in U.S.: Nation's largest minority overcomes hardships, exceeds expectations in health, language, studies say. *San Francisco Chronicle*, p. A1.

Hernandez, D. (2003a, July 15). Report shows how racial identities affect Latinos. *Los Ángeles Times*, p. A10.

Hernandez, D. (2003b, April 15). Tax day puts illegal immigrants in a special bind. *New York Times*, p. A19.

Hernandez, M. (2004, July 21–23). Evidence-based programs and cultural competence: What we know and do not know. Paper presented at the conference entitled "Promises and Challenges of Evidence-Based Practices for Latino Youth and Families" (July 21–23). Miami, Fl.

Hernandez, R. (2004a). On the age against the poor: Dominican migration to the United States. In D. Drachman and A. Paulino (Eds.), *Immigrants and social work: Thinking beyond the borders of the United States* (pp. 87–107). New York: Haworth Press. "Challenges of Evidence-Based Practices for Latino Youth and Families," Miami.

Hernandez, R. (2004b, December 21). Hispanics don't fit easy categories. *Herald News* (Passaic County, N.J.), p. B7.

Hernandez, R., Siles, M., and Rochin, R. (2000). Latino youth: Converting challenges to opportunities. In M. Montero-Sieburth and F. A. Villarruel (Eds.), *Making invisible Latino adolescents visible: A critical approach to Latino diversity* (pp. 1–28). New York: Palmer Press.

Heron, M. P., and Morales, L. S. (2002). *Latino health, nativity and socioeconomic status*. Santa Monica, Calif.: Rand Corporation.

Heubert, J. P. (2002). Disability, race, and high-stakes testing of students. In D. L. Losen and G. Orfield (Eds.). *Racial inequality in special education* (pp. 137–165). Cambridge, MA: Harvard University Press.

Heuer, L., Hess, C. W., and Klug, M. G. (2004). Meeting the health care needs of a rural Hispanic migrant population with diabetes. *Journal of Rural Health*, 20, pp. 265–270.

Hicks, L. S., Ayanian, J. Z., Orav, E. J., Soukup, J., McWilliams, J. M., Choi, S. S., and Johnson, P. A. (2005). Is hospital service associated with racial and ethnic disparities in experience with hospital care? *American Journal of Medicine*, 118, pp. 529–535.

Higuera, J. J. (2005, June 18). Hispanics advised to change beliefs to narrow wealth gap. *Arizona Republic*, p. 1.

Hill, T. D., Angel, J. L., Ellison, C. G., and Angel, R. J. (2005). Religious attendance and mortality: An eight-year follow-up of older Mexican Americans. *Journal of Gerontology*, 60, pp. S102–109.

Hispanic fusion market: Bilingual youth. (2002). *FutureScane*. Available at: http://www.findarticles.com/p/articles/mi_qa3908/is_200209/ai_n9089788/print. Accessed 5/23/05.

Hispanic vote, The. (2004, November 28). *St. Petersburg (Fla.) Times*, p. 2P.

Historical Society of Pennsylvania. (2005). *Latino identity: One name, many voices*. Available at: http://www.hsp.org/default.aspx?id-291. Accessed 4/12/05.

Hodgkinson, H. L. (2004). *Demographic trends*. Agency for Healthcare Research and Quality, U.S. Department of Health and Human Services, Washington, D.C. Available at: http:www.ahrq. gov/news/ulp/dispar/dispar1.htm. Accessed 6/10/05.

Hofstede, G. (1991). *Cultures and organizations: Software of the mind*. London: McGraw-Hill.

Hogan, P., Dall, T., and Nikolov, P. (2003). Economic costs of diabetes in the US in 2002. *Diabetes Care*, 26, pp. 917–932.

Holguin, F., Mannino, D. M., Anto, J., Mott, J., Ford, E. S., Teague, W. G., Redd, S. C., and Romieu, I. (2005). Country of birth as a risk factor for asthma among Mexican Americans. *American Journal of Respitory and Critical Care Medicine*, 171, pp. 103–108.

Holleran, L. K. (2003). Mexican American youth of the Southwest borderlands: perceptions of ethnicity, acculturation, and race. *Hispanic Journal of Behavioral Sciences*, 25, pp. 352–369.

Holleran, L. K., Taylor, M., Pomeroy, E. C., and Neff, J. A. (2005). Substance abuse prevention for high risk youth: Exploring culture and alcohol use and drug use. In M. Delgado (Ed.), *Latinos and alcohol use/abuse revisited: Advances and challenges for prevention and treatment programs* (pp. 165–184). New York: Haworth Press.

Holley, L. C. (2003a). Emerging ethnic agencies: Building capacity to build community. *Journal of Community Practice*, 11, pp. 39–57.

Holley, L. C. (2003b). The influence of ethnic awareness on ethnic agencies. *Administration in Social Work*, 27, pp. 47–63.

Holman, E. A., Silver, R. C., and Waitzkin, H. (2000). Traumatic life events in primary care patients: A study in an ethnically diverse sample. *Archives of Family Medicine*, 9, pp. 802–810.

Hom, M., and De Land, P. (2005). Prevalence and severity of symptomatic dry eye in Hispanics. *Optometry and Vision Science*, 82, pp. 206–208.

Homa, D. M., Mannino, D. M., and Lara, M. (2000). Asthma mortality in U.S. Hispanics of Mexican, Puerto Rican, and Cuban heritage, 1990–1995. *American Journal of Repiratory Critical Care Medicine*, 161, pp. 504–509.

Homedes, N., and Ugalde, A. (2003). Globalization and health in the United States–Mexico border. *American Journal of Public Health*, 93, pp. 2016–2022.

Hondagneu-Sotelo, P. (1994), *Gendered transitions: Mexican experiences of immigration*. Berkeley: University of California Press.

Hopkins, B. (2004, June 12). Specialty market: Drugstore catering to Latinos. *Daily News of Los Angeles*, p. B1.

Horowitz, C. R., Tuzzio, L., Rojas, M., Monteith, S. A., and Sisk, J. E. (2004). How do urban African Americans and Latinos view the influence of diet on hypertension? *Journal of Health Care of the Poor and Underserved*, 15, pp. 631–644.

Hough, R. L., Hazen, A. L., Soriano, F. I., Wood, P., McCabe, K., and Yeh, M. (2002). Mental health services for Latino adolescents with psychiatric disorders. *Psychiatric Services*, 53, pp. 1556–1562.

Hovell, M., Blumberg, E., Gil-Trejo, L., Vera, A., Kelley, N., Sipan, C., Hofstetter, C. R., Marshall, S., Berg, J., Friedman, L., Catanzaro, A., and Moser, K. (2003). Predictors of adherence to treatment for latent tuberculosis infection in high-risk Latino adolescents: A behavioral epidemiological analysis. *Social Science Medicine*, 56, pp. 1789–1796.

Hua, V. (2005, March 4). Big income divide among Asian Pacific Islanders. *San Francisco Chronicle*, p. B5.

Hubert, H. B., Snider, J., and Winklbey, M. A. (2005). Health status, health behaviors, and acculturation factors associated with overweight and obesity in Latinos from a community and agricultural labor camp survey. *Preventive Medicine*, 40, pp. 642–651.

Huerta, E. E., and Macario, E. (1999). Communicating health risk to ethnic groups: Researching Hispanics as a case study. *Journal of the National Cancer Institute Monographs*, 25, pp. 23–26.

Hunt, K. A., Gaba, A., and Lavizzo-Mourey, R. (2005). Racial and ethnic disparities and perceptions of health care: Does health plan type matter? *Health Services Research*, 40, pp. 551–576.

Hunt, L. M., Arar, N. H., and Akana, L. L. (2000). Herbs, prayer, and insulin: Use of medical and alternative treatments by a group of Mexican American diabetes patients. *Journal of Family Practice*, 49, pp. 216–223.

Hunt, L. M., Schneider, S., and Comer, B. (2004). Should "acculturation" be a variable in health research? A critical review of research on US Hispanics. *Social Science Medicine*, 59, pp. 973–986.

Huntington, S. P. (2004). *Who are we? The challenges to America's national identity*. New York: Simon and Schuster.

Hurtado, A. (1995). Variations, combinations, and evolutions: Latino families in the United States. In R. Z. Zambrana (Ed.), *Understanding Latino families: Scholarship, policy, and practice* (pp. 40–61). Thousand Oaks, Calif.: Sage.

Hurtig, J. D. (2000). Hispanic immigrant churches and the construction of ethnicity. In L. W. Livezey (Ed.), *Public religion and urban transformation: Faith in the city* (pp. 29–56). New York: New York University Press.

Hutchinson, E. O. (2005, June 26). A storm is brewing over L.A. 's Black-Latino divide: pretending it's not real won't solve L.A.'s racial issue. *Daily News of Los Angeles*, p. V1.

Hyde, C. A., and Hopkins, K. (2004). Diversity climates in human service agencies: A exploratory assessment. *Journal of Ethnic and Cultural Diversity in Social Work*, 13, pp. 25–43.

Idrogo, M., and Mazze, R. (2004). Diabetes in the Hispanic population: High risk warrants targeted screening and treatment. *Postgraduate Medicine*, 116, pp. 26–32, 35–36.

Iglehart, A. P., and Becerra, R. M. (1995). *Social services and the ethnic community*. Groveland, Ill.: Waveland Press.

Infant mortality rates. (2005, January 17). Editorial. *New York Times*, p. 16.

Intercultural Cancer Institute. (2005). *Hispanics/Latinos and cancer*. Houston: Author.

Interian, A., Guarnaccia, P. J., Vega, W. A., Gara, M. A., Like, R. C., Escobar, J. L., and Diaz-Martinez, A. M. (2005). The relationship between ataque de nervios and unexplained neurological symptoms: A preliminary analysis. *Journal of Nervous and Mental Disease*, 193, pp. 32–39.

Intrbartola, L. (2002, November 11). Hot clips: As the cut hair drops to the floor, dance music fills the air. *Home News Tribune* (Asbury, N.J.), p. 1.

Iowa's Hispanic population tops 100,000. (2005, August 12). Associated Press. Available at: http://web.lexis-nexis.com/universe/document?_m=ac8ff64dfc7f923. Accessed 8/15/05.

Istre, G. R., McCoy, M. A., Womack, K. N., Fanning, L., Dekat, L., and Stowe, M. (2002). Increasing the use of child restraints in motor vehicles in a Hispanic neighborhood. *American Journal of Public Health*, 92, pp. 1096–1099.

Jablon, R. (2003, February 6). Hispanic babies majority of newborns in California. Associated Press State and Local Wire, p. 1.

Jacobs, E. A., Shepard, D. S., Suaya, J. A., and Stone, E. L. (2004). Overcoming language barriers in health care: Costs and benefits of interpreter services. *American Journal of Public Health*, 94, pp. 866–869.

Jacoby, T. (2002, January 22). The immigrant second generation. National Democratic Leadership Council's Online Community. Available at: http://www.ndol.org/ndol_ci.cfm?contentid=250096andkaid=127andsubid=170. Accessed 5/9/05.

Jailed immigrants may go to Mexico prison. (2005, February 17). Associated Press.

Jaklevic, M. C. (2001). This side of the ethical border. Hospitals feel duty of keeping immigrants healthy despite federal limits. *Modern Health*, 3, pp. 52–54.

Jardine, J. (2005, March 19). Minority-owned firms a growing force in Valley. *Modesto (Calif.) Bee*, p. 12.

Jenkins, P. (2002). A new religious America. *First Things*, 125, pp. 25–28.

Jenrette, J., McIntosh, S., and Winterberger, S. (1999). "Carlotta!" Changing images of Hispanic-American Women in daytime soap operas. *Journal of Popular Culture*, pp. 37–48.

Johnson, B. (2004). An unlikely fit: Will the undocumented apply for a temporary status? *Immigration Policy Brief*, February, pp. 1–3.

Johnson, R. L., Saha, S., Arbelaez, J. J., Beach, M. C., and Cooper, L. A. (2004). Racial and ethnic differences in patient perceptions of bias and cultural competence in health care. *Journal of General Internal Medicine*, 19, pp. 101–110.

Johnson-Webb, K. D. (2000). *Recruiting Hispanic labor: Immigrants in nontraditional areas*. New York: LFB Scholarly.

Jolly, E. J. (2004). Beneath the surface: Working with the complexity of Latino American demography. *MOSAIC: An EDC Report Series*, spring, pp. 1–4. Newton, Mass.: Educational Development Center.

Jones, D. N. (2005, March 28). Latinos take their faith to the streets. *Pittsburgh Post-Gazette*, p. A8.

Jones, V. E. (2005, August 17). Sticking together: For some non-whites, socializing means making a choice. *Boston Globe*, pp. C1, C8.

Jones-Correa, M. (1998). *Between two worlds: The political predicament of Latinos in New York City*. Ithaca, N.Y.: Cornell University Press.

Jung, C. (2005, May 9). Wineries targeting Latino market. *San Jose Mercury News*, p. 1.

Kahn, R. S. (1996). *Other people's blood: U.S. immigration prisons in the Reagan decade*. Boulder, Colo.: Westview Press.

Kaniasty, K., and Norris, F. H. (2000). Help-seeking comfort and receiving social support: The role of ethnicity and context of need. *American Journal of Community Psychology*, 28, pp. 545–581.

Kaplan, M. S., Huguet, N., Newsom, J. T., and McFarland, B. H. (2004). The association between length of residence and obesity among Hispanic immigrants. *American Journal of Preventive Medicine*, 27, pp. 323–326.

Karliner, L. S., Perez-Stable, E. J., and Gildengorin, G. (2004). The language divide: The importance of training in the use of interpreters for outpatient services. *Journal of General Internal Medicine*, 19, pp. 175–183.

Karner, T. X., and Hall, L. C. (2002). Successful strategies for serving diverse populations. *Home Health Care Services Quarterly*, 21, pp. 107–131.

Kasindorf, M., and Puente, M. (1999, September 10). Hispanics, Blacks find futures entangled immigration. *USA Today*, p. 14.

Kataoka, S. H., Zhang, L., and Wells, K. B. (2002). Unmet need for mental health care among U.S. children: Variation by ethnicity and insurance status. *American Journal of Psychiatry*, 159, pp. 1548–1555.

Kates, B., and Wasserman, J. (2004, October 12). New immigrants sure mean business: More and more middle-class newcomers to city prospering as they start own commercial ventures. *New York Daily News*, p. 16.

Katrina's next expose: Immigration woes. (2005, October 14). *U.S.A. Today*, p. 23A.

Keefe, S. E., and Padilla, A. M. (1987). *Chicano ethnicity*. Albuquerque: University of New Mexico Press.

Keen, C. (2005, April 18). UF study: Latino groups face different prospects for health in the U.S. *University of Florida News*, p. 1.

Keiser Family Foundation. (2005). Latinos and HIV/AIDS. *HIV/AIDS Fact Sheet*, February, pp. 1–3.

Kelley, D. (2004, October 4). California cuts its population projection. *Los Angeles Times*, p. 1.

Kennedy, C. M. (2000). Television and young Hispanic children's health behaviors. *Pediatric Nursing*, 26, pp. 283–238, 292–294.

Kessler, M. L., Gira, E., and Poertner, J. (2005). Moving best practice to evidence-based practice in child welfare. *Families in Society* , 86, pp. 244–250.

Kilgannon, C. (2005, April 15). Immigrant populations with native remedies. *New York Times*, p. 1.

Kim, U., Triandis, H. C., Kagitcibasi, C., Choi, S. C., and Yoon, G. (1994). Introduction. In U. Kim, H. C. Triandis, C. Kagitchibasi, S. C. Choi and G. Yoon (1994),

Individualism and collectivism: Theory, methods, and applications (pp. 1–16). Thousand Oaks, Calif.: Sage.

Kitchen, A. (2005). Undocumented patients: Healthcare dilemma, social work challenge. *Social Work Today*, 5, pp. 32–35

Kitto, K. (2005, May 14). Catholics try to end mistrust of immigrants. *Herald-Sun* (Durham, N.C.), p. F1.

Kochhar, R. (2005). *Latino labor report: More jobs for new immigrants but at lower wages.* Washington, D.C.: Pew Hispanic Center.

Kochhar, R. (2004). *The wealth of Hispanic households.* Washington, D.C.: Pew Hispanic Center.

Kochhar, R., Suro, R., and Tafoya, S. (2005). *The new Latino South: The context and consequences of rapid population growth.* Washington, D.C.: Pew Hispanic Center.

Kornblum, J. (2003, January 4). More Hispanic Catholics losing their religion. *USA Today*, p. 1.

Kossak, S. N. (2005). Exploring the elements of culturally relevant service delivery. *Families in Society*, 86, pp. 189–195.

Koss-Chioino, J. D., and Vargas, L. A. (1999). *Working with Latino youth: Culture, development, and context.* San Francisco: Jossey-Bass.

Kotkin, J. (2003). Movers and Shakers: How immigrants are reviving neighborhoods given up for dead. In F. Siegel and H. Siegel (Eds.), *Urban society annual edition.* 12th ed. (pp. 106–111). Dubuque, Iowa: McGraw-Hill.

Kountz, D. S. (2004). Hypertension in ethnic populations: Tailoring treatments. *Clinical Cornerstone*, 6, pp. 39–46.

Kouyoumdjian, H., Zamboanga, B. L., and Hansen, D. J. (2003). Barriers to community mental health services for Latinos: Treatment considerations. *Clinical Psychology*, 10, pp. 394–422

Kravitz, R. L., Helms, L. J., Azari, R., Antonius, D., and Melnikow, J. (2000). Comparing the use of physician time and health care resources among patients speaking English, Spanish, and Russian. *Medical Care*, 38, pp. 728–738.

Krieger, N., Smith, K., Naishadham, D., Hartman, C., and Barbeau, E. M. (2005). Experiences of discrimination: Validity and reliability of a self-report measure for population health research on racism and health. *Social Science and Medicine*, 61, pp. 1576–1596.

Krissman, F. (2000). Immigrant labor recruitment: U.S. agribusiness and undocumented migration from Mexico. In M. Foner, R. G. Rumbaut, and S. J. Gold (Eds.), *Immigration research for a new century: Multidisciplinary perspectives* (pp. 277–300). New York: Russell Sage Foundation.

Kropp, R. Y., Montgomery, E. T., Hill, D. W., Ruiz, J. D., and Maldonado, Y. A. (2005). Unique challenges to preventing perinatal HIV transmission among Hispanic women in California: Results of a needs assessment. *AIDS Education and Prevention*, 17, pp. 22–40.

Kugel, S. (2002, February 24). The Latino culture wars. *New York Times*, p. A. 23.

Kullgren, J. T. (2003). Restrictions on undocumented immigrants' access to health services: The public health implications of welfare reform. *American Journal of Public Health*, 93, pp. 1630–1633.

Kuo, Y. F., Raji, M. A., Markides, K. S., Ray, L. A., Espino, D. V., and Goodwin, J. S. (2003). Inconsistent use of diabetes medications in older Mexican Americans over a seven- year period: Data from the Hispanic Established Population for the Epidemiologic Study of the Elderly. *Diabetes Care*, 26, pp. 3054–3060.

Labor Council for Latin American Advancement. (2005). *Latinos and Social Security*. Washington, D.C.: Author.

Lagana, K. (2003). Come bien, camina y no se preocupe—eat right, walk, and do not worry: Selective biculturalism during pregnancy in a Mexican American community. *Journal of Transcultural Nursing*, 14, pp. 117–124.

Laguzzi, A. L. (2004). Hardship in a new land can breed mental illness. *New York City Voices*, January/March, pp. 1–2.

Lahiri, T. (2004, June 30). A hometown away from home: Mexican migrants in New York unite to build projects back home. *New York Times*, p. C13.

Lakshmanan, I. A. R. (2005, April 13). A battle for souls in Latin America. *Boston Globe*, pp. A1, A8.

Lalwani, S. B. (2004, May 18). Latino immigrants scrimp to send money home. *Milwaukee Journal Sentinel*, p. 1.

Landrine, H., Klonoff, E. A., Fernandez, S., Hickman, N., Kashima, K., Parekh, B. Thomas, K., Brouillard, C. R., Zolezzi, M., Jensen, J. A., and Weslowski, Z. (2005). Cigarette advertising in Black, Latino, and White magazines, 1998–2002: An exploratory investigation. *Ethnicity and Disabilities*, 15, pp. 63–67.

Landsberg, M. (2005, October 4). L. A. Unified sued over race issues. *Los Angeles Times*, p. B4.

Lane, T., and Quigley, M. (2005, August 11). St. Lucie's Hispanic population growing explosively. *Palm Beach (Fla.) Post*, p. 1A.

Lane, W. G., Rubin, D. M., Monteith, R., and Christian, C. W. (2002). Racial differences in the evaluation of pediatric fractures for physical abuse. *Journal of the American Medical Association*, 288, pp. 1603–1609.

Lange, J. W. (2002). Methodological concerns for non-Hispanic investigators conducting research with Hispanic Americans. *Research and Nursing Health*, 25, pp. 411–419.

Lao-Montes, A., and Davila, A. (Eds.). (2001). *Mambo montage: The Latinization of New York*. New York: Columbia University Press.

Lara, M., Gamboa, C., Kahramanian, M. I., Morales, L. S., and Bautista, D. E. H. (2005). Acculturation and Latino health in the United States: A review of the literature and its sociopolitical context. *Annual Review of Public Health*, 26, pp. 367–397.

Lara-Cinisomo, S., Pebley, A. R., Valana, M. E., Maggio, E., Berends, M., and Lucas, S. R. (2004). *A matter of class: Educational achievement reflects family background more than ethnicity or immigration*. Santa Monica, Calif.: Rand Corporation.

Larkin, M. M. (1999). Nationality in Mexico. *Research Perspectives on Migration*, 2, pp. 15–16.

Larkey, L. K., Hecht, M. L., Miller, K., and Alatorre, C. (2001). Hispanic cultural norms for health-seeking behaviors in the face of symptoms. *Health Education Behavior*, 28, pp. 65–80.

Larmer, B. (1999, July 12). Latino America. *Newsweek*, pp. 50–58.

Larson, E. (2003). Racial and ethnic disparities in immunizations: Recommendations for clinicians. *Family Medicine*, 35, pp. 655–660.

Larson, R. W. (2001). How U.S. children and adolescents spend time: What it does (and doesn't) tell us about their development. *American Psychological Society*, 10, pp. 160–164.

Lasser, K. E., Himmelstein, D. U., Woolhandler, S. J., McCormick, D., and Bur, D. H. (2002). Do minorities in the United States receive fewer mental health services than whites? *International Journal of Health Services*, 32, pp. 567–578.

Latino Catholics: Presence, participation, and leadership in the Catholic Church. Executive summary. (2005). Available at: http://www.latinoleadership.org/research/reports/latinocatholics.html. Accessed 4/12/05.

Latino Coalition for a Healthy California (2004). *Latino health.* Sacramento, Calif.: Author.

Latino Commission on AIDS. (2002). *Key facts on HIV/AIDS in the Latino Community.* New York: Author.

Latino Commission on AIDS. (2001). Declaration of an HIV/AODS health emergency in the New York City Latino community. *Body Positive*, 14, pp. 1–5.

The Latino faith community. (2005). Brooklyn College. Available at: http://dephome.brooklyn.cuny.edu/risc/All%20of%20Part%201%2010_21– 021.pdf. Accessed 5/5/05.

Latino immigrants far more likely to use public transportation. (2005, July 19). *City News Service.* Available at: http://web.lexis-nexis.com/universe/document?_m=3849ea6bd5d668. Accessed 7/20/05.

Latinos decry Catholic bishops' silence on abuses and profits by Catholic hospitals. (2005, November 15). PR Newswire US. Available at: http://web.lexis.com/universe/document?_m=59846545f5e250. Accessed 11/20/05.

Latino youths take more risks with drinking and driving. (2003, August 14). *Connecticut Post* (Bridgeport), p. 1.

Lavender, A. D. (1988). Hispanic given names in five United States cities: Onomastics as a research tool in ethnic identity. *Hispanic Journal of Behavioral Sciences*, 10, pp. 105–125.

Law fails test on minority students. (2005, September 30). *U.S.A. Today*, p. 15A.

Laws, M. B., Heckscher, R., Mayo, S. J., Li, W., and Wilson, I. B. (2004). A new method for evaluating the quality of medical interpretations. *Medical Care*, 42, pp. 71–80.

Learner, N. (2004, July 28). Beyond salsa: More grocers cater to Hispanics. *Christian Science Monitor*, p. 1.

Leavitt, R. R. (1974). *The Puerto Ricans: Culture change and language deviance.* Tucson: University of Arizona Press.

Lecca, P. J., Gutierrez, J. A., and Tijerina, G. (1996). A model to improve the utilization of health and social services in Latino communities. *Journal of Health and Social policy*, 8, pp. 55–70.

Ledogar, R. J., Penchaszadeh, A., Garden, C. C., and Garden, I. (2000). Asthma and Latino cultures: Different prevalence reported among groups sharing the same environment. *American Journal of Public Health*, 90, pp. 929–935.

LeDuff, C. (2004, December 24). Just this side of the treacherous border, here lies Juan Doe. *New York Times*, p. A16.

Lee, J. W., Fitzgerald, K., and Ebel, B. E. (2003). Lessons for increasing awareness and use of booster seats in a Latino community. *Injury Prevention*, 9, pp. 268–269.

Lee, L. J., Batal, H. A., Maselli, J. H., and Kutner, J. S. (2002). Effect of Spanish interpretation method on patient satisfaction in an urban walk-in clinic. *Journal of General Internal Medicine*, 17, pp. 641–645.

Lee, M. Y., and Greene, G. J. (2003). A teaching framework for transformative multicultural social work education. *Journal of Ethnic and Cultural Diversity in Social Work*, 12, pp. 1–28.

Leith, S. (2005, April 24). A ripe market: With the Latino population maturing as a buying force, companies like Coco-Cola Enterprises are eager for a bigger share of the pie. *Atlanta Journal-Constitution*, p. 1E.

Leland, J. (2005, July 18). A church that packs them in, sixteen thousand at a time. *New York Times*, p. A1, A15.

Lerman-Garber, I., Villa, A. R., and Caballero, E. (2004). Diabetes and cardiovascular disease: Is there a true Hispanic paradox? *Revista Investigacion Clinica*, 56, pp. 282–296.

Lester, W. (2005, August 17). Hispanics in US divided on driver's license issue. *Boston Globe*, p. A14.

Levitt, P. (2002). Two nations under God? Latino religious life in the United States. In M. M. Suarez-Orozco and M. M. Paez (Eds.), *Latinos remaking America* (pp. 150–164. Los Angeles: University of California Press.

Levitt, P. (2001). *The transnational villagers*. Berkeley: University of California Press.

Levitt, P. (1995). A todos les llamo primo (I call everyone cousin): The social basis for Latino small businesses. In M. Halter (Ed.), *New migrants in the marketplace: Boston's ethnic entrepreneurs* (pp. 120–140). Amherst: University of Massachusetts Press.

Levy, C., Carter, S., Priloutskaya, G., and Gallegos, G. (2003). Critical elements in the design of culturally appropriate interventions intended to reduce health disparities: Immunization rates among Hispanic seniors in New Mexico. *Journal of Health and Human Service Administration*, 26, pp. 199–238.

Lewis, B. (1982). *The Muslim discovery of Europe*. New York: Norton.

Lewis-Fernandez, R., Das, A. K., Alfonso, C., Weissman, M. M., and Olfson, M. (2005). Depression in US Hispanics: Diagnostic and management considerations in family practice. *Journal of the American Board and Family Practice*, 18, pp. 282–296.

Lewis-Fernandez, R., Garrido-Castillo, P., Bennasar, M. C., Parrilla, E. M., Laria, A. J., Ma, G., and Petkova, E. (2003). Dissociation, childhood trauma, and ataque de nervios among Puerto Rican psychiatric outpatients. *American Journal of Psychiatry*, 159, pp. 1603–1605.

Leyva, M., Sharif, I., and Ozuah, P. O. (2005). Health literacy among Spanish-speaking Latino patients with limited English proficiency. *Ambulatory Pediatrics*, 5, pp. 56–59.

Lichter, S. R., and Amundson, D. R. (1994). *Distorted reality: Hispanic characters in TV entertainment*. Washington, D. C.: Center for Media and Public Affairs.

Lin, R. G., II. (2005, October 12). Nonprofit hospital chain gouges the uninsured. *Los Angeles Times*, p. B4.

Lindquist, C. H. (1999). Sociocultural determinants of physical activity among children. *Preventative Medicine*, 29, pp. 305–312.

Linquist, C. H., Reynolds, K. D., and Goran, M. I. (1999). Sociocultural determinants of physical activity among children. *Preventive Medicine*, 29, pp. 305–312.

Livezey, L. W. (2000). Communities and enclaves: Where Jews, Christians, Hindus, and Muslims share the neighborhoods. In L. W. Livezey (Ed.), *Public religion and urban transformation: Faith in the city* (pp. 133–162). New York: New York University Press.

Li-Vollmer, M. (2002). Race-representation in child-targeted television commercials. *Mass Communication and Society*, 5, pp. 207–228.

Lizarzaburu, J. L., and Palinkas, L. A. (2002). Immigration, acculturation, and risk factors for obesity and cardiovascular disease: A comparison between Latinos of Peruvian descent in Peru and in the United States. *Ethnicity and Disease*, 12, pp. 342–352.

Llorente, E. (2005, January 18). Reform plan will escalate detention of immigrants. *Record* (Bergen County, N.J.), p. A01.

Locke, D.C (1992). *Increasing multicultural understanding: A comprehensive world*. Newbury Park, Calif.: Sage.

Loera, J. A., Black, S. A., Markides, K. S., Espino, D. V., and Goodwin, J. S. (2001). The use of herbal medicine by older Mexican Americans. *Journal of Gerontology*, 56, pp. M714–M718.

Loera, J. E. (2005, July 4). Latino gifts to U.S. span history and recent days. *Fresno (Calif.) Bee*, p. B1.

Loera, J. E. (2004, September 6). Immigration study tells slanted story. *Fresno (Calif.) Bee*, p. B1.

Logan, J. R. (2003a). *Hispanic populations and their residential patterns in the metropolis*. Albany, N.Y.: University of Albany, Lewis Mumford Center for Comparative Urban and Regional Research.

Logan, J. R. (2003b). *How race counts for Hispanic Americans*. Albany, N.Y.: University of Albany, Lewis Mumford Center for Comparative Urban and Regional Research.

Logan, J. R. (2002a). *America's newcomers*. Albany, N.Y.: University of Albany, Lewis Mumford Center for Comparative Urban and Regional Research.

Logan, J. R. (2002b). *Separate and unequal: The neighborhood gap for Blacks and Hispanics in Metropolitan America*. Albany, N.Y.: University of Albany, Lewis Mumford Center for Comparative Urban and Regional Research.

Logan, J. R. (2001). *The new Latinos: Who they are, where they are*. Albany, N.Y.: University of Albany, Lewis Mumford Center for Comparative Urban and Regional Research.

Lohse, D., and Palmer, G. (2005, September 7). Not all home loans are equal. *San Jose (Calif.) Mercury News*, p. 1.

Lopes, A. A. (2004). Relationships of race and ethnicity to progression of kidney dysfunction and clinical outcomes in patients with chronic kidney failure. *Advanced Renal Replacement Therapy*, 11, pp. 14–23.

Lopez, B., Nerenberg, L., and Valdez, M. (2000). Migrant adolescents: Barriers and opportunities for creating a promising future. In M. Montero-Sieburth and F. A. Villlarruel (Eds.), *Making invisible Latino adolescents visible: A critical approach to Latino diversity* (pp. 289–307). New York: Falmer Press.

Lopez, I. H. (2004, December 29). The birth of a "Latino race." *Los Angeles Times*, p. 2.

Lopez, R. A. (2005). Use of alternative folk medicine by Mexican American women. *Journal of Immigrant Health*, 7, pp. 23–31.

Lorig, K. R., Ritter, P. L., and Jacquez, A. (2005). Outcomes of border health Spanish/English chronic disease self-management programs. *Diabetes Education*, 3, pp. 401–409.

Los Angeles elects first Latino mayor in 133 years. (2005, May 19). Reuters. National ed. Available at: http://web.lexisnexis.com/universe/document?_m=1a47c468634f0a. Accessed 5/20/05.

Losen, D. J., and Orfield, G. (2002). Racial inequity in special education. In D. J. Losen and G. Orfield (Eds.), *Racial inequity in special education* (pp. xv–xxxvii). Cambridge, Mass.: Harvard University Press.

Losen, D. J., and Welner, K. G. (2002). Legal challenges to inappropriate and inadequate special education for minority children. In D. J. Losen and G. Orfield (Eds.), *Racial inequity in special education* (pp. 167–194). Cambridge, Mass.: Harvard University Press.

Low, G., and Organista, K. (2000). Latinas and sexual assaults: Towards culturally sensitive assessment and interventions. *Journal of Multicultural Social Work*, 8, pp. 131–157.

Lowe, L. (1996). *Immigrant acts: On Asian cultural politics.* Durham, N.C.: Duke University Press.

Lown, E. A., and Vega, W. A. (2001). Intimate partner violence and health: Self-assessed health, chronic health, and somatic symptoms among Mexican American women. *Psychosomatic Medicine*, 63, pp. 352–360.

Lu, Y. E., Organista, K. C., Manzo, S. Wong, L., and Phung, J. (2001). Exploring dimensions of culturally sensitive clinical styles with Latinos. *Journal of Ethnic and Cultural Diversity in Social Work*, 10, pp. 45–66.

Lum, D. (2003). *Culturally competent practice: A framework for understanding diverse groups and justice issues.* 2nd ed. Pacific Grove, Calif.: Brooks/Cole.

Luna, E. (2003). Las que curan at the heart of Hispanic culture. *Journal of Holistic Nursing*, 21, pp. 326–342.

Lundgren, L. M., Capalla, L., and Ben-Ami, L. (2005). Alcohol use among adult Puerto Rican injection drug users. In M. Delgado (Ed.), *Latinos and alcohol use/abuse revisited: Advances and challenges for prevention and treatment programs* (pp149–164). New York: Haworth Press.

Ly, P. (2005, September 21). Immigrant twist on an American tradition: Service clubs adapt to changing demographics. *Washington Post*, p. B1.

Maas, C. (2004). Latino/Hispanic workers and alcohol abuse. *Journal of Employee Assistance*, September, p. 10.

MacGregor, H. (2005, February 7). Mainstream medicine is beginning to explore the aisles of botanicas; The shops, burgeoning in the Southland, sell herbs and remedies long used by Latinos. *Los Angeles Times*, p. F1.

Magana, S. M. (1999). Puerto Rican families caring for an adult with mental retardation: role of familism. *American Journal of Mental Retardation*, 104, pp. 466–482.

Magers, P. (2004, April 27). Analysis: Texas has new majority. United Press International. Available at: http://web.lexis-nexis.com/universe/document?_m= 8defdbba5714c2. Accessed 5/10/05.

Mahat, G., Scoloveno, M., and Whalen, C. (2002). Positive health practices of urban minority adolescents. *Journal of School Health*, 18, pp. 163–169.

Maher, J. E., Boysun, M. J., Rohde, K., Stark, M. J., Pizacani, B. A., Dilley, J., Mosbaek, C. H., and Pickle, K. E. (2005). Are Latinos really less likely to be smokers? Lessons from Oregon. *Nicotine Tobacco Research*, 7, pp. 283–287.

Mahler, S. J. (1995). *Salvadorans in suburbia: Symbiosis and conflict.* Needham Heights, Mass.: Allyn and Bacon.

Main, F., and Sweeney, A. (2005, April 22). Murder rate drops for young blacks: But numbers for Hispanic juveniles in city aren't budging. *Chicago Sun-Times*, p. 3.

Malentacchi, M. E., Cruz, N., and Wolfe, S. (2004). An assessment of Hispanic health status. *Connecticut Medicine*, 68, pp. 37–41.

Malgady, R. C., and Zayas, L. H. (2001). Cultural and linguistic considerations in psycho- diagnosis with Hispanics: The need for an empirically informed process model. *Social Work*, 46, pp. 39–49.

Mallonee, S. (2003). Injuries among Hispanics in the United States: Implications for research. *Journal of Transcultural Nursing*, 14, pp. 217–226.

Management Sciences for Health. (2003a). *Hispanics/Latinos and diabetes.* Washington, D.C.: Office of Minority Health and Bureau of Primary Health Care.

Management Sciences for Health. (2003b). *Hispanics/Latinos: Disparities overview.* Washington, D.C.: Office of Minority Health and Bureau of Primary Health Care.

Manoleas, P., Organista, K., Negron-Velasquez, G., and McCormick, K. (2000). Characteristics of Latino mental health clinicians: A preliminary examination. *Community Mental Health Journal*, 36, pp. 383–394.

Manos, M. M., Leyden, W. A., Resendez, C. I., Klein, E. G., Wilson, T. L., and Bauer, H. M. (2001). A community-based collaboration to assess and improve medical insurance status and access to health care of Latino children. *Public Health Reports*, 116, pp. 575–584.

Marcelli, E. A. (1999). Undocumented Latino immigrant workers: The Los Angeles experience. In D. W. Haines and K. E. Rosenblum (Eds.), *Illegal immigration in America: A reference book* (pp. 193–231). Westport, Conn.: Praeger.

Marcelli, E. A., and Lowell, B. L. (2005). Transitional twist: Pecuniary remittances and socioeconomic integration among authorized and unauthorized Mexican immigrants in Los Angeles County. *International Migration Review*, 39, pp. 69–102.

Marin, H. (2003). Hispanics and psychotropic medicines: An overview. *Psychiatric Times*, 20, pp. 1–4.

Marin, H., and Escobar, J. L. (2001). Special issues in the psychopharmacological management of Hispanic Americans. *Psychopharmacological Bulletin*, 35, pp. 197–212.

Marotta, S. A., and Garcia, J. G. (2003). Latinos in the United States in 2000. *Hispanic Journal of Behavioral Sciences*, 25, pp. 13–34.

Marquez, R. R., and Padilla, Y. C. (2004). Immigration in the life histories of women living in the United States-Mexico border region. In D. Drachman and A. Paulino (Eds.), *Immigrants and social work: Thinking beyond the borders of the United States* (pp. 11–29). New York: Haworth Press.

Marshall, A. (2003). Subgroups of working uninsured require different enrollment strategies. *Find Brief*, 6, pp. 1–3.

Marshall, G. N., and Orlando, M. (2002). Acculturation and peritraumatic dissociation in young adult Latino survivors of community violence. *Journal of Abnormal Psychology*, 111, pp. 166–174.

Marsiglia, F. F., Kulis, S., Hect, M. L., and Sills, S. (2004). Ethnicity and ethnic identity as predictors of drug norms and drug use among preadolescents in the US Southwest. *Substance Use and Misuse*, 39, pp. 1061–1094.

Marsiglia, F. F., Kulis, S., and Holleran, L. (2005, August 10–13). Acculturation and ethnic identity: Culturally-grounded prevention with Mexican-American youth. Paper presented at the annual meeting of the Society for Social Work Research, Miami.

Marsiglia, F. F., Kulis, S., Wagstaff, D. A., Eick, E., and Dran, D. (2005). Acculturation status and substance abuse prevention with Mexican and Mexican-American youth. In M. De La Rosa, L. Holleran, and L. A. Straussner (Eds.), *Substance abusing Latinos: Current research on epidemiology and treatment* (pp. 85–111). New York: Haworth Press.

Martinez, A. (2004, September 22). Hispanics in business: Small businesses boom, but little boardroom presence. Cable News Network, transcript no. 092203cb.105. Available at: http://web.lexis-nexis.com/universe/document?_m=18c50594b88a4b. Accessed 6/8/05.

Martinez, C. R., DeGarmo, D. S., and Eddy, J. M. (2004). Promoting academic success among Latino youths. *Hispanic Journal of Behavioral Sciences*, 26, pp. 128–151.

Martinez, E. (2005). *Black and brown workers alliance born in North Carolina*. Available at: http://zena.secureforum.com/Znet/zmag/octoomartinez.htm.

Martinez, G. J. (2001). Showcasing diversity: Cross-country drive unveils America's new face. *Hispanic Magazine*, June, pp. 3–6.

Mascaro, L. (2005, April 27). Twenty-five percent of Latino kids lack health plans. *Daily News of Los Angeles*, p. N1.

Mason, J. L. (1993). *Cultural competence self-assessment questionnaire*. Portland, Ore.: Portland State University, Multicultural Initiative Project.

Massey, D. S. (2005, August 12). From social sameness, a fascination with differences. *Chronicle of Higher Education*, p. 11.

Massey, D. S., Zambrana, R. E., and Bell, S. A. (1995). Contemporary issues in Latino families: Future directions for research, policy, and practice. In R. Z. Zambrana (Ed.), *Understanding Latino families: Scholarship, policy, and Practice* (pp. 190–204). Thousand Oaks, Calif.: Sage.

Matias-Carrelo, L. E., Chavez, L. M., Negron, G., Canino, G., Aguilar-Gaxiola, S., and Hoppe, S. (2003). The Spanish translation and cultural adaptation of five mental health outcome measures. *Cultural Medicine and Psychiatry*, 27, pp. 291–313.

Mattson, S., and Rodriguez, E. (1999). Battering in pregnant Latinas. *Issues in Mental Health Nursing*, 20, pp. 405–422.

Maxwell, B., and Jacobson, M. (1989). *Marketing disease to Hispanics: The selling of alcohol, tobacco, and junk foods*. Washington, D.C.: Center for Science in the Public Interest.

Mayo, Y. (1997). Machismo, fatherhood and the Latino family: Understanding the concept. *Journal of Multicultural Social Work*, 4, pp. 49–61.

Mazor, S. S., Hampers, L. C., Chande, V. T., and Krug, S. E. (2002). Teaching Spanish to pediatric emergency physicians: Effects on patient satisfaction. *Archives of Pediatric and Adolescent Medicine*, 156, pp. 693–695.

Mazur, R. E., Marquis, G. S., and Jensem H. H. (2003). Diet and food insufficiency among Hispanic youths: Acculturation and socioeconomic factors in the third National Health and Nutrition Examination Survey. *American Journal of Clinical Nutrition*, 78, pp. 1120–1127.

McCarthy, K. F., and Vernez, G. (1997). *Immigration in a changing economy: California's experience*. Santa Monica, CA: RAND.

McCartt Hess, P., and Mullen, E. J. (1995). Bridging the gap: Collaborative considerations In practitioner-researcher knowledge-building partnerships. In P. McCartt Hess and E. J. Mullen (Eds.), *Practitioner-researcher partnerships: Building knowledge from, in, and for practice* (pp. 1–30). Washington, D.C.: NASW Press.

McCormick, E., and Holding, R. (2004, October 3). Too young to die. *San Francisco Chronicle*, p. A19.

McDonald, E. J., McCable, K., Yeh, M., Lau, A., Garland, A., and Hough, R. L. (2005). Cultural affiliation and self-esteem as predictors of internalizing symptoms among Mexican American adolescents. *Journal of Clinical Child and Adolescent Psychology*, 34, pp. 163–171.

McGavin, G. (2005, September 23). Latinos: Obstacles hinder access to health services, advocates say, breaking barriers. *Press Enterprise* (Riverside, Calif.), p. B1.

McGlade, M. S., Saha, S., and Dahlstrom, M. E. (2004). The Latina paradox: An opportunity for restructuring prenatal care delivery. *American Journal of Public Health*, 94, pp. 2062–2065.

McKay, E. (2002). *Literature review circles of support: Orphans and unwanted children*. Cambridge, Mass.: ABT Associates.

McKenna, M. A. J. (2005, July 27). Immigrants subsidize care: Medical study debunks myth on health costs. *Atlanta Journal-Constitution*, p. 1F.

McKnight, J. (1995). *The careless society: Community and its counterfeits*. New York: Basic Books.

McKnight, J., and Kretzmann, J. (1991). *Mapping community capacity*. Evanston, Ill.: Northwestern University, Center for Urban Policy Affairs and Research.

McLaughlin, H. J., Liljestrom, A., Lim, J. H., and Meyers, D. (2002). Learn: A community study about Latino immigrants and education. *Education and Urban Society*, 34, pp. 212–232.

McNary, S. (2005, May 3). Latinos gain jobs, lose pay. *Press Enterprise* (Riverside, Calif.), p. A01.

McNeece, C. A., Falconer, M. K., and Springer, D. (2002). Impact of immigration on health and human services: Florida's experience. *Social Work in Health Care*, 35, pp. 501–522.

McNeill, D., and Kelley, E. (2005). How the national healthcare quality and disparities reports can catalyze quality improvement. *Medical Care*, 43, pp. 182–188.

McNutt, J. G., Queiro-Tajalli, I., Boland, K. M., and Campbell, C. (2001). Information poverty and the Latino community: Implications for social work practice and social work education. *Journal of Ethnic and Cultural Diversity in Social Work*, 10, pp. 1–20.

McQuiston, C., and Flaskerud, J. H. (2003). "If they don't ask about condoms, I just tell them": A descriptive case study of Latino lay health advisors' helping activities. *Health Education Behavior*, 30, pp. 79–96.

McTaggart, J. (2004, October 15). Coast to coast, chains are vying to leave no Hispanic customer behind, but for the independents it's second nature. *Progressive Grocer*, p. 1.

Melgar-Quinoez, H., Kaiser, L. L., Martin, A. C., Mtez, D., and Olivarez, A. (2003). Inseguridad alimentaría en latinos de California: Observaciones de grupos focales. *Salud Publica Mexico*, 45, pp. 198–205.

Melwani, L. (2004, November 24). The new New Yorkers: City agencies and local groups are using indirect methods to inform immigrants of health-care services. *Newsday*, p. A44.

Mena, M. (1989). Cultural sensitivity and work with Latino teen fathers. *Men's Reproductive Health*, 3, pp. 4–6.

Mendelson, C. (2003). Creating healthy environments: Household-based health behaviors of contemporary Mexican American women. *Journal of Community Nursing*, 20, pp. 147–159.

Mendoza, L. (1980). Hispanic helping networks: Techniques of cultural support. In R. Valle and W. A. Vega (Eds.), *Hispanic natural support systems: Mental health promotion perspective* (pp. 55–63). Sacramento: State of California Department of Mental Health.

Mensah, G. A., Mokdad, A. H., Ford, E. S., Greenlund, K. J., and Croft, J. B. (2005). State of disparities in cardiovascular health in the United States. *Circulation*, 111, pp. 1233–1241.

Meyerson, H. (2004). A tale of two cities. *American Prospect*, June, p. A8.

Mezzich, J. E., Ruiz, P., and Munoz, R. A. (1999). Mental health care for Hispanic Americans: A current perspective. *Cultural Diversity and Ethnic Minority Psychology*, 5, pp. 91–102.

Mibourn, T. (2004, September 24). Business, politics passing Latinos by: Marketing efforts made, but no local offices held. *Modesto (Calif.) Bee*, p. B1.

Mikhail, N., Wali, S., and Ziment, I. (2004). Use of alternative medicine among Hispanics. *Journal of Alternative and Complementary Medicine*, 10, pp. 851–859.

Miller, S. B. (2005, April 13). Boston develops melting-pot politics. *Christian Science Monitor*, p. 02.

Miller, S. B. (2004, February 6). Planting new churches, Latinos alter religious land-scape. *Christian Science Monitor*, p. 1.

Miller-Day, M., and Barnett, J. M. (2004). "I'm not a druggie": Adolescents' ethnicity and (erroneous) beliefs about drug use norms. *Health Communication*, 16, pp. 209–228.

Milne-Tyte, A. (2005, August 30). Mexican immigrant develops Internet job board for unskilled immigrants. *Marketplace Morning Report*, 7:50 A.M. EST SYND. Available at: http://web.lexis.com/universe/document?_m=fea8de61bea407. Accessed 9/1/05.

Minnis, A. M., and Padian, N. S. (2001). Reproductive health differences among Latin American– and US-born young women. *Journal of Urban Health*, 78, pp. 627–637.

Minsky, S., Vega, W., Miskimen, T., Gara, M., and Escobar, J. (2003). Diagnostic patterns in Latino, African American, and European American psychiatric patients. *Archives of General Psychiatry*, 60, pp. 637–644.

Miranda, A. O., and Matheny, K. B. (2000). Socio-psychological predictors of acculturative stress among Latino adults. *Journal of Mental Health Counseling*, 22, pp. 306–317.

Miranda, C. (2005). Brief overview of Latino demographics in the twenty-first century: Implication for alcohol related services. In M. Delgado (Ed.), *Latinos and alcohol use/abuse revisited: Advances and challenges for prevention and treatment programs* (pp. 9–27). New York: Haworth Press.

Mirande, A. (1988). Chicano fathers: Traditional perceptions and current realities. In P. Bronstein and C. P. Cowan (Eds.), *Fatherhood today: Men's changing role in the family* (pp. 93–106). New York: Wiley.

Mishra, R. C. (1994). Individualist and collectivist orientations across generations. In U. Kim, H. C. Triandis, C. Kagitchibasi, S. C. Choi, and G. Yoon (Eds.), *Individualism and collectivism: Theory, methods, and applications* (pp. 225–238). Thousand Oaks, Calif.: Sage.

Mizio, E. (1998). Staff development: An ethical imperative. In M. Delgado (Ed.), *Latino elders and the twenty-first century: Issues and challenges for culturally competent research and practice* (pp. 17–32). New York: Haworth Press.

Modern Latin: Pizza patron's new brand- building ad campaign targets the young Latino market. (2004). *Business and Industry Chain Leader*, 9, p. 26.

Molgaard, C. A., Rothrock, J., Stang, P. E., and Golbeck, A. L. (2002). Prevalence of migraine among Mexican Americans in San Diego, California: Survey 1. *Headache*, 42, pp. 878–882.

Montalvo, F. (2004). Surviving race: Skin color and the socialization and acculturation of Latinas. *Journal of Ethnic and Cultural Diversity in Social Work*, 13, pp. 25–43.

Montalvo, F. (1999). The critical incident interview and ethnoracial identity. *Journal of Multicultural Social Work*, 7, pp. 19–43.

Montero-Sieburth, M., and Villarruel, F. A. (2000a). Afterword: Pensamientos. In M. Montero-Sieburth and F. A. Villarruel (Eds.), *Making invisible Latino adolescents visible: A critical approach to Latino diversity* (pp. 333–337). New York: Palmer Press.

Montero-Sieburth, M., and Villarruel, F. A. (Eds.). (2000b). *Making invisible Latino adolescents visible*. New York: Falmer Press.

Montiel, M. (Ed.). (1978). *Hispanic families: Critical issues for policy and programs in human services.* Washington, D.C.: National Coalition of Hispanic Mental Health and Human Services Organizations.

Montoya, L. J. (2002). Gender and citizenship in Latino political participation. In M. M. Suarez-Orozco and M. M. Paez (Eds.), *Latinos remaking America* (pp. 410–429). Los Angeles: University of California Press.

Mora, J. K. (2002). *Debunking English-only ideology: Bilingual educators are not the enemy.* Available at: http://coe.sdsu./people/Prop227/EngOnly.htm. Accessed 5/7/05.

Moracco, K. E., Hilton, A., Hodges, K. G., and Frasier, P. Y. (2005). Knowledge and attitudes about intimate partner violence among immigrant Latinos in rural North Carolina: Baseline information and implications for outreach. *Violence against Women*, 11, pp. 337–352.

Morales, L. S., Cunningham, W. E., Brown, J. A., Liu, H., and Hays, R. D. (1999). Are Latinos less satisfied with communication by health care providers? *Journal of General Internal Medicine*, 14, pp. 409–417.

Morales, L. S., Cunningham, W. E., Galvan, F. H., Andersen, R. M., Nakazono, T. T., and Shapiro, M. F. (2004). Sociodemographic differences in access to care among Hispanic patients who are HIV infected in the United States. *American Journal of Public Health*, 94, pp. 1119–1121.

Morales, L. S., Gutierrez, P., and Escarce, J. J. (2005). Demographic and socioeconomic factors associated with blood lead levels among Mexican-American children and adolescents in the United States. *Public Health Report*, 120, pp. 448–454.

Morano, C. L. (2003). The role of appraisal and expressive support in mediating strain and gain in Hispanic Alzheimer's disease caregivers. *Journal of Ethnic and Cultural Diversity in Social Work*, 12, pp. 1–18.

Morin, R. (2004, December 19). The salmon effect. *Washington Post*, p. B05.

Morton, P. (2005, April 12). The Latino cash connection: Money transfers to Latin America often outstrip foreign and tourism dollars. *National Post's Financial Post and FP Investing* (Canada), p. FP24.

Moscoso, E. (2005, April 15). Hispanics heed call of evangelicals: More are moving to Protestant churches that place emphasis on faith in Christ. *Austin American-Statesman*, p. A15.

Munet-Villaro, F. (1998). Grieving and death rituals of Latinos. *Oncological Nurses Forum*, 10, pp. 1761–1763.

Munoz, J. C. (2004, May 18). North America: Church anticipates launching Latino TV programming. *Adventist News Network*, pp. 1–2.

Munoz, R. (2004, July 17). Latinos rejecting Bush in greater numbers. *People's Weekly World Newspaper*, p. 1.

Murdock, S. H. (1998). *American challenge*. Washington, D.C.: Heritage Foundation.

Murguia, A., Peterson, R. A., and Zea, M. C. (2003). Use and implications of ethnomedical health care approaches among Central American immigrants. *Health and Social Work*, 28, pp. 43–51.

Murphy, D. A., Roberts, K. J., Hoffman, D., Molina, A., and Lu, M. C. (2003). Barriers and successful strategies to antiretroviral adherence among HIV-infected monolingual Spanish-speaking patients. *AIDS Care*, 15, pp. 217–230.

Murphy, D. F. (2005, May 29). California looks ahead, and doesn't like what it sees. *New York Times*, Week in Review, pp. 1, 5.

Murr, A. (2005, May 30). The survivor's story: Antonio Villaraigosa likes building bridges. First, he had to find his own way. *Newsweek*, pp. 32, 34.

Murray, B. (2005). Latino religion in the U.S.: Demographic shifts and trends. *Faith and Public Life*. Available at: http://www.facsnet.org/issues/faith/espinosa.php.

Murray, D. E., and Banerjee, N. (2005, April 11). Catholics in U.S. keep faith, but live with contradictions. *New York Times*, pp. A1, A16.

Murray, S. (2004, March 25). The American dream gets a Latin beat: Advertising. *Financial Times* (London), p. 13.

Muzyk, A. J., Muzyk, T. L., and Barnett, C. W. (2004). Counseling Spanish-speaking patients: Atlanta pharmacists' cultural sensitivity, use of language-assistance services and attitudes. *Journal of the American Pharmacist Association*, 44, pp. 366–374.

NAHJ discouraged by the overall lack of coverage of Latinos on the network evening news. (2004, December 13). PR Newswire Association. Available at: http://web.lexis.nexis.com/universe/document?_m=627e2d73a36fel. Accessed 5/28/05.

Napoles-Springer, A. M., Santoyo, J., Houston, K., Perez-Stable, E. J., and Stewart, A. L. (2005). Patients' perceptions of cultural factors affecting the quality of their medical encounters. *Health Expectations*, 8, pp. 4–17.

NASW. (2003a). *Social work speaks*. 6th ed. *NASW policy statements 2003–2006*. Washington, D.C.: Author.

NASW. (2003b). *Time and access to research findings: Barriers to translating research to social work practice*. Washington, D.C.: Author.

National agenda for Latino cancer prevention and control revealed. (2005, July 11). *Clinical Oncology Week*, p. 65.

National Council of La Raza. (2004, October 14). *Lost opportunities: The reality of Latinos in the U.S. justice system*. Washington, D.C.: Author.

National Latino Alliance for the Elimination of Domestic Violence. (2001). *Forum on Latinos who batter: Hope for those who hurt others*. Executive summary, April 27–28. Pasadena, Calif.: Author.

Navarrette, R. (2005a, April 10). Illegal immigrants and Social Security. *San Diego Union-Tribune*, p. G3.

Navarrette, R. (2005b, February 1). *Study finds discrimination across Spanish-speaking Latinos seeking access to medical benefits at D.C. Department of Human Services*. Washington, D.C.: Civil Rights Coalition.

Navarro, M. (2003a, November 9). Going beyond black and white, Hispanics choose "other." *New York Times*, p. 2B.

Navarro, M. (2003b, April 28). In New York's cultural mix, Black Latinos carve out niche. *New York Times*, p. 1B.

Navarro, M. (2002, May 16). Trying to get beyond the role of maid. *New York Times*, p. 1E.

Neary, S. R., and Mahoney, D. F. (2005). Dementia caregiving: The experiences of Hispanic/Latino caregivers. *Journal of Transcultural Nursing*, 16, pp. 163–170.

Negy, C., Shreve, T. L., Jenses, B. J., and Uddin, N. (2003). Ethnic identity, self-esteem, and ethnocentrism: A study of social identity versus multicultural theory of development. *Cultural Diversity and Ethnic Minority Psychology*, 9, pp. 333–344.

Nelson, J. (2005, January 31). Feds should pay counties for illegal-immigrant inmates. *San Francisco Chronicle*, p. NP.

Nelson, J. A., Chiasson, M. A., and Ford, V. (2004). Childhood overweight in a New York City WIC population. *American Journal of Public Health*, 94, pp. 458–462.

Nemoto, T., Operario, D., Keatley, J., Han, L., and Soma, T. (2004). HIV risk behaviors among male-to-female transgender persons of color in San Francisco. *American Journal of Public Health*, 94, pp. 1193–1199.

Newcomb, M. D., and Carmona, J. V. (2004). Adult trauma and HIV status among Latinas: Effects upon psychological adjustment and substance use. *AIDS Behavior*, 8, pp. 417–428.

Newcomb, M. D., Locke, T. F., and Goodyear, R. K. (2003). Childhood experiences and psychosocial influences on HIV risk among adolescent Latinas in southern California. *Cultural Diversity and Ethnic Minority Psychology*, 9, pp. 219–235.

New Latino nation. (2005, May 30). *Newsweek*, pp. 28–31.

New nationwide Hispanic education initiative launched. (2005, November 16). *Business Wire*. Available at: http://web.lexis-nexis.com/universe/document?_m=59846545f5e250. Accessed 11/20/05..

Nezami, E., Unger, J., Tan, S., Mahaffey, C., Ritt-Olson, A., Sussman, S., Nguyen-Michel, S., Baezconde-Garbanati, L., Azen, S., and Johnson, C. A. (2005). The influence of depressive symptoms on experimental smoking and intention to smoke in a diverse youth sample. *Nicotine Tobacco Research*, 7, pp. 243–248.

Ngo-Metzger, O., Massagli, M. P., Clarridge, B. R., Manocchia, M., Davis, R. B., Iezzoni, L. I., and Phillips, R. S. (2003). Linguistic and cultural barriers to care. *Journal of General Internal Medicine*, 18, pp. 44–52.

Niebuhr, G. (1999, May 13). Youthful optimism powers Mormon missionary engine. *New York Times*, pp. 1, 24.

Niemann, Y. F., Romero, A. J., Arredondon, J., and Rodriguez, V. (1999). What does it mean to be "Mexican"? Social construction of an ethnic identity. *Hispanic Journal of Behavioral Sciences*, 21, pp. 47–60.

NIMH expands public health education effort. (2005, October 7). *State News Service*. Available at: http://web.lexis-nexis.com/universe/document?_m=68092d40aa9a4?. Accessed10/11/05.

Novak, K., and Riggs, J. (2004). *Hispanic/Latinos and Alzheimer's disease*. Washington, D.C.: Alzheimer's Association.

Nurse, D. (2005, March 3). Catering to Latinos: Risky business of the past a success today. *Atlanta Journal-Constitution*, p. 2JF.

Oboler, S. (1995). *Ethnic labels, Latino lives: Identity and the politics of (re)presentation in the United States*. Minneapolis: University of Minnesota Press.

O'Connor, T., Loomis, D., Runyan, C., Abboud dal Santo, J., and Schulman, M. (2005). Adequacy of health and safety training among young Latino construction workers. *Journal of Occupational and Environmental Medicine*, 47, pp. 272–277.

O'Donnell, L., O'Donnell, C., Wardlaw, D. M., and Stueve, A. (2004). Risk and resiliency factors influencing suicidality among urban African American and Latino youth. *American Journal of Community Psychology*, 33, pp. 37–49.

Olivarez, A. (1998). Studying representations of U.S. Latino culture. *Journal of Communication Inquiry*, 22, pp. 426–437.

Omi, M. A. (2001). The changing meaning of race. In N. J. Smelser, W. J. Wilson, and F. Mitchell (Eds.), *America becoming: Racial trends and their consequences* (vol. I, pp. 243–263). Washington, D.C.: National Academy Press.

One in seven U.S. workers born abroad: New study. (2005, November 11). Agence France Presse—English. Available at: http://web.lexis-nexis.com/universe/document?_m=27a6f7855fe515a. Accessed 11/14/05.

Onimura, S. (2004, July 4). Women in business; Latinas providing jobs; women balance family and community demands with entrepreneurial dreams. *Business Press/California*, p. 14.

Opler, L. A., Ramirez, P. M., Dominguez, L. M., Fox, M. S., and Johnson, P. B. (2004). Rethinking medication prescribing practices in an inner-city Hispanic mental health clinic. *Journal of Psychiatric Practice*, 10, pp. 134–140.

Oppenheimer, G. M. (2001). Paradigm lost: Race, ethnicity, and the search for a new population taxonomy. *American Journal of Public Health*, 91, pp. 1049–1055.

Oquendo, M. A., Dragatsi, D., Harkavy-Friedman, J., Derview, K., Currier, D., Burke, A. K., Grunebaum, M. F., and Mann, J. J. (2005). Protective factors against suicidal behavior in Latinos. *Journal of Nervous Disorders*, 193, pp. 438–443.

Ordonez, F. (2005, July 17). Banks covet untapped market: Programs target illegal immigrants. *Boston Globe*, p. H1, H4.

Ordonez, J. (2005, May 30). "Speak English. Live Latin." *Newsweek*, p. 30.

Oropesa, R. S., and Landale, N. S. (2000). From austerity to prosperity? Migration and child poverty among mainland and island Puerto Ricans. *Demography*, 37, pp. 323–338.

O'Rourke, L. M. (2005, July 14). Latinos lag in saving: Most fail to plan for retirement, must rely on Social Security. *Sacramento Bee*, p. D1.

Orozco, M. (2004). *The remittance marketplace: Prices, policy and financial institutions.* Washington, D.C: Pew Hispanic Center.

Ortega, A. N., Rosenheck, R., Alegria, M., and Desai, R. A. (2000). Acculturation and the lifetime risk of psychiatric and substance use disorders among Hispanics. *Journal of Nervous Disorders*, 188, pp. 736–740.

Ortega, R. M. (2000, September 21–22). *Latinos and child well-being: Implications from child welfare.* Paper presented at the Research Symposium on Child Well-Being, University of Illinois, Urbana-Champaign.

Ortiz, C. B. (1973). *Esperanza: An ethnographic study of a peasant community in Puerto Rico.* Tucson: University of Arizona Press.

Ortiz, L., Arizmendi, L., and Cornelius, L. J. (2004). Access to health care among Latinos of Mexican descent in colonias in two Texas counties. *Journal of Rural Health*, 20, pp. 246–252.

Ortiz, V. (1995). The diversity of Latino families. In R. Z. Zambrana (Ed.), *Understanding Latino families: Scholarship, policy, and practice* (pp. 18–39). Thousand Oaks, Calif.: Sage.

Ostir, G. V., Eschbach, K., Markides, K. S., and Goodwin, J. S. (2003). Neighbourhood composition and depressive symptoms among older Mexican Americans. *Journal of Epidemiology and Community Health,* 57, pp. 897–992.

Ottenbacher, K. J., Ostir, G. V., Peek, M. K., and Markides, K. S. (2004). Diabetes mellitus as a risk factor for stroke incidence and mortality in Mexican American older adults. *Journal of Gerontology,* 59, pp. M640–M645.

Oyserman, D., Coon, H. M., and Kemmelmeier, M. (2002). Rethinking individualism and collectivism: Evaluation of theoretical assumptions and meta-analyses. *Psychological Bulletin,* 128, pp. 3–72.

Pabon, E. (2005). Creating circulos del cuidad for AOD Latino juvenile offenders. In M. Delgado (Ed.), *Latinos and alcohol use/abuse revisited: Advances and challenges for prevention and treatment programs* (pp. 131–147). New York: Haworth Press.

Padilla, A. M. (2004). Developmental processes related to intergenerational transmission of culture: Growing up with two cultures in the United States. In U. Schonpflug (Ed.), *Perspectives on cultural transmission* (pp. 16–44). Oxford: Oxford University Press.

Padilla, A. M. (2002). Hispanic psychology: A twenty-five-year retrospective book. In W. J. Lonner, D. L. Dinnel, S. A. Hayes and D. N. Sattler (Eds.), *Online readings in psychology and culture,* unit 3, chap. 3. Bellingham, Wash.: Western Washington University. Available at: http://www.wwu.edu/-culture. Accessed 5/19/05.

Padilla, E. R., and Padilla, A. M. (Eds.). (1978). *Transcultural psychiatry: An Hispanic perspective.* Los Angeles: UCLA Spanish Speaking Mental Health Research Center.

Palloni, A., and Arias, E. (2004). Paradox lost: Explaining the Hispanic adult mortality advantage. *Demography,* 41, pp. 385–415.

Pandey, D. K., Labarthe, D. R., Goff, D.C, Chan, W., and Nichaman, M. Z. (2001). Community-wide coronary heart disease mortality in Mexican Americans equals or exceeds that in non-Hispanic whites: The Corpus Christi Heart Project. *American Journal of Medicine,* 110, pp. 81–87.

Parker, V. L. (2005, September 27). Poultry job illnesses: injuries higher than believed in N.C. *News and Observer* (Raleigh, N.C.), p. 1.

Parrish, T. (2002). Racial disparities in the identification, funding, and provision of Special education. In D. J. Losen and G. Orfield (Eds.), *Racial inequity in special education* (pp. 15–38). Cambridge, Mass.: Harvard University Press.

Pascual, A. M. (2004, July 7). Baby boom: High birth rate among women in Georgia's burgeoning Latino community. *Atlanta Journal-Constitution,* p. 1F.

Passel, J. S. (2005). *Estimates of the size and characteristics of the undocumented population.* Washington, D.C.: Pew Hispanic Center.

Passel, J. S., and Clark, R. L. (1998). *Immigrants in New York: Their legal status, incomes, and taxes.* Washington, D.C.: Urban Institute.

Pate, R. R., Heath, G. W., Dowda, M., Trost, S. G. (1996). Associations between physical activity and other health behaviors in a representative sample of U.S. adolescents. *American Journal of Public Health,* 86, pp. 1577–1581.

Patterson, T. L., Bucardo, J., McKibbin, C. L., Mausbach, B. T., Moore, D., Barrio, C., Goldman, S. R., and Jeste, D. V. (2005). Development and pilot testing of a new psychosocial intervention for older Latinos with chronic psychosis. *Schizophrenia Bulletin*, pp. 922–930.

Pavlik, V. N., Hyman, D. J., Wendt, J. A., and Orengo, C. (2004). Association of a culturally defined syndrome (nervios) with chest pain and DSM-IV affective disorders in Hispanic patients referred for cardiac stress testing. *Ethnic Disabilities*, 14, pp. 505–514.

Paz-Bailey, G., Teran, S., Levine, W., and Markowitz, L. E. (2004). Syphilis outbreak among Hispanic immigrants in Decatur, Alabama: Association with commercial sex. *Sexual Transmitted Diseases*, 31, pp. 20–25.

Pear, R. (2005, August 12). Racial and ethnic minorities gain in nation as a whole. *New York Times*, p. A16.

Pearce, C. W. (1998). Seeking a healthy baby: Hispanic women's views of pregnancy and prenatal care. *Clinical Excellence in Nurse Practice*, 2, pp. 352–361.

Peifer, K. L., Hu, T., and Vega, W. (2000). Help seeking by persons of Mexican origin with functional impairments. *Psychiatric Services*, 51, pp. 1293–1298.

Penchaszadeh, V. B. (2001). Genetic counseling issues in Latinos. *Genetic Testing*, 5, pp. 193–200.

Pentz, M. A., Rothspan, S., Turner, G., Skara, S., and Voskanian, S. (1999). Multiethnic approaches to substance abuse prevention: A multicultural perspective. In S. B. Kar (Ed.), *Substance abuse prevention: A multicultural perspective* (pp. 43–75). Amityville, N.Y.: Baywood.

Perera, F. P., Illman, S. M., Kinney, P. L., Whyatt, R. M., Kelvin, E. A., Shepard, P., Evans, D., Fullilove, M., Ford, J., Miller, R. L., Meyer, H. H., and Rauh, V. A. (2002). The challenge of preventing environmentally related disease in young children: Community-based research in New York City. *Environmental Health Perspective*, 110, pp. 197–204.

Perez, M. (2001, March 14). Hispanics and Blacks must be partners, not rivals. *Record* (Bergen County, N.J.), p. A3.

Perez, W., and Padilla, A. M. (2000). Cultural orientation across three generations of Hispanic adolescents. *Hispanic Journal of Behavioral Sciences*, 22, pp. 390–398.

Perez-Stable, E. J., Ramirez, A., Villareal, R., Talavera, G. A., Trapido, E., Suarez, L., Marti, J., and McAlister, A. (2001). Cigarette smoking behavior among US Latino men and women from different countries of origin. *American Journal of Public Health*, 91, pp. 1424–1430.

Perez-Stable, E. J., and Salazar, R. (2004). Issues in achieving compliance with antihypertensive treatment in the Latino population. *Clinical Cornerstone*, 6, pp. 49–61.

Perez Williams, D., and McPherson, H. A. (2000). Providing culturally sensitive care to Hispanic patients in Arkansas. *Journal of the Arkansas Medical Society*, 96, pp. 312–314.

Perkins, H. S., Shepherd, K. J., Cortez, J. D., and Hazuda, H. P. (2005). Exploring chronically ill seniors' attitudes about discussing death and postmortem medical procedures. *Journal of the American Geriatric Society*, 5, pp. 895–900.

Pew Hispanic Center. (2005). *Hispanics: A people in motion.* Washington, D.C.: Author.

Pew Hispanic Center. (2004). *Hispanic school achievement: Catching up requires running faster than white youth.* Washington, D.C.: Author.

Pew Hispanic Center. (2002a). *Hispanic health: Divergent and changing.* Pew Hispanic Center Fact Sheet. Washington, D.C.: Author.

Pew Hispanic Center. (2002b). *Latinos share distinctive views and attachment to heritage, but attitudes differ by language and place of birth, assimilation across generations.* Washington, D.C.: Author.

Pew Hispanic Center. (2002c). *U.S.-born Hispanics increasingly drive population developments.* Washington, D.C.: Author.

Pew Hispanic Center/Keiser Family Foundation. (2002, December 17). *2002 survey of Latinos.* Washington, D.C..: Author.

Pfeffer, M. J. (1994). Low-wage employment and ghetto poverty: A comparison of African American and Cambodian day-haul farm workers in Philadelphia. *Social Problems, 41,* pp. 9–29.

Phillips, J. A. (2002). White, black, and Latino homicide rates: Why the difference? *Social Problems, 49,* pp. 349–373.

Phillips, T. (2005a, September 9). Study finds Latinos behind in education percentage of third-generation graduates less than Asians, Whites. *Modesto(Calif.) Bee,* p. A1.

Phillips, T. (2005b, September 10). Trying to fill the Latino education gap: Programs opening doors for kids of immigrants. *Modesto(Calif.) Bee,* p. A1.

Phipps, E. J., True, G., and Murray, G. F. (2003). Community perspectives on advance care planning: Report from the Community Ethics Program. *Journal of Cultural Diversity, 10,* pp. 118–123.

Pickel, M. L. (2005, August 10). Illegal immigration polarizes Christians. *Atlanta Journal-Constitution,* p. 1F.

Pietz, C. A., Mayes, T., Naclerio, A., and Taylor, R. (2004). Pediatric organ transplantation and the Hispanic population: Approaching families and obtaining their consent. *Transplantation Proceedings, 36,* pp. 1237–1240.

Pleck, J. H., and O'Donnell, L. N. (2001). Gender attitudes and health risk behaviors in urban African American and Latino early adolescents. *Maternal and Child Health Journal, 5,* pp. 265–272.

Pluralism Project Harvard University. (2003). *The emerging Latino Muslim community in America.* Cambridge, Mass.: Pluralism Project.

Poe, J. (2003, August 6). Being Latin and Black: Afro-Latinos grapple with labels in U.S. *Atlanta Journal-Constitution,* p. 1.

Pogrebin, R. (2005, October 17). Lured by the work but struggling to be paid. *New York Times,* p. A19.

Pole, N., Best, S. R., Metzler, T., and Marmar, C. R. (2005). Why are Hispanics at greater risk for PTSD? *Cultural Diversity and Ethnic Minority Psychology, 11,* pp. 144–161.

Pollack, M. A. (2004, May 1). Say "hola" to Hispanic customers. *Retail Traffic.* Available at: http://web.lexis-nexis.com/universe/document?_m=3c3457f917c5f. Accessed 6/13/05.

Poole, S. M. (2004, September 18). Reports finds language not only barrier to Latino health care. *Atlanta-Journal Constitution,* p. 3A.

Poon, A. W., Gray, K. V., Franco, C. C., Cerruti, D. M., Schreck, M. A., and Delgado,

E. D. (2003). Cultural competence: Serving Latino patients. *Journal of Pediatric Orthopedics*, 23, pp. 546–549.

Porter, E. (2005a, April 5). Illegal immigrants are bolstering social security with billions. *New York Times*, pp. A1, C6.

Porter, E. (2005b, June 7). Migrants' Social Security sideline: Number rentals. *New York Times*, pp. A1, C3.

Porter, E., and Malkin, E. (2005a, August 4). Mexicans at home and abroad: Will millions retire here or go south of border? *New York Times*, pp. C1, C6.

Porter, E., and Malkin, E. (2005b, September 30). Way north of the border: In Minnesota, a community of Mexican immigrants takes root. *New York Times*, pp. C1–C2.

Portes, A., and Rumbaut, R. G. (2001). *Legacies: The story of the immigrant second generation*. Berkeley: University of California Press.

Portes, A., and Sensebrenner, J. (1993). Embeddedness and immigration: Notes on the social determinants of economic action. *American Journal of Sociology*, 98, pp. 1320–1350.

Portillo, C. J., Villarruel, A., De Leon Siantz, M. L., Peragallo, N., Calvillo, E. R., and Eribes, C. M. (2001). Research agenda for Hispanics in the United States: A nursing perspective. *Nursing Outlook*, 49, pp. 263–269.

Portugal, C., Cruz, T. B., Espinoza, L., Romero, M., and Baezconde-Garbanati, L. (2004). Countering tobacco industry sponsorship of Hispanic/Latino organizations through policy adoption: A case study. *Health Promotion Practice*, 5, no. 3 suppl., pp. 1435–1565.

Poss, J., and Jezewski, M. A. (2002). The role and meaning of susto in Mexican Americans' explanatory model of type 2 diabetes. *Medical Anthropology Quarterly*, 16, pp. 360–377.

Posternak, M. A., and Zimmerman, M. (2005). Elevated rates of psychosis among treatment-seeking Hispanic patients with major depression. *Journal of Nervous Mental Disorders*, 193, pp. 66–69.

Potocky-Tripodi, M. (2002). *Best practices for social work with refugees and immigrants*. New York: Columbia University.

Predatory lending in the Big Apple. (2005, April 24). Ascribe Newswire. Available at: http://web.lexi-nexis.com/universe/document?_m=bf456334d38398. Accessed 5/26/05.

President's Commission on Mental Health. (1979). Report. Washington, D.C.: U.S. Government Printing Office.

PR Newswire Association. (2005, May 13). Wells Fargo becomes first major U.S. bank to offer consumer remittance services to El Salvador and Guatemala. Available at: http://web.lexis-nexis.com/universe/document?_m=9c09dales8349501. Accessed 5/20/05.

PR Newswire Association. (2005, September 15). Wells Fargo to lend $5 billion to Latino business owners by 2010; Latino-owned businesses surge to 1.6 million, up 31 percent. Available at: http://web.lexis-nexis.com/universe/document?_m=9752bdeof63335. Accessed 9/19/05.

Purdum, T. S. (2000, July 4). Shift in the mix alters the face of California. *New York Times*, pp. A1, A12.

Quinones, S. (2005, October 5). Shooting in South L.A. store brings new tensions to area where some seek unity. *Los Angeles Times*, p. B3.

Rabinowitz, P. M., and Duran, R. (2001). Is acculturation related to use of hearing protection? *AIHAJ*, 62, pp. 611–614.

Raffaelli, M., Zamboanga, B. L., and Carlo, G. (2005). Acculturation status and sexuality among female Cuban American collage students. *Journal of American College Health*. 54, pp. 7–13.

Ramirez, N. (2003). Views towards organizational arrangements for ethnic-sensitive supervision in clinical settings serving Latino persons. *Journal of Ethnic and Cultural Diversity in Social Work*, 12, pp. 1–18.

Ramos, B., Jaccard, J., and Guilamo-Ramos, V. (2003). Dual ethnicity and depressive symptoms: Implications of being Black and Latino in the United States. *Hispanic Journal of Behavioral Sciences*, 25, pp. 147–173.

Randall, H., and Csikai, E. (2003). Issues affecting utilization of Hospice services by rural Hispanics. *Journal of Ethnic and Cultural Diversity in Social Work*, 12, pp. 79–94.

Ranney, M. J., and Aranda, M. P. (2001). Factors associated with depressive symptoms among Latino family dementia caregivers. *Journal of Ethnic and Cultural Diversity in Social Work*, 10, pp. 1–21.

Rassin, D. K., Markides, K. S., Baranowski, T., Bee, D. E., Richardson, C. J., Mikrut, W. D., and Winkler, B. A. (1993). Acculturation and breastfeeding on the United States–Mexico border. *American Journal of Medical Sociology*, 306, pp. 28–34.

Reaching out to the down low: A look inside the clubs where men have secret gay sex reveals why many can't be convinced to play safe. (2004, August 17). *Advocate*, p. 32.

Records, K., and Rice, M. (2002). Childbearing experiences of abused Hispanic women. *Journal of Midwifery and Women's Health*, 47, pp. 97–103.

Reed, M. C., and Margraves, J. L. (2003). Prescription drug access disparities among Working-age Americans. Issue Brief, 73. Washington, D. C.: Center for Studying Health System Change.

Rehm, R. S. (2003). Cultural intersections in the care of Mexican American children with chronic conditions. *Pediatric Nursing*, 29, pp. 434–439.

Rein, M. (1977). Social planning: The search for legitimacy. In N. Gilbert and H. Specht (Eds.), *Planning for social welfare: Issues, models, and tasks* (pp. 50–69). Englewood Cliffs, N.J.: Prentice-Hall.

Revolutionary Worker. (2000, March 26). *Latinos and the urban landscape*. Chicago: Author.

Reyes, M. (1998). Latina lesbians and alcohol and other drugs: Social work implications. In M. Delgado, M. (Ed.), *Alcohol use/abuse among Latinos: Issues and examples of culturally competent services* (pp. 179–192). New York: Haworth Press.

Reyes, R. (2005, September 2). What is the proper mission of Spanish departments? *Chronicle of Higher Education*, p. 17.

Rhoades, J. A. (2004). The uninsured in America, 2003: Estimates for the U.S. population under age sixty-five. *Medical Expenditure Panel Survey*. Available at: http://www.meps. ahrq.gov/papers/st41/stat41.htm. Accessed 6/1/05.

Rich, S. S., DiMarco, N. M., Huettig, C., Essery, E. V., Andersson, E., and Sanborn, C. F. (2005). Perceptions of health status and play activities in parents of overweight Hispanic toddlers and preschoolers. *Family and Community Health*, 28, pp. 130–141.

Richardson, D. B., Loomis, D., Bena, J., and Bailer, A. J. (2004). Fatal occupational injury rates in Southern and non-Southern states, by race and Hispanic ethnicity. *American Journal of Public Health*, 94, pp. 1756–1761.

Richardson, L. (2005, August 12). Anti-illegal immigration group's forum plan foiled: Concerns over racism thwart Save Our State's effort to find allies in the black community. *Los Angeles Times*, p. B1.

Riolo, S. A., Nguyen, T. A., Greden, J. F., and King, C. A. (2005). Prevalence of depression by race/ethnicity: Findings from the National Health and Nutrition Examination Survey III. *American Journal of Public Health*, 95, pp. 998–1000.

Rios, D. J. (2003). U.S. Latino audiences of "telenovelas." *Journal of Latinos and Education*, 2, pp. 59–65.

Risen, C. (2005, November 7). Going South. *New Republic*, p. 10.

Rivadeneyra, R., Elderkin-Thompson, V., Silver, R. C., and Waitzkin, H. (2000). Patient centeredness in medical encounters requiring an interpreter. *American Journal of Medicine*, 108, pp. 470–474.

Rivera, H. P. (2002). Developing collaborations between child welfare agencies and Latino communities. *Child Welfare*, 81, pp. 371–384.

Rivera, J. O., Chaudhuri, K., Gonzalez-Stuart, A., Tyroch, A., Chaudhuri, S. (2005). Herbal product use by Hispanic surgical patients. *American Surgery*, 71, pp. 71–76.

Roberts, A. R., and Yeager, K. R. (Eds.). (2004). *Evidence-based practice manual*. New York: Oxford University Press.

Roberts, D. E. (2002). *Racial disproportionality in the U.S. child welfare system: Documentation, research on causes, and promising practices*. Evenston, Ill.: Northwestern University School of Law, Institute for Policy Research.

Roberts, R. E., Alegria, M., Roberts, C. R., and Chen, I. G. (2005). Mental health problems of adolescents as reported by their caregivers: A comparison of European, African, and Latino Americans. *Journal of Behavioral Health Services Research*, 32, pp. 1–13.

Robertson, T. (2005, April 16). Pentecostalism luring away Latino Catholics. *Boston Globe*, pp. A1, A16.

Robert Wood Johnson Foundation. (2001). *Language barriers contribute to health dare disparities in the United States of America*. Princeton, N.J.: Author.

Robles, B. J. (2003). *Latino families: Income*. Austin: University of Texas, LBJ School of Public Affairs.

Roche, M. J. L., and Shriberg, D. (2004). Diversity in consultation: High stakes exams and Latino students: Toward a culturally sensitive education for Latino children in the United States. *Journal of Educational and Psychological Consultation*, 15, pp. 205–223.

Rodriguez, C. (2005, July 26). Immigrants aren't the real issue. *Denver Post*, p. 1F.

Rodriguez, C. (2001, February 15). Revised census estimates points to total of 285m. *Boston Globe*, p. A3.

Rodriguez, C. E. (2000). *Changing race: Latinos, the Census, and the history of ethnicity in the United States.* New York: New York University Press.

Rodriguez, C. E. (Ed.). (1997). *Latin looks: Images of Latinas and Latinos in the U.S. media.* Boulder, Colo.: Westview Press.

Rodriguez, G. (2005, May 30). Why we're the new Irish: Mexican-Americans, too, began apart—and are now a thread in the tapestry. *Newsweek,* p. 35.

Rodriguez, G. (2002, April 7). It's Latino immigrants who can save the Catholic Church. *Los Ángeles Times,* p. 11.

Rodriguez, L. (2005a, July 1). Latinos must take responsibility for dropout rates. *Morning Call* (Allentown, Pa.), p. A9.

Rodriguez, L. (2005b, May 2). Shifting demographics: Latinos bringing change to black neighborhoods. *Houston Chronicle,* p. 1.

Rodriguez, L. (2004, October 6). How acculturation impacts health and education. Paper presented at the Annual Conference of the Center for Latino Achievement and Success in Education (CLASE), Athens, Georgia.

Rodriguez, M. C., and Morrobel, D. (2004). A review of Latino youth development research and a call for an asset orientation. *Hispanic Journal of Behavioral Sciences,* 26, pp. 107–127.

Rodriguez, Y. (2004, August 18). Bank on it: Latinos can count on being wooed as a red-hot, untapped market segment. *Atlanta Journal-Constitution,* p. 1F.

Rodriguez-Reimann, D. I., Nicassio, P., Reimann, J. O., Gallegos, P. I., and Olmedo, E. L. (2004). Acculturation and health beliefs of Mexican Americans regarding tuberculosis prevention. *Journal of Immigrant Health,* 6, pp. 51–62.

Rojas, A. (2000, January 20). Education gap for Latinos a daunting problem in state. *Sacramento Bee Capital Bureau* (California). Available at: www.sacbee.com/state/archive/news/projects/leftbehind/dayth. Accessed 6/27/05.

Rollins, G. (2002). Translation, por favor. *Hospital Health Network,* 76, pp. 46–50, 1. Romero, A. J., and Roberts, R. E. (1998). Perception of discrimination and ethnocultural variables in a diverse group of adolescents. *Journal of Adolescence,* 21, pp. 641–656.

Romero, A. J., Robinson, T. N., Haydel, K. F., Mendoza, F., and Killen, J. D. (2004). Associations among familism, language preference, and education in Mexican-American mothers and their children. *Journal of Development and Behavioral Pediatrics,* 25, pp. 34–40.

Romero, M., and Habell-Pallan, M. (2002) *Latino/a popular culture.* New York: New York University Press.

Romero, S. (2005, July 20). Patrolling the border for migrants from Mexico, with a humanitarian goal. *New York Times,* p. A11.

Romero-Gwynn, E., and Gwynn, D. (1997). *Dietary patterns among Latinos of Mexican descent.* Research report no. 23. East Lansing: Michigan State University, Julian Samora Research Institute.

Root, L. (2004). Literature review and implications for social work practice with Hispanic dialysis patients. *Advance Renal Replacement Therapy,* 11, pp. 92–96.

Rosenberg, R. (2005, May 25). Largest minority: The U.S. Hispanic population is Growing rapidly—and so are the telecom opportunities. Insight Research Cor-

poration. Available at: http://www.intelecard.com/features/03features.asp?
A_ID=198. Accessed 5/25/05.

Rosenblum, K. E. (1999). Rights at risk: California's Proposition 187. In D. W. Haines
and K. E. Rosenblum (Eds.), *Illegal immigration in America: A reference book* (pp.
367–382). Westport, Conn.: Praeger.

Rowland, C. (2004, October 24). Parmacies in Canada zero in on US Latinos. *Boston Globe*, pp. F1, F5.

Rozemberg, H. (2005, January 25). Latinos turning to Islam: Curiosity spawned by
9–11 leads some to convert. *San Antonio Express-News*, p. 1A.

Rucibwa, N. K., Modeste, N., Montgomery, S., and Fox, C. A. (2003). Exploring family
factors and sexual behaviors in a group of Black and Hispanic adolescent males.
American Journal of Health Behavior, 27, pp. 63–74.

Ruiz, P. (2002). Hispanic access to health/mental health services. *Psychiatric Quarterly, 73,* pp. 85–91.

Russell, J. (2004). The entrepreneur as folk hero. *Hispanic Business Magazine*, April,
pp. 2–3.

Russell, L. D., Alexander, M. K., and Corbo, K. F. (2000). Developing culture-specific
interventions for Latinas to reduce HIV high-risk behaviors. *Journal of the Association of Nurses in AIDS Care, 11,* pp. 70–76.

Sachs, S. (2002, August 11). Immigrants see path to riches in phone cards. *New York Times*, p. A20.

Saenz, R. (2005). *Latinos and the changing face of America.* Washington, D.C.: Population Reference Bureau.

Salabarria-Pena, Y., Trout, P. T., Gill, J. K., Morisky, D. E., Muralles, A. A., and Ebin,
V. J. (2001). Effects of acculturation and psychosocial factors in Latino adolescents' TB-related behaviors. *Ethnicity and Disability, 11,* pp. 661–675.

Saleebey, D. (1996). The strengths perspective in social work practice: Extensions
and cautions. *Social Work, 41,* pp. 296–305.

Saleebey, D. (Ed.). (1992). *The strengths perspective in social work practice.* New York:
Longman.

Sanchez, C. D. (1987). Self-help: Model for strengthening the informal support system of the Hispanic elderly. *Journal of Gerontological Social Work, 9,* pp. 117–130.

Sanchez, G. J. (2002). ã Y tu. Que?" (Y2K): Latino history in the new millennium.
In M. M. Suarez-Orozco and M. M. Paez. (Eds.), *Latinos remaking America*
(pp. 45–58). Los Angeles: University of California Press.

Sanchez, J. P., Meacher, P., and Beil, R. (2005). Cigarette smoking and lesbian and
bisexual women in the Bronx. *Journal of Community Health, 30,* pp. 23–37.

Sanchez, J. W. (2005, August 8). A little bit of Mexico: Salt Lake panaderia offers
Latinos some traditional food, chance to speak Spanish. *Salt Lake (Utah) Tribune*, p. B1.

Sanchez-Ayendez, M. (1988). Puerto Rican elderly women: The cultural dimension
of social support network. *Women and Health, 14,* pp. 239–252.

Sanchez-Johnsen, L. A. P., Fitzgibbon, M. L., Martinovich, Z., Stolley, M. R., Dyer,
A. R., and Horn, L. V. (2004). Ethnic differences in correlates of obesity between
Latin- American and Black women. *Obesity Research, 12,* pp. 652–660.

Sandelur, G. D., Martin, M., Eggerling-Boeck, J., Mannon, S. E., and Meier, A. N. (2001). An overview of racial and ethnic demographic trends. In N. J. Smelser, W. J. Wilson, and F. Mitchell (Eds.), *America becoming: Racial trends and their consequences* (vol. 1, pp. 40–102). Washington, D.C.: National Academy Press.

Sanderson, M., Coker, A. L., Roberts, R. E., Tortolero, S. R., and Reininger, B. M. (2004). Acculturation, ethnic identity, and dating violence among Latino ninth-grade students. *Preventive Medicine*, 39, pp. 373–383.

Santiago, L. C. (2004). *Acculturation and gender roles in intimate partner violence among Latinas*. Milwaukee: Helen Bader School of Social Welfare.

Santisteban, D. A., Dillon, F., Mena, M. P., Estrada, Y., and Vaughan, E. L. (2005). Psychiatric, family, and ethnicity-related factors that can impact treatment utilization among Hispanic substance abusing adolescents. In M. De La Rosa, L. Holleran, and L. A. Straussner (Eds.), *Substance abusing Latinos: Current research on epidemiology and treatment* (pp. 133–155). New York: Haworth Press.

Sarmiento, O. L., Miller, W. C., Ford, C. A., Schoenbach, V. J., Viadro, C. L., Adimora, A. A., and Suchindran, C. M. (2005). Disparities in routine physical examinations among in-school adolescents of differing Latino origins. *Journal of Adolescent Health*, 35, pp. 310–320.

Sastry, N., and Pebley, A. R. (2003). *Neighborhood and family effects on children's health in Los Angeles*. Santa Monica, Calif.: Rand Corporation.

Saver, B. G., Doescher, M. P., Symons, J. M., Wright, G. E., and Andrilla, C. H. (2003). Racial and ethnic disparities in the purchase of nongroup health insurance: The roles of community and family-level factors. *Health Services Research*, 38, pp. 211–231.

Schechter, D. S., Marshall, R., Salman, E., Goetz, D., Davies, S., and Liebowitz, M. R. (2000). Ataque de nervious and history of childhood trauma. *Journal of Trauma and Stress*, 13, pp. 529–534.

Schifter, J., and Madrigal, J. (2000). *The sexual construction of Latin youth: Implications for the spread of HIV/AIDS*. New York: Haworth Press.

Schitai, A. (2004). Caring for Hispanic patients interactively: Simulations and practices for allied health professionals. *Journal of Nurses Staff Development*, 20, pp. 50–55.

Schmid, C. L. (2001). Educational achievement, language-minority students, and the new second generation. *Sociology of Education, Supplement: Currents of thought: Sociology of education at the dawn of the twenty-first century* (pp. 71–87). ProQuest Database. Retrieved 7/7/05.

Schmitt, E. (2001, April 1). Portrait of a nation: U.S. now more diverse, ethnically and racially. *New York Times*, p. 18.

Schneider, D., Freeman, N. C., and McGarvey, P. (2004). Asthma and respiratory dysfunction among urban, primarily Hispanic school children. *Archives of Environmental Health*, 59, pp. 4–13.

Schneider, A. C. (2002, December 23). A changing America has changing tastes. *Kiplinger Business Forecasts*, p. 1.

Schodilski, V. J. (2003, October 21). Hispanic population in America growing, assimilating fast. *Chicago Tribune*, p. 1.

Schoenbaum, M., Miranda, J., Sherbourne, C., Duan, N., and Wells, K. (2004). Cost-effectiveness of interventions for depressed Latinos. *Journal of Mental Health Policy and Economics*, 7, pp. 69–76.

Schultz, M. (2005, February 4). CDC backs study on how Latino youth adjust to U.S. *Herald-Sun* (Durham, N.C.), p. C4.

Schuster, C. (2005, May 25). Latina adolescent health. *Advocates for Youth*, pp. 1–4.

Scommegna, P. (2004). *U.S. growing bigger, and more diverse*. Washington, D.C.: Population Reference Bureau.

Scott, G., and Ni, H. (2004). Access to health care among Hispanic/Latino children: United States, 1998–2001. *Advance Data*, 344, pp. 1–20.

Scott, J. (2003, May 6). Census numbers for Hispanic subgroups rise. *New York Times*, p. A19.

Scott, J. (2001, June 27). Adjusted census question is blamed for miscount: Total for some Hispanic groups seems low. *New York Times*, A21.

Scott, J. F., and Delgado, M. (1979). Planning mental health programs for Hispanic communities. *Social Casework: Journal of Contemporary Social Work*, 60, 451–436.

Second national reports on quality and disparities find improvements in health care quality, although disparities remain. (2005, February 22). U.S. Newswire. Available at: http://web.lexis-nexis.com/universe/document?_m=alb4fb25a98326. Accessed 5/11/05.

Seelye, K. Q. (1997, March 27). The new U.S.: Grayer and more Hispanic. *New York Times*, p. A32.

Sellers, J. M. (2003). Hispanic churches primed to be more socially active. *Christianity Today.Com*. Available at: http://www.christianitytoday.com. Accessed 5/28/05.

Seper, J. (2004, August 26). Illegals' costs outpace tax payments, report says. *Washington Times*, p. A03.

Sequist, T. D., Narva, A. S., Stiles, S. K., Karp, S. K., Cass, A., and Ayanian, J. Z. (2004). Access to renal transplantation among American Indians and Hispanics. *American Journal of Kidney Disease*, 44, pp. 344–352.

Sered, S. S., and Fernandopulle, R. (2005). *Uninsured in America: Life and death in the land of opportunity*. Berkeley: University of California Press.

Sevilla Matir, J. F., and Willis, D. R. (2004). Using bilingual staff members as interpreters. *Family Practice Management*, 11, pp. 34–36.

Shann, M. H. (2001). Students' use of time outside of school: A case for after school programs for urban middle school youth. *Urban Review*, 33, pp. 339–356.

Shapiro, J., Monzo, L. D., Rueda, R., Gomez, J. A., and Blacher, J. (2004). Alienated advocacy: Perspectives of Latina mothers of young adults with developmental disabilities on service systems. *Mental Retardation*, 42, pp. 37–54.

Sharma, S., Malarcher, A. M., Giles, W. H., and Myers, G. (2004). Racial, ethnic and socio- economic disparities in the clustering of cardiovascular disease risk factors. *Ethnic Disparities*, 14, pp. 43–48.

Shaw, J. A., Lewis, J. E., Loeb, A., Rosado, J., and Rodriguez, R. A. (2001). A comparison of Hispanic and African American sexually abused girls and their families. *Child Abuse and Neglect*, 25, pp. 1363–1379.

Shedlin, M. G., and Deren, S. (2002). Cultural factors influencing HIV risk behavior among Dominicans in New York City. *Journal of Ethnicity in Substance Abuse*, 1, pp. 71–95.

Sheehan, D., and Cardenas, J. (2005, July 24). New culture in old coal town; Hazleton's Hispanic influx is part of a national trend. *Morning Call* (Allentown, Pa.), p. A1.

Sheppard, H. (2005, February 8). Population growth slows in L.A. *Daily News of Los Angeles*, p. N1.

Shingh, G. K., and Siahpush, M. (2002). Ethnic-immigrant differentials in health behaviors, morbidity, and cause-specific mortality in the United States: An analysis of two national data bases. *Human Biology*, 74, pp. 83–109.

Shinnar, R. S. (2005, March 3–4). Career progression among Mexican immigrants. Paper presented at University Center for International Studies at the University of North Carolina, Chapel Hill, North Carolina.

Shipman, C. (2005, September 25). Latino nation: Latinos now nation's largest ethnic minority. *Good Morning America*. Available at: http://web.lexis-nexis.com/universe/document?_m=1ab9d55710a1f1f. Accessed 9/27/05.

Shogren, E. (2005, January 13). Ruling could free hundreds of immigrants. *Los Angeles Times*, p. 24.

Sidime, A. (2005, August 11). Latino students get less in financial aid than other groups. *San Antonio Express-News*, p. 1.

Siegel, J. T., Alvaro, E. M., and Jones, S. P. (2005). Organ donor registration preferences among Hispanic populations: Which modes of registration have the greatest promise. *Health Education Behavior*, 32, pp. 242–252.

Siegel, T. (2005, June 24). Behind-the-camera Latinos breaking through. *Herald News* (Passaic County, N.J.), p. E08.

Sifuentes, E. (2004, November 16). Latinos spending power to increase to $670 billion in San Diego area. *North County News*. Available at: http://web.lexis-nexis.com/universe/document?_m=dc5f89efa842.

Sikkink, D., and Hernandez, E. I. (2003). *Religion matters: Predicting schooling success among Latino youth*. Terre Haute, Ind.: University of Notre Dame, Center for the Study of Latino Religion .

Simon, C. M., and Kodish, E. D. (2005). Step into my zapatos, Doc: Understanding and reducing communication disparities in the multicultural informed consent setting. *Perspectives in Biology and Medicine*, 48, pp. S123–S138.

Sirocchi, A. (2005, May 4). Latinos left behind in U.S. economic growth. *Tri-City Herald* (Kennewick, Wash.), p. 1.

Size of California's obesity problem grows. (2004, October 22). United Press International. Available at: http://web.lexis-nexis.com/universe/document?_m=ae966967b2a99b. Accessed 5/16/05.

Slusser, W. M., Cumberland, W. G., Browdy, B. L., Winham, D. M., and Neumann, C. G. (2005). Overweight in urban, low-income, African American and Hispanic children attending Los Angeles elementary schools: Research stimulating action. *Public Health Nutrition*, 8, pp. 141–148.

Smart, G. (2005, March 6). Bilingualism and the bottom line: Led by car dealers, local businesses are learning that catering to Latino customers can boost sales. *Sunday News* (Lancaster, Pa.), p. D1.

Smedley, B. D., Stith, A. Y., and Nelson, A. R. (Eds.). (2003). *Unequal treatment: Confronting racial and ethnic disparities in health care*. Washington, D.C.: National Academics Press.

Smith, C. (2005, January 13). Gay caballeros: Inside the secret world of Dallas' mayates. *Dallas Observer* , p. 1.

Smith, E. P., Walker, K., Fields, L., Brookins, C. C., and Seay, R. C. (1999). Ethnic identity and its relationship to self-esteem, perceived efficacy and prosocial attitudes in early adolescence. *Journal of Adolescence*, 22, pp. 867–880.

Smith, J. P. (2003). Assimilation across the Latino generations. *American Economic Review*, 93, pp. 315–319.

Smith, L. A., Hatcher-Ross, J. L., Wertheimeir, R., and Katin, R. S. (2005). Rethinking race/ethnicity, income, and childhood asthma: Racial/ethnic disparities concentrated among the very poor. *Public Health Reports*, 120, pp. 109–116.

Smith, V. (2005, May 7). Hispanic migration finally hits northern Appalachia. Associated Press. Available at: http://web.lexis-nexis.com/universe/document?_m=d508f10a34e035. Accessed 7/27/05.

Smith, W. E., Day, R. S., and Brown, L. B. (2005). Heritage retention and bean intake Correlates to dietary fiber intakes in Hispanic mothers—Que Sabrosa Vida. *Journal of the American Dietary Association*, 105, pp. 404–411.

Smokowski, P. R., Bacallao, M. L., Ma, M., and Chapman, V. (2005a, August 10–13). Acculturation risk and protective factors: Mediating and moderating processes in the development of mental health problems in Latino adolescents. Paper presented at the annual meeting of the Society for Social Work Research, Miami.

Smokowski, P. R., Bacallao, M. L., Ma, M., and Chapman, V. (2005b, August 10–13). Operationalizing biculturalism: Comparing simplistic measures of a complex construct. Paper presented at the annual meeting of the Society for Social Work Research, Miami.

Snowden, L. R., Cuellar, A. E., and Libby, A. M. (2003). Minority youth in foster care: Managed care and access to mental health treatment. *Medical Care*, 41, pp. 264–274.

Social Security tab: Even illegal immigrants don't escape taxes. (2005, April 7). *San Diego Union-Tribune*, p. B10.

Sociologist: Young Latinos need to achieve in school. (2005, October 5). Associated Press State and Local Wire. Available at: http://web.lexis-nexis.com/universe/document?_m=68092d40aa9a42. Accessed 10/11/05.

Sodders, L. M. (2005, July 17). Two-year colleges Latinos' start; study finds local campuses are a "pipeline" to Ph.D.s. *Daily News of Los Angeles*, p. N3.

Sodders, L. M. (2004, June 23). Study: Latinos lag in degrees: Fewer earning a bachelor's. *Pasadena (Calif.) Star-News*, p. 1.

Solis, D. (2005a, October 19). Greyhound illegal immigrant policy threatens relationship with Latino groups. *Dallas Morning News*, p. 1.

Solis, D. (2005b, August 11). Grocery chains tweak formats, offerings to lure Latinos. *Dallas Morning News*, p. 11.

Solis, H. L. (2005). Social Security and the Latino Community. Available at: http://solis.house.gov/HoR/CA32/English/Issues/Social+Securityan. Accessed 5/13/05.

Sommer, D. (2002). American projections. In M. M. Suarez-Orozco and M. M. Paez (Eds.), *Latinos remaking America* (pp. 457–461). Los Angeles: University of California Press.

Sosa, L. (2003). *Social work services for the Latino elderly: A framework*. New York: Fordham University Graduate School of Social Services.

Soto, J. J. (2000, May 30). Mental health services issues for Hispanics/Latinos in rural America. *Motion Magazine*, pp. 1–3.

Source of immigration problem. (2005, August 14). *Chattanooga (Tenn.) Times Free Press*, p. F5.

Sowers, C. (2004, August 16). Latinos logging on and loving it. *Arizona Republic*, p. 1.

Spinelle, J. (2005, February 18). Latino speech at Penn State breaks racial, diverse barriers. *Daily Collegian*, p. 1.

Stanton-Salazar, R. D. (2000). The development of coping strategies among Urban Latino youth: A focus on help-seeking orientation and network-related behavior. In M. Montero-Sieburth and F. A. Villarruel (Eds.), *Making invisible Latino adolescents visible: A critical approach to Latino diversity* (pp. 203–238). New York: Palmer Press.

Stavan, I. (2005, July 29). The challenges facing Spanish departments. *Chronicle of High Education*, p. 6.

St. Clair, S. (2005, November 7). More Latinos live in suburbs: Drawn by opportunities, middle class leaves Chicago in droves. *Chicago Daily Herald*, p. 1.

Steidel, A. G. L., and Contreras, J. M. (2003). A new familism scale for use with Latino populations. *Hispanic Journal of Behavioral Sciences*, 25, pp. 312–330.

Stepick, A., and Stepick, C. D. (2002). Becoming American, constructing ethnicity: Immigrant youth and civic engagement. *Applied Developmental Science*, 6, pp. 246–257.

Stevens, J., Harman, J. S., and Kelleher, K. J. (2004). Ethnic and regional differences in primary care visits for attention-deficit hyperactivity disorder. *Journal of Developmental Behavior Pediatrics*, 25, pp. 318–325.

Stevens-Arroyo, A. M., and Diaz-Stevens, A. M. (1993). Latino churches and schools as urban battlegrounds. In S. W. Rothstein (Ed.), *Handbook of schooling in urban America* (pp. 245–270). Wesport, Conn.: Greenwood Press.

Stevenson, L., Faucher, Y., Hewlett, S., Klemm, K., and Nelson, D. (2004). Chronic hepatitis C virus and the Hispanic community: Cultural factors impacting care. *Gastroenterol Nursing*, 5, pp. 230–238.

Streng, J. M., Rhodes, S. D., Ayala, G. X., Eng, E., Areco, R., Phipps, S. (2004), Realidad Latina: Latino adolescents, their school, and a university use photovoice to examine and address the influence of immigration. *Journal of Interprofessional Care*, 18, pp. 403–415.

Strength in numbers. (2005, February 24). *Washington Times*, p. A18.

Strug, D. L., and Mason, S. E. (2001). Social service needs of Hispanic immigrants: An exploratory study of the Washington Heights community. *Journal of Ethnic and Cultural Diversity in Social Work*, 10, pp. 69–88.

Suarez, Z. E. (1993). Cuban Americans. In H. P. McAdoo (Ed.), *Family ethnicity: Strength in diversity* (pp. 164–176). Newbury Park, Calif.: Sage.

Suarez-Orozco, M. M., and Paez, M. M. (Eds.), (2002). *Latinos remaking America*. Los Angeles: University of California Press.

Suber, J., Galea, S., Ahern, J., Blaney, S., and Fuller, C. (2003). The association between multiple domains of discrimination and self-assessed health: A multilevel analysis of Latinos and blacks from four low-income New York City neighborhoods—measured issues in social determinates. *Health Services Research*, 38, pp. 1735–1759.

Subervi-Velez, F. A. (1999). Spanish-language television coverage of health news. *Howard Journal of Communications*, 10, pp. 207–228.

Suggs, E. (2005, May 20). Remarks unite Latinos, blacks: Jackson multicultural group to form. *Atlanta Journal-Constitution*, p. 2D.

Suleiman, L. P. (2003). Beyond cultural competence: Language access and Latino civil rights. *Child Welfare*, 82, pp. 185–200.

Suleiman Gonzalez, L. P. (2004). Children, families and foster care: Commentary 5. *Future of Children*, 14, pp. 21–29 .

Sullivan, W. P. (1992). Reconsidering the environment as a helping resource. In D. S. Saleebey (Ed.), *The strengths perspective in social work practice* (pp. 148–157). New York: Longman.

Sundquist, J., and Winkleby, M. (2000). Country of birth, acculturation status and abdominal obesity in a national sample of Mexican-American women and men. *International Journal of Epidemiology*, 29, pp. 470–477.

Suro, R. (2005a). *Attitudes towards immigrants and immigration policy: Surveys among US Latinos and in Mexico.* Washington, D.C.: Pew Hispanic Center.

Suro, R. (2005b). Latino power? It will take time for the population boom to translate. *Washington Post*, p. B01.

Suro, R. (2003a). *Billions in motion: Latinos, immigrants and the remittance in the U.S.* Washington, D.C.: Pew Hispanic Center.

Suro, R. (2003b). *Remittance senders and receivers: Tracking the transnational channels.* Washington, D.C.: Pew Hispanic Center.

Suro, R., and Tafoya, S. (2004). *Dispersal and concentration: Patterns of Latino residential settlement.* Washington, D.C.: Pew Hispanic Center.

Swall, S., Cabrera, A. F., and Lee, C. (2004). *Latino youth and the pathway to college.* Washington, D.C.: Pew Hispanic Center.

Swarns, R. I. (2004, October 24). Hispanics debate census plan to change racial grouping. *New York Times*, p. 21.

Swarns, R. I. (2003a, June 17). Asylum seekers suffer psychological setbacks, study finds. *New York Times*, p. A23.

Swarns, R. I. (2003b, June 25). Immigrants feel the pinch of post–9/11 laws. *New York Times*, p. A14.

Szalacha, L. A., Erkut, S., Coll, C. G., Alarcon, O., Fields, J. P., and Ceder, I. (2003). Discrimination and Puerto Rican children's and adolescents' mental health. *Cultural Diversity and Ethnic Minority Psychology*, 9, pp. 141–155.

Szapocznik, J., Santisteban, D. A., Perez-Vidal, A., Kurtines, W. M., and Hervis, O. E. (1986). Bicultural Effectiveness Training. *Hispanic Journal of Behavioral Sciences*, 8, pp. 303–330.

Tafoya, S. (2004). *Shades of belonging.* Washington, D.C.: Pew Hispanic Center.

Talamantes, M. A., and Aranda, M. F. (2004). *Cultural competency in working with Latino Family caregivers.* San Francisco: Family Caregiver Alliance, National Center on Caregiving.

Talaschek, M. L., Peragallo, N., Norr, K., and Dancy, B. L. (2004). The context of risky behaviors for Latino youth. *Journal of Transcultural Nursing*, 15, pp. 131–138.

Tambiah, S. J. (2000). Transnational movements, diaspora, and multiple modernities. *Daedalus*, 129, pp. 163–183.

Tanaka, R. (2005, March 21). Area busting at the seams? *San Gabriel Valley (Calif.) Tribune*, p. 1.

Taylor, A. (2004). A cultural exploration of the Latino community. *NASP* (National Association of School Psychologists), 33, pp. 1–5.

Taylor, J. P., and Suarez, L. (2000). Prevalence and risk factors of drug-resistant tuberculosis along the Mexico-Texas border. *American Journal of Public Health*, 90, pp. 271–273.

Taylor, K. (2004, October 14). Clamoring for Spanish. *Oregonian*, p. 1.

Teichert, N. W. (2005, May 31). Aging Latinos' future clouded increasing percentage of state population will face touch medical-care issues. *Modesto (Calif.) Bee*, p. A1.

Temple, J. (2005a, November 6). Latino homeownership rising rapidly. *Contra Costa Times* (Walnut Creek, Calif.), p. 1.

Temple, J. (2005b, November 6). Realtors respond to growing Latino housing market. *Contra Costa Times* (Walnut Creek, Calif.), p. 1.

Texeira, E. (2005, July 18). Hispanics lag in education, struggle with funding, language support. Associated Press. Available at: http://web.lexis.com/universe/document?_fb363dc99e3a3a. Accessed 7/20/05.

The trial of Latino migration: A desert crossing. (2003, October 1). National Public Radio. Available at: http://www.npr.org/templates/story.php?storyID=1451521.

Three degrees of acculturation. (2005). Entrepreneur.com. Available at: http://www.entrepreneur.com/article/0,4621,228754–3,00.html. Accessed 5/7/05.

Timmins, C. L. (2002). The impact of language barriers on the health care of Latinos in the United States: A review of the literature and guidelines for practice. *Journal of Midwifery and Women's Health*, 47, pp. 80–96.

Tocher, T. M., and Larson, E. B. (1999). Do physicians spend more time with non-English-speaking patients? *Journal of General Internal Medicine*, 14, pp. 303–309.

Top ten places of one hundred thousand or more population with the highest percent Hispanic, 2000. (2005). *High Beam Research*. Available at: http://www.infoplease.com/ipa/A0904147.html. Accessed 8/4/05.

Torres, B. (2005, June 24). Consumer scams target Latinos. *Baltimore Sun*, p. 3.

Torres, J. (2005, June 30). Network news shows shirk coverage of Latino life Scripps Howard News Service. Available at: http://web.lexis-nexis.com/universe/document?_m=d5f73f291896a4. Accessed 7/13/05.

Torres, J. B., Solberg, V. S., and Carlstrom, A. H. (2002). The myth of sameness among Latino men and their machismo. *American Journal of Orthopsychiatry*, 72, pp. 163–181.

Torres, V. (2003). Influences on ethnic identity development of Latino college students in the first two years of college. *Journal of College Student Development*, 44, pp. 532–547.

Torres-Saillant, S. (2002). Problematic paradigms: Racial diversity and corporate identity in the Latino community. In M. M. Surarez-Orozco and M. M. Paez

(Eds.), *Latinos remaking America* (pp. 435–455). Los Angeles: University of California Press.

Tschann, J. M., Flores, F., Marvin, B. V., Pasch, L. A., Baisch, E. M., and Wibbelsman, C. J. (2002). Interpersonal conflict and risk behaviors among Mexican American adolescents: A cognitive-emotional model. *Journal of Abnormal Child Psychology*, 30, pp. 373–385.

Tu, J. I. (2005, January 29). A thirst for Spanish-language mass. *Seattle Times*, p. B1.

Turner, T. (2005, August 11). Nationwide aims new ads at Black, Latino markets. *Columbus (Ohio) Dispatch*, p. 01E.

Turning immigrants into Virginians. (2005, August 15). *Roanoke (Va.) Times*, p. B6.

Two Feathers, J., Kieffer, E. C., Guzman, R., Palmisano, G., Anderson, M., Sinco, B., Janz, N., Heisler, M., Spencer, M., Thompson, J., Wisdom, K. D., and James, S. (2005). Racial and ethnic approaches to community health (REACH) Detroit partnership: Improving diabetes-related outcomes among African American and Latino adults. *American Journal of Public Health*, 95, pp. 1552–1560.

Ulloa, E. C., Jaycox, L. H., Marshall, G. N., and Collins, R. L. (2004). Acculturation, gender stereotypes, and attitudes about dating violence among Latino youth. *Violence and Victims*, 19, pp. 273–287.

Umana-Taylor, A. J. (2004). Ethnic identity and self-esteem: Examining the role of social context. *Journal of Adolescence*, 27, pp. 139–146.

Umana-Taylor, A. J., Diversi, M., and Fine, M. A. (2002). Ethnic identity and self-esteem among Latino adolescents: Distinctions between the Latino populations. *Journal of Adolescent Research*, 17, pp. 303–327.

Undocumented immigrants need labor protection. (2005, June 28). *Buffalo News*, p. A7.

Unger, J. B., Reynolds, K., Shakib, S., Spruijt-Metz, D., Sun, P., and Johnson, C. A. (2004). Acculturation, physical activity, and fast-food consumption among Asian- American and Hispanic adolescents. *Journal of Community Health*, 29, pp. 467–481.

United States Hispanic Leadership. (2004). *Almanac of Latino politics*. Chicago: Author.

Unzueta, M., Globe, D., Wu, J., Paz, S., Zen, S., and Varma, R. (2004). Compliance with recommendations for follow-up care in Latinos: The Los Angeles Eye Study. *Ethnicity and Disease*, 14, pp. 285–291.

Uranga, R. (2005a, August 15). L. A. region national capital of influential Latinos. *Daily News of Los Angeles*, p. N1.

Uranga, R. (2005b, August 27). Latino marchers to protest Iraq war, today's injustices. *Daily News of Los Angeles*, p. N1.

Uranga, R. (2004, March 28). More Latino Catholics turning to evangelism. *Daily News of Los Angeles*, p. N1.

U.S. Bureau of the Census. (2005). *Asian Pacific American heritage month*. Washington, D.C.: Author.

U.S. Bureau of the Census. (2003). *African American history month*. Washington, D.C.: Author.

U.S. Bureau of the Census. (2001). *The Hispanic population in the United States: Population characteristics*. Washington, D.C.: Author.

U.S. Department of Health and Human Services. (2004). *Minority health disparities at a glance*. Washington, D.C.: Author.

Utsey, S. O., Cahe, M. H., Brown, C. F., and Kelley, D. (2002). Effect of ethnic group membership on ethnic identity, race-related stress, and quality of life. *Cultural Diversity and Ethnic Minority Psychology*, 8, pp. 366–377.

Vaeth, P. A., and Willett, D. L. (2005). Level of acculturation and hypertension among Dallas County Hispanics: Findings from the Dallas Heart Study. *Annals of Epidemiology*, 15, pp. 373–380.

Valle, R., and Vega, W. A. (Eds.). (1980). *Hispanic natural support systems: Mental health promotion perspectives.* Sacramento: State of California Department of Mental Health.

Valle, R., Yamada, A. M., and Barrio, C. (2004). Ethnic differences in social network help-seeking strategies among Latino and Euro-American dementia caregivers. *Aging and Mental Health*, 8, pp. 535–543.

Vandervort, E. B., and Melkus, G. D. (2003). Linguistic services in ambulatory clinics. *Journal of Transcultural Nursing*, 14, pp. 358–366.

Van Hook, J., Brown, S. L., and Kwenda, M. N. (2004). A decomposition of trends in poverty among children of immigrants. *Demography*, 41, pp. 649–670.

Van Houtven, C. H., Voils, C. L., Oddone, E. Z., Weinfurt, K. P., Friedman, J. Y., Schulman, K. A., and Bosworth, H. B. (2005). *Journal of General Internal Medicine*, 20, pp. 578–583.

Van Soest, D., and Garcia, B. (2003). *Diversity education for social justice: Mastering teaching skills.* Alexandria, Va.: Council on Social Work Education.

Varas-Diaz, N., Serrano-Garcia, I., and Toro-Alfonso, J. (2005). AIDS-related stigma and social interaction: Puerto Ricans living with HIV/AIDS. *Qualitative Health Research*, 15, pp. 169–187.

Varney, J. (2005, October 18). Nuevo Orleans? An influx of Hispanic workers in the wake of Hurricane Katrina has some officials wondering why locals aren't on the front lines of recovery. *Times-Picayune* (New Orleans), p. 1.

Vaughn, B. (2001). Mexico in the context of the slave trade. *Dialogo*, 5. Available at: http://condor.depaul.edu/-dialogo/back_issues/issue_5/mexico_slave_. Accessed 6/6/05.

Vazquez, L., and Swan, J. H. (2003). Access and attitudes toward oral health care among Hispanics in Wichita, Kansas. *Journal of Dental Hygiene*, 77, pp. 85–96.

Vega, W., and Scribney, W. M. (2005). Seeking care for alcohol problems: Patterns of need and treatment among Mexican-origin adults in Central California. In M. Delgado (Ed.), *Latinos and alcohol use/abuse revisited: Advances and challenges for prevention and treatment programs* (pp. 29–51). New York: Haworth Press.

Vega, W., Scribney, W. M., Aguilar-Gaxiola, S., and Kolody, B. (2004). Twelve-month prevalence of DSM-III-R psychiatric disorders among Mexican Americans: Nativity, social assimilation, and age determinants. *Journal of Nervous Mental Disorders*, 192, pp. 532–541.

Vega, W. A. (2005). The future of culturally competent mental health care for Latino immigrants. In M. J. Gonzalez and G. Gonzalez-Ramos (Eds.), *Mental health care for new Hispanic immigrants: Innovative approaches in contemporary clinical practice* (pp. 191–198). New York: Haworth Press.

Vega, W. A. (1995). The study of Latino families: A point for departure. In R. Z.

Zambrana (Ed.), *Understanding Latino families: Scholarship, policy, and practice* (pp. 3–17). Thousand Oaks, Calif.: Sage.

Vega, W. A., and Amaro, H. (1994). Good health, uncertain prognosis. *Annual Review of Public Health*, 15, pp. 39–67.

Vega, W. A., and Kolody, B. (1985). The meaning of social support and the mediation of stress across cultures. In W. A. Vega and M. R. Miranda (Eds.), *Stress and Hispanic mental health: Relating research to service delivery* (pp. 48–75). Rockville, Md.: National Institute of Mental Health.

Vega, W. A., and Lopez, S. R. (2001). Priority issues in Latino mental health services research. *Mental Health Services Research*, 3, pp. 189–200.

Vega, W. A., and Miranda, M. R. (Eds.), (1985). *Stress and Hispanic mental health: Relating research to service delivery*. Rockville, Md.: National Institute of Mental Health.

Vega, W. A., Valle, R., Kolody, B., and Hough, R. (1987). Hispanic social network prevention intervention study: A community-based randomized trial. In R. E. Munoz (Ed.), *Depression prevention: Research directions* (pp. 217–231). New York: Hemisphere Press.

Veh, M., Hough, R. L., McCabe, K., Lau, A., and Garland, A. (2004). Parental beliefs about the causes of child problems: Exploring racial/ethnic patterns. *Journal of the American Academy of Child and Adolescent Psychiatry*, 43, pp. 605–612.

Velazquez, L. C. (2003). *Some facts about Hispanics and education in the USA*. Available at: http://cls.coe.utk.edu/lpm/esltoolkit/101Hispanic.html. Accessed 8/2/05.

Velez, C. G. (1980). Mexicano/Hispano support systems and confianza: Theoretical issues of cultural adaptation. In R. Valle and W. A. Vega (Eds.), *Hispanic natural support systems: Mental health promotion perspectives* (pp. 45–54). Sacramento: State of California Department of Mental Health.

Verble, M., and Worth, J. (2003). Cultural sensitivity in the donation discussion. *Progressive Transplant*, 13, pp. 33–37.

Vergara, C., Martin, A. M., Wang, F., and Horowitz, S. (2004). Awareness about factors that affect the management of hypertension in Puerto Rican patients. *Connecticut Medicine*, 68, pp. 269–276.

Vicevich, R. (2004, July 28). Culture leads Latino mothers to prefer heavier babies. University Wire. Available at: http://web.lexis-nexis.com/universe/document?_129c5ae6a3775). Accessed 5/6/05.

Vigeland, T. (2004, December 14). Report says some Southern states are not equipped to educate the children of a growing number of Latino immigrants in their states. *Marketplace Morning Report*. Available at: http://web.lexis.com/universe/document?_m=f27269bc0a88.

Viglucci, A., and Henderson, T. (2003, July 19). Hispanics pass blacks as largest U.S. minority. *Miami Herald*, p. 1.

Villasenor, Y., and Waitzkin, H. (1999). Limitations of a structured psychiatric diagnostic instrument in assessing somatization among Latino patients in primary care. *Medical Care*, 37, pp. 637–646.

Virgin, B. (2005, August 12). Startup bank to serve Hispanics. *Seattle Post-Intelligencer*, p. C1.

Viscidi, L. (2003). Latino muslims a growing presence in America. *Washington Report on Middle East Affairs*, 22, pp. 56, 58, 59.

Vitullo, M. W., and Taylor, A. K. (2002). Latino adults' health insurance coverage: An examination of Mexican and Puerto Rican subgroup differences. *Journal of Health Care for the Poor and Underserved*, 13, pp. 504–525.

Waites, C., Maegowan, M. J., Pennell, J., Carlton-LaNey, L., and Weil, M. (2004). *Social Work*, 49, pp. 291–300.

Waldinger, R., and Bozorgmohr, M. (Eds.). (1996). *Ethnic Los Angeles*. New York: Russell Sage Foundation.

Waldinger, R., and Lee, J. (2001). New immigrants in urban America. In R. Waldinger (Ed.), *Strangers at the gates: New immigrants in urban America* (pp. 30–79). Berkeley: University of California Press.

Wall, T. P., and Brown, L. J. (2004). Dental visits among Hispanics in the United States, 1999. *Journal of the American Dental Association*, 135, pp. 1036–1038.

Walsh, A. M. S. (2003). *Latino Pentecostal identity: Evangelical faith*. New York: Columbia University Press.

Wang, E. (2003, June 29). Ad agencies cash in on growing interest in reading Latino consumers. Cox News Service. Available at: http://web.lexis-nexis.com/universe/document?_m=2e4b8a55b5ad15. Accessed 5/20/05.

Warda, M. R. (2000). Mexican Americans' perceptions of culturally competent care. *Western Journal of Nursing Research*, 22, pp. 203–224.

Washington, L. (2005, March 14). A Latino mayor? It's a crazy idea whose time has come. *Chicago Sun-Times*, p. 45.

Wasow, B. (2002). Setting the record straight: Social Security works for Latinos. *Social Security Network*, May, pp. 1–3.

Waters, J. A., Fazio, S. L., Hernandez, L., and Segarra, J. (2002). The story of CURA, a Hispanic/Latino drug therapeutic community. *Journal of Ethnicity in Substance Abuse*, 1, pp. 113–134.

Watkin, D. J. (2002, January 2). Ranks of Latinos turning to Islam are increasing. *New York Times*, p. 1.

Weathers, A., Minkovitz, C., O'Campo, P., and Diener-West, M. (2004). Access to care for children of migratory agricultural workers: Factors associated with unmet need for medical care. *Pediatrics*, 113, pp. 276–282.

Wedam, E. (2000). "God doesn't ask what language I pray in": Community and culture on Chicago's Southwest side. In L. W. Livezey (Ed.), *Public religion and urban transformation: Faith in the city* (pp. 107–132). New York: New York University Press.

Wedner, D. (2005, May 1). Sharing a dream; Latinos have become a fast-growing segment of the home-buying market. *Los Angeles Times*, p. K1.

Weinick, R. M., Jacobs, E. A., Stone, L. C., Ortega, A. N., and Bustin, H. (2004). Hispanic healthcare disparities: Challenging the myth of a monolithic Hispanic population. *Medical Care*, 42, pp. 313–320.

Weinick, R. M., and Krauss, N. A. (2000). Racial/ethnic differences in children's access to care. *American Journal of Public Health*, 90, pp. 1771–1774.

Weinstein, H. (2005, May 19). L.A.'s new mayor: Big numbers that finally add up. *Los Angeles Times*, p. A21.

Weintraub, D. (2005, March 20). The path of immigration: Each generation of Latinos does better in California. *Sacramento Bee*, p. E1.

Weisberg, L. (2005, January 23). Where Latinos live; many reside in neighborhoods where they are not in majority. *San Diego Union-Tribune*, p. I1.

Weiss, C. O., Gonzalez, H. M., Kabeto, M. U., and Langa, K. M. (2005). Differences in amount of informal care received by non-Hispanic Whites and Latinos in a nationally representative sample of older Americans. *Journal of the American Geriatric Society*, 53, pp. 146–151.

Weiss, R. (2003). Boosting organ donation among Hispanics. *Health Progress*, 84, pp. 13–14.

Wells, K., Klap, R., Koike, A., and Sherbourne, C. (2001). Ethnic disparities in unmet need for alcoholism, drug abuse and mental health care. *American Journal of Psychiatry*, 158, pp. 2027–2032.

Whitaker, D., and Bruin, D. (2005, July 18). UCLA Chicana/o study released. University Wire. Available at: http://web.lexis-nexis.com/universe/document?_m=56a67c6c3fb4c7. Accessed 7/20/05.

White, A. (2005, October 22). Incorporating Islam Latino converts say becoming Muslim adds to, not supplants, their identity. *Modesto (Calif.) Bee*, p. G1.

White, B. (2004, November 26). Pursuing Hispanic wealth: Latinos' clout grows with their income. *Washington Post*, p. E01.

White, J. (2005, March 20). Seasonal worker shortage hurts businesses. *Times-Picayune* (New Orleans), p. 1.

Wiederholt, K. (2005, April 12). Increasing numbers of Latinos leaving the Catholic Church and turning to evangelical churches. National Public Radio. Available at: http://web.lexis-nexis.com/universe/document?_m=84875bc09ed817.

Wildermuth, J. (2005, June 28). Latino growth not reflected at polls. *San Francisco Chronicle*, p. A5.

Wilkinson, A. V., Spitz, M. R., Strom, S. S., Prokhorov, A. V., Barcenas, C. H., Cao, Y., Saunders, K. C., and Bondy, M. L. (2005). Effects of nativity, age at migration, and acculturation on smoking among adult Houston residents of Mexican descent. *American Journal of Public Health*, 95, pp. 1043–1049.

Williams, D. R., and Jackson, J. S. (2000). Race/ethnicity and the 2000 census: Recommendations for African American and other black populations in the United States. *American Journal of Public Health*, 90, pp. 1728–1730.

Williams, J. K., Wyatt, G. E., Resell, J., Peterson, J., and Asuan-O'Brien, A. (2004). Psycho-social issues among gay- and non-gay-identifying HIV-seropositive African American and Latino MSM. *Cultural Diversity and Ethnic Minority Psychology*, 10, pp. 268–286.

Wilson, A. H., Pittman, K., and Word, J. L. Listening to the quiet voices of Hispanic migrant children about health. *Journal of Pediatric Nursing*, 15, pp. 137–147.

Wilson, W. J. (2003). *The roots of racial tension: Urban ethnic neighborhoods.* Cambridge, Mass.: Harvard University Press.

Winkleby, M. A., Snider, J., Davis, B., Jennings, M. G., and Ahn, D. K. (2003). Cancer-related health behaviors and screening practices among Latinos: Findings from a community and agricultural labor camp survey. *Ethnic Disabilities*, 13, pp. 376–386.

Wong, W., Tambis, J. A., Hernandez, M. T., Chaw, J. K., and Klausner, J. D. (2003). Prevalence of sexually transmitted diseases among Latino immigrant day laborers in an urban setting—San Francisco. *Sexually Transmitted Diseases, 30,* pp. 661–663.

Wood, D. B. (2005, August 11). L.A.'s blacks, Latinos see answers in alliance. *Christian Science Monitor,* p. O2.

Workers' value not undocumented by the government. (2005, April 7). *Arizona Republic,* p. 1.

Wu, J. H., Haan, M. N., Liang, J., Ghosh, D., Gonzalez, H. M., and Herman, W. H. (2003). Diabetes as a predictor of change in functional status among older Mexican Americans: A population-based cohort study. *Diabetes Care, 26,* pp. 314–319.

Wyatt, G. E., Myers, H. F., Williams, J. K., Kitchen, C. R., Loeb, T., Carmona, J. V., Wyatt, L. E., Chin, D., and Presley, N. (2002). Does a history of trauma contribute to HIV risk for women of color? Implications for prevention and policy. *American Journal of Public Health, 92,* pp. 660–665.

Yan, M. C., and Wong, Y.-L. R. (2005). Rethinking self-awareness in cultural competence: Toward a dialogic self in cross-cultural work. *Families in Society, 86,* pp. 181–188.

Yancey, A. K., Siegel, J. M., and McDaniel, K. L. (2002). Role models, ethnic identity, and health-risk behaviors in urban adolescents. *Archives of Pediatric and Adolescent Medicine, 156,* pp. 55–61.

Yarbrough, M. M., Williams, D. P., and Allen, M. M. (2004). Risk factors associated with osteoporosis in Hispanic women. *Journal of Women and Aging, 16,* pp. 91–104.

Yoon, J., Grumbach, K., and Bindman, A. B. (2004). Access to Spanish-speaking physicians in California: Supply, insurance, or both. *Journal of the American Board of Family Practitioners, 17,* pp. 165–172.

Young, J., Flores, G., and Berman, S. (2004). Providing life-saving health care to undocumented children: Controversies and ethical issues. *Pediatrics, 114,* pp. 1316–1320.

Younge, G. (2005, March 22). Number of illegal migrants in US tops ten million. *Guardian* (London), p. 15.

Yu, S. M., Nyman, R. M., Kogan, M. D., Huang, Z. J., and Schwalberg, R. H. (2004). Parent's language of interview and access to care for children with special health care needs. *Ambulatory Pediatrics, 4,* pp. 181–187.

Zambrana, R. E. (Ed.). (1995). *Understanding Latino families: Scholarship, policy, and practice.* Thousand Oaks, Calif.: Sage.

Zambrana, R. E., and Carter-Pokras, O. (2004). Improving health insurance coverage for Latino children: A review of barriers, challenges and state strategies. *Journal of the National Medical Association, 96,* pp. 508–523.

Zambrana, R. E., Cornelius, L. J., Boykin, S. S., and Lopez, D. S. (2004). Latinas and HIV/ AIDS risk factors: Implications for harm reduction strategies. *American Journal of Public Health, 94,* pp. 1152–1158.

Zambrana, R. E., and Logie, L. A. (2000). Latino child health: Need for inclusion in the US national discourse. *American Journal of Public Health, 90,* pp. 1827–1833.

Zapata, J., and Shippee-Rice, R. (1999). The use of folk healing and healers by six Latinos living in New England: A preliminary study. *Journal of Transcultural Nursing,* 10, pp. 136–142.

Zayas, L., Jaen, C. R., and Kane, M. (1999). Exploring lay definitions of asthma and inter-personal barriers to care in a predominantly Puerto Rican, inner-city neighborhood. *Journal of Asthma,* 36, pp. 52–537.

Zayas, L., Kaplan, C., Turner, S., Romero, K., and Gonzalez-Ramos, G. (2000). Under standing suicide attempts by adolescent Hispanic females. *Social Work,* 45, pp. 53–63.

Zea, M. C., Reisen, C. A., and Diaz, R. M. (2003). Methodological issues in research on sexual behavior with Latino gay and bisexual men. *American Journal of Community Psychology,* 31, pp. 281–291.

Zea, M. C., Reisen, C. A., Poppen, P. J., Echeverry, J. J., and Bianchi, F. T. (2004). Disclosure of HIV-positive status to Latino gay men's social networks. *American Journal of Community Psychology,* 33, pp. 107–116.

Zernike, K., and Thompson, G. (2003, June 29). Deaths of immigrants uncover makeshift world of smuggling. *New York Times,* pp. 1, 23.

Zsemik, B. A., and Fennell, D. (2005). Ethnic variations in health and the determinants of health among Latinos. *Social Science Medicine,* 61, pp. 53–63.

Zuniga, M. (2004). Mexican immigrants: "Would you sacrifice your life for a job?" In D. Drachman and A. Paulino (Eds), *Immigrants and social work: Thinking beyond the borders of the United States* (pp. 119–137). New York: Haworth Press.

Zunker, C., Rutt, C., and Cummins, J. (2004). Older women on the U.S.-Mexico border: Exploring the health of Hispanics and non-Hispanic Whites. *Journal of Women and Aging,* 16, pp. 105–117.

INDEX

abortion, 95
abuse
  childhood, consequences of, 139–
    140, 153–154
  substance (*see* substance abuse)
academic achievement. *See*
    educational attainment
access, to services, 127–140
  child welfare system and, 139–140
  complex dimensions of, 73, 127–
    128, 135
  correctional supervision system and,
    138–139
  cultural, 136–137
  cultural approaches for, 129–135
  geographical, 135–136
  for health care, 73–83, 93, 128, 137
  historical overview of, 128–129
  operational, 137–138
  in partnerships, 170
  physical, 135–136
  psychological, 136
accidents
  death rates related to, 39
  employment-related, 27, 78–79
accommodation, of ethnic identities, 15
acculturation, 15, 118
  adaptation modes for, 118, 142
  Catholic Church role, 145–147, 155
  dietary practices related to, 87–88
  dissonant, 117–118
  gender relations and, 155–157

as health care influence, 74–76
  impact on practice, 111, 224–225
  of individualism vs. collectivism,
    165–166
  mediating effects of, as best practice,
    103, 117–122
  remittance and, 61
  as research construct, 17
  sociodemographic factors
    influencing, 118–119, 194
  terminology for, 117
  three-stage continuum of, 119
  U.S.-born Latinos and, 29–31
acculturative stress, 119–120
  best practices consideration of, 111–
    112, 117
  alcohol use related to, 106, 121
  ethnic identity and, 115–116
action-orientation, of practice, 110
adaptation modes, of immigrants, 118,
    142
adolescents. *See* youth
advocacy movement, 32, 128
affective disorder, 153
African Americans
  civil rights for, 4, 98, 224
  coalitions with, 5, 225
  educational attainment of, 49–51
  as group of color, 15–16
  in Latino demographics, 24–25, 39,
    42, 45–46
  social dimensions of, 53, 67, 87

groups of color
    avoidance of social work services,
        128
    ethnic identity and, 15–16, 18–19
    in Latino demographics, 24–25, 39,
        42, 45–46
    Guatemalans, 25, 50

health care, 72–96
    access barriers to, 73–76, 128, 137
    data collection on, 72–74, 128–129
    demographics impact on, 26–27,
        48
    emergency room dynamics, 153,
        160–161
    emerging topics for, 95–96
    folk medicine coinciding with, 152–
        153
    insurance factor of, 72, 74, 76–79,
        147
    racism and discrimination in, 72–
        73, 96–98
    sociopolitical context of, 76–81
health education, outreach campaigns
    for, 132–133, 216–217
health insurance
    costs of providing, 72, 74
    lack of, 76–79, 137
    "price gouging" for, 147–148
    state programs for children, 74, 77–
        78
health knowledge
    lack of, 74
    Spanish materials on, 82–83
health legislation, importance of, 74
health needs/status, 71–99
    acculturation impact on, 74–76,
        120
    conceptual context for, 71–72, 99
    data collection on, 72–73, 75, 128–
        129
    disease/illness-specific, 85–92
    disparities in, 72–73, 128–129
    health care systems for, 72–96
    Latino paradox of, 38, 75, 87
    mental health-related, 92–95
    racism and discrimination related
        to, 72–73, 96–98
    television watching impact on, 66–
        67
health outcomes, disparities in, 72–74

health practices
    ethnic identity development and,
        115–116
    folk beliefs and, 152
    "healthy migrant hypothesis," 75
Healthy People 2010, 74
hepatitis C, 85
herbal medications, 131, 152, 171
    botanical shop example of, 193–221
heterogeneity, as professional
    challenge, 8, 14, 129
heuristics, of acculturation, 119
high school education
    drop out rate, 49, 109
    Latino representation in, 49–50
Hispanic Decade, 225
Hispanic natural support systems,
    169–176. See also natural
    support systems
"Hispanic paradox," 38, 75, 87
Hispanicization of America, 116
    language in, 109, 111, 226–228
Hispanics, definition of, 11–12
HIV/AIDS
    botanical shop initiative for, 197–
        198, 212–217, 219
    community education project on,
        216–217
    health care needs related to, 83–85
    social dimensions of, 120, 133, 152,
        155, 176
HIV testing
    community-based training on, 214–
        215
    community referral system for, 215–
        216, 219
home ownership, 53, 57
home visits, 135
hometown associations, 63, 171
homicide, death rate from, 37
hospice care, 95, 98
hospital systems, of religious
    organizations, 147–148
household income, 53, 66
household structure, familismo
    influence on, 160
houses of worship. See religion/
    religiosity
human services, 12
    cultural competence for, 6–7, 229
Hurricane Katrina, 36

labor market. *See* employment
language
  health care services and, 72, 76, 80–83, 98
  in Hispanicization of America, 109, 111, 226–228
  as professional challenge, 7, 103, 225, 231
  service access barriers related to, 129–130, 137, 153
  use of, as acculturation factor, 119–121, 142, 147
language of preference, 106, 108
Latin Americans
  demographic trends of, 25, 28
  remittance trends of, 61–62
Latino community, 165–166
  assets of (*see* community cultural assets)
  decision making role, 103, 143, 178, 230–231
  dynamic changes of, 42, 229
  identification with, 143
  importance of reaching, 3–4
  increase in size of, 6–7, 23–24
  interdependence of (*see* collaboration)
  research participation by, 229–230
"Latino epidemiological paradox," 38, 75, 87
Latino pride, 15–16, 116, 227
Latinos
  culturally competent interventions for, 6–7
  definition of, 11–16, 224, 231
  diversity of (*see* subgroups)
  learning about, 228–229
  legal status of, 3
  population trends of (*see* demographics)
Latinos for Peace, 54
lead, blood levels of, 95
legal status
  acculturative stress related to, 120
  health care services and, 76, 79, 97
  as professional challenge, 3, 7
libraries, cultural access and, 137
life expectancy, "Hispanic paradox" of, 38, 75, 87
linguistics. *See* language

loans, for Latinos
  business, 55, 57–58
  mortgage, 57
  as predatory, 60
long-term care programs, bias in, 73
longevity, "Hispanic paradox" of, 38, 75, 87

machismo, 8, 155–156
mammograms, 76
mapping stage, for culture-specific interventions, 180, 182–183
  barbershop example, 208, 210
  botanical shop example, 206–211
  context setting for, 205–206
  practice applications of, 210–211
marginalized communities
  access to higher education, 51–52
  access to services for, 3, 7–8, 111, 128
  dynamic factors of, 20, 121–122, 168, 226, 230
marianismo, 8, 155–156
marketing strategies, for targeting Latinos, 56–60
marriage/marital status
  Catholic doctrines on, 145–146
  intergroup vs. out-group, 16
  as professional challenge, 17, 224
  retirement benefits and, 26–27
Maryland, demographic trends in, 33
Massachusetts
  cultural asset examples situated in, 192–194
  demographic trends in, 16, 193–194
media campaigns
  as acculturation factor, 119, 158–159
  for community services, 132–133, 218
media representation, of Latinos, 65–68
  music and, 56, 65–66
  television themes and, 67–68
  television watching by children, 66–67
median age, of population, 25
Medicaid, 31, 74, 77
Medicare, 26, 36–37
memorial murals, as cultural asset, 199–201, 219

obesity, 85–88
occupational injuries, 27, 78–79
operational access, to services, 137–138
opinion polls, national, 6, 14
    on health care discrimination, 96
oppression, 97, 132
organ donation/transplantation, 95
organizational policy
    as access factor, 130–131, 137–138
    for best practices support, 50, 103, 136
    on community asset engagement, 177
osteoporosis, 95
other than Mexicans (OTM), demographics of, 25, 41
outreach efforts. *See* community outreach

padrinos, 159–160
pain management, 153
Paisanos al Rescate (Countrymen to the Rescue), 33
parole, access to services and, 138–139
participatory models
    for best practices determination, 231
    for research, 229–230
patient education, bilingual strategies for, 80–83
Pennsylvania Historical Society, definition of Latino, 12–13
pension benefits, undocumented immigrants and, 36–37
Pentecostals, influence of, 149, 192, 204, 208
personal information, sharing of, 165
personal relationships, in partnerships, 170
personalismo, 155, 164–165, 168, 213
personalization, of interpersonal relationships, 143
Peruvians, 15, 25
Pew Hispanic Center
    demographic studies of, 27–28, 42
    national poll of, 6, 14, 96
pharmacists, language barriers for, 80
phenotype, ethnic identity and, 19, 225
photography, for community outreach, 132–133

physical abuse, childhood, 139–140, 153–154
physical access, to services, 135–136
physician visits, language impact on, 80–81
plastic surgery, appeal to Latinos, 59
political power
    for communities of color, 225–226
    cultural aspects of, 17–18
    of Hispanic/Latino term, 12–13, 225
    Latino exercising of, 64–65
population groups. *See* subgroups
population profile. *See* demographic profile
posttraumatic stress disorder (PTSD), 94
poverty
    demographics and, 26–27, 54
    health care and, 73–74, 86
precontact stage, for culture-specific interventions, 180–181
    botanical shop example, 197–198
    context setting for, 196–197
    memorial mural example, 199–201
    practice applications of, 201–202
predatory lending, 60
pregnancy, biculturalism benefits with, 107–108
preschool programs, racial inequality in, 49
prescription drugs, 78, 80, 95
President's Commission on Mental Health, 169
preventive health care, 73–74, 89
"price gouging," for health insurance, 147–148
pride, cultural, 15–16, 116, 227–228
privacy, family-based, 158
probation, correctional, access to services and, 138–139
procreation, as cultural value, 155–156
product lines, Latino markets for, 56–57
    from country of origin, 58
professional development
    best practices and, 101–102
    for effective collaboration, 178, 186
    resources for, 137, 228–229
professional expertise. *See* best practices

professional issues
  complexity as, 223–224
  current, 3–4, 6–9, 132
  historical, 3
professional practice. *See* social work
professional standards, for social work,
    101, 136
project staff, best practice principles
    for, 103–104
Proposition 187, of California, 5, 97
Protestants, influence of, 147–149
psychiatric disorders, 93–94, 98
psychological access, to services, 136
psychosis, 93–94, 98
psychotherapy
  barrier to health services and, 128,
    131
  folk techniques congruence with,
    152–154
public art, as cultural asset, 199–201,
    219
public health, international trade
    cooperation for, 73
public policy, demographics impact on,
    29, 42
  politics of, 64–65
Puerto Ricans, 8, 14–16, 18
  demographic trends of, 24–25
  educational attainment of, 50
  legal status of, 3, 30
  mortality rate of, 38–39
purchasing power, economic, of
    Latinos, 55–60

racial diversity
  in census data, 23–24, 39, 45, 47
  combined identities in, 14–15, 18–19
  impact on practice, 224–225
  as professional challenge, 3–4, 6–7
racism
  educational attainment and, 49–52
  in health care, 72–73, 96–98
  Mexicans and, 15
  modified practices based on, 104–
    105, 132, 225
reciprocity, 110
referral system, for HIV testing, 215–
    216, 219
relationship building stage, for
    culture-specific interventions,
    180, 183–184

beauty parlor example, 212–213
botanical shop example, 211–212
context setting for, 211
practice applications of, 213–214
religion/religiosity, 144–151
  Catholic Church influence, 144–
    148
  as cultural asset, 204, 208
  evangelical influence, 147–148
  faith-based federal initiatives and,
    149
  folk beliefs coexisting with, 151
  fundamentalist influence, 149–150
  Islam influence, 150
  modified practices based on, 111–
    112, 131–132
  Mormon influence, 150
  in natural support systems, 114,
    144–145, 170–171
  Pentecostal influence, 149, 204, 208
  as professional challenge, 8, 17, 231
  Protestant influence, 147–149
  social perspectives of, 108, 147, 151,
    168, 178
religious organizations, hospital
    systems of, 147–148
remittance
  to country of origin, 61–63
  ethnic identity development and,
    115
Republican Party, conservative values
    of, 5
research
  access to undocumented
    immigrants, 230–231
  for best practices, 100–102, 112,
    230
  culture constructs for, 17, 19, 191–
    192, 220
  participatory models for, 229–230
  practice shaped by, 8, 10, 191, 220,
    229–231
  support for, 12, 103, 128, 220–221,
    226
resource directories, of cultural assets,
    202
respect
  for clients, 110
  in partnerships, 170, 183–184
respecto, 155, 162–163, 168
restaurants, as cultural asset, 193, 208

vision care, 95
volunteers/volunteering, civic, 54–55
voter initiatives, 4
voting, Latino patterns of, 64–65

wages, undocumented Latinos impact
    on, 5, 34–35
Washington, birth rates in, 40
wealth. *See* economic power
weddings, significance of, 145–146,
    164–165
West Virginia, demographic trends in,
    42
whites
    in demographic trends, 29, 38–39,
      45, 47–48
    ethnic identity and, 15–16, 18
wisdom, as best practice, 101
Women, Infants, and Children (WIC)
    program, 86
women's rights, 225

workplace violence, 96
workshops, for social workers, 229–230

youth
    acculturation of, 29–31
    assets possessed by, 112–114, 176–
      177
    biculturalism benefits for, 107
    bilingualism importance for, 108–
      109
    health care for, 74, 91, 94–95, 153
    health insurance programs for, 74,
      77–78
    health outcomes of, 72, 74–75, 86–
      87
    media impact on, 65–68, 75
    relationships importance to, 105,
      111, 158–159
    second-generation, 14–15, 28–29
    trauma impact on, 139–140, 153–
      154